Power, Order, and Change in World Politics

Are there recurring historical dynamics and patterns that can help us understand today's power transitions and struggles over international order? What can we learn from the past? Are the cycles of rise and decline of power and international order set to continue? Robert Gilpin's classic work, *War and Change in World Politics*, offers a sweeping and influential account of the rise and decline of leading states and the international orders they create. Now, some thirty years on, this volume brings together an outstanding collection of scholars to reflect on Gilpin's grand themes of power and change in world politics. The chapters engage with theoretical ideas that shape the way we think about great powers, with the latest literature on the changing US position in the global system, and with the challenges to the existing order that are being generated by China and other rising non-Western states.

G. JOHN IKENBERRY is the Albert G. Milbank Professor of Politics and International Affairs at Princeton University in the Department of Politics and the Woodrow Wilson School of Public and International Affairs. He is also Co-Director of Princeton's Center for International Security Studies. Professor Ikenberry is also a Global Eminence Scholar at Kyung Hee University in Seoul, Korea, and in 2013–2014 he was the 72nd Eastman Visiting Professor at Balliol College, Oxford.

Professor Ikenberry has written and edited several books, including *After Victory: Institutions, Strategic Restraint, and the Rebuilding of Order after Major Wars* (2001), which won the 2002 Schroeder-Jervis Award presented by the American Political Science Association for the best book in international history and politics, and *International Relations Theory and the Consequences of Unipolarity* (Cambridge University Press, 2011).

Power, Order, and Change in World Politics

Edited by

G. John Ikenberry

CAMBRIDGE
UNIVERSITY PRESS

CAMBRIDGE
UNIVERSITY PRESS

University Printing House, Cambridge CB2 8BS, United Kingdom

Cambridge University Press is part of the University of Cambridge.

It furthers the University's mission by disseminating knowledge in the pursuit of education, learning and research at the highest international levels of excellence.

www.cambridge.org
Information on this title: www.cambridge.org/9781107421066

© Cambridge University Press 2014

First published 2014

A catalogue record for this publication is available from the British Library

Library of Congress Cataloguing in Publication data
Power, order, and change in world politics / edited by G. John Ikenberry.
    pages   cm
ISBN 978-1-107-07274-9 (Hardback) – ISBN 978-1-107-42106-6 (Paperback)
1. International relations.   2. World politics.   3. Balance of power.
4. Hegemony.   5. Gilpin, Robert. War and change in world politics.
I. Ikenberry, G. John, author, editor of compilation.
JZ1310.P694 2014
327.1′12–dc23   2014010353

ISBN 978-1-107-07274-9 Hardback
ISBN 978-1-107-42106-6 Paperback

Table of contents

Contributors

BARRY BUZAN is Emeritus Professor of International Relations at the LSE (formerly Montague Burton Professor), honorary professor at Copenhagen and Jilin Universities, and a Senior Fellow at LSE IDEAS. In 1998 he was elected a fellow of the British Academy. He has written, co-authored, or edited over two dozen books, and written or co-authored more than 120 articles and chapters, mainly around themes of international security and international relations theory.

DANIEL DEUDNEY is Associate Professor and Director of Undergraduate Studies at Johns Hopkins University where he teaches political science, international relations, and political theory. He is the author of the prize-winning book, *Bounding Power: Republican Security Theory from the Polis to the Global Village* (2007).

JOHN A. HALL is the James McGill Professor of Comparative Historical Sociology at McGill University in Montreal. He is the author of many books, most recently *Ernest Gellner: An Intellectual Biography* (2010) and *The Importance of Being Civil* (2013). He is working on a book on the links between nations, states, and empires.

G. JOHN IKENBERRY is the Albert G. Milbank Professor of Politics and International Affairs in the Woodrow Wilson School and Department of Politics at Princeton University, and Co-Director of the Center for Internatonal Security Studies. He is also Global Eminence Scholar at Kyung Hee University in Seoul, Korea. His most recent books are *Liberal Leviathan: The Origins, Crisis, and Transformation of the American World Order* (2011) and *The Rise of Korean Leadership: Emerging Powers and Liberal International Order* (2013).

JONATHAN KIRSHNER is the Stephen and Barbara Friedman Professor of International Political Economy in the Department of Government and Director of the Reppy Institute for Peace and Conflict Studies at Cornell University. His most recent book is *American Power After the Financial Crisis*.

CHARLES A. KUPCHAN is Professor of International Affairs at George-town University and Whitney H. Shepardson Senior Fellow at the Council on Foreign Relations. His most recent books are *No One's World: The West, the Rising Rest, and the Coming Global Turn* (2012) and *How Enemies Become Friends: The Sources of Stable Peace* (2010).

DAVID A. LAKE is the Jerri-Ann and Gary E. Jacobs Professor of Social Sciences, Distinguished Professor of Political Science, Associate Dean of Social Sciences, and Director of Yankelovich Center for Social Science Research at the University of California, San Diego. He has written widely in the field of international relations. Lake is the former chair of the International Political Economy Society and past president of the International Studies Association. The recipient of UCSD Chancellor's Associates Awards for Excellence in Graduate Education (2005) and Excellence in Research (2013), he was elected to the American Academy of Arts and Sciences in 2006.

MICHAEL MASTANDUNO received his PhD from Princeton University and is currently Nelson A. Rockefeller Professor of Government and Dean of the Faculty of Arts and Sciences at Dartmouth College. His recent work examines US–China economic and security relations and US foreign policy in the post-Cold War international system.

WILLIAM C. WOHLFORTH is the Daniel Webster Professor in the Department of Government at Dartmouth College. He is editor of *Status and World Politics* (Cambridge University Press, 2014) with T. V. Paul and Deborah Larson. He is currently writing a book with Stephen Brooks entitled *America Abroad: The United States' Global Role in the 21st Century*.

Acknowledgments

The idea for this book started with a conversation in the hallways of Bendheim Hall at Princeton University. Wolfgang Danspeckgruber, Director of the Liechtenstein Institute on Self-Determination, remarked to me that the thirtieth anniversary of Robert Gilpin's *War and Change in World Politics* was fast approaching. We agreed that this would be a perfect occasion to assemble a group of scholars to reflect on the book's grand themes of power and change in world politics. The goal has not been to produce a Festschrift, but to invite scholars to grapple with the theory and vision that Gilpin advances. With Gilpin's book as a starting point, how can we make sense of today's great shifts in power and global order?

Work on this book began on the twenty-ninth anniversary of *War and Change in World Politics*, and it was completed on the thirty-third anniversary. So the book has been long in the making, but it has been a decidedly joyful undertaking for everyone involved. The authors in this volume have been driven by several motivations. One has been to honor Robert Gilpin and his groundbreaking book. Most of the scholars who have contributed essays, including myself, have pursued our work "in the shadow" of *War and Change*. It is a book that has inspired and provoked us. Gilpin's book provides a framework in which many of us have either built on or pushed off against. So the book reflects our efforts to acknowledge a debt to Robert Gilpin. Another motivation has been to showcase the range of current research and debates that flow out of Gilpin's book. Building on realist theory, Gilpin constructed a framework for thinking about great shifts in the global system. It has provided a conceptual language and large-scale hypotheses for inquiry into the rise and fall of international order. The authors in this volume have taken up the challenge of thinking in new ways about the logic of order and change in world politics, doing so with a focus on contemporary power shifts and struggles over order.

When Gilpin wrote his book, the Cold War was not yet ended and Japan was on the rise. Today, the Soviet Union no longer exists and it is

x   Acknowledgments

China that is on the rise. The cast of leading states on the world stage has changed but the drama over power and order remains. The struggle over global order continues. For this reason, Gilpin's last words in his book seem profoundly relevant today. "The supreme task for statesmen in the final decades of the twentieth century is to build on the positive forces of our age in the creation of a new and more stable international order."

I would like to acknowledge the generous financial assistance of the Liechtenstein Institute on Self-Determination, the Center for International Security Studies, and the Program on the Future of Multilateralism, all at the Woodrow Wilson School of Public and International Affairs at Princeton University. Thanks also go to Wolfgang Danspeckgruber and Aaron Friedberg for their support. I also acknowledge the excellent assistance of Lindsay Woodrick, Cynthia Ernst, and Alexander Lanoszka.

G. John Ikenberry

Introduction: power, order, and change in world politics

G. John Ikenberry

Introduction

The global system is in the midst of a great transformation. The distribution of power is shifting. Great powers are rising and declining. For almost a century, the United States dominated world politics. But today, China and other rising non-Western states, such as India and Brazil, are growing in wealth, power, influence, and ambition. The old order – led by the United States and its allies – is still a commanding presence in the global system. But the power once concentrated in the hands of the United States is diffusing outward and, as a result, new struggles are emerging over global rules and institutions. In the midst of these changes, scholars have been asking basic questions about the logic and character of contemporary international order. How profound is the change that is underway in global order? If the United States is losing its position of preeminence, will the order that it created weaken and break apart, giving way to a new type of global order? Or will non-Western rising states ultimately become stakeholders in the existing order? Do rising states want great authority and privileges in the existing international order or do they want to use their growing power to reorganize the basic principles and norms of the system?

The struggles underway today over international order are, of course, not new. The rise and decline of great powers and convulsive shifts in international order have played out many times over the centuries. In past eras, states have risen up, fought wars, and built international order. Spain, France, Great Britain, Germany – each of these states grew in power in a past century and made a bid to dominate Europe and the wider world. In turn, each declined or was defeated in war, triggering a renewal of geopolitical struggle over leadership and the organizing rules and arrangements of global order. Over the centuries, the actors on the global stage have changed but the scripts and plot lines of struggle over order have appeared and reappeared many times. As a result, scholars are asking questions about the past. Are there recurring historical dynamics and patterns that can help us understand today's power transitions and struggles over international order? What can we learn from the past? Is the past prolog? Are we doomed to repeat endlessly the cycles of rise and decline of power and international order that is found in our past?

This volume brings together nine leading scholars to explore these grand questions of global order and change. The starting point of each of these scholars is Robert Gilpin's classic work, *War and Change in World Politics*.[1] More than any other modern book on international relations theory, Gilpin's thirty-three-year-old classic offers the most sweeping, elegant, and influential account of the rise and decline of leading states and the international orders they create. Power, order, war, hegemony, and the transformation of world politics – these are the terms of reference in Gilpin's landmark work. In the three decades that have followed, the great debates over power transitions and the governance of world order have directly or indirectly built upon and engaged Gilpin's sweeping historical and theoretical vision.

The chapters that follow are not scholarly discussions, narrowly speaking, of Gilpin's *War and Change in World Politics*. The book is simply their point of departure. Each chapter begins by engaging an aspect of Gilpin's book, using it as a springboard for making original arguments about order and change. Some of the authors find Gilpin's framework as a useful foundation for exploring contemporary dynamics of global change. Other authors make their arguments by critiquing the limits or blind spots in Gilpin's theoretical vision. Together, the chapters demonstrate the richness of analysis and debate that flows from the engagement with Gilpin's classic statement.

As a collection, the chapters offer a striking portrait of order and change in the global system. They do so by exploring the deep theoretical ideas that shape the way we think about great powers and the global orders they create. They also do so with a special eye on the changing American position in the global system and the challenges to the existing order that are being generated by China and other rising non-Western states. Together, the chapters move beyond Gilpin's original conception of war and change in world politics. Most of the authors argue against a rigid cyclical view of the rise and decline of states and international order. The distribution of material capabilities – and its shifts over time – provides the setting and resources for states as they struggle over the

---

[1] Robert Gilpin, *War and Change in World Politics* (New York, NY: Cambridge University Press, 1981).

terms of world order. But grand shifts in the character of states, societies, capitalism, technologies, violence, and ideas are not cyclical. They change and evolve over the centuries. As a result, the future is never simply a reproduction of the past, not least international order.

In this introduction, I begin by looking at Robert Gilpin's theoretical vision of power, order, and change in world politics. After this, I locate the three great thematic areas of debate about order that lie at the heart of Gilpin's work, thematic areas that are explored in the chapters that follow. The first theme focuses on hegemonic power and the problem of rule or governance of international order. Here the questions concern the various ways that leading states project power and ideas into the global system and establish their rule over the system. The second theme focuses on the rise and decline of great powers and the logic of order formation and change. Here the questions are directed at the dynamics of power transitions and the opportunities these transitions create for struggles over order. The third theme focuses on system change and the foundations of world order. The focus here is on the great world historical shifts in the basic units and structures of global order – nation-states, empires, transnational society, and the transformations in these units and structures in the wake of political and technological revolutions. In each of these areas, I highlight the arguments advanced by the authors in this volume. Finally, I offer a more general portrait of our scholarly knowledge about order and change in world politics. The chapters in this book illuminate our current understandings of the logic of power and order – and they also illuminate the dilemmas and pathways of change in the current era of American-led world order.

The rise and fall of states and order

Robert Gilpin's *War and Change in World Politics* has had an enduring impact on how scholars think about international order. A dominant tendency within the realist tradition has been to think about order in terms of anarchy. International order is seen as the result of the balancing interaction of states competing for security in a decentralized state system. Order is manifest as a power equilibrium. No state – not even a strong one – rules the system.

Gilpin's *War and Change in World Politics* offered a different view, one in which powerful states rise up, create, and direct international order. States – strong ones – do rule the system. Building on a different strand of realist thinking, Gilpin sees world politics as a succession of ordered systems created by leading – or hegemonic – states that emerge after war with the opportunity and capabilities to organize the rules and arrangements of interstate relations.[2]

The Gilpin view about war and the rise and fall of international order has opened up a rich set of theoretical and historical issues. Order is not simply a "resultant" – it is created by leading states. Order is not simply "non-war" made possible by a balancing of power – it is infused with rules, institutions, and organizational principles. Order is not simply the crystallization of the distribution of power – it is constituted with authority relations, shared expectations, and settled practices through which states do business. Order is not built on the balance of power but on a structured asymmetry of power. To be sure, there is ambiguity in Gilpin's theoretical vision about the degree to which international order goes beyond the power and coercion that the leading state wields in creating that order. Gilpin does suggest that order can be and often is based on more than coercive lead-state control. Ideology and mutual interests matter in various ways. In Gilpin's vision, international order is a sort of primitive system of politics. It may look more Hobbesian than Lockean – but it is, nonetheless, a vision of international political order organized around hegemonic leaders, differential roles, authority relations, and complex moving parts.

In *War and Change in World Politics*, Gilpin seeks to provide a systematic theory of international political change. He does not claim to have discovered the "laws of change" in world politics, but he does offer a framework for thinking about war and change, one that he argues can help "identify recurrent patterns, common elements, and general tendencies in the major turning points in international history."[3] When and why do great shifts in international order occur? This is Gilpin's question. His conviction is that there are patterns and regularities to global change. Ironically, Gilpin can make this claim about identifying the logic of international change because of his simultaneous insistence that when it comes to the "fundamental nature of international relations," change has in fact *not* occurred over the centuries and millennia.[4] At a deep level, Gilpin insists, the problem of change today is not unlike

[2] The alternative realist conception of order, defined in terms of anarchy and sustained by the balance of power, is articulated in Kenneth Waltz, *The Theory of International Politics* (New York, NY: Wiley, 1979). While Gilpin offers a narrative of change, Waltz provides a theory of continuity: why wars reoccur, why balances of power form and reform, and why attempts at military hegemony fail. For a discussion of these two influential theories of order, both realist but offering very different accounts, see William C. Wohlforth, "Gilpinian Realism and International Relations," *International Relations*, Vol. 25, No. 4 (December 2011), pp. 499–511.
[3] Gilpin, *War and Change in World Politics*, p. 3.   [4] *Ibid.*, p. 7.

the problem of change in the ancient world or the eras that followed. Thucydides' account of the Peloponnesian War is as relevant today for understanding war and change as it was when it was written in the fifth century BC. As Gilpin sees it, the nature of contemporary international relations is what it has always been, "a recurring struggle for wealth and power among independent actors in a state of anarchy."[5]

Gilpin's conceptual framework illuminates the timeless search by political actors for political order. The most powerful actors in a social system – or states within the international system – are driven to secure and advance their interests through the establishment of institutions and regularized relationships. The resulting political order serves the interests of the leading actors. Indeed, it is established precisely for this purpose. This is what happens in international relations. A powerful state rises up in the system and creates order, doing so to protect and advance its interests. Over time, however, the distribution of power and wealth changes, driven by the diffusion of technology and production. The old order still exists, but the underlying distribution of material capabilities that supported it has eroded. In Gilpin's language, a "disequilibrium" emerges between international order and the underlying distribution of power and interests. Eventually, the state or states that are growing more powerful and wealthy will seek to change the order to reflect their interests. At great historical junctures, this change is brought on by hegemonic wars in which a rising state violently takes command of the global system and overturns the old order. The resulting order reflects a new equilibrium between power and interests. As Gilpin puts it, "the process of international political change ultimately reflects the efforts of individuals or groups to transform institutions and systems in order to advance their interests."[6]

The framework Gilpin sketches in *War and Change in World Politics* provides a striking image of power and order in world politics. Like other theorists working in the areas of long cycles, power transitions, and hegemony, Gilpin sees global order moving through cycles of leadership and domination.[7] The global system is built around powerful states who

[5] *Ibid.*, p. 7.   [6] *Ibid.*, p. 10.
[7] The focus of *War and Change in World Politics* on recurring cycles of power and order places it in the company of several large literatures on power transitions, long cycles, and hegemonic stability theory. On power transitions, see A.F.K. Organski, *World Politics* (New York, NY: Knopf, 1958); Organski and Jacek Kugler, *The War Ledger* (University of Chicago Press, 1980); and Ronald Tammen, Jacek Kugler, and Douglas Lemke, et al., *Power Transitions: Strategies for the 21st Century* (New York, NY: Chatham House, 2000). On long cycles, see George Modelski, *Long Cycles in World Politics* (Seattle, WA: University of Washington Press, 1987); George Modelski, ed., *Exploring Long Cycles* (Boulder, CO: Lynne Rienner Publishers, 1987); William R. Thompson, *On Global*

construct hierarchical systems of political order. These hierarchical orders can persist for decades and even centuries. But eventually, underlying material conditions of power shift and transform, and the hierarchies of world politics break apart, sometimes quite violently.

Gilpin's *War and Change in World Politics* is a useful starting point to illuminate the logic and character of international order and change for several reasons. First, one of the great challenges of international relations theory is to find analytic frameworks that allow scholars to explore similarities and differences in patterns of conflict and cooperation across historical eras. How do great powers operating in the seventeenth or eighteenth century compare with their counterparts in the twentieth or twenty-first century? How does the nature of international order change or evolve over the centuries as the character of the great powers who build and uphold international order change? In *War and Change*, Gilpin identifies two deep and recurring dynamics that appear and reappear across the centuries – the dynamic of power concentration and diffusion and the dynamic of war and order building. This twin focus allows scholars to move back and forth across eras to compare and assess how power and order have moved and shifted.

Second, Gilpin's theoretical vision focuses the study of international relations on the basic sources of political order. Powerful states build international order – this is Gilpin's contention. The material capabilities of states are the building blocks – the resources – that states use to build order. This is a very useful starting point for theory and debate about the structure and functioning of world politics. It allows scholars to think about the global system as a type of political order or political system. States operate in this order. It is not just an abstract "anarchy" or the epiphenomenal outcome resulting from the interaction of states. Political orders have rights and rules and institutions, even if they are ultimately the product of powerful states pursuing their interests. In this sense there is a sort of "base-superstructure" aspect to Gilpin's vision. Material capabilities – and their changing distribution among states – provide the base or

War: Historical-Structural Approaches to World Politics (Columbia, SC: University of South Carolina Press, 1988); and Karen Rasler and William R. Thompson, *The Great Powers and Global Struggle, 1490–1900* (Lexington, KY: University of Kentucky Press, 1994). On hegemonic stability theory, see Charles Kindleberger, *The World in Depression, 1929–39* (Berkeley, CA: University of California Press, 1974); Stephen D. Krasner, "State Power and the Structure of International Trade," *World Politics*, Vol. 28, No. 3 (April 1976), pp. 317–347; Robert Keohane, "The Theory of Hegemonic Stability Theory and Changes in International Economic Regimes," in Ole R. Holsti, Randolph M. Siverson, and Alexander L. George, ed., *Change in the International System* (Boulder, CO: Westview, 1980); and Robert Gilpin, *The Political Economy of International Relations* (Princeton University Press, 1987).

foundation for superstructural political relationships and institutions to form. These aspects of Gilpin's theory provide a useful starting point for developing more complicated sorts of theories about power and order.

Beyond this, Gilpin's *War and Change* offers three major "problems" about power and order that provide the thematic organization for this book. First, there is the "problem" of rule and domination within international orders. How do states that sit on top of global power hierarchies establish their dominance and run the order? What do hegemonic states do when they are being hegemonic? The second "problem" concerns the great-power shifts within a global system and the rise and decline of imperial and hegemonic orders that result. This is the problem of power transitions, hegemonic wars, and construction and destruction of international order. The focus is on the transition from one hegemonic-led order to another. Finally, and most generally, there is the "problem" of the macro-shifts in the global system – that is, in the basic units and organizing logic of the global system. What accounts for the great shifts from global systems organized around, say, city-states or universal empire to a system of sovereign states? The focus at this macro-level is not on the changes in leadership of the global system. Rather, the focus is on the deeper "revolutions" in the units and organizing character of the global system itself. In each of these thematic areas, three authors offer historical and theoretical arguments. The intellectual architecture of Gilpin's *War and Change* provides the foundation and starting point for new inquiries into the nature of power, order, and change. We can briefly summarize these contributions.

Types of international orders and strategies of rule

The first part of the book explores variations in types of international orders and the strategies hegemonic states employ to rule these orders. The focus here is on the different ways in which hegemonic powers can create order. If all orders are a mix of coercion and consent, what choices and circumstances lead hegemonic states to create one mix or another mix? Global hierarchical orders can be built around imperial or liberal logics. How do these types of hierarchies differ and what explains why one or the other emerges within a particular historical era? How do we compare and evaluate the performance of international orders? We are also interested in the way leading states "manage" or "govern" international order. What does it mean when we say that leading states "run" or "rule" an international order? If the United States has pursued a "liberal strategy" of order building and governance, what sort of strategy of governance might China pursue?

In the first chapter, Charles A. Kupchan explores the types of national values, cultural orientations, and societal interests that leading states bring to the building of international order. Kupchan argues that Gilpin, along with most other scholars of hegemony, relies exclusively on material variables: order emerges from disparities of power and hierarchies enforced by the leading state. But Kupchan suggests that hegemonic orders vary widely in their "packages of ordering ideas and rules." These ideas and rules exhibit normative orientations and they are imbued with cultural and ideological dispositions. It follows that the American liberal world order is not an expression of universal values or ideals. Rather, it is imbued with cultural and political ideals unique to American society. With the decline of American power and the weakening of the liberal international order, Kupchan argues that rival and successor hegemonic states will bring forward their own cultural values and political ideals – leading to a more pluralistic, diversified, and regionalized world order. Kupchan unpacks these claims through an examination of four hegemonic powers – the Ottomans, Imperial China, Great Britain, and the United States.

In the second chapter, David A. Lake explores unresolved questions that flow from Gilpin's conception of hegemonic order. First, noting that coercion is actually quite rare in world politics, Lake poses the question of why states in fact comply with the rules and institutions of international order. What provides the basis for command and rule? Lake argues that "authority" is the key feature of hierarchy orders. Legitimate domination is more desirable as a source of stable rule than coercion – and hierarchical orders reflect this fact. Second, Lake asks the question of why liberal hierarchical orders were the most successful over the last two hundred years.

Here Lake argues that the domestic constitutional limits of the abuse of power within liberal democracies make them more effective at establishing authoritative rule within international order. Finally, Lake asks the question of why there is so little "war and change" in the contemporary global system. His answer leads him to explore the role of "vested" interests in the existing order. In effect, order becomes self-reinforcing. In each of these theoretical claims, Lake finds implications for how China and other rising states might reconcile themselves and become stakeholders within the prevailing global order.

In the third chapter, G. John Ikenberry steps back to look at the various ways in which leading states have created international order, noting the distinctive character of the American "liberal hegemonic" order. The chapter goes on to explore the reasons and circumstances that lead major states to seek to construct international order – identifying the incentives,

constraints, opportunities, and tools that are associated with these potential order-building moments. While Gilpin sees an endless cycle of rising
and falling orders, Ikenberry argues that it is possible to see order
building as an evolutionary or unfolding process driven by the order-
building "projects" of the Westphalian system and the liberal ascendency. Seen in this light, the American-led liberal international order is
not simply a "creature" of American power, but is responsive to these
deeper unfolding logics of order building. Ikenberry argues that for an
international order to be durable, it needs to be built around three
features. It must be supported by a configuration of power, wielded by
one or several leading states. There must be some measure of legitimacy
to the rule and institutions that mark the order. And the order must
provide functional returns to participating states. That is, it must solve
collective action problems or provide services and benefits to states
within the order. Ikenberry argues that if these claims are correct, the
American-led international order may have more life in it than is generally thought. China and other states may grow more powerful but an
alternative order that harnesses the power of leading states may not exist
for decades to come.

Power transition and the rise and decline
of international order

The second part of the book focuses on power transitions and the rise
and decline of international orders. This cyclical drama is at the heart of
Gilpin's vision of world politics. Powerful states are never powerful
forever. The ground upon which they stand is always moving – and at
critical moments, power shifts create the conditions for war, upheaval,
and the reordering of global politics. As Gilpin argues, these power
transitions are moments that are fraught with danger and frequently
laced with violence. The powerful but declining state – which has built
and ruled the international order – is now losing ground to a rising state
or group of states that increasingly seek to challenge the old order. As
Gilpin sees it, these passages from an international order dominated by
one state to one dominated by another are typically marked by hegemonic wars. Three chapters explore these issues of power transition and
order, each building on but also complicating the basic Gilpin vision.

In Chapter 4, William C. Wohlforth explores the logic of hegemonic
decline. This has remained an understudied question within the broader
literature of the rise and decline of international order. Wohlforth asks
the question: is the pursuit of hegemony self-defeating? The conventional
answer is yes. Drawing on Gilpin's *War and Change*, Kennedy's *Rise and*

Fall, and a number of other key works, scholars routinely maintain that asserting and sustaining leadership over an international system inevitably becomes a losing proposition that causes the hegemon to decline faster than it otherwise would. Wohlforth shows that this conventional wisdom rests on weak foundations. Scholars have failed to distinguish between causes of decline that are exogenous to hegemony and the international system and those that are causally connected to being the hegemon or pursuing hegemony. Mechanisms of decline that really stem from being the hegemon or pursuing hegemony have rarely been identified, and those that have are weakly grounded in logic and poorly supported by evidence. A new wave of scholarship has emerged over the last two decades showing that, if anything, hegemons can use their position to slow decline and mitigate its effects. The implications for the debate on the US grand strategy are straightforward: think long and hard before giving up hard-won positions of systemic leadership and embarking on heedless retrenchment.

In Chapter 5, Jonathan Kirshner argues that *War and Change* remains, properly, a vital and relevant text for students and practitioners of world politics, despite the fact that it was rooted in the Cold War concerns of the later 1970s and raised alarming expectations that failed to materialize. But there was always more – much more – to *War and Change* than the derivation of a deductive theory to be judged on its predictive power. It was also a summary statement of classical realism, an attribute obscured by the fact that the book attempted to offer a hybrid of classical and structural theorizing. This chapter first situates Gilpin and *War and Change* in the context of classical realism, which differs from structural realism in its treatment of politics, history, ideology, and the motivations of states and relevance of statesmen. A second section then considers the distinct classical treatment of actors' rationality and their capacity for prediction. A renewed emphasis on these elements advances our understanding of *War and Change* (and world politics) by resolving two basic unresolved puzzles generated by the book, rooted in problematic assumptions regarding the efficiency of hegemonic expansion, and under-theorized explanations for the challenges of decline and the difficulty of retrenchment. Resolving these loose ends by emphasizing the classical realist elements of *War and Change* yields improved and enduring insights into perennial (and contemporary) problems posed by rising states and declining great powers. A concluding section briefly summarizes some of the enduring lessons of *War and Change*.

In Chapter 6, Michael Mastanduno explores the "grand bargains" that are part of the underside of hegemonic orders. As Gilpin argues, a powerful state does not simply create order through force. At least in the British and American eras, order resulted in part through bargains and negotiations with other great powers. Mastanduno offers a depiction of the American-era grand bargains with European and Asian states that laid the foundation for the postwar world order, and he explores the various ways in which these bargains are unraveling today. America built postwar order with Germany and Japan as junior partners. But today, it is China that is the second-largest economy and whom increasingly the United States must turn to. Mastanduno argues that a grand bargain with China is problematic and unstable. Germany and Japan were security allies and the American provision of alliance security facilitated the wider set of bargains over rules, institutions, and the governance of the world economy. The United States is now entering an era where China is a growing security rival and American-led hegemonic grand bargains will be difficult to sustain.

Systems change and global order

The last section of the book explores systems change and global order. Here the focus is on the basic organizational units and macro-structures of world politics. Over the millennia, the global system has been made up of different sorts of political units – city-states, empires, universal religious groupings. In the modern era, the Westphalian state system has been the dominant organizational form of world politics. What are the causes of these great changes in the basic units of the system? In particular, what accounts for the rise of the state system – as it both emerged as a tool of empire and a deep organizational change to it? How have states competed with alternative organizing logics and dealt with the rise of modernity and functional imperatives of world politics that alter and transform states and the states system? Three chapters explore aspects of these questions.

In Chapter 7, Daniel Deudney examines arguments about hegemony and liberal hegemony from the perspective of the nuclear revolution. Gilpin's argument is that war has been the prime mover of global change. Long-term shifts in the distribution of power among states set the stage for wars and order building. Deudney looks at the ways in which the changing "composition" of power influences the shaping and reshaping of international order, focusing in particular on the ways in which the nuclear revolution has shaped the contemporary character of the global power hierarchy. In some respects, nuclear weapons – to the extent they have radically reduced the likelihood of great-power war – have essentially brought to an end the cycles of hegemonic war that Gilpin sees as integral to the rise and fall of international order. As Deudney notes, nuclear weapons have simultaneously made states more secure and more insecure, less vulnerable and more vulnerable. The presence of nuclear deterrence also has important implications for the durability of the liberal international order that have been underappreciated. How this dual dynamic plays out in the era of American hegemonic dominance will matter for the pathways of global order and change.

In Chapter 8, Barry Buzan critically engages Gilpin's dynamic theory of global change. Gilpin's conception of order and change is decidedly realist in orientation. It is an endless dynamic of great-power rise and fall driven forward by material shifts in power capabilities and the competitive dynamics of an anarchic state system. Buzan argues that Gilpin acknowledges but fails to fully appreciate the impact of industrial capitalism and the evolving character of international society on global order and change. The cyclical logic of *War and Change* misses the ways in which modernity and "the long nineteenth century" have altered the states system. The deep evolutionary logic of modern industrialism and capitalism has transformed the social structural underpinnings of world politics. Industrial modernization impacts the capacities and character of states and societies – wealth generation, transportation and communication, weapons and security, and the rise and fall of great powers. Buzan focuses in particular on global processes of functional differentiation, given force by modernity, and the ways in which this organizes and reorganizes state relationships. Out of this "historical sociological" perspective, Buzan traces the ways in which the long nineteenth century has transformed world politics. If this critique is correct, Buzan argues, the structure of world politics is not best understood as a cyclical dynamic as Gilpin suggests but rather as an evolving and transforming global socio-political whole. The unfolding global system is unlike anything seen before.

In Chapter 9, John A. Hall takes up the classic question of how to understand the world historical transition from empire to nation-state. This transition is at the heart of Gilpin's notion of systems change – the moments when the nature of the units themselves shift. In the simplest formulation, the modern era is defined by the transition from imperial forms of rule to the Westphalian state system. It is a narrative of global change that emphasizes the growing capacities of states to harness "the nation" and compete within a European – and later global – system of nation-states. John Hall revisits this global transformation, and he argues that the different logics – of states and empires – are more complexly related than often understood. States made empires but empires also made states. Indeed, the rise of Westphalian states in early modern Europe gave impetus to empire rather than offering a systemic alternative to them. Hall offers a particular view of the role of nationalism. Nationalism is not simply a modern development which reinforced the primacy and capacity of states. Nationalism is in part the consequence of state action driven by geopolitical need.

Themes and conclusions

Together, these chapters provide an illuminating portrait of the state of our scholarly knowledge about order and change in world politics. The chapters show that Gilpin's theoretical vision provides a useful "baseline" position or framework to do this sort of theoretical updating. Gilpin's *War and Change* provides a language and conceptual architecture with which scholars can argue and compare notes. The debates about order and change are more coherent and our knowledge can accumulate because of the shared terms and master hypotheses that Gilpin's book provides. We are able to move across historical eras with more analytic precision. We are able to more clearly distinguish alternative views of the role of power, war, ideas, and authority in the making and remaking of international order. And we are able to deploy these theories and scholarly expectations to better make sense of the "power transition" that is unfolding today.

Several broad arguments emerge in these chapters that speak to ongoing theoretical debates about the rise and fall of international orders – and to current debates about the future of the American-led order. First, many of the chapters take issue with the cyclical theory of power shifts and order change. Barry Buzan makes perhaps the most sweeping challenge to the cyclical view by focusing on the evolutionary – and indeed revolutionary – impact of industrialism and modernizing capitalism on the character of states and their relationships. The structural setting within which states rise and fall and build order is itself transforming – altering the social character and complex organizing relationships within the international system. Ikenberry also finds evidence of an evolutionary logic. The cycles of rise and decline are not simply a recurring dynamic generated by the diffusion and concentration of power. Rather the changing nature of the states and the learning and adaptation that occur in the building and rebuilding of order give the historical process contingent evolutionary markings as well as cyclical form. The twin dynamics of the Westphalian project of building a functioning state system and the "liberal ascendancy" have altered the rise and decline logic. David Lake also argues that the liberal character of the American-led order is different from past non-liberal forms of international order, and this has implications for the incentives and constraints that today's rising non-Western states face. Daniel Deudney also argues that nuclear weapons have altered the power transition dynamic by making great-power war less likely. If hegemonic war is taken off the table of history, the Gilpin vision of war and order building is decisively altered.

Second, several of the chapters seek to engage and modify Gilpin's commitment to a materialist power theory of order and change. Material power matters, of course, but so too do ideas and culture, at least in the view of some authors. Gilpin's own work opens the door to this sort of complicating view of order. John Hall shows that nationalism – not just power – can be a powerful shaping influence on war and order building. Hall argues that the ideational impact of nationalism is felt at specific historical junctures in the modern era, such as at the end of the nineteenth century in Europe. Nationalism and geopolitics became intertwined, creating world-shattering dynamics. Jonathan Kirshner argues that Gilpin is more of a "classical realist" than a "structural realist," and this means that Gilpin does in fact appreciate the way that domestic politics, ideas, and political traditions will influence and shape the way great powers project power and seek to build order. Charles Kupchan's chapter takes this "theoretical invitation" to explore the impact of ideas and culture and goes further. Kupchan sees quite distinct types of international orders across the centuries, driven by the divergent cultural and ideological orientation of the states that seek to build order. These arguments complicate the more materialist version of Gilpin's theory. They suggest that the "superstructure" of politics and institutions might have a more independent standing as a source of order – and this modified view opens up new ideas about the continuity and durability of particular international orders. After all, if rising states share the same ideas and cultural orientations that are embedded in the existing international order, they might not seek to confront and overturn it. But the focus on ideas and culture might also complicate the arguments of authors such as Ikenberry and Lake who see a special robustness in today's American-led liberal international order. If Kupchan is right, these liberal characteristics of order may be more parochial than Ikenberry and Lake think. If ideas and culture can be used by the hegemonic state to legitimate international order, clashes over ideas and culture can also serve to undermine international order.

Third, these chapters show that there are more "moving parts" within hegemonic orders than Gilpin's vision allows. Gilpin provides a masterful account of the hierarchical character of ancient and modern regional and global orders. There are leading states and subordinate states. But some of the chapters in this book show that the "vertical relations" between states in these hierarchical orders can actually be quite complicated. Michael Mastanduno shows the complex "grand bargains" that provided the basis for consensus and partnership in American-led postwar order. The American hegemonic order was not simply a unipolar directorship. There was a sort of hierarchically organized "concert" of liberal democracies. Different states within the order had different roles and responsibilities, and the order itself was tied together with strategic bargains and understandings about leadership and collaboration. The United States provided public goods related to security and the maintenance of economic openness, and other states shouldered responsibilities of economic adjustment and burden sharing. The Ikenberry and Lake chapters serve to reinforce this idea that political order – at least in the modern liberal era – can be much more open, legitimate, and reciprocally governed than a more straightforward realist model of order would suggest.

Fourth, several of the chapters illuminate the problem of retrenchment within hegemonic systems. Gilpin's book provides a striking vision of the "beginnings" of international orders. War and a newly dominant lead-state create the circumstances for a new organization of rules and institutions. But Gilpin's vision of the "endings" of orders is a bit more obscure. Wars, again, play a decisive role. But what actually brings an international order to the edge of war? And how do orders end if hegemonic wars no longer operate as an instrument of global change? William Wohlforth offers new thinking about the problems of hegemonic decline and prospects for hegemonic retrenchment. How might states that are in decline – yet still hegemonic – find ways to slow or reverse their strategic plight? Gilpin hints at this problem in *War and Change*, indicating that past hegemonic states have sometimes sought to extract more tribute or "hegemonic tax" from weaker and junior states within the order. Wohlforth builds on this idea and explores the wider array of tools and opportunities that leading states might have to influence the dynamics of rise and decline. Mastanduno and Kirshner also explore ways in which strategic bargains might be renewed or renegotiated to generate support within a prevailing hegemonic system.

Finally, the chapters all step back and offer ideas about the basic "problem" of international order. Gilpin's vision is clear. Hegemonic states build orders so as to protect and advance their interests. Order building is in effect an exercise in power. This classic formulation is not directly contested by the authors in this volume. But various authors do seek to elaborate and add complexity to this idea. David Lake sees the problem of order as a more functional exercise in creating legitimate authority. The leading state and others within the order are motivated by the search for functional and efficient sharing of power and authority.

Contracts and institutions – decidedly hierarchical – provide an efficient and stable environment within which states achieve their interests. Barry Buzan also sees the problem of order in functional terms. It is not great-power politics and anarchy that drive the rise and decline of international order. Order emerges more as a result of ongoing deep shifts in the logic and organization of capitalism and modernity.

Taken together, these chapters suggest that grand shifts in order in the twenty-first century will not follow any straightforward cyclical pathway. The dominance of liberal democracies and capitalism reinforce the existing international order. The order itself is "wider and deeper" than past international orders. Nuclear weapons both deter global war and generate incentives for great powers to negotiate stability in the face of mutual vulnerability. China and other non-Western rising states are putting pressure on the old international order. But China and these other new powers have profoundly complicated and ambivalent relationships with the old American-led liberal order. They are both tied to it and constrained by it. They bring antagonist values and cultural orientations to the old liberal world order. They look at liberal order and, at least to some extent, see a Western-oriented imperial order. They bring ideas about order that emerge out of an anti-imperial and anti-colonial heritage. In all these ways, international order is continuously impacted by forces of continuity and change. Gilpin's *War and Change* brilliantly maps many of these basic forces and pressures. Building on these insights, the authors in this book offer a message: the past cycles of rise and decline of international order do illuminate the global pathways and future prospects for change, but the grand forces of liberalism, democracy, capitalism, nationalism, civilization, and modernity are pushing and pulling history in new directions. Future international order will bear the markings of the past and ongoing power transitions will inevitably alter the array of leading states, but future international order will almost surely recreate itself in new and surprising ways.

Part I

Varieties of international order and strategies of rule

1 Unpacking hegemony: the social foundations of hierarchical order

Charles A. Kupchan[1]

Introduction

Since its publication over three decades ago, Robert Gilpin's *War and Change* has definitively shaped scholarly debate about the rise and fall of great powers. According to Gilpin's seminal work, the main cause of the cyclical rise and decline of hegemonic powers is the inevitable shift in the locus of power from the core to the periphery of the international system. As the gap between reigning hegemon and rising challenger closes, the order derived from hierarchy gives way to competition over position and status. A new hegemon ultimately rises to primacy, and order is again established through hierarchy. This account of systemic change has become a foundational pillar of the contemporary study of international relations.

Gilpin's theory of international change relies exclusively on material variables. Order comes from asymmetries of power, and instability and war come when changes in the distribution of power trigger rivalry among states seeking to sit atop a new international hierarchy. Gilpin's emphasis on the distribution of material power as the main determinant of order is in line with many other works on the subject. The field of international relations has a well-developed body of knowledge on power transitions, with most scholars joining Gilpin in focusing heavily on material variables in their analysis.[2]

---

[1] For their comments on earlier drafts of this chapter, the author would like to thank G. John Ikenberry and the other contributors to this volume; participants in seminars at the University of Wisconsin, the University of Michigan, and the Transatlantic Academy; and the editors and anonymous reviewers at Cambridge University Press and *Security Studies*. This chapter draws on Charles A. Kupchan, "The Normative Foundations of Hegemony and the Coming Challenge to *Pax Americana*," *Security Studies*, Vol. 23, No. 2 (June 2014), pp. 219–258.

[2] See, for example, A.F.K. Organski, *World Politics* (New York, NY: Knopf, 1968); Paul Kennedy, *The Rise and Fall of the Great Powers: Economic Change and Military Conflict from 1500 to 2000* (New York, NY: Random House, 1987); George Modelski, *Long Cycles in World Politics* (Seattle, WA: University of Washington Press, 1987); and Joshua Goldstein, *Long Cycles: Prosperity and War in the Modern Age* (New Haven, CT: Yale University Press, 1988).

However, understanding and managing international change requires examining not just shifts in material power, but also the associated contest among competing norms of order. Transitions in the international distribution of power produce not only novel hierarchies, but also novel brands of international order that rest on the social and ideological proclivities of newly powerful states in the system. To be sure, the states in a regional or global system that wield a preponderance of material power are usually the ones that establish and enforce the rules of the prevailing order. But that reality does not obviate the need to examine the substantive content of the norms that shape that order.

On this front – the normative dimensions of hegemonic order – existing scholarship provides a much more embryonic intellectual foundation.[3] The material focus of most studies of hegemonic transition has led to the scholarly neglect of other dimensions of order. As Ayşe Zarakol aptly notes, "the lack of attention given to the particular cultural and historical origins of the modern international system may just be the most glaring oversight in mainstream International Relations."[4] Hegemonic systems, whether coercive or more consensual, have a distinctive normative character; order emerges not just from hierarchy, but also from packages of ideas and rules that inform the nature of a given order and govern social relations within that order.

These packages of ordering ideas and norms vary widely across different hegemonic systems, be they regional or global. Moreover, the norms propagated by these ideational packages are consequential; they affect the character, stability, and durability of hegemonic orders, and may

---

[3] Works on the normative dimensions of hegemony are growing in number, but they do not provide a systematic and cumulative treatment of the subject. These works include Antonio Gramsci, *Selections from the Prison Notebooks* (New York, NY: International Publishers, 1971); John Gerard Ruggie, "International Regimes, Transactions, and Change: Embedded Liberalism in the Postwar Economic Order," *International Organization*, Vol. 36, No. 2 (Spring 1982), pp. 379–415; Hedley Bull and Adam Watson, ed., *The Expansion of International Society* (Oxford: Clarendon Press, 1987); Robert Cox, *Production, Power, and World Order* (New York, NY: Columbia University Press, 1987); G. John Ikenberry and Charles A. Kupchan, "Socialization and Hegemonic Power," *International Organization*, Vol. 44, No. 3 (Summer 1990), pp. 283–315; David Skidmore, ed., *Contested Social Orders and International Politics* (Nashville, TN: Vanderbilt University Press, 1995); Peter Katzenstein, ed., *Civilizations in World Politics: Plural and Pluralist Perspectives* (New York, NY: Routledge, 2010); Daniel Nexon, *The Struggle for Power in Early Modern Europe: Religious Conflict, Dynastic Empires, and International Change* (Princeton University Press, 2009); John Owen, *The Clash of Ideas in World Politics: Transnational Networks, States, and Regime Change, 1520–2010* (Princeton University Press, 2010); and Ayşe Zarakol, *After Defeat: How the East Learned to Live with the West* (Cambridge University Press, 2011); Ted Hopf, "Common-sense Constructivism and Hegemony in World Politics," *International Organization*, Vol. 67, No. 2 (April 2013), pp. 317–354.
[4] Zarakol, *After Defeat*, p. 6.

well shape the nature of the transition that ensues when one order gives way to another. The "normative distance" between a particular hegemonic order and the one that follows it could affect whether a change in hierarchy might fundamentally disrupt the international system.[5] The transition from Pax Britannica to Pax Americana, for example, may have been uniquely peaceful because both orders rested on an "Anglo-Saxon" package of ordering ideas and rules. It may also be the case that the normative differences between successive orders have diminished over time due to a convergence produced by systemic pressures. Such issues will loom large in the coming decades. As China's ascent continues, the character of its relationship with the United States may well turn on whether Beijing embraces, or instead seeks to overturn, the ordering norms associated with US hegemony.

The content of the norms that shape international order may well be more important today than at any previous point in history. Globalization has fostered interdependence and diminished the consequences of geographic separation. As Western primacy gives way to the onset of a world with multiple centers of power, the international system, for the first time in history, will be globalized and interdependent, but without the normative anchor afforded by the West's material and ideological dominance.[6] To be sure, previous historical eras played host to multiple regional hegemonies. During the seventeenth century, for example, the Holy Roman Empire, Ottoman Empire, Mughal Empire, Qing Dynasty, and Tokugawa Shogunate each governed according to its own rules and cultural norms. These imperial zones were, however, largely self-contained; there was little interaction among them, and thus little need to agree upon a set of common norms to preserve order. The onset of globalization during the nineteenth century then coincided with – indeed, was a product of – the West's ascent, meaning that Europe and, thereafter, the United States have overseen the international system in place since the end of the Napoleonic Wars. The next world will thus be the first in which diverse orders intensely and continuously interact with each other in the absence of Western hegemony. In a world that will be both interdependent and multipolar, global governance will be more vital – but also more elusive.

---

[5] On the relationship between ideological difference and the potential for conflict, see Mark Haas, *The Ideological Origins of Great Power Politics, 1789–1989* (Ithaca, NY: Cornell University Press, 2005); and Mark Haas, *The Clash of Ideologies: Middle Eastern Politics and American Security* (New York, NY: Oxford University Press, 2012).

[6] See Charles A. Kupchan, *No One's World: The West, the Rising Rest, and the Coming Global Turn* (New York, NY: Oxford University Press, 2012), pp. 46–73, 182–186.

This chapter seeks to advance the task of unpacking the normative content of different hegemonic orders.[7] It examines the norms shaping the social relations that are the sinews of hegemony. In the service of developing an anatomy of order-producing norms, the chapter explores four dimensions of hegemonic order:

1. Geopolitical logic – the metropole's architecture of order and hegemonic design.
2. Socioeconomic logic – the structure of the metropole's socioeconomic order and its replication of that order within its zone of hegemony.
3. Cultural logic – the metropole's approach to cultural attributes (inclusive or exclusive on matters of race, religion, and ethnicity).
4. Commercial logic – the metropole's structuring of economic relations within and beyond its hegemonic zone.

The following section elaborates this chapter's theoretical underpinnings. The chapter contends that as great powers rise, they as a matter of course seek to extend to their expanding spheres of influence the norms that provide order within their own polities. They do so to advance their ideological as well as material interests. The chapter next provides empirical support for this argument by exploring the substantive differences among the logics of geopolitics, socioeconomics, culture, and commerce across four hegemonic powers: the Ottoman Empire, Imperial China, Great Britain, and the United States. Investigation of these four cases affords considerable temporal, geographic, and cultural variation.

---

[7] With its focus on international norms and the social character of interstate relations, the constructivist literature provides a useful foundation for pursuing this task. See, for example, Martha Finnemore, *National Interests in International Society* (Ithaca, NY: Cornell University Press, 1996); Emanuel Adler and Michael Barnett, ed., *Security Communities* (Cambridge University Press, 1998); Alexander Wendt, *Social Theory of International Politics* (Cambridge University Press, 1999); Patrick Jackson, *Civilizing the Enemy: German Reconstruction and the Invention of the West* (Ann Arbor, MI: University of Michigan Press, 2006); and Christian Reus-Smit, *The Moral Purpose of the State: Culture, Social Identity, and Institutional Rationality in International Relations* (Princeton University Press, 2009). This chapter advances the constructivist literature by investigating in a systematic way the normative dimensions of hegemony, a subject that has received relatively little attention from constructivists. It also represents a synthesis of constructivist and rationalist approaches by demonstrating how ideational, cultural, and material interests combine to shape the social purpose of hegemonic powers. Constructivist scholars often distance themselves too far from materialist explanations, failing to appreciate that ideational and normative preferences are often derivative of materialist incentives and socioeconomic trajectories. Finally, this chapter advances the constructivist agenda by being primarily empirical rather than theoretical in its focus. The study of norms and ideas can be empirically challenging; identifying the different logics that shape hegemony and specifying their substantive content helps fill out the social theory that informs constructivism.

The cases also offer potential insight into the future, illuminating through historical inquiry the different approaches to order that may prevail in the Middle East, China, and among Western democracies. Indeed, the concluding section of the chapter draws on China's imperial past to reflect on how Chinese conceptions of hegemony might evolve in the twenty-first century.

The chapter reveals the starkly different normative orientations of these four hegemonic powers. Ottoman rulers governed through a hub-and-spoke imperial structure that rested on vertical lines of authority; drawing on Islamic tradition, the sultan wielded both temporal and religious authority, keeping tight control over administration, commerce, and social inclusion. The long era of Chinese hegemony in East Asia took the form of a highly ritualized hegemonic order based on concentric circles of Sinicization; geopolitical architecture depended more on cultural than material dominance, with Confucian tradition providing the basis for normative consensus. In contrast, the British Empire rested on horizontal linkages among a global network of peripheral strongpoints, reflecting its commercial origins as well as its cultural universalism. The United States embraced different geopolitical architectures in different theaters; it was motivated more by strategic necessity than commercial opportunity. The United States upheld the British preference for a liberal trading system, but the more open and consensual character of US hegemony reflected America's more egalitarian social order as well as its ideological commitment to democratization.

Based on the normative diversity of these four hegemonic zones, the chapter concludes by challenging the proposition, popular among policy-makers and scholars alike, that emerging powers are likely to embrace the liberal international order on offer from the West.[8] Instead, today's rising powers – as have their predecessors throughout history – will craft hegemonic aspirations informed by their own histories, cultures, and social norms. As Peter Katzenstein notes, societies are today following "different programs of modernity" instead of "converging on a common path involving capitalist industrialism, political democracy ... and pluralizing secularisms."[9] China is a case in point. As its economic and military strength grows, China will seek to push outward to its sphere of influence its own ordering norms. China's quest to restore a Sinocentric brand of hegemony in East Asia, its adherence to one-party rule, and its

[8] See, for example, G. John Ikenberry, "The Future of the Liberal World Order: Internationalism after America," *Foreign Affairs*, Vol. 90, No. 3 (May/June 2011), pp. 56–68.
[9] Katzenstein, *Civilizations in World Politics*, p. 17.

commitment to state capitalism at home and mercantilism abroad will challenge the foundational norms of Pax Americana. Far from embracing the current international order, China and other emerging powers will seek to advance alternative norms that further their ideological preferences and material interests.

If a rules-based global order is to emerge as multipolarity advances, that order will have to reflect the cultural and political diversity of the major powers that shape and comprise it. The pathway most likely to afford stability may well be a more regionalized world, one in which multiple hegemonic powers exercise material and normative sway in their respective spheres of influence. Global governance would entail a mixture of tolerance and coordination among these disparate regional orders.

Norms and social relations in hegemonic orders

Most work on the logics and structures of hegemony rests on rationalist and materialist foundations. Gilpin's *War and Change* unambiguously identifies shifts in the distribution of material power as the underlying causal engine of the cyclical rise and fall of hegemonies. Charles Kindleberger and Robert Keohane explore the impact of material decline on hegemonic stability.[10] Alfred Mahan and Halford Mackinder debate the relative merits of sea power versus land power in projecting hegemonic control.[11] Ronald Robinson and John Gallagher argue that indirect rule pays more handsomely than direct rule, providing imperial powers with incentives to opt for formal as opposed to informal empire only when resistance in the periphery forces them to do so.[12] John Ikenberry distinguishes between liberal hegemony (rule by consent) and empire (rule by command), and David Lake explores the role of legitimate authority in sustaining hegemonic order.[13] Ikenberry and Lake both focus on the functional and material advantages afforded by strategic restraint and the exercise of hegemony through authority rather than coercion. Indeed,

---

[10] Charles Kindleberger, *The World in Depression, 1929–1939* (Berkeley, CA: University of California Press, 1986); Robert Keohane, *After Hegemony: Cooperation and Discord in the World Political Economy* (Princeton University Press, 1984).

[11] Halford J. Mackinder, "The Geographical Pivot of History," *Geographical Journal*, Vol. 23, No. 4 (April 1904), pp. 421–437; Alfred T. Mahan, *The Influence of Sea Power upon History, 1660–1783* (Boston, MA: Little, Brown, 1890).

[12] John Gallagher and Ronald Robinson, "The Imperialism of Free Trade," *The Economic History Review*, Second series, Vol. 6, No. 1 (1953), pp. 1–15.

[13] See their chapters in this volume, as well as G. John Ikenberry, *Liberal Leviathan: The Origins, Crisis, and Transformation of the American World Order* (Princeton University Press, 2011); and David Lake, *Hierarchy in International Relations* (Ithaca, NY: Cornell University Press, 2011).

Ikenberry's optimism that the Western order will endure even as the West's material primacy wanes arises from his confidence in the functional advantages of its liberal character.[14]

Such efforts to unpack the material costs and benefits of different dimensions of hegemony have yielded important insights; the character and durability of hegemony indeed vary as a consequence of the functional advantages of specific modes of control. But the nature of hegemony, however, is also shaped by normative dimensions of order. Gilpin, for one, recognizes as much, noting that major states "enter social relations and create social structures in order to advance particular sets of political, economic, or other types of interests."[15] As Gilpin acknowledges, states that enjoy a preponderance of power as a matter of course exercise their ability to structure social relations within their hegemonic zones. These "social structures" serve as the infrastructure of hegemonic order. They give hierarchy and hegemony social character and enable the hegemon to assert its normative preferences. Put differently, these social structures bring to life hegemonic rule in the same way that ordering norms shape and inform political and social relations inside a unitary state.

A chief objective of this chapter is to build on this core insight and to demonstrate that hegemonic orders are shaped by normative as well as material preferences. The allure of advancing security and prosperity matters a great deal; material considerations provide the main incentives for great powers to expand, and they heavily influence when and where such expansion occurs. At the same time, normative preferences and social and cultural orientations affect the character of hegemony and the nature of the rule that metropoles exercise over their peripheries. Neither material considerations nor norms are determinative. Rather, material incentives and normative preferences work in tandem to shape hegemonic rule.

This chapter contends that the norms informing hegemonic orders are often derivative of the metropole's own domestic order. As Martha Finnemore and Kathryn Sikkink note, "domestic norms ... are deeply entwined with the working of international norms. Many international norms began as domestic norms ..."[16] For a number of reasons, metropoles export to their zones of influence the norms and rules that prevail at home. They press outward the norms that shape their domestic orders because hegemonies, just like unitary states, are social entities, not just material instruments of control; they reflect the hegemon's own values

---

[14] Ikenberry, *Liberal Leviathan*, Chapter 8.   [15] Gilpin, *War and Change*, p. 9.
[16] Martha Finnemore and Kathryn Sikkink, "International Norm Dynamics and Political Change," *International Organization*, Vol. 52, No. 4 (Autumn 1998), pp. 887–917, 893.

and norms as well as its preponderant power. Such norms are the sources of order and strength in the metropole and are deemed appropriate to serve the same function in the periphery. Moreover, the norms that provide order at home are the ones that metropolitan elites know and practice. These elites as a matter of course bring these norms with them when they exert power abroad, thereby conveying the metropole's social preferences to peripheral states.

Metropoles also replicate their own ordering norms throughout their spheres of influence because it is in their material interest to do so. The Ottomans constructed a hub-and-spoke economy controlled from Istanbul, the Soviets erected a command economy throughout the Eastern Bloc, and the United States propagated market capitalism because fashioning the periphery in the metropole's image furthered its economic and strategic objectives. If the metropolitan economy depends on controlled supply and prices, then it stands to reason that imperial authorities would seek to erect compatible economic structures in the periphery. If the metropole operates according to market principles, then it would seek a hegemonic order whose economy rests on similar economic norms and practices. By seeking to reproduce in the periphery the socioeconomic order that prevails at home, the metropole advances the interests of its own political and economic elites. In this respect, hegemonic zones reflect both the social norms and material interests of the states that construct and oversee them; social ideals intimately intertwine with material incentives in shaping hegemonic order.[17]

Inasmuch as hegemonies represent normative orders and not just material hierarchies, hegemonic transitions entail competition over norms and rules as well as position and status. As a great power rises, it seeks to push outward to its expanding sphere of influence a set of ordering norms unique to its own cultural, socioeconomic, and political orientations. The defining characteristics of a particular hegemonic zone "bubble up" from the normative proclivities of the great power that establishes it. For this reason hegemonic transitions are usually ideological contests, not just material ones, as amply demonstrated by World War II and the Cold War, which pitted fascism and communism, respectively, against liberal democracy.[18] It is also for this reason that the redistribution of power currently unfolding will challenge not just the international pecking order, but also the founding norms of Pax Americana. As China and other emerging powers ascend, each will seek to propagate norms

[17] See Ikenberry and Kupchan, "Socialization and Hegemonic Power."
[18] On the ideological foundations of great-power rivalry, see Haas, *The Ideological Origins of Great Power Politics*.

and rules that emerge from its unique domestic milieu. Accordingly, the universalization of the Western order is not in the offing. On the contrary, if the coming transition in global power is to occur peacefully, the West will have to make room for the alternative ordering norms that emerging powers will press outward as they rise.

In mapping out the normative dimensions of hegemony, this chapter focuses on four main logics of order: geopolitical, socioeconomic, cultural, and commercial. Geopolitical logic – the architecture of order – varies widely from one hegemony to the next.[19] Some great powers erect a hub-and-spoke pattern of control over subjugated peripheries, while others build up their peripheries as interconnected points of strength. Some hegemons construct hierarchies consisting of concentric circles of control emanating from the metropole, while others exert control in a less uniform and more variegated fashion. Some great powers aim to vanquish or transform challengers, while others seek primarily to balance against adversaries. These and other variations in geopolitical logic are to some extent determined by geography and material considerations. But they are also shaped by normative preferences and social orientations.

The Ottoman Empire, for example, relied on a hub-and-spoke pattern of rule radiating outward from Istanbul. The priority assigned to hierarchy meant that the Ottomans generally sought to eliminate adversaries rather than balance against them. This type of order had functional utility – the effective maintenance of imperial authority – but it also had normative origins. Islam provided the sultan not only legitimacy, but also broad control over virtually all aspects of imperial rule. Islamic norms of governance as well as functionality shaped the architecture of empire. Britain's architecture of order represented a sharp contrast. Pax Britannica explicitly avoided direct control of neighboring territory in continental Europe and rested instead on horizontal linkages among peripheral strongpoints. The British also tended to balance against adversaries rather than seek to defeat them. This geopolitical logic was partly material in origin; as an island nation, Britain focused on naval hegemony rather than contiguous continental expansion and normally lacked the ground forces needed to conquer enemies. But this logic also had social origins. The notion of "splendid isolation" from the Continent, which came to anchor British grand strategy, emerged from a conception of hegemony focused primarily on commercial rather than strategic objectives. So too did the practice of balancing against other

---

[19] On structures of empire and hegemony, see Daniel Nexon and Thomas Wright, "What's at Stake in the American Empire Debate?" *American Political Science Review*, Vol. 101, No. 2 (May 2007), pp. 253–271.

centers of power become an embedded norm for Britain's political class. The Ottoman and British empires represent only two of many possible architectures of order.

Hegemonic zones also rest on a particular socioeconomic logic.[20] Within their spheres of influence, great powers tend to replicate the social hierarchies that shape the distribution of wealth and power in their own polities. Metropoles with social orders in which wealth and status are highly restricted and concentrated are likely to encourage the same in their peripheries; in such hegemonic zones, metropolitan elites tend to undermine independent sources of wealth and status in the periphery. In contrast, metropoles with more stratified social orders are likely to encourage similar social hierarchy in their peripheries. In such cases, metropolitan elites tend to coopt peripheral elites as collaborators.[21] The tendency of great powers to replicate their social orders internationally is partly a product of material interest – societal compatibility facilitates control and trade. It is also, however, a consequence of normative orientation; hegemons as a matter of course want their hegemonic orders to reflect their own political and social values.

Wealth and power in the Ottoman realm were concentrated in the hands of the sultan; other imperial agents – administrators, *ulema* (Islamic scholars), the Janissaries, the cavalry – all served at the pleasure of the sultan and depended upon him for their status and income. Imperial relations with the periphery followed. By stripping landed aristocrats of their holdings, regularly rotating imperial administrators, and preventing the accumulation of wealth in the provinces, Ottoman authorities ensured that no alternative center of power would emerge as a counterweight to Istanbul. In contrast, Britain sought to replicate its own stratified social hierarchy throughout its empire. Colonial envoys cultivated peripheral collaborators, many of whom were local notables. Britain also invested in a peripheral elite trained in English and in British administration and law. London sought to build up rather than undermine socioeconomic hierarchy in the periphery, using that hierarchy as a source of local order. Both at home and in the periphery, independent wealth was viewed as a key element of imperial strength.

Hegemonic zones also rest on a cultural logic that shapes the ordering role played by religion, race, and ethnicity. Some hegemonies are particularistic and exclusive – they serve the interests of a privileged in-group. Others are based on cultural inclusivity and a universalizing ambition.

[20] See Skidmore, *Contested Social Orders*.
[21] Social orders in the periphery as well as in the metropole shape the nature of the interface between metropolitan agents and colonized elites. See Michael Doyle, *Empires* (Ithaca, NY: Cornell University Press, 1986), pp. 162–231.

In general, great powers that embrace an exclusivist conception of membership within the metropole do the same throughout their hegemonic zones; peripheral populations are subject to not just political subjugation, but also cultural subjugation. Social inclusion runs along ethnic, racial, and religious lines. Great powers that embrace an inclusive conception of membership within the metropole do the same in their hegemonies; political subjugation is often the pathway to social inclusion irrespective of ethnic, racial, and religious differences. Such hegemonies are vehicles for the exportation of values and identity across cultural dividing lines.

The Ottoman Empire was an Islamic polity for and of Muslims. The expansion of the empire at times led to religious conversion – as in the Balkans. But many non-Muslims also resided within the empire's territorial boundaries. Indeed, Byzantine Christians often rose to influential positions within the imperial apparatus, and Armenians, Jews, and other minorities were prominent merchants. These subjects were grouped along confessional lines; social inclusion was defined by religion. In contrast, the British Empire espoused universalist ambition and incorporated on an ostensibly equal basis many races, religions, and ethnic groups. To be sure, Anglo-Saxons from the metropole sat atop a de facto social hierarchy, Christian missionaries proselytized in many parts of the imperial periphery, and Britain sought to export its legal system, education system, and bureaucratic traditions. But social inclusion ran along political and territorial, not cultural, lines.

Finally, trade and financial matters within hegemonic zones are shaped by a particular commercial logic. Metropoles with command economies keep tight rein over all aspects of imperial commerce, including prices, trade, capital flows, and the accumulation of wealth. These great powers are usually mercantilist in their foreign economic policies. Other hegemons operate according to market principles and support open trade at home, within their zones of hegemony, and with other countries. In between lie hybrid hegemonies that mix market principles with state control. Differences in commercial logic reflect contrasting social norms toward the appropriate relationship between states and markets and between public and private wealth.

In the Ottoman Empire, Istanbul controlled virtually all aspects of commerce, setting prices for commodities, regulating trade, and blocking the accumulation of wealth outside the imperial apparatus. Ottoman authorities viewed independent wealth in the core as well as the periphery as a threat to imperial rule. Financial instruments were rudimentary compared with the innovations that emerged in Europe, due in part to Islamic law and traditions. In contrast, Britain during its imperial ascent abandoned mercantilism in favor of a principled commitment to free trade. London not only backed relatively open markets for trade and finance, but also provided the protected sea lanes and other public goods needed for such markets to operate. This switch in commercial strategy had material foundations in Britain's search for raw materials for its factories and markets for its goods. But it was also precipitated by socioeconomic and ideational change – the growing political power of Britain's commercial class and the broadening influence of Adam Smith and other economic liberals.

As stated above, the central claim of this chapter is *not* that normative considerations alone determine these logics of hegemony; rather, social norms and material conditions together inform the character of hegemony. For normative as well as functional reasons, great powers structure social relations within their zones of hegemony in very different ways. The normative dimensions of hegemonic order are now examined in greater depth through a discussion of the Ottoman Empire, Imperial China, Great Britain, and the United States. Table 1.1 summarizes the discussion that follows, identifying the main normative characteristics of these four hegemonic powers.

The Ottoman Empire

Geopolitical logic. Imperial authority within the Ottoman realm was vested in the sultan, who from the early sixteenth century onward also served as the caliph, the leader of the Islamic world. The sultan enjoyed a divine mandate and wielded absolute power through the interpretation and implementation of *sharia*, which informed not only religious affairs but also matters of politics, security, and justice. He controlled the imperial administration and all appointees – from high-ranking advisers in Istanbul to low-ranking emissaries in the periphery. The state held tight rein over economic, religious, political, and military affairs, seeking to ensure that the provinces were run directly from Istanbul. Major trunk routes connected the center to the periphery, serving as conduits of control and commerce. According to Karen Barkey, the empire operated as a "hub-and-spoke network structure, where the rim is absent," a system that "made peripheral elites dependent on the center, communicating only with the center rather than with one another."[22]

This architecture of order, which was founded upon an Islamic conception of absolute authority and the merging of religious and secular power, had a profound effect on social relations within the empire. Power ran exclusively along vertical lines, with authority extending downward

[22] Karen Barkey, *Empire of Difference: The Ottomans in Comparative Perspective* (Cambridge University Press, 2008), pp. 9, 18.

Table 1.1: *Logics of hegemonic order*

	Geopolitical	Socioeconomic	Cultural	Commercial
Ottoman Empire	Hub-and-spoke; vertical lines of control; eliminate adversaries	Rigid socioeconomic hierarchy; suppression of independent sites of wealth or social status	Islamic polity; inclusion defined along confessional lines; pragmatic incorporation of minorities through *millet* system	Mercantilist; commerce and trade controlled by imperial authorities
Imperial China (Ming and Qing Dynasties)	Concentric circles of control centered on imperial core; hierarchy a function of cultural more than material dominance; Sinicize adversaries	Rigid socioeconomic hierarchy; Confucian exam system as pathway to social mobility; social order in empire replicated through tributary system	Confucian foundations; assimilation in imperial core; Sinicization through tributary system	Mercantilist; government control of markets, but with accommodation of free enterprise
Great Britain	Horizontal linkages among peripheral strongpoints; avoidance of continental commitment; balance against adversaries	Class hierarchy at home replicated abroad; cultivation and cooptation of peripheral collaborators; encouragement of peripheral wealth	Universalism; inclusion determined by territorial boundaries; racial and ethnic categorization; spread of British culture, language, and religion	Initially mercantilist, subsequently laid foundation for liberal trading order
United States	Variable architecture dependent on strategic circumstances; transform adversaries	Egalitarian aspirations in both core and periphery	Universalism; principled commitment to self-determination; democratizing ambition	Free trade; dismantling of colonial empires; erection of international financial architecture

from the sultan, through the imperial bureaucracy, to cavalry and administrators in the periphery. Officials assigned to the provinces rotated to new areas every three years to ensure that they would not develop strong ties to the local population and organize potential resistance to central authority.[23] Neither merchants nor local notables were able to amass wealth or build local political or commercial networks.[24] Istanbul deliberately forestalled the development of horizontal social linkages that could have developed into counterweights to the sultan's power. To be sure, the imperial administration did not always succeed in extending central authority to remote locations. But instances of regional autonomy were generally the product of distance and local resistance, not imperial design.

The maintenance of hierarchical order similarly informed Ottoman strategy toward adversaries beyond imperial territory. After the Safavid Dynasty came to power in Persia in 1501, Istanbul spent the better part of the sixteenth century seeking to defeat its new rival on the battlefield. To their west, the Ottomans went to war against the Venetians, Hungarians, Austrians, and other Europeans, in 1683 making their final unsuccessful attempt to conquer Vienna – long prized by Istanbul as the strategic key to controlling Central Europe. The Ottomans were generally intent on dominating their adversaries, not on establishing a stable balance of power with them.

Socioeconomic logic. Ottoman society was patrimonial in structure; the sultan sat atop the social hierarchy and both civil administrators and the military effectively served as his personal staff. The sultan and his court enforced the vertical exercise of authority by adopting strategies of governance that neutralized alternative sites of wealth and status. Istanbul not only blocked horizontal social linkages from forming, but also undermined the power base of social sectors that could potentially challenge the sultan's authority. Imperial administrators expropriated the land of aristocratic families and converted it to state-owned property. Land and wealth could no longer be passed from one generation to the next. The power of the landed elite was effectively transferred to administrators and cavalry, to whom the sultan assigned the right to draw

---

[23] *Ibid.*

[24] This system changed over the course of the eighteenth century, when local notables (*ayans*) were granted life tenure as tax collectors. This reform increased central revenue, but also gave rise to a provincial elite that was able to amass wealth and challenge imperial authority. The growing power of the *ayans* was then followed by a period of recentralization in the 1800s. See Carter Vaughn Findley, *Turkey, Islam, Nationalism, and Modernity: A History, 1789–2007* (New Haven, CT: Yale University Press, 2010), pp. 28–29; and Kemal Karpat, "The Transformation of the Ottoman State, 1789–1908," *International Journal of Middle East Studies*, Vol. 3, No. 3 (July 1972), pp. 243–281.

revenue from farms. In return for their service, imperial appointees could tax agricultural production, keeping some of the income for themselves and sending the rest to the central treasury.[25]

Merchants, artisans, and professionals operated only within the confines of the hierarchical state. They were unable to accumulate significant wealth or to raise their social status. Some government functionaries were able to amass considerable savings. They were, however, firmly ensconced within the imperial apparatus, depended upon their posts for their affluence, and could not pass their assets on to their offspring. These restrictions prevented the evolution of powerful and wealthy family lines.

Even the Janissaries – the sultan's personal army – were recruited in a manner intended to prevent their potential emergence as a threat to imperial authority. Initially, the ranks of the Janissaries were filled by young men of Christian background who were prisoners of war. In the early fifteenth century, a system of conscription (*devsirme*) was put into place. The Janissaries were not permitted to come from Muslim families or to marry; these proscriptions ensured that this elite corps could not develop into a hereditary warrior class capable of undermining the sultan's authority. On the contrary, the Janissaries' unique privilege and status engendered loyalty to the sultan.

Over time, the strict protocols that sustained this trustworthy militia began to loosen; during the later empire, the Janissaries were allowed to marry and have children. As the court had initially feared, a loyal imperial guard developed into a hereditary institution that became a potent counterweight to the sultan. This threat to centralized control eventually evoked a harsh reaction. In the early nineteenth century, Mahmud II abolished the Janissary system and killed most of its serving members. Istanbul rigidly enforced socioeconomic hierarchy as a means of preserving imperial unity.

Cultural logic. In keeping with Islamic tradition, the Ottoman realm made no distinction between the secular and the sacred. *Ulema* were key advisers to the sultan, and *sharia* profoundly shaped imperial governance. Islamic law informed virtually all aspects of daily life, including commerce, education, and the justice system. Membership and status within the empire were defined by religion; the cultural foundations of hegemony were particularistic, not universal, in scope. The Ottoman realm was a Muslim polity.

Despite its religious foundations, the Ottoman realm did not exclude non-Muslims. On the contrary, the Ottoman court bolstered hierarchical

---

[25] On changes to land tenure over time, see Findley, *Turkey*, pp. 51–56.

rule by embracing religious heterodoxy. Osman, who founded the empire and ruled from 1299 until 1324, forged political compacts across religious boundaries, incorporating into the empire not only Muslims who embraced diverse traditions, but also Orthodox Christians from the Byzantine Empire – some of whom enjoyed influential positions within the imperial administration. Sunni doctrine and practice were dominant throughout the Ottoman realm, but Shiites and Sufis were generally treated with tolerance.[26]

Accommodations were also made for non-Muslims. The *millet* system allowed non-Muslim communities to retain their own religious and political institutions even as it incorporated them into the empire's hierarchical system of control. Armenians, Greek Orthodox, and Jews, for example, maintained separate courts and religious laws.[27] At the same time, the heads of these minority populations functioned as intermediaries between imperial authorities and their local communities; minority leaders directed their allegiance to Istanbul even as they enjoyed significant autonomy on matters of communal governance. The *millet* system was a pragmatic response to the reality that Ottoman territory was host to a varied population. By defining political status along confessional lines, the Ottomans were able to balance the Islamic character of the empire with the religious diversity of its subjects.

Commercial logic. The Ottoman Empire pursued a mercantilist economic policy. Istanbul's control of commerce was as tight as its oversight of imperial administration. Imperial officials set the prices of goods and regulated the flow of trade, in no small part to fill the central treasury and ensure that the government could secure commodities at preferential cost.[28] Foreign trade was somewhat less regulated than commerce within the empire, but it was handled primarily by Greeks, Jews, Armenians, and other non-Muslims. Moreover, the Ottomans did not develop a modern banking system – a consequence of the constraints imposed by Islamic legal practices – instead relying on informal networks of lending and, eventually, on European financiers doing business in

---

[26] William McNeill, *The Rise of the West* (University of Chicago Press, 1963), p. 626. The toleration of religious diversity gradually diminished after the Safavid Dynasty came to power in neighboring Persia in the early sixteenth century, putting Shiites in control of a principal geopolitical competitor to the Ottomans. Thereafter, Ottoman authorities no longer viewed Shiites as just religious dissenters, but instead saw them as a direct internal and external threat to the empire.

[27] Daniel Goffman, *The Ottoman Empire and Early Modern Europe* (Cambridge University Press, 2002), p. 73.

[28] Hendrik Spruyt, *The Sovereign State and Its Competitors* (Princeton University Press, 1994), p. 16; and Suraiya Faroqhi, *The Ottoman Empire and the World Around It* (New York, NY: I.B. Tauris, 2007), pp. 16–17, 94, 156.

Ottoman lands.[29] The Ottomans thus subcontracted specific commercial functions to outsiders who would not threaten imperial power or contravene Islamic traditions – meanwhile keeping tight control of commerce among the bulk of the population.

Ottoman reliance on centralized control of religious, political, and economic life preserved imperial unity for centuries. Istanbul's hub-and-spoke mode of rule, its enforcement of a rigid socioeconomic hierarchy, its approach to managing confessional diversity, and its mercantilist economic policies had clear functional utility. At the same time, they were imbued with norms derived from Islamic traditions. Indeed, the staying power of those normative orientations became clear over the course of the nineteenth century, when Ottoman rulers resisted change even after the realm's eclipse by a rising Europe had exposed the disadvantages of the Ottoman approach to hegemonic rule. The *Tanzimat* reform movement sought to import European practices in order to revitalize the Ottoman realm, but the empire's social norms were too deeply embedded and its institutions too inflexible. By the late 1800s, the rigidity of its normative order, rather than preserving imperial unity, was contributing to hegemonic decline.

Imperial China

Chinese hegemony in East Asia spans many centuries. Its origins date to the Shang era in the fifteenth century BCE. China's last imperial dynasty – the Qing – officially collapsed in 1912. Over the course of the centuries in between, different dynasties embraced varying approaches to managing hegemony. Nonetheless, the evolution of the tributary system and the normative anchor provided by Confucian conceptions of order and governance made for important continuities. This section provides a distillation of China's logic of imperial management, drawing heavily on the Ming (1368–1644) and Qing (1644–1912) dynasties. In important respects, these final dynasties represent the culmination of the tributary system and the long era of Chinese domination of East Asia.[30]

---

[29] For a comprehensive study of Ottoman commercial and financial practices, see Timur Kuran, *The Long Divergence: How Islamic Law Held Back the Middle East* (Princeton University Press, 2011). Kuran's main argument is that "The Middle East fell behind the West because it was late in adopting key institutions of the modern economy." Quotation from p. 5.

[30] See Yongjin Zhang and Barry Buzan, "The Tributary System as International Society in Theory and Practice," *Chinese Journal of International Politics*, Vol. 5, No. 1 (Spring 2012), pp. 3–36, 22–23; and Mark Mancall, "The Ch'ing Tribute System: An Interpretive Essay," in John Fairbank, ed., *The Chinese World Order* (Cambridge, MA: Harvard University Press, 1968), pp. 63–89, 66.

Geopolitical logic. The tributary system established a hierarchical order in which hegemony was arrayed in concentric circles around the imperial core. In the innermost circle – China proper – imperial authorities and soldiers exercised direct control. The empire did not maintain fixed borders: they waxed and waned as continuing struggles with nomadic peoples in the north and west produced fluid frontiers. Expansion was particularly pronounced during the Qing, which more than doubled the size of the territory that had been under direct imperial rule during the preceding Ming.[31] When such expansion occurred, imperial authorities exercised tight vertical control by extending the central bureaucracy into new areas. In order to forestall the emergence of local centers of power that could challenge central rule, top provincial officers had to come from regions other than the one in which they served. As in the Ottoman Empire, they also rotated to new posts every three years.[32]

Although central authorities maintained strictly vertical lines of rule, the imperial bureaucracy was limited in size and governed with a relatively light touch. The Chinese army was also comparatively small given the size of the territory under its protection. Confucian tradition placed considerable value on lean and efficient governance – in the words of John Bryan Starr, "a minimal state with maximal reach."[33] Beyond imperial territory, China exercised only indirect rule over subordinate parties; hierarchy was more the product of deference and legitimate authority than of coercive control of the sort exercised within the Ottoman Empire. As William Wohlforth and his co-authors conclude, order within the tributary system rested on a combination of "a unipolar distribution of capabilities centered on China with a ramified cultural and normative overlay."[34]

The tributary system was strictly bilateral; it created a hub-and-spoke pattern of relations with peripheral states. Delegations from these states regularly visited the Chinese court to pay tribute. The gifts brought by these delegations did not represent an onerous tax, but were primarily ritualistic and symbolic in nature – a sign of respect and acknowledgment of China's material and cultural dominance.[35] In return, tribute

---

[31] William Rowe, *China's Last Empire: The Great Qing* (Cambridge, MA: Harvard University Press, 2009), p. 1.

[32] *Ibid.*, pp. 38–39.

[33] John Bryan Starr, *Understanding China: A Guide to China's Economy, History, and Political Structure* (New York, NY: Hill and Wang, 1997), p. 41.

[34] William Wohlforth, et al., "Testing Balance-of-Power Theory in World History," *European Journal of International Relations*, Vol. 13, No. 2 (June 2007), pp. 155–185, 173.

[35] See Joseph Esherick, "China and the World: From Tribute to Treaties to Popular Nationalism," in Brantly Womack, ed., *China's Rise in Historical Perspective* (Lanham, MD: Rowman and Littlefield, 2010), pp. 19–38, 19–20.

states enjoyed the benefits of inclusion in China's hegemonic sphere of influence, including lucrative trade links and military protection. Nonetheless, these states enjoyed significant autonomy over their own domestic affairs and foreign policy; Imperial China treated tribute states as subordinates, but did not seek to control them.

Cultural more than geographic proximity determined whether tribute states stood in the inner or outer circle of Chinese hegemony. Japan, Korea, the Ryukyu Islands, and Vietnam were in the inner circle. These states all embraced significant elements of Chinese script and vocabulary, Confucian learning, and China's exam system and meritocratic bureaucracy. Japan, which was more determined to resist Sinicization than Vietnam and Korea, was accorded lower status and permitted to send fewer tribute missions to China.[36] States in the outer ring, such as Cambodia, Borneo, Burma, Siam, and Indonesia, were significantly less Sinicized than states in the inner ring. The geopolitical structure of the tributary system was thus heavily informed by cultural norms. According to Yongjin Zhang and Barry Buzan, "There was clear acknowledgment of the legitimacy of the authority of Chinese hegemony derived from its cultural achievements, and not from material power."[37] David Kang agrees that "cultural achievement in the form of status was as important a goal as was military or economic power."[38]

The geopolitical logic that informed Chinese conceptions of hegemony also allowed for considerable flexibility as to inclusion. The boundaries of the empire fluctuated regularly. While some non-Han populations were Sinicized and incorporated into imperial territory, others exited; the imperial frontier was adjusted accordingly.

The tributary system was similarly flexible; states could begin or end their participation at will. According to Zhang and Buzan, "The tributary system ... has open access and is also inherently elastic."[39] Such malleability was in part a function of the cultural content of Chinese conceptions of hegemony. Since Chinese power stemmed more from political and moral suasion than coercion, states exiting China's sphere of influence were demonstrating their own cultural shortcomings, not posing a challenge to Chinese authority.

China's unique conception of hegemonic order and the elasticity of that order had distinct pacifying effects. Although both the Ming and

---

[36] David Kang, *East Asia Before the West: Five Centuries of Trade and Tribute* (New York, NY: Columbia University Press, 2010), pp. 59–60.
[37] Zhang and Buzan, "The Tributary System," p. 25.
[38] Kang, *East Asia Before the West*, p. 8.
[39] Zhang and Buzan, "The Tributary System," p. 19.

Qing engaged in regular skirmishes with nomads along the imperial frontier, war among major states in the tributary system was, by comparative standards, quite rare. Between the middle of the fourteenth century and the middle of the nineteenth, only two brief wars occurred – between China and Vietnam from 1402 to 1428, and between Japan and Korea from 1592 to 1598.[40]

Socioeconomic logic. The socioeconomic order of Imperial China was highly stratified. Qing society consisted of five classes: aristocrats, officials, degree-holding literati, free commoners, and debased persons (such as criminals, beggars, and prostitutes). The upper classes were thinly populated, and entry was highly restrictive. The main vehicle for upward mobility was the exam system, and only a select few were able to pass these rigorous tests of Confucian learning. During the later Qing, the expansion of markets and the spread of literacy opened up new opportunities for social advancement. But a nascent middle class remained within the confines of the traditional social hierarchy. Indeed, imperial authorities coopted newly empowered actors – such as wealthy families and merchant and artisan guilds – to reinforce social control at the local level.[41]

The Confucian emphasis on patrilineal traditions and the centrality of the nuclear family played a significant role in producing social stasis. A societal order deeply rooted in ritual and normative consensus preserved hierarchy even in the face of commercialization and greater opportunities for upward mobility. As William Rowe notes, imperial authorities were adept "in the use of normative and ritual means for social control."[42] Ritualized practice and normative consensus mattered more than the distribution of wealth in shaping China's domestic socioeconomic order.

China's socioeconomic order in many respects served as a blueprint for the tributary system; the metropole pressed outward to its zone of hegemony the Confucian norms that provided order at home. According to Brantly Womack, the moral, ritualistic, and hierarchical character of China's own social order was a model for the norms, rituals, and hierarchical order that informed relations with tribute states.[43] Within the empire as well as within China's broader zone of hegemony, order

---

[40] See Kang, *East Asia Before the West*, pp. 82–106.

[41] William Rowe, "Social Stability and Social Change," in Willard Peterson, ed., *The Cambridge History of China: The Ch'ing Empire to 1800*, Vol. 9, Part 1 (Cambridge University Press, 2003), pp. 473–562; and Rowe, *China's Last Empire*, p. 33.

[42] Rowe, *China's Last Empire*, p. 33

[43] Brantly Womack, "Introduction," in Womack, ed., *China's Rise in Historical Perspective*, p. 4.

was the product of cultural and social norms at least as much as the exercise of preponderant material power.

Cultural logic. Imperial China's claim to hegemony rested on a logic of cultural superiority as well as material primacy. Indeed, the Chinese saw themselves as representing not just a higher civilization, but *the* civilization – the global standard bearer.[44] The empire was traditionally referred to as *Zhongguo*, which means "central kingdom" or "center of civilization." In keeping with this culturally informed conception of imperial power, the civil service exams – the main pathway to a post in the imperial apparatus – tested primarily knowledge of Confucian texts and poetry, not matters of administration or policy. Schooling in Chinese culture and morality was the principal qualification for positions of leadership and responsibility.[45] In similar fashion, participation in the tributary system entailed deference to Chinese culture and the embrace of Chinese ritual. As mentioned above, states that were part of the tributary system were divided into two categories depending upon their level of Sinicization. "Cooked" or "inner" barbarians, such as the Koreans, adhered more closely to Chinese culture. "Raw" or "outer" barbarians, such as the populations of Southeast Asia and Central Asia, were seen as more distant culturally and thus of lower status within the tributary system.[46]

Sinicization took place not just among tribute states, but also through imperial expansion into China's borderlands. Indeed, it was along the imperial frontier that China most intently pursued cultural assimilation. Imperial authorities at times aspired to "turn the frontier into a fixed border and expand institutional control outward from the center."[47] But Tibetans, Uighurs, Mongols, Khitans, Manchus, and other nomadic groups confronted China with a daunting ethnic and cultural diversity. Accordingly, imperial administrators sought to ensure that China's language, marriage and burial rites, patrilineal customs, and education system – along with other cultural practices – moved in step with the frontier. The Ming Dynasty put particular emphasis on inter-marriage; although the provision was not always enforced, minorities were required to marry Han Chinese.[48] The Qing orchestrated migration of Han to the periphery, encouraged frontier populations to embrace Confucian ritual, and usually paired officials of non-Han background with a Han

---

[44] Zhang and Buzan, "The Tributary System," p. 11.

[45] Rowe, *China's Last Empire*, pp. 45–46.

[46] *Ibid.*, pp. 133–134. See also Kang, *East Asia Before the West*, pp. 47–54.

[47] Kang, *East Asia Before the West*, p. 157.

[48] Ping-ti Ho, "In Defense of Sinicization: A Rebuttal of Evelyn Rawski's 'Reenvisioning the Qing,'" *The Journal of Asian Studies*, Vol. 57, No. 1 (February 1998), pp. 123–155, 141.

counterpart. The central government also arranged pilgrimages, trade missions, and participation in the Imperial Hunt as means of drawing non-Han populations into China's cultural sphere of influence.[49]

Acculturation was, of course, not a one-way street. The practices and rituals that emerged in frontier regions represented a cultural amalgam, not a pure form of Sinicization. As the empire expanded, Han populations not only propagated their rituals in the borderlands, but also absorbed the traditions of nomadic peoples. Some outlying regions also enjoyed a significant measure of cultural autonomy. Mongols and Tibetans, for example, tended to maintain their own systems of local administration. Frontier regions were thus characterized by complexity and fluidity on matters of culture, identity, and ethnicity.[50] Nonetheless, borderlands that enjoyed relative cultural autonomy were the exception; Imperial China for the most part pursued a purposeful and determined strategy aimed at Sinicizing its non-Han populations.

It is also the case that even military victors over China acquiesced to Chinese culture rather than vice versa. The Manchus that ruled during the Qing era adopted the Chinese language, jettisoned their own marriage and burial ceremonies in favor of Chinese practices, and accepted the Confucian canon as the foundation for governance and the civil service exam. According to Evelyn Rawski, "No one can deny that the Manchus portrayed themselves as Chinese rulers."[51] Ping-ti Ho agrees that "Manchu success at [governing] ... was achieved in large measure by drawing upon a Chinese tradition of policies and institutions."[52]

Imperial China had little regular contact with states beyond the tributary system until the late Qing. Such states were beyond the Sinic sphere of influence – and hence alien. From this perspective, Imperial China embraced a particularistic, not universalistic, conception of its culture. Through assimilation and/or subordination, other peoples – barbarians of one sort or another – could enter China's sphere of hegemony. But China had no interest in exporting its political system or values beyond the tributary system. Unlike Britain and the United States, which embraced universalizing creeds, Imperial China adhered to an exceptionalist notion of its cultural uniqueness and superiority.

[49] Rowe, "Social Stability and Social Change," p. 507; and Rowe, *China's Last Empire*, pp. 38–40.
[50] Evelyn Rawski, "Presidential Address: Reenvisioning the Qing: The Significance of the Qing Period in Chinese History," *The Journal of Asian Studies*, Vol. 55, No. 4 (November 1996), pp. 829–850, 833, 841–842; and Rowe, "Social Stability and Social Change," p. 511.
[51] Rawski, "Reenvisioning the Qing," p. 834.
[52] Ho, "In Defense of Sinicization,", p. 125.

Commercial logic. Imperial China was broadly mercantilist and the central government oversaw a command economy; economic activity was to serve the purposes of the state. The main source of imperial revenue was taxation of agricultural production. Tribute missions, official trade (commerce under the auspices of the tributary system), and private trade (which was subject to duties) also contributed to imperial wealth. Even though Qing authorities oversaw a command economy, they were less intrusive and rent-seeking than their Ottoman counterparts. Confucian standards of governance encouraged the central government to be sensitive to the material wants of its population. Moreover, the need to increase agricultural production to keep pace with the population growth of the Qing era prompted imperial authorities to tap market incentives. Local merchants and prominent families had expanding latitude to engage in private commerce. By the end of the eighteenth century, roughly 10% of grain production and 25% of cotton production were traded on the open market.[53] The same approach applied to foreign trade. The central government generally looked askance at private commerce with foreign parties but nonetheless permitted it.[54]

Even as private markets expanded, however, they did so within the context of a command economy and a socioeconomic order shaped by Confucian tradition. Wealthy merchants sought not to overturn or circumvent that order, but to ascend the social hierarchy by joining the educated elite.[55] As markets for grain and other commodities grew, imperial authorities intervened to stabilize prices and to oversee their distribution. In Rowe's words, "the Qing strategy was to use the market to control the market."[56] China thus has a long tradition of intermixing commercial markets with state control.

China's long run of hegemony in East Asia rested on a highly ritualized order informed by Confucian norms. Its geopolitical architecture consisted of concentric circles radiating outward from the imperial core; hierarchical control was a function of China's cultural dominance as much as its material superiority. A stratified and ritualized socioeconomic order at home was replicated abroad through the tributary system. A particularistic conception of inclusion informed the character of Chinese hegemony, with assimilation and Sinicization serving as key elements of social and political control. Imperial China embraced a hybrid commercial logic that mixed state control with market mechanisms.

---

[53] Rowe, *China's Last Empire*, p. 123.
[54] Dwight H. Perkins, "China's Prereform Economy in World Perspective," in Womack, ed., *China's Rise in Historical Perspective*, p. 111.
[55] Rowe, *China's Last Empire*, pp. 127–133.   [56] *Ibid.*, p. 56.

Great Britain

Geopolitical logic. In contrast to the Ottomans and Chinese, who built contiguous, hub-and-spoke imperial zones, the British erected a seaborne empire that rested on naval mastery and a network of horizontal linkages among far-flung peripheral strongpoints. London deliberately eschewed strategic commitments on its neighboring landmass. Instead, the British relied on diplomacy, assistance, and occasional and temporary bouts of military intervention to maintain an equilibrium of power on the Continent that would leave Britain free to keep its army small and focus its attention and resources on the imperial periphery. Also in contrast to the Ottomans and Chinese, who often sought to eliminate or assimilate adversaries, Britain regularly sought to maintain stable balances of power – not dominion – in key strategic theaters, including Europe, the western Atlantic, and the Far East.

This hegemonic architecture was heavily influenced by geography. England was an island nation afforded protection by the Channel; seaborne expansion would play to its comparative advantage. In the early sixteenth century, Henry VIII's advisers spelled out a principle that would guide the country's grand strategy for centuries to come: "Let us in God's name leave off our attempts against the *terra firma*. The natural situation of islands seems not to consort with conquests of that kind. England alone is a just Empire. Or, when we would enlarge ourselves, let it be that way we can, and to which it seems the eternal Providence hath destined us, which is by the sea."[57] As shipbuilding and navigation improved in quality, English merchants and emigrants, eventually backed by the Royal Navy, ventured ever farther from the home islands.

Geography alone, however, is not sufficient to explain the evolution of a hegemonic architecture resting on seaborne linkages among peripheral strongpoints.[58] Other island nations – Japan, for example – pursued imperial ambitions on its neighboring mainland. Britain's unique imperial structure was in part a product of its distinctively commercial origins.

From the outset, imperial expansion was meant to be a paying proposition. Colonies were to provide markets and raw materials for the

[57] J.H. Rose, A.P. Newton, and E.A. Benians, *The Cambridge History of the British Empire*, Vol. 1 (Cambridge University Press, 1929), p. 95.
[58] On the foundations of Britain's imperial architecture, see Lance Davis and Robert Huttenback, *Mammon and the Pursuit of Empire: The Political Economy of British Imperialism, 1860–1912* (Cambridge University Press, 2009); and Mark Brawley, *Liberal Leadership: Great Powers and Their Challengers in Peace and War* (Ithaca, NY: Cornell University Press, 1994).

metropolitan economy. Indeed, India, the "jewel in the crown," was for decades under the administration of the British East India Tea Company and became a formal colony only in 1813. Unlike the Ottoman Empire, which was structured primarily to maximize hierarchical control, the British Empire was more regularly structured to maximize profits.[59] London cherry-picked territories that would provide commercial opportunities and afford the Royal Navy control over the main transportation chokepoints. Linkages among these chokepoints produced the horizontal strategic network that stands in stark contrast to the vertical, hub-and-spoke lines of control maintained by Ottoman authorities.

It is also the case that British reliance on sea power and the notion of "splendid isolation" from the Continent became a deeply embedded norm in the official and public mind. The degree to which avoidance of continental commitments was a social norm that imbued strategic culture – and not just a rationalist strategy born of material conditions – became clear after Germany unified in 1871 and soon thereafter overturned a stable balance of power in Europe. In the years leading up to World War I, the British government maintained ambiguity about its readiness to undertake a continental commitment – principally out of fear of a political backlash. London's stance, even if inadvertently, encouraged German adventurism; Berlin's decision to launch the invasion that started World War I presumed British neutrality.[60] Britain's attachment to overseas empire and aversion to continental commitments were even more costly during the inter-war period, when London directed available resources to peripheral defenses and woefully neglected preparation for a land war against Nazi Germany. Following the toll taken by World War I, the British embraced a "never again" attitude toward participating in armed conflict on the Continent while remaining heavily invested – psychologically, politically, and materially – in overseas empire. Britain defended its imperial possessions even when doing so came at the expense of the security of the metropole.[61] Social norms were overriding a rationalist calculation of material interest.

Unlike the Ottomans and Chinese, who generally preferred to deal with adversaries and enforce order through the application of preponderant

---

[59] The Scramble for Africa in the late nineteenth century was a notable exception. Rapid British and French expansion was motivated in large part by strategic rivalry.

[60] See Scott Sagan, "1914 Revisited: Allies, Offense, and Instability," in Steven Miller, Sean Lynn-Jones, and Stephen Van Evera, ed., *Military Strategy and the Origins of the First World War* (Princeton University Press, 1991), pp. 109–133, 126.

[61] See Michael Howard, *The Continental Commitment: The Dilemma of British Defence Policy in the Era of the Two World Wars* (London: Ashfield Press, 1989).

power, the British regularly relied on a balance of power as a key source of order. In the words of Esme Hoard, balance-of-power thinking was "a corner-stone of English policy, unconsciously during the sixteenth, subconsciously during the seventeenth, and consciously during the eighteenth, nineteenth and twentieth centuries."[62] The Peace of Westphalia in 1648 effectively institutionalized as an ordering norm the maintenance of power balances in Europe. At the close of the Napoleonic Wars in 1815, London operationalized this norm through the Concert of Europe, securing a rules-based order that both preserved a stable balance on the Continent and enabled Britain to concentrate its resources on the imperial periphery. It also accepted, and even encouraged, stable balances of power in primary overseas theaters. At the end of the nineteenth century, Britain made way for US naval primacy in the western Atlantic and welcomed America's arrival as an imperial power in the Pacific. In the Far East, Britain fashioned a naval alliance with Japan in 1902 in order to maintain an effective balance against France and Russia. The British Empire certainly fought its fair share of wars, but London frequently resorted to either balancing against or coopting other centers of power – not defeating them.

Socioeconomic logic. In Ottoman and Chinese societies, wealth and political power were highly concentrated. In contrast, wealth and power in Britain were more broadly distributed across the monarchy, landed aristocracy, and commercial class. Following England's seventeenth-century civil wars and the Glorious Revolution (1688) that brought the conflicts to an end, Parliament not only checked the power of the monarchy, but also increasingly represented the interests of the rising commercial class. The monarchy needed to tax the commercial elite to fund the modern state, but in return had to grant this new elite more political voice. Britain's emergence as a leading imperial power thus coincided with the evolution of a social order resting on a compact among these three agents of social power – monarchy, aristocracy, and rising bourgeoisie.[63]

Britain replicated such socioeconomic compacts in its periphery. Whereas the Ottomans and Chinese undercut sites of social power that could challenge imperial authority, the British actively cultivated social hierarchy in their periphery. In instances of formal empire, colonial governors ruled through local elites who were often schooled in Britain's

---

[62] Sir Esme Hoard, "British Policy and the Balance of Power," *American Political Science Review*, Vol. 19, No. 2 (May 1925), pp. 261–267, 261; and Victoria Hui, *War and State Formation in Ancient China and Early Modern Europe* (Cambridge University Press, 2005), Chapter 3.

[63] On the evolution of this social order, see Mark Kishlansky, *A Monarchy Transformed: Britain 1603–1714* (New York, NY: Penguin, 1997).

language, laws, and administrative traditions. In instances of informal empire, colonial emissaries worked through collaborators – existing political and economic elites – in the periphery. Britain's system of colonial rule reflected the social stratification and horizontal compacts among privileged sectors that anchored metropolitan society.

It is also the case that changes in Britain's socioeconomic order translated into changes in imperial management. By the middle of the nineteenth century, Britain had switched from mercantilism to free trade. The main driver of this shift in commercial strategy was the rise of the country's industrial and financial class and the consequent formation of an influential constituency in favor of open markets. Urbanization and industrialization had shifted political power away from monarchy and aristocracy – defenders of statist policies – toward social sectors that would most benefit from free trade. The result was Britain's readiness to provide the open markets and protected sea lanes essential to establishing a liberal international trading order. A changing socioeconomic order in the metropole was producing an accompanying change in the practice of hegemony.[64]

Cultural logic. The British Empire was home to peoples of diverse religion, ethnicity, and race. Unlike the Ottomans, who accommodated minorities within an Islamic polity, and the Chinese, who sought to assimilate minorities, the British were culturally inclusive and embraced a universalizing mission; they sought to export across cultural dividing lines their own language, religion, and way of life. According to Percival Spear, "Britain's supreme function has been that of a cultural germ carrier... The introduction of the English language provided a vehicle for western ideas, and English law a standard of British practice. Along with English literature, came western moral and religious ideas, and the admission of missionaries provided, as it were, a working model of western moral precepts."[65] Peripheral collaborators were to serve as the main source of cultural transmission. In the words of Lord Thomas Babington Macaulay, "We must at present do our best to form a class who may be interpreters between us and the millions whom we govern; a class of persons Indian in blood and colour, but English in taste, in opinions, in morals, and in intellect."[66]

---

[64] See Anthony Howe, *Free Trade and Liberal England, 1846–1946* (Oxford University Press, 1998).

[65] Percival Spear, *The Oxford History of Modern India, 1740–1975*, 2nd edn. (New Delhi: Oxford University Press, 1978), p. 7. See also Stanley Wolpert, *India*, 3rd edn. (Berkeley, CA: University of California Press, 2005), pp. 44–55.

[66] Angela Partington, ed., *Oxford Dictionary of Quotations*, 4th edn. (Oxford University Press, 1991), p. 435.

Despite its cultural inclusivity and universalizing ambition, matters of religion, race, and ethnicity still had a significant impact on Britain's management of its imperial domain. Throughout much of the imperial periphery, the British categorized populations into new communal categories – a practice of social engineering that had lasting effects.[67] In addition, the British Empire rested on a political and cultural hierarchy imbued with the notion of Anglo-Saxon superiority.[68] Colonies and former colonies whose populations were primarily of European extraction consistently enjoyed a privileged relationship with the metropole. During rapprochement with the United States in the late nineteenth century, for example, both sides of the Atlantic were awash with talk of the supremacy of the Anglo-Saxon race. Concurrently, Britain was fashioning a naval alliance with Japan – but that relationship enjoyed none of the cultural affinity that helped foster Anglo-American amity. Indeed, British officials complained that alliance with a non-European power damaged British prestige. As Admiral Cyprian Bridge, one of the officers coordinating the naval compact with the Japanese, remarked, "I feel no social or moral affinity with them and I would rather live with any branch of the Caucasian race, even the Russian, than I would with them." When Britain dropped the alliance in the early 1920s, race unambiguously played a part. London's ambassador to Tokyo argued in favor of alignment with "our great White Outposts in the Pacific" and "our great White Neighbour" – the United States.[69]

It is also the case that British enthusiasm for the inculcation of its values among colonial populations was regularly tempered by peripheral resistance. Even in India, where Britain made perhaps its most valiant attempts to Anglicize the populace, setbacks eventually convinced London that socializing Indians was a lost cause. After the Sepoy Mutiny in 1857, for example, the British scaled back efforts to export their culture to India. As Karuna Mantena writes, the rebellion "would mark the decisive *turning away* from an earlier liberal, reformist ethos that had furnished nineteenth-century empire its most salient moral justification."[70]

---

[67] See Benedict Anderson, *Imagined Communities: Reflections on the Origin and Spread of Nationalism* (London: Verso, 1991), pp. 163–185.

[68] See Stuart Anderson, *Race and Rapprochement: Anglo-Saxonism and Anglo-American Relations, 1894–1904* (East Brunswick, NJ: Associated University Presses, 1981); and Peter Katzenstein, *Anglo-America and Its Discontents: Civilizational Identities beyond West and East* (New York, NY: Routledge, 2012).

[69] See Charles Kupchan, *How Enemies Become Friends: The Sources of Stable Peace* (Princeton University Press, 2010), pp. 154–155.

[70] Karuna Mantena, *Alibis of Empire: Henry Maine and the End of Liberal Imperialism* (Princeton University Press, 2010), p. 1.

Cultural norms thus pulled the British in competing directions. On the one hand, Britain embraced a universalistic conception of inclusion, and expansion was guided by commercial and strategic considerations, not religious, ethnic, or racial ones. On the other hand, religious, ethnic, and racial categorization informed imperial management and key decisions about imperial strategy were shaped by cultural norms. So too did resistance in the periphery ultimately call into question the effectiveness and utility of Britain's efforts at socialization.

Commercial logic. The Ottomans, and to a lesser extent the Chinese, prevented the accumulation of wealth outside imperial structures, kept tight rein over markets and trade, and feared that economic gain in the periphery would eventually generate challenges to imperial power. In contrast, the British, after initially embracing mercantilist policies, supported generally free markets at home and open trade abroad. Moreover, London viewed economic development in the periphery as a desirable objective, one that would both further the wealth of the metropole through trade and investment and promote stability in overseas possessions. Effectively, Britain was the first hegemon to erect and defend a global system of open markets and liberal trade.

The architecture and management of Britain's empire was heavily influenced by the commercial logic prevailing in the metropole. London's concern that empire was to be a paying proposition directed metropolitan agents to lucrative peripheral markets. As Robinson and Gallagher argue, cost sensitivity also meant that the British often preferred informal rule if possible and formal rule only if necessary.[71] Coincident with the mounting economic and political power of Britain's business community, London dropped mercantilism in favor of free trade and began to focus not just on markets for goods, but also greater investment opportunities for the surplus capital accumulating in the metropole. As mentioned, Britain's changing socioeconomic order at home had a direct impact on the conduct of imperial strategy in the periphery. During the second half of the nineteenth century, Britain began to fashion and enforce the rules-based liberal system that would later provide a foundation for the integrated global economy associated with Pax Americana.

Pax Britannica was based on a geopolitical architecture that relied on the preservation of a stable balance of power in Europe coupled with a network of horizontal linkages among peripheral strongpoints. Britain's social compacts at home were replicated abroad through social

---

[71] Gallagher and Robinson, "The Imperialism of Free Trade."

stratification in the periphery and the nurturing of political and economic collaborators. The British Empire embraced cultural universalism and was open to all ethnicities, races, and religions, but cultural dividing lines nonetheless shaped the contours of British hegemony. As for its commercial logic, the British Empire was the first to promote free markets and an open system of international trade. A combination of material conditions and social norms shaped these defining features of British hegemony.

The United States

Geopolitical logic. Rather than adhering to a unified geopolitical architecture, the United States after World War II has constructed hegemony in parts, relying on different geopolitical logics in different strategic theaters. In the Western Hemisphere, America's material preponderance, backed up by occasional bouts of intimidation and military intervention, has enabled the United States to exert centripetal force throughout the region; hegemony follows naturally from hierarchy. In a Europe threatened by the Soviet Union, Washington deployed a sizable military presence on the Continent while also supporting multilateral integration through NATO and the European Community. The United States served as an on-shore balancer, and its security umbrella enabled its allies to bind themselves to each other in pursuit of economic and political union. The success of that strategy, despite Russia's recent adventurism in Ukraine, has permitted a marked reduction in the US presence in Europe. In East Asia, the United States constructed a hub-spoke architecture based primarily on bilateral alliances and off-shore reservoirs of US power. As in the Ottoman Empire, this hub-spoke structure lacked a rim; regional states within America's sphere of influence were encouraged to deepen ties with the United States, not with each other.

Elsewhere, Washington has relied on strongpoint defense, using a mix of forwardly deployed forces and regional proxies to secure its interests in strategically important areas. A primary example of this logic has been security arrangements in the Persian Gulf.

Such variation in geopolitical logic was in part a product of pragmatic responses to geopolitical realities. In the Western Hemisphere, the United States faced no peer competitors; it enjoyed hegemony by default. In Europe, the United States needed a forwardly deployed military presence to help protect the industrial heartland in Germany and France from potential Soviet attack. Moreover, America's European allies were ready to set aside their rivalries and pursue regional integration, providing Washington a compelling rationale for opting for a multilateral architecture. In contrast, Asia's main center of power – Japan – was off-shore, and historical animosities stood in the way of regional integration, favoring a hub-and-spoke structure. In the Persian Gulf, the United States initially found willing regional proxies in Iran and Saudi Arabia, enabling it to maintain a relatively small and largely off-shore military presence. The wars in Iraq and Afghanistan dramatically increased the US presence in the region, but US strategy seems again headed toward reliance on regional proxies and a largely off-shore presence.

Social purpose, and not just pragmatic response to geopolitical realities, has informed the structure and character of US hegemony. In contrast with Great Britain, whose empire was primarily commercial and extractive in origin, American hegemony was founded on a combination of geopolitical imperative and ideological ambition. Amid World War II and then the Cold War, Washington's primary objective in building a hegemonic sphere of influence was to prevent the domination of major areas of economic and military strength by a hostile power. Indeed, it took Japan's attack on Pearl Harbor to coax the United States out of its isolationist shell, and the peacetime overseas presence that took shape during the late 1940s was a direct response to the threat posed by the Soviet Union. The location and nature of US commitments and the conduct of US strategy emerged accordingly. To be sure, American corporations and the nation's economic interests were ultimately well served by the era of US hegemony. But America's hegemonic ambitions arose as a check against peer competitors, not as a vehicle for pursuing either public or private interests of a commercial nature.

The character of US hegemony was also informed by ideological objectives. The British aimed to marshal sufficient strength to protect imperial possessions and the sea lanes of communication that connected them to the metropole. In contrast, the United States embraced strategies that required the strength needed not just to balance against adversaries, but to vanquish and democratize them as well. This objective meant that the United States sought to amass preponderant power against enemies rather than an equilibrium of power. The ambition to transform enemies stemmed in part from a conviction that regime type was a potent determinant of a state's foreign policy; to spread democratic rule would be to advance the nation's geopolitical interests. This objective was also grounded in a national creed that took the spread of freedom to be central to America's identity and its role in the world.[72]

---

[72] See Ernest Lee Tuveson, *Redeemer Nation: The Idea of America's Millennial Role* (University of Chicago Press, 1968); Susan Matarese, *American Foreign Policy and the Utopian Imagination* (Amherst, MA: University of Massachusetts Press, 2001); and

The ideological and transformative ambitions of America's hegemonic order produced a more activist and expensive grand strategy than that pursued by the British. This difference helps explain why the maintenance of Pax Britannica at its zenith cost the metropole roughly 2–3% of national income, while US defense spending has averaged about 5% of GDP since the 1960s.[73]

Socioeconomic logic. Since its founding era, the United States has sought to construct an egalitarian socioeconomic order – one that would depart from Europe's social stratification and class immobility. This social norm has not only shaped the evolution of American society, but also contributed to the transformational ambition of US hegemony. When the United States occupied Germany and Japan at the end of World War II, it set about dismantling Germany's industrial cartels and Japan's *zaibatsu*. Both were seen as contributors to militarism and as socially regressive. The United States continues to demonstrate enmity toward regimes marked by illiberal politics and economic oligarchy – and on occasion has resorted to the use of force to topple such regimes. Through its dominating position in international financial institutions, the United States has also sought to export the Washington Consensus, propagating to the developing world its neoliberal approach to economic policy.

The private sector played its part in shaping a brand of hegemony aimed at exporting economic liberalism. Although they overstate their case, revisionist historians of the Cold War provide ample evidence that the interests of US companies did figure in the architecture of order that emerged after World War II – particularly in Western Europe. Commercial and financial opportunities provided US companies strong incentives to expand their overseas presence, ultimately serving as a vehicle for the replication abroad of America's domestic socioeconomic order.[74] Nonetheless, the private sector operated within the confines of a geopolitical architecture primarily defined by strategic and ideological objectives.

Cultural logic. With a few notable exceptions – the burst of overseas expansion at the end of the nineteenth century and the 2003 invasion and consequent occupation of Iraq among them – the United States has opted for what Ikenberry calls "liberal hegemony" rather than formal

Jonathan Monten, "The Roots of the Bush Doctrine: Power, Nationalism, and Democracy Promotion in US Strategy," *International Security*, Vol. 29, No. 4 (Spring 2005), pp. 112–156.
[73] Paul Kennedy, *The Rise and Fall of British Naval Mastery* (London: Macmillan, 1983), p. 150.
[74] See, for example, Michael Hogan, *The Marshall Plan: America, Britain, and the Reconstruction of Western Europe, 1947–1952* (New York, NY: Cambridge University Press, 1987).

empire.[75] More often than not, Pax Americana has been enforced through persuasion instead of coercion. This distinguishing feature of US hegemony rests in part on social norms supportive of the autonomy of all peoples – regardless of their race, ethnicity, or religion. From the eighteenth century onward, Americans embraced a republican identity that set them against the imperial ambitions of Europe's great powers, particularly in the Western Hemisphere.[76] As it became a major naval power, the United States did colonize the Philippines in 1898 and used brute force against the tenacious insurgency that followed. Congress and the public, however, readily soured on the material and moral costs of formal empire. Soon thereafter, President Woodrow Wilson began a campaign to spread self-determination and end colonialism worldwide, a goal US leadership ultimately brought to fruition with the dismantling of European empires after World War II.

The United States is also an immigrant and multicultural nation and is therefore, to use a phrase coined by Henry Nau, "at home abroad."[77] Like Great Britain, the United States has embraced a brand of hegemony with universalizing ambition and cultural inclusivity. Moreover, ethnic, racial, and religious categories have figured less prominently in the character of US hegemony than they did during the era of Pax Britannica. The British saw themselves as steeping inferior peoples in British law, education, religion, and administration – a process that would ultimately produce societies recreated in Britain's image. In contrast, the United States has seen itself as freeing foreign peoples to realize universal values. Shepherding the citizens of other countries to the ballot box has been an act of liberation, not one of inculcation.

In this respect, the United States has long based its foreign policy on belief, perhaps naïve, in the universality of liberal political values across all cultures. The reproduction internationally of America's defining creed at home is regularly deployed as a justification for the sacrifice of blood and treasure abroad. Such ambition has noble intent and has produced many positive outcomes – for example, the defeat and democratization of Nazi Germany and Imperial Japan. But this transformational instinct has also drawn the United States into some of its most frustrating episodes of nation-building – the inconclusive conflicts in Afghanistan and Iraq among them.

---

[75] See Ikenberry, *Liberal Leviathan.*
[76] See Robert Kagan, *Dangerous Nation: America's Place in the World from Its Earliest Days to the Dawn of the Twentieth Century* (New York, NY: Knopf, 2006), pp. 40–46.
[77] Henry Nau, *At Home Abroad: Identity and Power in American Foreign Policy* (Ithaca, NY: Cornell University Press, 2002).

Americans have not always embraced such cultural universalism. Indeed, the impact of racial attitudes on US foreign policy has evolved in step with societal attitudes toward race on the home front. In the nineteenth century, racism acted as a major impediment to overseas expansion: Americans did not want to incorporate into their union or rule over "inferior peoples."[78] A surge in feelings of Anglo-Saxon solidarity accompanied rapprochement with Great Britain at the end of the nineteenth century. In the early twentieth century, the United States opposed including a racial equality clause in the Versailles Treaty and imposed strict quotas on immigration. It was only during the second half of the twentieth century, as the civil rights movement advanced at home, that Washington became a major supporter of the international promotion of racial and gender equality and deployed the nation's economic and military power in the service of building liberal societies abroad.

Commercial logic. The United States inherited from the British the task of providing the public goods needed to sustain a liberal international trading order. But Washington also implemented two significant changes to that order. First, as mentioned above, it insisted on the dismantling of colonial empires, viewing them not only as antithetical to its own political identity and values, but also as a main cause of the economic nationalism that helped spawn World War II. Second, Washington put new emphasis on the institutionalization of liberal multilateralism, overseeing at the close of World War II the flurry of diplomacy that ultimately produced the financial architecture born at Bretton Woods in 1944. The General Agreement on Tariffs and Trade followed in 1947. The United States was in important respects replicating internationally its domestic reliance on a liberal and institutionalized framework for managing trade and finance.[79]

As was the case with Britain, America's preference for open trade was conditioned by its underlying socioeconomic order. During the nineteenth century, the United States imposed trade tariffs to protect its growing industrial base. As industrialization proceeded and manufacturers became globally competitive, protectionism gave way to free trade.[80] This change of course was further advanced by the development of a robust financial industry strongly supportive of open commerce. Moreover, the pro-growth and anti-monopoly policies that succeeded in

[78] See Reginald Horsman, *Race and Manifest Destiny: The Origins of American Racial Anglo-Saxonism* (Cambridge, MA: Harvard University Press, 1981).
[79] See Brawley, *Liberal Leadership.*
[80] See Peter Trubowitz, *Defining the National Interest: Conflict and Change in American Foreign Policy* (University of Chicago Press, 1998).

ameliorating the class cleavages of the New Deal era were exported to Europe after World War II with the aim of speeding recovery and fostering social stability in America's expanding zone of hegemonic influence.[81]

American hegemony has been distinguished by its diversity. Motivated primarily by the objective of checking and ultimately pacifying peer competitors, the United States has applied different geopolitical logics in different theaters. Its rejection of social hierarchy at home has been reflected in its effort to promote more egalitarian social orders in the periphery. America's multiculturalism and democratizing creed have contributed to its universalizing and transformational ambition abroad. And the US commitment to free-market capitalism at home produced a brand of hegemony aimed at establishing an open trading order globally.

Hegemonic transitions, normative diversity, and the rise of China

This chapter has sought to shed light on the diverse set of ordering norms that informed Ottoman, Chinese, British, and American brands of hegemony. Each of these four great powers erected hegemonic zones that rested on unique geopolitical, socioeconomic, cultural, and commercial logics. To be sure, in these and all other cases of hegemony, power asymmetry provided the essential foundation for hierarchical order. But this chapter makes clear that hegemony also rests on packages of ordering norms and ideas that affect its character, stability, and durability, as well as its relationship with other centers of power. Although he left the issue unexplored, Gilpin was on target in pointing out that major states "create social structures in order to advance particular sets of political, economic, or other types of interests."[82] The pervasive effects of normative preferences and socioeconomic structures on hegemonic order mean that transitions from one hegemony to the next are not just about changes in hierarchy, but also about changes in political and social norms.

In order to advance understanding of the normative dimensions of hegemony, this chapter has thus far examined different orders in isolation rather than focusing on the interaction among them. However, extending the analysis to periods of systemic transition, when hegemons intensely interact with one another, only confirms this chapter's core

---

[81] Charles Maier, "The Politics of Productivity: Foundations of American International Economic Policy after World War II," *International Organization*, Vol. 31, No. 4 (Autumn 1977), pp. 607–633, 609–618.

[82] Gilpin, *War and Change*, p. 9.

claims. During hegemonic transitions, great powers compete not just over the international pecking order, but also over the norms and rules that each power seeks to enforce internationally. After the Roman Empire split into eastern and western halves in the fourth century, competition between Rome and Constantinople was about governance, culture, and religious doctrine as much as status or territory. The conflict that raged between the Ottoman Empire and Safavid Persia during much of the sixteenth century was rooted in competition between Sunni and Shiite traditions. World War I, World War II, and the Cold War were contests over ideology as well as hierarchy and territory, with liberal democracies generally lining up against monarchic, fascist, and communist alternatives. It can hardly be accidental that the only peaceful power transition in history occurred between Great Britain and the United States; the baton was passed "within the family," from one Anglo-Saxon great power to another.

It is of important geopolitical consequence that hegemony has normative dimensions and that power transitions entail clashes among competing norms. The world is entering a period of transformation as power shifts from the West to the rising rest. One school of thought – which dominates in Washington – holds that emerging powers are poised to embrace the existing international order; Western norms are universal norms, and the dictates of globalization are ensuring their worldwide spread. According to Ikenberry, "The United States' global position may be weakening, but the international system the United States leads can remain the dominant order of the twenty-first century." The West should "sink the roots of this order as deeply as possible" to ensure that the world continues to play by its rules even as its material preponderance wanes. "China and other emerging great powers," he concludes, "do not want to contest the basic rules and principles of the liberal international order; they wish to gain more authority and leadership within it."[83]

The analysis in this chapter suggests that such conventional wisdom is illusory; emerging powers will not readily embrace the order on offer from the West. Regardless of the presumed functionality of the current order from a liberal, transactional perspective, emerging powers – China, India, Brazil, Turkey, to name a few – are following their own paths to modernity based on their own cultural, ideological, and socioeconomic trajectories. Their normative and social orientations will produce quite disparate approaches to building and managing international order.

[83] G. John Ikenberry, "The Rise of China and the Future of the West," *Foreign Affairs*, Vol. 87, No. 1 (January/February 2008), pp. 23–37, 25, 37; and Ikenberry, "The Future of the Liberal World Order," p. 57.

Unlike during earlier periods of multipolarity, when different hegem-onies often operated independently of each other, in today's globalized world multiple hegemonic zones will intensely and continuously interact with each other.

In light of its growing economic and military power, China is likely to pose the most significant challenge to the ordering norms of Pax Ameri-cana. It is true that China for now is not challenging many of the rules associated with the Western liberal order, particularly when it comes to commerce. But as all great powers have done throughout history, China will likely seek to recast that order when it has the power to do so. Indeed, China is set to become the world's leading economy by the end of the next decade.[84] Drawing on its historical, cultural, and socioeconomic trajectory, Beijing is poised to bring to the fore a set of ordering norms that contrast sharply with those of Pax Americana.

The normative orientation of China's past approach to exercising hegemony is hardly a reliable predictor of the ordering norms that might shape a Chinese sphere of influence in the future. Nonetheless, the historical record provides a basis for informed speculation.[85] China may well aspire to resurrect in East Asia a sphere of influence that is arrayed in concentric circles around a Sinicized core. Through this tiered struc-ture, China might attempt to exercise a brand of regional hegemony modeled on the tributary system. China's material primacy would serve as the foundation for its economic, strategic, and cultural centrality. Its neighbors would demonstrate deference to Beijing through both policy and ritual – but they would maintain their autonomy and their independent relations with each other. Nonetheless, China would become the region's strategic and economic hub, playing a role similar to that of the United States in the Americas. Beijing could well unfurl its own version of the Monroe Doctrine, laying claim to primacy in North-east Asia and guardianship of the region's sea lanes. Indeed, Beijing has already ramped up maritime activities in the East China Sea and South China Sea and rejected Washington's call for addressing the area's territorial disputes through multilateral negotiation.

Such a Sinocentric brand of hegemony in East Asia is of course incom-patible with the current security architecture, in which the United States

---

[84] Kupchan, *No One's World*, pp. 75–76.

[85] On the growing influence of traditional strategic conceptions on contemporary Chinese policy, see Fei-Ling Wang, "Between *Tianxia* and Westphalia: China Searches for Its Position in the World," paper presented at the Annual Meeting of the American Political Science Association, Seattle, WA, September 2011; and Martin Jacques, *When China Rules the World: The End of the Western World and the Birth of a New Global Order* (New York, NY: Penguin, 2009), pp. 369–399.

continues to serve as the region's geopolitical hub. Accordingly, the United States and China have strong incentives to turn to diplomacy to tame their relationship over the course of this decade – before the naval balance in the western Pacific becomes more equal. On the table will have to be both the material and the normative dimensions of order. If Beijing and Washington succeed in reaching a meeting of the minds, a peaceful power transition in East Asia may be in the offing. If not, a historic confrontation may well loom.

Should diplomacy fail to avert rivalry, Sino-American competition may nonetheless fall short of the bipolar enmity of the Cold War. China and the United States are economically interdependent whereas the Soviet Union and the United States carved out separate economic blocs. Moreover, China's geopolitical ambition, at least for the foreseeable future, seems focused primarily on East Asia, suggesting that rivalry with the United States could be more contained than the global competition that ensued between the United States and the Soviet Union. China's regional ambitions are, however, poised to clash head-on with America's determination to maintain strategic primacy in Northeast Asia. Even if it does not match the hostility of the Cold War, the resulting confrontation could well resemble the naval race between Great Britain and Germany that commenced at the turn of the twentieth century.[86] Although Wilhelmine Germany did not threaten the global dominance of the Royal Navy, its naval buildup in the European theater fueled a spiral of hostility that culminated in World War I.

On the socioeconomic front, China has successfully fashioned a stable compact between its ruling elite and its rising bourgeoisie. During the eighteenth and nineteenth centuries, Imperial China was particularly adept at coopting a rising merchant class into the existing political order. The same goes for the Chinese Communist Party (CCP) today; the CCP has deliberately incorporated China's rapidly expanding middle class into the centralized state, ensuring at least for now that the spread of private wealth does not undermine the party's unitary grip on power. As Kellee Tsai notes, "China's capitalists are pragmatic and creative but they are not budding democrats." "Economic growth," she concludes, "has not created a prodemocratic capitalist class."[87] The status quo certainly faces

---

[86] On the prospects for naval rivalry between China and the United States, see Michael Swaine, et al., "China's Military and the US-Japan Alliance in 2030: A Strategic Net Assessment," Carnegie Endowment for International Peace, May 6, 2013, available at: http://carnegieendowment.org/2013/05/03/china-s-military-and-u.s.-japan-alliance-in-2030-strategic-net-assessment/g1wh.

[87] Kellee Tsai, *Capitalism without Democracy: The Private Sector in Contemporary China* (Ithaca, NY: Cornell University Press, 2007), pp. 4, 201. See also Bruce Dickson, *Red*

challenges from economic inequality, corruption, environmental degrad-ation, factional strife within the CCP, and restive minority populations. But meritocratic entry into public service, the continued competence of China's leaders, and governance that is broadly aimed at shared societal gains rather than rent-seeking augur in favor of political stasis.

From this perspective, China's ascent should not be expected to trans-form its socioeconomic order along Western lines any time soon. On the contrary, its domestic order is likely to continue shaping its economic and geopolitical ascent, favoring policies that advantage the compact between the party and the middle class. If so, China is poised to emerge as a hegemonic power well before it democratizes, meaning that the world's leading economy will not ascribe to the dominant political norms associ-ated with the Western liberal order. To be sure, the CCP's partial embrace of a market economy and its growing concern with legitimacy and accountability do moderate the "ideological distance" between Beijing and Washington.[88] Nonetheless, China and the United States remain miles apart on fundamental norms, including human rights, the rule of law, and representative government. That gap may necessitate inter-national deliberation about what constitutes legitimate forms of gover-nance. One option would be to associate legitimacy with responsible governance rather than procedural democracy. States that govern so as to meet the needs and fulfill the aspirations of their citizens, not just those that hold multiparty elections, would be considered in good standing.[89] Such revision to the normative foundations of Pax Americana may be needed to promote normative consensus as Western hegemony wanes.

The ethnocentrism of China's imperial past suggests that a new era of Chinese hegemony would likely be characterized by cultural particu-larism, not universalism.[90] As it has already begun to do, Beijing will continue to develop a worldwide commercial network affording the extraction of raw materials and the development of export markets. But China shows few signs of wanting to export globally its own cultural and ideological norms – in sharp contrast with the universalizing ambi-tion of both Britain and the United States.

Capitalists in China: The Party, Private Entrepreneurs, and Prospects for Political Change (Cambridge University Press, 2003).

[88] For an optimistic view of the prospects for normative convergence between China and the United States, see Edward Steinfeld, *Playing Our Game: Why China's Rise Doesn't Threaten the West* (New York, NY: Oxford University Press, 2010).

[89] On the need for revision of prevailing conceptions of international legitimacy, see Charles Kupchan and Adam Mount, "The Autonomy Rule," *Democracy: A Journal of Ideas*, No. 12 (Spring 2009), pp. 8–21.

[90] See Peter Katzenstein, ed., *Sinicization and the Rise of China: Civilizational Processes beyond East and West* (New York, NY: Routledge, 2012).

In this respect, China's ascent may mean that cultural dividing lines will matter more than they have during the era of American hegemony. China would accept – and perhaps even encourage – a global order characterized by pluralism. Whereas the United States has sought to construct an international order that rests on universal rules, norms, and institutions, China might favor greater diversity and the devolution of authority to regional bodies that represent cultural groupings. Just as China has long argued that America's political and social values are not appropriate for the Chinese, so too would a hegemonic China likely deem it inappropriate and unnecessary for the Chinese to propagate their own norms beyond a Sinicized sphere of influence in East Asia. In this respect, a hegemonic China would likely welcome a more variegated global order, with different regions guided by their own cultural, social, and political norms. Contra Samuel Huntington's prediction of a clash of civilizations, regional groupings that fall along civilizational lines are by no means destined to collide with one another.[91] However, managing relations among them would require a level of political and ideological pluralism inconsistent with the universalism of Pax Americana.

As for its commercial orientation, China's ongoing economic success rests on a hybrid economic model that combines state control with market mechanisms. So-called "state capitalism" has afforded multiple advantages, including long-range strategic planning, programmatic investment in infrastructure, and a regulatory framework that has helped mitigate the financial turbulence that has recently plagued the more open economies of the democratic West. To be sure, the Chinese economy faces multiple vulnerabilities, including unfavorable demographic trends, a relationship among the state, industry, and finance that impairs competition, and a lack of entrepreneurial innovation. Nonetheless, success breeds continuity. Beijing will likely continue to place a premium on the profitability of the export sector and state-owned enterprises, which enriches party elites as well as private entrepreneurs. It will also concentrate on expanding international access to the energy supplies and raw materials needed to fuel its manufacturing and industrial base. Its foreign economic policy is poised to remain extractive and mercantilist, with little emphasis on using economic penetration as an instrument of political reform.

State-planning at home and mercantilism abroad are set to be enduring features of Beijing's commercial strategy. As its economy continues to expand, China will remain interested in embracing, at least to some

[91] See Samuel Huntington, *The Clash of Civilizations and the Remaking of World Order* (New York, NY: Simon & Schuster, 2011).

degree, the rules of open multilateralism. It is worth keeping in mind, however, that although China joined the World Trade Organization over a decade ago, it is continuing to practice a state-led brand of capitalism – the state sector still produces some 40% of the country's GDP – and to exploit concessions won during accession negotiations to use the body to its advantage.[92] In this respect, it would be illusory to expect Beijing to bend increasingly to prevailing international rules as China's power rises. On the contrary, as Chinese power grows, Beijing will likely bend the rules to favor China's political and economic needs and norms – just as all great powers before it have done as they emerge as hegemons. Indeed, China's leading role in the Shanghai Cooperation Organization and the BRICS grouping, as well as its support for a regional trade group that excludes the United States, reveal that Beijing is already seeking to circumvent institutions dominated by the West, not work within them.

China will not be alone among rising powers in pursuing a new brand of international governance that reflects its own interests and normative orientations. A key challenge for coming decades will be to forge a consensus among major powers that embrace a broad array of different ordering norms. As Zarakol warns, "there may be a limit to how long the majority of the world's population will tolerate living under an international system whose rules they have very little input in."[93] The West will have to make room for the alternative approaches and visions of rising powers and prepare for an international system in which its principles no longer serve as the primary ideational and normative anchor. If the next international system is to be characterized by a rules-based order rather than competitive anarchy, it will have to be predicated on great-power consensus and toleration of political and social diversity rather than universalization of the liberal international order erected during the West's watch.

Multipolarity and normative diversity suggest the onset of a more regionalized international system.[94] Major powers – or supranational polities, as in the case of the European Union – would each seek to push outward its normative preferences within its regional sphere of influence. In the interdependent world of the twenty-first century, effective global

[92] Keith Bradsher, "China's 10-Year Ascent to Trading Powerhouse," *New York Times*, December 8, 2011.
[93] Zarakol, *After Defeat*, p. 253.
[94] See Joseph Nye, *Peace in Parts: Integration and Conflict in Regional Organization* (Boston, MA: Little, Brown, 1971); Charles Kupchan, "After Pax Americana: Benign Power, Regional Integration, and the Sources of a Stable Multipolarity," *International Security*, Vol. 23, No. 2 (Autumn 1998), pp. 42–79; and Peter Katzenstein, *A World of Regions: Asia and Europe in the American Imperium* (Ithaca, NY: Cornell University Press, 2005).

governance would require a combination of tolerance and coordination among such regional groupings. As the world's two leading powers, China and the United States would have a unique role to play in shaping this hybrid order – one that would at once recognize the political autonomy and normative diversity of different regions but also rest on a working consensus among them. China has a long tradition of regional hegemony. The United States is skilled at constructing hegemony in parts and in acting as a hemispheric power. These experiences may serve both countries well as they seek to manage peacefully the transition to a new and more regionalized international order.

2   Dominance and subordination in world politics: authority, liberalism, and stability in the modern international order

David A. Lake

Introduction

Order is a fundamental feature of world politics, but it is not a constant. It waxes and wanes with corresponding ebbs and flows, yet not in any predictable lunar cycle. Where order exists, as in the so-called developed or first world since 1945, peace and prosperity are possible. In this "Western" system, states have escaped the Hobbesian state-of-nature for an international society. Where order is absent, as in present-day Africa, war and suffering often abound. In the absence of an international civil society, as Hobbes wrote, "life is solitary, poor, nasty, brutish, and short."[1]

Order arises in many forms and from many sources. In Chapter 1, Charles Kupchan emphasizes the normative orientations of leading states. In Chapter 3, John Ikenberry highlights the confluence of American power and liberal ideals. I do not disagree with their perspectives or their core interpretations of modern international orders. In this chapter, however, I examine the role of authority and international hierarchy in the creation and maintenance of international order. In this focus, norms and ideals follow from and facilitate transfers of authority from subordinate to dominant states, but are not primary drivers of international order.

The discipline of international relations has largely ignored international authority. Blinkered by the assumption that the international system is anarchic, scholars of international relations and even contemporary policy makers have failed to see or understand the importance of authority by states over other states in international history.[2] There is no clearer example of how paradigmatic assumptions blind scholars to reality.[3]

---

[1] Chris Brown, et al., eds., *International Relations in Political Thought: Texts from the Ancient Greeks to the First World War* (New York, NY: Cambridge University Press, 2002), p. 337.

[2] David A. Lake, *Hierarchy in International Relations* (Ithaca, NY: Cornell University Press, 2009).

[3] Thomas S. Kuhn, *The Structure of Scientific Revolutions* (University of Chicago Press, 1970).

International hierarchy is an important determinant of the degree and character of international order. Indeed, political order is the glue that holds dominant and subordinate states together in authority relationships.

This chapter proceeds in four steps. Using Robert Gilpin's *War and Change in World Politics*[4] (hereafter *WCWP*) as a point of departure, I identify three key unresolved questions in the study of international order. I then address each of the questions in separate sections, and show how an understanding of authority is central to their answers. The conclusion then briefly applies the answers generated to the case of China as a possible peer competitor to the United States.

War, change, and international order

In the three decades since its publication, Gilpin's classic *WCWP* has become received wisdom in international relations. As a reflection of its profound influence, many scholars – especially younger theorists – have absorbed the ideas developed in the book without now recognizing or acknowledging their origins. The approach developed in *WCWP* has only gained in importance. Written in a time of American decline, it remains relevant to our current era of unipolarity and the continuing rise of China. Even though the challenge of the Soviet Union and the competition with Japan both passed without major war, and were followed by a period of American renewal, Gilpin forecasts – perhaps presciently – a bleak future of competition and struggle between Washington and Beijing. *WCWP* is well worth revisiting.

Gilpin's core insight is that states seek to build international orders that reflect their interests. As coalitions of coalitions, states have unique preferences and aim to shape the rules of international order to the point where the marginal costs equal the marginal benefits of action. Small to medium powers are "rule takers" for the most part, but great powers have the potential to provide order and craft rules that privilege their domestic coalitions over those in other countries. International order, in this now broadly accepted view, is not neutral but reflects the interests and perhaps the compromises of the major powers. Order matters to world politics, as do the rules that comprise that order. Thus, countries struggle over the basic rules and benefits of world politics.

Somewhat more controversially, Gilpin posited that the dynamic distribution of capabilities is the primary driver of change and war. Unlike

---

[4] Robert Gilpin, *War and Change in World Politics* (New York, NY: Cambridge University Press, 1981).

neo-realists who gave pride of place to the static distribution,[5] Gilpin argued that countries were subject to the "law of uneven growth," which produced an ever evolving and unstable set of relative capabilities and power. Technologically advanced states initially enjoy rapid rates of economic growth and increased capabilities, and thus greater influence over the international order. But the diffusion of technology and economic convergence, as well as the burdens of international leadership, eventually lead to relative economic decline. Benefiting from the advantages of backwardness and new technological innovations, other powers begin to grow more rapidly and challenge the earlier "generation." As these rapidly growing powers rise, their interests almost inevitably clash with the rules of the existing international order. Declining states could give way, Gilpin observed, but rarely do so. The conflicts between declining and rising powers, he concluded, have been resolved historically by hegemonic war. *WCWP* emphasized the decline of the United States in the 1970s, but was vague on the challengers to American rule, although in other works Gilpin pointed more directly to Japan and the European Union[6] and China.[7] Both the Soviet Union in the Cold War and Japan afterwards turned out to be failed competitors who never rose to equality with the United States. Gilpin's model of world politics, however, resonates with current fears of a rising China which does appear on track to overtake the United States within coming decades.

Though important to the discipline of international relations and still relevant today, *WCWP* left several key questions unresolved. Drawing on scholarship in the intervening decades, I sketch preliminary answers in each of three sections below. First, *why do states comply with biased international orders*, or why is there so little coercion in world politics? Gilpin introduced the concept of a hierarchy of prestige within the anarchic international system, which itself relied on a reputation for power or coercion.[8] Going beyond Gilpin's sophisticated but still fundamentally realist view of world politics, I argue that international order can rest on the authority of a dominant state over subordinate states who recognize its rule as legitimate. Although relations occur within the shadow of coercion, as in all authoritative political systems, dominant states do not require coercion to obtain preferred outcomes or even to

[5] Kenneth N. Waltz, *Theory of International Politics* (Reading, MA: Addison-Wesley, 1979).
[6] Robert Gilpin, *The Political Economy of International Relations* (Princeton University Press, 1987).
[7] Robert Gilpin, *The Challenge of Global Capitalism: The World Economy in the 21st Century* (Princeton University Press, 2000).
[8] Gilpin, *War and Change in World Politics*, pp. 29–32.

enforce their rules on a day-to-day basis in relations with subordinate states. Authority is a more efficient form of rule than is coercion.

Second, *why are hegemons liberal* and, in turn, why have the most successful international orders of the last two centuries been liberal? This is the great unanswered question of hegemonic stability theory, with which Gilpin is often associated. The answer follows from the authoritative nature of international order. To accept the authority of another state over more or less of one's own policies is an awesome decision, perhaps the most important one a state can make. The power to set rules for subordinates is also the power to abuse those rules. Subordinate states will likely accept the authority of a dominant state only if that state can credibly commit not to act opportunistically or exploit them at some future date. Because the domestic authority of their own governments is limited and, by necessity, they must rely on market-based rules, liberal states are more credible in their promises to govern others lightly and fairly. Hegemons need not be liberal, and being hegemonic does not necessarily make a state market-oriented. Rather, the correlation between hegemony and liberalism emerges because of an underlying selection mechanism: liberal states are simply better able to acquire and sustain authority over other states.

Third, *why is there so little war and change*, or why is international order so robust? As Gilpin recognized, and Ikenberry[9] has argued in more detail, international orders lock in particular sets of interests that then endure over time. But why do rules stick in what remains an anarchic and "thinly" institutionalized international system? Both states and private actors adapt to particular authorities and their rules of order. As a social construct, authority is an equilibrium, a set of behaviors by ruler and ruled – or dominant and subordinate states – that neither has an incentive to change. Once that mutual equilibrium is reached, actors take the rules of order as "given" and adjust their investments and assets accordingly. Having done so, these actors then acquire an interest in preserving the rules as they exist. In short, the actors become vested in that order. It is not just power that is dynamic, as for Gilpin, but interests as well, and these interests tend over time to conform to prevailing rules. In this way, order becomes self-reinforcing. Vesting does not overturn the law of uneven growth on which Gilpin focused, but it does explain why order can endure long after the dominant state has declined in power capabilities

---

[9] G. John Ikenberry, *After Victory: Institutions, Strategic Restraint, and the Rebuilding of Order after Major Wars* (Princeton University Press, 2001); G. John Ikenberry, *Liberal Leviathan: The Origins, Crisis, and Transformation of the American World Order* (Princeton University Press, 2011).

or prestige. It also suggests the possibility that potential challengers can be converted into supporters as they too become vested in the existing international order. This possibility is central to the debate over the future of China, which I examine in the Conclusion to this chapter.

Why do states comply with biased international orders?

Gilpin[10] argues that, even within anarchy, states are ranked in a "hierarchy of power and prestige." As the "reputation for power," prestige "refers primarily to the perceptions of other states with respect to a state's capacities and its ability and willingness to exercise its power." This perception, in turn, ultimately rests on the "successful use of power, and especially through victory in war." Although possessing a moral and functional basis, the hierarchy of prestige is, in the end, determined by the coercive capabilities of states. Along with the distribution of power itself, the hierarchy of prestige is central to the construction and maintenance of international order.

Yet, in an oft-cited critique of hegemonic stability theory, McKeown[11] argued that hegemons – Great Britain and the United States, in particular – rarely if ever appear to use coercion to create or maintain international order. The mechanism central to the theory is, thus, inconsistent with the historical record. Although there are notable examples – the Suez Crisis of 1956, sanctions against Cuba and other "rogue" states – there is just not enough coercion by dominant states to support the conclusion that order is created and sustained solely by the use of force by one country over others. In this way, the hierarchy of prestige is inadequate to explain the widespread and relatively stable international order – and importantly, the compliance with that order – that we observe.[12]

Gilpin posits that prestige is "the functional equivalent of the role of authority in domestic politics." In limiting prestige to its "equivalent," he is hampered by a residual realism. In a classic fallacy of composition, Gilpin assumes that since the system is anarchic, all relations between units must likewise be anarchic and that, as a result, there can be no

---

[10] Gilpin, *War and Change in World Politics*, pp. 29–32.
[11] Timothy J. McKeown, "Hegemonic Stability Theory and 19th Century Tariff Levels in Europe," *International Organization*, Vol. 37, No. 1 (1989), pp. 73–91.
[12] This is, of course, a glass half-empty/half-full conclusion. There is clearly some coercion in international relations, but theory is vague about just how often we should observe coercion in practice and we do not have good measures (or even definitions) of coercion (as some non-actions, such as deterrence, can be understood as coercive as well). Nonetheless, violence between states is not self-evidently higher than political violence within states (i.e., civil wars).

authority by one state over another. Although sensitive to the need for legitimacy in international orders, Gilpin stops short of recognizing the important role of authority in world politics.

Authority is, simply put, rightful rule. As a bundle of rights and obligations, authority entails (a) the right by a ruler, in this case a dominant state, to issue certain limited commands, (b) the duty by the ruled, here a collective of individuals organized into a subordinate state, to comply with these rules to the extent they are able, and (c) the right of the ruler or dominant state to enforce its commands in the event of non-compliance.[13] In domestic political systems, authority is typically understood to follow from formal–legal institutions. The leader's ability to command citizens, and the citizen's willingness to comply, follow from the lawful position or office that the leader holds. Although perhaps useful for analyzing established domestic hierarchies, this formal-legal conception suffers from a chicken-and-egg problem that makes it of dubious utility for the study of international relations. If political authority derives from lawful office, law must precede authority. But if political authority creates law, then authority must precede lawful office. Neither law nor authority can explain its own creation, and thus in all political systems authority must originate in something other than a formal-legal order.

Authority can derive from many other sources, including charisma, tradition, and religion. In international relations, authority mostly rests on social contracts in which dominant states provide political orders to subordinate states of sufficient value to offset their loss of autonomy.[14] Both dominant and subordinate states are better off than they would be in their next best alternative, reasonably assumed in international relations to be a state-of-nature. Authority relations, in turn, condition the behaviors of dominant and subordinate states alike in important ways.[15] Dominant states must produce the promised order, even when it is costly to do so. One manifestation of this responsibility is that dominant states are significantly more likely to join crises in which a subordinate state is involved. Dominant states must also credibly commit not to abuse their authority over subordinates, a task made more difficult in unipolarity and, thus, possibly driving the United States to tie its hands even more firmly through multilateralism today than in the past.[16] Enjoying the fruits of the

---

[13] Lake, *Hierarchy in International Relations*, pp. 17–21.
[14] *Ibid.*, pp. 34–40.   [15] *Ibid.*, Chapters 4 and 5.
[16] As an out-of-equilibrium event, the importance of tying hands through multilateralism was made clear by President George W. Bush's attempt to break free from the international fetters constraining the United States during the Iraq War, and the vociferous international opposition that followed.

political order, subordinate states relative to non-subordinates spend less on defense and engage in higher levels of international trade, especially with others tied to the same dominant state. Legitimating the policies of their protector, subordinates are also more likely to follow dominant states into wars and especially to join coalitions of the willing, even though they often contribute little beyond their verbal support and could easily free ride on the efforts of others. Finally, dominant states discipline subordinates who violate their commands both by intervening to replace local leaders – their agents – and ostracizing them from normal political intercourse through sanctions or other barriers to exchange (e.g., US-Cuba). This syndrome of behaviors by both dominant and subordinate states is not predicted nor easily explained by attributes other than authority.

The gains from entering an international civil society, however, are unlikely to be distributed evenly or even fairly between dominant and subordinate states; after all, as Gilpin recognized, the ability to write the rules of international order is a power that few states fail to exploit for their own benefit. It is here that international power matters in setting the terms of the international order in which members are embedded. Power is the ability of A to get B to do something he or she would otherwise not do.[17] Authority, in turn, is a type of power, defined as the legitimate use of force.[18] But in creating authority, other forms of power may also play a role and determine the degree of bias in the corresponding international

[17] Robert A. Dahl, "The Concept of Power," *Behavioral Science*, Vol. 2, No. 3 (1957), pp. 201–215.
[18] Authority differs from coercion in being fundamentally a collective or social construct. Although the social meaning of coercion may vary, as do the social norms governing its use (on interventions, see Martha Finnemore, *The Purpose of Intervention* (Ithaca, NY: Cornell University Press, 2003)), the physical ability to impose violence on another state exists independently of the self-understanding of the actors themselves. With authority, on the other hand, the right to punish non-compliance ultimately requires the collective acceptance or *legitimacy* of the dominant state's right to rule. As Thomas Hobbes himself recognized, "the power of the mighty (the Leviathan) hath no foundation but in the opinion and belief of the people" (quoted in Michael C. Williams, "The Hobbesian Theory of International Relations: Three Traditions," in Beate Jahn, ed. *Classical Theory in International Relations* (Cambridge University Press, 2006), p. 265). If recognized as legitimate, the dominant state acquires the ability to punish individuals within the subordinate state because of the broad backing of others (Richard E. Flathman, *The Practice of Political Authority: Authority and the Authoritative* (University of Chicago Press, 1980), p. 30). The dominant state, for instance, can enforce specific edicts even in the face of opposition if its general body of commands is accepted as legitimate by a sufficiently large number of the members of the subordinate state (Harold D. Lasswell and Abraham Kaplan, *Power and Society* (New Haven, CT: Yale University Press, 1950, p. 133); Chester L. Bernard, *The Functions of the Executive* (Cambridge, MA: Harvard University Press, 1962), p. 169).

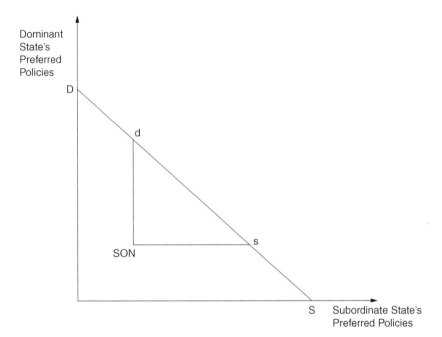

Figure 2.1: Power, bargaining, and international order: how the gains from order lock states into biased sets of rules

order. The idea here is nicely illustrated in Figure 2.1.[19] By entering the international order and escaping the state-of-nature (SON), both the dominant and subordinate states move toward the Pareto frontier (the negatively sloped line DS), improving their welfare. At the same time, however, each state has different preferences over the exact nature of that order, with the dominant state preferring a set of rules and behaviors closer to D and the subordinate state preferring outcomes closer to S. Any result between d and s leaves both parties better off than in the SON. Yet, even as both parties may be better off under an international order, power determines the bias in that order. Although the dominant state will typically bias the order in its favor (closer to d), different subordinates will get better or worse "deals" depending on their available alternatives, including possible relationships with other potentially dominant states, and the ability of the subordinate to withstand coercive pressure from the dominant state. Overall, subordinate countries with

---

[19] Stephen D. Krasner, "Global Communications and National Power: Life on the Pareto Frontier," *World Politics*, Vol. 43, No. 3 (1991), pp. 336–366.

highly specific assets necessary to the dominant state – sometimes referred to as "strategic" assets in the international relations literature – are likely to obtain sets of rules and required behaviors closer to their ideal points (S) than countries with less specific assets.[20].

Once created, moreover, international order is likely to be self-enforcing. The further both states are from the SON in Figure 2.1 (the closer they are to the Pareto frontier or the further that frontier is from the SON), the more they have to lose if that order and the authority on which it is premised decays. States – and especially subordinate states – follow the rules of international order even when they are biased in favor of the dominant state because of the gains from civil society. Even so, the balance of power in the relationship, and the authority exercised by the dominant state, will evolve over time. The dominant state may become even more dependent on the specific asset of the subordinate, shifting the rules of order in favor of the latter, or vice versa. The subordinate state might also lose a possible outside option, shifting the balance of power in the dominant state's favor, as happened for the United States after the implosion of the Soviet Union in 1991. Authority and order are dynamic relationships that respond to shifting circumstances in world politics, even as both parties are locked into the relationship by the gains from political order.

As an equilibrium, authority naturally entails relatively high levels of compliance, even if the rules issued by the dominant state are biased in its favor. Compliance occurs not just because rule is rightful; indeed, legitimacy is, in many ways, nothing more than the recognition by subordinates that it is in their interests to respect the rules of the dominant state. Rather, given the alternatives, as well as the community's acceptance of the dominant state's right to enforce its rules, states comply because they are better off doing so than not. Subordinates value order over chaos, even if the order that exists favors the ruler more than the ruled. And as long as the community of which they are part grants the dominant state the right to punish defectors, individual subordinates are deterred from breaking the rules or even challenging the dominant state's right to make rules. In domestic politics, Levi[21] has described this equilibrium as quasi-voluntary compliance. The same holds for authority between states. Once authority is established, states comply and follow rules as if this were of their own choosing, but compliance occurs always

---

[20] David Lake, *Entangling Relations: American Foreign Policy in Its Century* (Princeton University Press, 1999).

[21] Margaret Levi, *Of Rule and Revenue* (Berkeley, CA: University of California Press, 1988), p. 52.

in the shadow of legitimate enforcement. Establishing authority comes at substantial cost to the dominant state. It must agree to tie its own hands and restrict its freedom of action (see above). It must also produce order, protect subordinates, and maintain an enforcement capability. Nonetheless, authority is a more efficient form of rule than is coercion alone in generating compliance. The existence of authority across a large number of possible dyads within the international system under both the Pax Britannica and Pax Americana helps explain the presence of widespread order – and compliance with that order – despite the bias in the rules and the absence of high levels of coercion between states.

Why are hegemons liberal?

For Gilpin, liberalism that supports an open international market economy is the product of hegemony and efficiency in production. Both are necessary conditions. As he writes,

Hegemony without efficiency tends to move toward imperial-type economies, as is the case in the Soviet bloc. National economic efficiency without a corresponding political-military strength may not be able to induce other powerful societies to assume the costs of a market system... Because the precondition of combined political hegemony and economic efficiency has infrequently existed, it is not surprising that market systems have been few in the past and that the two great champions of market systems in the modern world have been Great Britain in the nineteenth century and the United States in the twentieth.[22]

Although both hegemony and efficiency are likely related to the law of uneven growth, liberalism is in Gilpin's view largely a product of internal developments in Britain and the United States that propelled both to hegemony and made them the most efficient states of their eras.[23] By implication, lacking a liberal domestic political tradition, Chinese hegemony if attained will look quite different than in centuries past.

The link between hegemony and efficiency and international economic openness was always the Achilles' heel of hegemonic stability theory. According to economic theory, larger (and more powerful) countries are more likely to have positive optimal tariffs, not lower tariffs than average, and all countries have a comparative advantage, so absolute advantage as implied by the concept of efficiency should not matter. A number of attempts were made to theorize why especially large states

---

[22] Gilpin, *War and Change in World Politics*, pp. 129–130.
[23] Robert Gilpin, "Economic Interdependence and National Security in Historical Perspective," in K. Knorr and F. N. Trager, ed., *Economic Issues and National Security* (Lawrence, KS: Regents Press of Kansas, 1977), pp. 19–66.

will have stronger interests in free trade than others, but none were entirely satisfactory.[24] A focus on authority, however, reverses the causal arrow and suggests that hegemony does not cause liberalism but liberalism is more likely to lead to hegemony. To put this another way, great power does not produce liberalism; liberalism is likely to produce greater international authority.

Clearly, basic power capabilities are necessary for a dominant state to earn international authority by producing order, defending subordinates, and enforcing rules. The ability to "police" an international order requires some minimum coercive ability. But the scope of the order provided – and specifically the number and range of countries covered by that order – can be adjusted to fit national capabilities. The United States, for instance, did not begin its rise to dominance by creating a global order. Rather, it started by constructing a regional order in the Western Hemisphere, assuming control over the region from Britain starting in the 1890s. It then modified this order, making it more clearly liberal, and extended it to Western Europe and Northeast Asia after 1945. It even attempted to expand the order to include the Middle East starting in the 1970s and more significantly in the 1990s. At the same time, it has never sought to produce significant order nor govern subordinates in Africa, South Asia, or – with the exception of Vietnam – Southeast Asia. The United States, like Britain before it, tailored its rule to its capabilities, albeit imperfectly.

Once established, moreover, authority and order tend to attract additional subordinates. Although the metaphor is inapt, one might think of order as a black hole. On the supply side, producing order, defending subordinates, and enforcing rules tend to have large economies of scale, explaining why authority tends to cluster at the regional level or why most states in an area become subordinate to the same dominant state at roughly the same time.[25] As the dominant state benefits from order, it also increases its capabilities and willingness to bear the costs of rule. Order begets greater order. On the demand side, the benefits of order draw prospective subordinates into that order, much as the success of NATO and the open international economy pulled in virtually all of the former Soviet subordinates in Eastern Europe. Hegemons often start

[24] David Lake, "Leadership, Hegemony, and the International Economy: Naked Emperor or Tattered Monarch with Potential?" *International Studies Quarterly*, Vol. 37, No. 4 (1993), pp. 459–489.
[25] Lake, *Entangling Relations*; David Lake, "Regional Hierarchies: Authority and Local International Order," *Review of International Studies*, Vol. 35 (Supplement S1) (2009), pp. 35–58.

"small" and then cast a broader net, suggesting that above some threshold relative capabilities are neither determinative nor exogenous.

Instead, liberal states appear more likely than non-liberal states to gain authority over other countries. Liberal states, first of all, generally possess greater capabilities and enjoy greater success in mobilizing resources for international power.[26] Where power sometimes repels, in turn, liberalism attracts. If subordinates must "sell" their sovereignty, they will want to do so to the state offering the greatest order for the lowest price – in this case, the fewest constraints on their sovereignty. Liberal states govern more lightly (with less hierarchy). Because liberal states possess smaller public spheres, more internal checks and balances or veto points, and are more credible in their commitments, countries are more willing to subordinate themselves to liberal than other possible dominant states. Thus, if hegemons are dominant countries with a wide range of subordinate states, they attain this status because they are liberal, not vice versa.[27]

Central to any authority relationship is the subordinate's transfer of decision rights to the dominant state. Such transfers of sovereignty are fraught. Having given another state the right to command and enforce obedience, the subordinate is now vulnerable to opportunism by a dominant state that subsequently governs not as the subordinate might like but in its own self-interest. To yield sovereignty, therefore, the subordinate must be confident that the dominant state will not exploit it at some future date. A liberal state, in turn, can commit more credibly than nearly all other types of states to live within rules that bind its own behavior.[28] The idea here is presaged in North and Weingast's famous argument about tying the sovereign's hands.[29] Here, the tighter are the fetters on the dominant state, the better able it is to attract subordinates.

Liberal states have, by definition, small public spheres in which they wield authority. In polities with large public spheres (small private spheres), the state possesses authority over a wide range of issues and

---

[26] David Lake, "Power Pacifists: Democratic States and War," *American Political Science Review*, Vol. 86, No. 1 (1992), pp. 24–37; Dan Reiter and Allan C. Stam, *Democracies at War* (Princeton University Press, 2002).

[27] This does not preclude totalitarian hegemons, but their rule relies more on coercion and is more fragile.

[28] Lisa L. Martin, *Democratic Commitments: Legislatures and International Cooperation* (Princeton University Press, 2000); Charles Lipson, *Reliable Partners: How Democracies Have Made a Separate Peace* (Princeton University Press, 2003).

[29] Douglass C. North and Barry R. Weingast, "Constitutions and Commitment: The Evolution of the Institutions of Public Choice in 17th Century England," *Journal of Economic History*, Vol. 49, No. 4 (1989), pp. 803–832. See also, Kenneth A. Schultz and Barry R. Weingast, "The Democratic Advantage: Institutional Foundations of Financial Power in International Competition," *International Organization*, Vol. 57, No. 1 (2003), pp. 3–42.

practices. At an extreme, in totalitarian societies the state claims the authority to regulate legitimately all human interactions, although this is usually not possible in practice. In polities with small public spheres (large private spheres), the state possesses only limited and highly constrained authority. Liberal states, thus, possess only limited legitimate powers over their own people, and are explicitly denied the right to regulate many social, religious, "personal," and even political practices. The limited state is enshrined in the rights of free speech, association, religion, and others often associated with the first ten amendments to the US Constitution. Small public spheres, in turn, are associated with a larger reliance on market forces. Rather than regulating the behavior of many private actors, liberal states must rely on the discipline of the market. The small public sphere in liberal states, in turn, is defended by powerful domestic constituencies who govern their own areas within society, be these owners of firms who regulate their own business practices and relations with employees or clan or religious leaders who set and enforce rules on the social behaviors of their members. This is a type of "compliance constituency" first discussed in the literature on international law, but applied at the domestic level.[30]

Dependent on markets, and accustomed to large realms of private authority, liberal states then generalize their own governance systems to the international level, if possible.[31] They desire access to the markets of subordinate states, but for the same reasons as at home are not necessarily interested in or able to regulate large areas of social and economic relations. States that are liberal at home are likely to be liberal abroad. By extension, the same domestic constituencies that enforce limits on the state at home also enforce limits on the home state when it controls policy areas in subordinates in which they are invested. Private firms, for instance, who oppose government regulation in their domestic economy will likewise oppose attempts by their government to regulate their actions in the subordinate states, and will even press their home government to constrain regulation by the subordinate state government to the extent it retains sovereignty within the relevant issue area. The same for religious and other social groups; religious organizations that enforce the separation of church and state at home will oppose home government attempts to limit their proselytizing within subordinate states.

---

[30] Miles Kahler, "Conclusion: The Causes and Consequences of Legalization," in J. Goldstein, M. Kahler, R.O. Keohane and A.-M. Slaughter, ed., *Legalization and World Politics* (Cambridge, MA: MIT Press, 2001), pp. 291–293.

[31] David Lake, "Global Governance: A Relational Contracting Approach," in A. Prakash and J.A. Hart, ed., *Globalization and Governance.* (New York, NY: Routledge, 1999), pp. 31–53; Ikenberry, *After Victory*; Ikenberry, *Liberal Leviathan.*

Although "democratic imperialism" is not unknown, it nearly always takes less hierarchical forms than in its more authoritarian variants and occurs most frequently when the subordinate population can be more clearly differentiated from the home population by clear racial or ethnic categories and unequal treatment can be intellectually or politically justified.[32]

In addition, liberal states have a larger number of veto players than non-liberal states, and these points of potential blockage make it harder for such states to deviate from the status quo.[33] This makes promises to preserve an essentially liberal policy toward the subordinate more credible. It also ensures that any veto player can block efforts to exploit the subordinate in the future. Neither limited states nor large numbers of veto players are guarantees against opportunism by the dominant state, but they do serve as checks and balances that limit capricious decisions that may harm the interests of subordinate states.

These checks and balances within liberal states, in turn, make it easier for subordinates to transfer sovereignty and accept their authority. Since it is more difficult for liberal states to deviate from their liberalism, they are more reliable and predictable rulers. As a result, liberal states are more likely to become dominant over more subordinates. Through this selection process, liberal states are more likely to become hegemonic, and thus we are more likely to observe hegemonic states pursuing liberal policies. Hegemons need not be liberal – as Gilpin's reference above to the imperial role of the Soviet Union in Eastern Europe suggests. But liberal states are – all else constant, including relative capabilities – more likely to become hegemonic. And as hegemons, they are more likely to be constrained by their own societies to act in ways consistent with their liberal foundations, even in subordinates. This affinity between liberalism and hegemony, in turn, helps explain the correlation between hegemony and liberal market economies.

Why is there so little war and change?

For Gilpin, international order is transient and nearly always destroyed in hegemonic war, only like the phoenix to rise again from the ashes. Once order is established, the hegemon will eventually suffer slower

---

[32] Neta C. Crawford, *Argument and Change in World Politics: Ethics, Decolonization, and Humanitarian Intervention* (New York, NY: Cambridge University Press, 2002).

[33] Peter F Cowhey, "Domestic Institutions and the Credibility of International Commitments: Japan and the United States," *International Organization*, Vol. 47, No. 2 (1993), pp. 299–326; George Tsebelis, *Veto Players: How Political Institutions Work* (Princeton Press, 2002).

economic growth, higher costs of protection, increased consumption at the expense of investment, a shift to less productive services, and the corrupting effects of affluence and preeminence.[34] As these effects mount, the hegemon can no longer sustain its leadership. Although it could increase the resources devoted to maintaining its international position or retrench by reducing its international commitment, these strategies simply forestall the inevitable decline and may, in fact, either worsen rates of internal investment or stimulate challengers.[35] With the declining hegemon holding to the status quo, change usually occurs only through a global conflagration over control of the system. This dynamic view of international power nonetheless neglects the problem of "hegemonic afterglow" in which the hegemon continues to provide order and, more importantly, subordinates continue to comply with its rules long after they "should."[36] It also fails to account for challenges that do not occur, including the United States against Britain in the late nineteenth century and Japan against the United States in the late twentieth century.

As above, power sets the terms and some minimal level of coercive capability is necessary to sustain international order, but the relationship between power capabilities and authority is not tightly correlated. Powerful countries can abuse their authority and lose their right to rule, much as the Soviet Union did in Eastern Europe. Conversely, dominant states can lose some of their coercive capabilities without an erosion of international order and, thus, the basis of their authority. Subordinates who benefit from that order can emerge to support the declining hegemon as it declines, as did the United States in the late nineteenth century for Britain and Japan and Germany did in the 1970s for the United States.[37] Even more important, however, is that international order transforms the political economies of subordinate states and creates interests vested in that particular international order. Once this happens, challenges to the hegemon decline and compliance naturally increases. This does not imply that order lasts forever. Gilpin is likely right that declining capabilities and conflicts of interest will eventually provoke challenges to the international order from those least embedded in its rules – as were Germany and Russia in the Pax Britannica and Russia and China have been in the Pax Americana. But order can have strong dynamic

[34] Gilpin, *War and Change in World Politics*, p. 166.   [35] *Ibid.*, p. 188.

[36] Stephen D. Kranser, "State Power and the Structure of International Trade," *World Politics*, Vol. 28, No. 3 (1976), pp. 317–347; Mark R. Brawley, *Afterglow or Adjustment: Domestic Institutions and Responses to Overstretch* (New York, NY: Columbia University Press, 1999).

[37] David A. Lake, *Power, Protection, and Free Trade: The International Sources of American Commercial Strategy, 1887–1939* (Ithaca, NY: Cornell University Press, 1988).

effects that allow it to "entrap" some challengers and endure long after the hegemon's coercive capabilities have waned.

Political authority is largely self-enforcing because of the vested interests – a term of opprobrium to political reformers – that accumulate in the societies of both dominant and subordinate states.[38] The effect of vested interests is seen most easily, perhaps, in the contrast between liberal market economies (LMEs) and organized market economies (OMEs).[39] LMEs have large private spheres of authority, rely more on market-based allocation systems, and offer fewer social protections. In turn, both firms and workers develop flexible economic strategies that discourage investments in specific processes or skills, creating a large pool of "generic" capital and labor that flows (relatively) easily across sectors. Having invested in flexible production and skills, however, society has little motivation to press government for policies that encourage long-term holding of assets, apprenticeship programs tailored to long-term employment contracts, and other features common in OMEs. Adapted for flexibility, changing policies are of less import for societal actors and, in turn, the political arena is characterized by institutions that if they do not amplify at least do not dampen political swings, such as single-member electoral districts and majority party rule. The economy and its political actors are vested in a particular, self-reinforcing mode of production in which liberal markets yield more liberal markets. OMEs, by contrast, have larger public spheres, rely less on market forces, and have more counter-cyclical social protection programs. Both firms and workers expect to be engaged in long-term relationships, so both have incentives to invest in specific skill and asset acquisition. Having invested in high skill-oriented production, in turn, both firms and workers have incentives to press government for a steady flow of equally well-trained workers and counter-cyclical social programs that will tide them through

---

[38] Vested interests are an explanation for the apparent lack of cycling in "institutionalized" polities. William Riker ("Implications from the Disequilibrium of Majority Rule for the Study of Institutions," *American Political Science Review*, Vol. 74, No. 2 (1980), pp. 432–446) posed a fundamental critique of the structure-induced equilibrium approach of Kenneth Shepsle ("Institutional Arrangements and Equilibrium in Multidimensional Voting Models," *American Journal of Political Science*, Vol. 23, No. 1 (1979), pp. 27–60) and others. Riker's ("The Heresthetics of Constitution-Making: The Presidency in 1787, with Comments on Determinism and Rational Choice," *American Political Science Review*, Vol. 78, No. 1 (1984), pp. 1–16) own solution to the problem of cycling – heresthetics – focused more on rhetoric than the vested interest approach outlined here.

[39] Peter A. Hall and David Soskice, ed., *Varieties of Capitalism: The Institutional Foundations of Comparative Advantage* (New York, NY: Oxford University Press, 2001); Peter Gourevitch and James Shinn, *Political Power and Corporate Control: The New Global Politics of Corporate Governance* (Princeton University Press, 2005).

market downturns and sustain investment in these specific assets. Since policy instability would threaten to undermine these incentives, the political system is structured for centrism, either through proportional representation electoral systems or coalition governments in which centrist parties are pivotal. Organized markets follow organized markets. In both LMEs and OMEs, policies breed self-interests in maintaining the political authorities that produce those policies.[40]

Over time, subordinate states have become vested in the American-led international order. As within countries, states develop interests in sustaining the international order to which they have adapted and from which they have prospered. Through such vesting, the international order also becomes self-enforcing. At the most general level, globalization rewards winners and punishes losers, tilting the political playing field over time in favor of the former and against the latter.[41] Export interests and others that benefit from an open world economy grow and expand their political influence. Import-competing sectors and others that lose steadily shrink in size and influence; textiles and shoes, once core industries in the protectionist coalition in the United States, are no longer a political force.[42] Exporters become ever more dependent on world markets and the national economy becomes increasingly specialized. These "internationalist" interests, in turn, develop stronger interests in maintaining market openness, both at home and abroad.[43] International liberalism becomes self-sustaining and perhaps even expands. This incremental process of political realignment transformed both postwar Germany and Japan. Both were, of course, totalitarian and imperialist challengers to the decaying Pax Britannica. After being soundly defeated in World War II, it was not obvious that they would reemerge as democratic states deeply embedded in a liberal international economy. Yet, the former imperialist segments of the societies that supported totalitarianism were deeply delegitimated by defeat, opening the possibility for fundamental change. In turn, the United States and other occupying powers promoted moderate internationalists within both – the Christian Democrats in Germany, the

---

[40] In this same way, Social Security is the "third rail" of American politics because so many individuals have premised their lifetime consumption and savings patterns on its future. Farm subsidies everywhere are hard to reform because any reduction would not only affect the current income of farmers but also the value of their land, often their single biggest asset.

[41] Ronald Rogowski, *Commerce and Coalitions: How Trade Affects Domestic Political Alignments* (Princeton University Press, 1989).

[42] Oona Hathaway, "Positive Feedback: The Impact of Trade Liberalization on Industry Demands for Protection," *International Organization*, Vol. 52, No. 3 (1998), pp. 575–612.

[43] Helen V. Milner, *Resisting Protectionism: Global Industries and the Politics of International Trade* (Princeton University Press, 1988).

Liberal Democrats in Japan – against the left. With US backing, these moderates took firm control of their societies and, following the rules of the US-led order, opened themselves to international trade and especially promoted export-led growth, upending their political economies over time. Comparatively disadvantaged sectors were swept away, assets were redeployed toward comparatively advantaged sectors, and raw materials – previously obtained through imperialism and bilateral balancing – were freely acquired on US-protected international markets. Over time, many segments of German and Japanese society became dependent on and implicated in the US-led international order. This dependence eventually became so deep that both Germany and Japan became vigorous champions and fervent supporters of the liberal international economy that was imposed on them in the early postwar period. Thus, the American-led international order has – slowly but inexorably – reshaped the domestic political economies of subordinate states, an effect that is deeper and more dramatic the higher the level of integration. Now highly dependent on international markets, subordinates have become important forces in sustaining those markets, and indirectly the American-produced order.

This process of vesting interests in international order can be further illustrated by the recent American attempt to expand further its authority into the Middle East. Many Europeans were quite reluctant to follow the United States into the region, and some subordinates obviously resisted in the case of the Iraq War. But there were still few significant dissenters from American ambition. Beginning under Britain and then expanded by the United States after World War II, the international economy has thrived on access to cheap oil from the Middle East. This relatively inexpensive energy source, in turn, is deeply integrated into the economic and social structures of every advanced industrialized country, as any attempt to regulate CO_2 emissions today makes abundantly clear. All societies – and especially those in which oil is relatively cheap, like the United States – have developed infrastructures premised on continued access to stable and inexpensive supplies. This infrastructure is a significant "specific asset." Individuals, in turn, have invested in automobiles and homes in suburban areas, which together are often their most valuable assets, and these individually owned assets create a continuing political demand for cheap oil. For both of these reasons, voters in the United States support policies intended to ensure continued access to oil supplies in the Middle East and bolster local regimes that are friendly toward the West. The need for oil has driven Washington into support for the Shah of Iran (overthrown in the Iranian Revolution in 1979), continuing political alliances with autocratic regimes in Saudi Arabia and the Persian Gulf, the 1991 Persian Gulf War, and finally the 2003 Iraq War. Oil companies generally lack the political clout to drive a nation like the United States to war. Rather, the dependence on oil is structural and, as such, a deep motivation for policy of which voters may not even be aware.[44]

Importantly, states subordinate to the United States are also deeply vested in cheap oil from the Middle East and have frequently joined the US-led incursions into the region, especially Great Britain which assumed a prominent role as a supporter of the United States in both 1991 and 2003. Although attention focused on those subordinates like Germany that "defied" the Bush Administration in 2003 – an odd term if relations truly are anarchic that was frequently invoked prior to the war – subordinates were more than twice as likely to join the "coalition of the willing" than non-subordinates.[45] This was in part symbolic obeisance, a form of legitimating American rule, but it also reflects the deeply vested nature of the subordinates in the international order created and maintained by the United States. Subordinates were compelled to support the United States not by force but by the dependence of their own economies and societies on the particular order built by Washington in the Middle East. They are "locked in" to the American order not by institutions, but their own domestic constituencies that benefit from the existing structure of rules and the corresponding outcomes.

The main point here is that the interests of subordinate states are not fixed or exogenous but are endogenous to international order. As order and its attendant benefits are created, groups within subordinate countries become vested in that order and will encourage their governments to both comply with the rules and support that order should it start to erode or come under challenge. This allows order to persist long after the initial distribution of capabilities on which it originally rested has changed. The international institutions on which others have focused, and that are constructed within that order, clearly have some residual effects in reinforcing order, as old institutions continue to provide value by facilitating cooperation and are a sunk cost that must be paid anew if a different order is to be created.[46] But what ultimately makes those

---

[44] This parallels instrumental vs. structural Marxist accounts of foreign policy. See Stephen D. Krasner, *Defending the National Interest: Raw Materials Investments and US Foreign Policy* (Princeton University Press, 1978).

[45] David A. Lake, "Relational Authority and Legitimacy in International Relations," *American Behavioral Scientist*, Vol. 53, No. 3 (2009), pp. 331–353.

[46] Robert O. Keohane, *After Hegemony: Cooperation and Discord in the World Political Economy* (Princeton University Press, 1984); Ikenberry, *After Victory.*

institutions and order robust are the social interests vested in that order who have compelling reasons to follow the rules and support the order in general against possible challengers.

Today, many countries are deeply vested in the American-led order. Hegemony is less fragile than the distribution of capabilities alone would suggest. As a result, political change and the deep conflicts of interest that can lead to hegemonic war are less frequent than expected by a focus on coercion alone.

Conclusion: will China be a spoiler or supporter?

With its vast population, large territory, and rapidly growing economy, China's aggregate GDP will soon surpass that of the United States.[47] Although it will still be a "poor" country with an average per capita income far below that in developed states, its sheer economic size will soon permit it to be a major player on the world scene and to deploy a global military reach equal to that of the United States.[48] This increase in Chinese power will almost certainly give rise to new demands for greater influence in international affairs, including over the rules of the American-led order.[49] Although the United States might prefer to retain its current position as the leading power, there is little it can do to arrest this future shift in power capabilities.[50]

The authoritative nature of international order, however, creates the possibility for integrating China into the American-led international system. Embedding China into an order that protects territorial integrity and generates prosperity for all from secure property rights, monetary stability, and trade openness, promises benefits to Beijing from living within this system that will likely exceed those of a Chinese-led alternative, especially if this can only be obtained by forcibly challenging the United States;[51] if so, the benefits of consenting to American authority,

[47] C. Fred Bergsten, *China's Rise: Challenges and Opportunities* (Washington, DC: Peterson Institute for International Economics, et al., 2009).

[48] John J. Mearsheimer, *The Tragedy of Great Power Politics* (New York, NY: W.W. Norton, 2001); Bergsten, *China's Rise*.

[49] Aaron L. Friedberg, "The Future of US-China Relations: Is Conflict Inevitable?" *International Security*, Vol. 30, No. 2 (2005), pp. 7–45.

[50] Mark Beeson, "Hegemonic Transition in East Asia? The Dynamics of Chinese and American Power," *Review of International Studies*, Vol. 35, No. 1 (2009), pp. 95–112.

[51] Martin Jacques, *When China Rules and World: The End of the Western World and the Brith of a New Global Order* (New York, NY: Penguin Press, 2009); Stefan Halper, *The Beijing Consensus: How China's Authoritarian Model Will Dominate the Twenty-First Century* (New York, NY: Basic Books, 2010).

or at least participating in a system of American-made rules, may be greater than the prospects of a costly confrontation.

China is also developing – perhaps unwittingly – its own compliance constituencies that hold out the promise of transforming Beijing over time into a supporter of the American system. Following the path of Japan, South Korea, and the other Asian "tigers," China is pursuing a strategy of export-led growth that depends on the continued openness and health of an open world economy dominated by the United States and its subordinates and governed by rules agreed upon by those same countries. Although China is not a "small country" in absolute terms, it is still both a "price taker" in world markets and a "policy taker" in international institutions. To date, it is largely conforming to the existing system as it develops.[52] In turn, it is also accumulating domestic interests that are vested in the current international order and who may, in the years ahead, become an important political force that backs living within rather than challenging the American order.[53]

This is the promise of cooperation rather than confrontation with China, often left implicit and seldom linked to issues of authority by its proponents. Like postwar Germany and Japan, the more deeply China is integrated into the current world order, the less likely it will be to challenge America's authority in the future, even as its coercive capabilities grow. The United States succeeded Britain as hegemon without undue conflict, perhaps because both were relatively liberal states that shared similar preferences over the nature of international order. As a non-liberal state, China's preferred international order is less likely to mirror that constructed by the United States, and greater political tensions are probably inevitable in the years ahead. Nonetheless, integrating China into the open world economy is likely to create compliance constituencies that support the American-led order, and may actually serve to liberalize China over time. Future relations will be conditioned on whether China can be vested into the existing American-led international order. We may not know this for a decade or more, but the potential

---

[52] Alastair Iain Johnston, "Is China a Status Quo Power?" *International Security*, Vol. 27, No. 4 (2003), pp. 5–56; Alastair Iain Johnston, "How New and Assertive is China's New Assertiveness?" *International Security*, Vol. 37, No. 4 (2013), pp. 7–48; Daniel W. Drezner, "The New New World Order," *Foreign Affairs*, Vol. 86, No. 5 (2007), pp. 34–46.

[53] Thomas G. Moore and Dixia Yang, "Empowered and Restrained: Chinese Foreign Policy in the Age of Economic Interdependence," in D.M. Lampton, ed., *The Making of Chinese Foreign and Security Policy in the Era of Reform.* (Palo Alto, CA: Stanford University Press, 2001); Susan Shirk, *China: Fragile Superpower: How China's Internal Politics Could Derail Its Peaceful Rise* (New York, NY: Oxford University Press, 2007).

payoffs seem sufficiently high that it is worth running some risk that trade now will enhance the wealth and power of a possibly autonomous and antagonistic China in the future. The larger, more vibrant, and more prosperous the American order, the larger the incentives for China to join with rather than challenge the United States. This holds out a hope that, while change is inevitable, hegemonic war is not.

3   The logic of order: Westphalia, liberalism,
     and the evolution of international order
     in the modern era

G. John Ikenberry

Introduction

In *War and Change in World Politics*, Robert Gilpin offers a sweeping
account of the rise and decline of states and international order. It is a
cyclical theory of war and order building.[1] Wars create winners and
losers, opening up opportunities for a leading state to emerge hegemonic
and organize the system. Over time, power and wealth eventually diffuse,
new challengers emerge, and hegemonic war follows – and a new order is
forged in its wake. States rise up and build international order – and they
rule over that order until they grow weak and are challenged by a newly
powerful state. This is a strikingly evocative vision of power, order, and
change in world politics. But the character of order and the logic of
change remain sketchy in Gilpin's vision. What precisely are the sources
of international order and its persistence? If order is based on more than
material capabilities, what role do ideology and legitimate authority play?
There has also been a wide variation in the types of international order
that have made appearances across the centuries and within various
regions. What accounts for the variations in the types of orders that major
states have built? In the last two centuries, liberal capitalist states have
risen to global dominance. How has this liberal ascendency shaped or
influenced the logic and character of great-power rise and decline and
international order building?

Gilpin's *War and Change* provokes questions about the past and the
great upheavals in world order. But it also provokes questions about the
current era of world politics and the approaching future. The American
post-1945 hegemonic order looks very different from past international
orders. It is deeper and wider than the ancient and early modern
international orders. It can be described as a hierarchical order with
liberal characteristics or as a liberal international order with hegemonic

---

[1] Robert Gilpin, *War and Change in World Politics* (New York, NY: Cambridge University
Press, 1981).

characteristics. It is not a traditional balance of power order, nor is it a traditional imperial order. So how do we depict and explain historical variations in international order and the rise of the American liberal hegemonic order? And how do the answers to these questions help us predict what comes next? Indeed, the rise of China provokes questions about whether and how China might be able to grow powerful and preside over the reorganization of international order. If the Gilpin logic of hegemonic war is removed from history, how will China translate its power into order? And to what extent can and will China want to alter the existing international order?

To answer these questions, this chapter offers a series of arguments about how to think about international order, the American postwar system of order, and the relationship between power transitions and the liberal ascendency. I make four sets of arguments. First, I define international order and suggest ways to distinguish between and evaluate different types of international order. Second, I explore why leading states might want to build international order and the incentives, constraints, opportunities, and tools that are associated with these potential order-building moments. Third, I suggest that there are ways to see order building as an evolutionary or unfolding process driven by the order-building projects of the Westphalian system and the liberal ascendency. Fourth, I look more directly at the United States order-building project – and the liberal hegemonic order that was built and which continues to operate more or less at the global level today. I offer a way of looking at how the rise of China will interact with this larger and evolving liberal-oriented Westphalian international system.

My central argument is that large, durable, and expansive international orders are built around three features. One is a configuration of power. A leading state or group of states can only create and lead an international order if it or they have material capabilities to coerce and entice other states into the order. Second, there must be some measure of legitimacy to the rules and institutions that mark the order. The leading state must in some sense gain the normative approbation of participating states. Finally, the order must provide functional returns to participating states. The order must solve collective problems or provide services and benefits to states within the order. The critical characteristics of a durable order need not exist on some absolute scale. They need only exist relative to alternative orders that might be on offer. Orders may be more or less built around a dominant power, more or less based on a normative consensus, and more or less able to provide functional benefits and services. But international orders will rise and fall to the extent these characteristics are manifest or not.

If this argument is correct, the old American-led international order may have more life in it than is generally thought. Liberal internationalism retains features of legitimacy and functionality and it is embraced by a wide and growing array of stake holders in both rising and declining states. China and other states may grow more powerful but alternative orders that harness the power of leading states, that are widely seen as legitimate, and that have macro-structural functionality may not exist for decades to come.

Varieties of international order

International order refers to the settled arrangements that define and guide relations between states. War and upheaval between states – that is, disorder – is turned into order when stable rules and arrangements are established by agreement, imposition, or other means. Order exists in the patterned relations between states. States operate according to a set of organizational principles that define roles and the terms of their interaction. International order breaks down or enters into crisis when the settled rules and arrangements are thrown into dispute or when the forces that perpetuate order no longer operate.[2]

The explicit discussion of international order can be found in classical realist literatures, diplomatic history, and the English school. Henry Kissinger's study of the Congress of Vienna and Hedley Bull's *The Anarchical Society* are emblematic of these historical and theoretical literatures that place "the problem of order" at the center of the study of world politics. State power, anarchy, insecurity – these realist features of world politics are never very far from center stage. But the focus is on how states create rules and arrangements for ongoing relations of competition and cooperation. World politics is not simply states operating in anarchy – it is an active political order with rules, institutions, authority relations, and accumulated understandings and expectations.[3]

Gilpin's contribution was to offer a grand account of the rise and fall of international order. As Gilpin argues, world politics can be seen as a sequence of historical cycles or eras punctuated by great-power wars.

---

[2] This section draws on Ikenberry, *Liberal Leviathan: The Origins, Crisis, and Transformation of the American World Order* (Princeton University Press, 2011).

[3] The notion of international order is an old one, but it is not a term that has been central to dominant theoretical literatures in international relations. Realist theories of the balance of power build their arguments around notions such as anarchy, alliances, security dilemmas, and self-help dynamics. Liberal theories have tended to focus on notions such as complex interdependence, regimes, and institutional cooperation.

War destroys the old order – indeed, war itself reflects the failure of the old order. Winners and losers emerge. The power distribution shifts. A new leading state or group of states makes peace and, in one way or another, establishes a new international order. As Gilpin argues, these periodic wars "resolve the question of which state will govern the system, as well as what ideas and values will predominate."[4] At these rare moments, basic questions are placed on the world diplomatic table about who commands and who benefits. The rules and institutions of order are hammered out. In this idealized vision, international orders look a lot like domestic political orders. There are founding moments. States are born. Polities are forged. Governments are established. In the same way, there are moments in world politics where basic principles and organizational logics are put in place.

The iconic moments of order building, of course, are the European and world war settlements – 1648, 1713, 1815, 1919, and 1945. The wars that triggered these order-building moments are the ones that Gilpin identifies as "hegemonic wars." As Gilpin notes, "[a]t issue in each of these great conflicts was the governance of the international system."[5] Peace conferences and settlement agreements followed these wars. Institutions, rules, and practical arrangements were proposed as tools to manage the peace. Victorious states were given opportunities to organize and lead the system. Along the way, power and chaos were turned into order.

In this sense, to talk about international order – its rise, fall, and evolution in character – is to focus on the organizational logic of international relations. The character of states and the nature of their relations are defined, embedded in the rules and norms of the system. International order provides settled answers to the big questions. How is sovereignty arrayed across the system? What is the distribution of rights and authority among states? What are the rules and institutions for "doing business" – i.e., facilitating cooperation, fostering collective action, resolving conflicts, avoiding war? More generally, international order is a functioning political order – however primitive and power-based – which establishes the terms by which states command, follow, benefit, and suffer.

Seen in this light, international orders can be distinguished and compared in many ways. International orders can differ in terms of their *geographic scope*. They can be global or regional. They can encompass the entire world or exist among a smaller set of states. International orders

---

[4] Gilpin, *War and Change in World Politics*, p. 203.   [5] *Ibid.*, p. 200.

can differ in terms of their *functional scope*. They can be organized simply around security protection – manifest, for example, in a simple balance of power order. Or they can be more elaborate orders in which economic, social, political, and other aspects of life are organized and coordinated among states. International orders can differ in terms of their *institution-alization*. They can be orders with little explicit or formal rules and institutions. Or they can be highly institutionalized, with elaborate, formal, and legalistic specifications of the terms of state relations. International orders can be more or less *hierarchical*. Relations between states can be highly hierarchical, with vertically organized differential rights and authority roles and relationships between superordinate and subordinate states. Or international orders can be less hierarchical in which states operate according to more equal and horizontally organized rights and authority. Likewise, the *distribution of power* in international orders can also vary. Power can be centralized or decentralized. Order can be organized around various poles of power – multipolar, bipolar, or uni-polar.[6] The challenge for scholars is to use these various features or dimensions to capture the alternative logics and changing characteristics of international order.[7]

An important dimension that distinguishes types of international order is the source of stable relations. What makes the order endure? In this regard, there are at least three major sources. Order can be based on the balance of power. Here the problem of order is security, and the solution is establishing countervailing power to check or neutralize the power or threats of other states. Stable order exists when there is an equilibrium of power. This form of order can be more or less explicit and institutional-ized. In some instances, balancing is a sort of unintended and unacknow-ledged outcome – and as such, there is only a marginal sense in which the order is truly a functioning political order. Or a balance of power order

---

[6] On regional and global systems of order, see Barry Buzan and Ole Waever, *Regions and Power: The Structure of International Security* (New York, NY: Cambridge University Press, 2003); and Peter Katzenstein, *A World of Regions: Asia and Europe in the American Imperium* (Ithaca, NY: Cornell University Press, 2005). On variations in the institutionalization of international order, see Stephen Krasner, ed., *International Regimes* (Ithaca, NY: Cornell University Press, 1982). On variations in hierarchy, see David Lake, *Hierarchy in International Relations* (Ithaca, NY: Cornell University Press, 2009). On variations in polarity and the distribution of power, see Edward D. Mansfield, "Concentration, Polarity, and the Distribution of Power," *International Studies Quarterly*, Vol. 37, No. 1 (March 1993), pp. 105–128; and Barry Buzan, *The United States and the Great Powers* (London: Polity, 2004), Chapter 3.

[7] International orders can also be compared in terms of their "solidarist" character, that is, the degree to which order – and international society – is infused with shared notions of law and justice. See Andrew Hurrell, *On Global Order, Power, Values, and the Constitution of International Society* (Oxford University Press, 2007).

can be more explicit and acknowledged by the states operating within it. The international orders that followed 1713 and 1815 were more or less of this sort.[8]

Order can also be based on command. Disparities of power allow a lead state to dominate and control lesser states. States are integrated vertically in superordinate and subordinate positions. Command-based order can vary widely in terms of the degree to which the hierarchical terms of order are enforced through coercion or if there are also elements of autonomy, bargaining, and reciprocity. The great empires of the ancient and modern world were hierarchical orders, manifesting various strategies of rule and "repertories of imperial power."[9] The British- and American-led international orders were also hierarchical with a distinct mix of imperial and liberal characteristics.

Finally, order can be based on consent. In these instances, international order is organized around agreed-upon rules and institutions that allocate rights and limits on the exercise of power. Frameworks of rules and arrangements are constructed that provide authoritative arrangements for international relations. State power is not extinguished in a consent-based order, but it is circumscribed by agreed-upon rules and institutions. Disparities of power between states may still matter in the structuring of consensual, rule-based order, but the rules and institutions nonetheless reflect reciprocal and negotiated agreements between states. The British- and American-led liberal orders have been built in critical respects around consent. The contemporary European Union is also a political order of this sort.

This discussion of aspects or types of international order allows us to make several observations. First, international order is not simply "created" by leading states. Some orders more than others are indeed based on the strategy and design of a leading state or group of states. But order can also be shaped by the multiple and independent adjustments that states make to a given distribution of power. When a state becomes powerful, lots of reactions by other states are triggered – all the more if the state is truly a world-class state without or with few peers. Adjustments may take the form of balancing or strategies of engagement and integration. These adjustments may be small or large, incremental or strategic. But their sum total generates patterns of relations that over time can give

---

[8] For an important survey of the balance of power logic across world history, see Stuart J. Kaufman, Richard Little, and William C. Wohlforth, ed., *The Balance of Power in World History* (New York, NY: Palgrave, 2007).

[9] Jane Burbank and Frederick Cooper, *Empires in World History: Power and the Politics of Difference* (Princeton University Press, 2010), Chapter 1.

shape to international order. This can happen without a war or a peace conference. But an international order – whether based on balance, command, consent, or a combination of these features – takes shape.

Second, because international orders differ in character from one era or geographic location to another, it is possible to assess or evaluate them. Some international orders have been more coherent, durable, and consent-based than others. Some international orders more than others have been organized and run "from the center." In the same way, it is possible to draw conclusions about which international orders have been most successful in terms of generating security, prosperity, or social advancement. For example, the American-led order built after World War II provided the conditions for more security, welfare, and wealth creation than the troubled order built after World War I. Scholars – and policy makers – can draw lessons about what works and what does not.

Third, the fact that international order can – and has – come in so many varieties means that a simple rise and decline model of world politics and order building is inadequate. The idea that leading states have periodically found themselves in a position to build international order is not in dispute. But the explanation for variations in the character of the orders that they build is. At the very least, we need more variables to explain the "outcome" – i.e., the resulting international order. Why have some eras and geographical locations manifest imperial or command-based orders and others manifest liberal consent-based orders? Beyond this, can we talk about an "evolution" in the character of international order building? How has the rise of democracy and capitalism – or the wider and deeper transformations yielded by modernization – shaped and reshaped the logics of international order building? Gilpin's framework opens up these questions for debate.

Fourth, we can place the American-led order within this typological context. The Western international order that emerged after World War II was a hybrid. It was partly built on the balance of power. The rise of the Cold War was a catalyst for alliance building and a wide array of military, economic, and political commitments and undertakings. It was also built on command. The United States organized relations with allied states within a hierarchy of relations. Allies, special relationships, and client states were all part of this system. And the postwar American-led order had features of consent-based order. In relations with other Western democracies, the United States engaged in diffuse reciprocity and pursued widely beneficial agendas of trade and institutionalized cooperation. The features of balance, command, and consent were arrayed differentially across regions and across time. Moreover, the fact that the American-led order was a hybrid – and was based on mutual and reinforcing logics of order – is surely relevant in discussions about why that order has been so durable, surviving the end of the Cold War and remaining salient in the face of the rise of non-Western developing states, including China.

The evolution of international order

In the long succession of international orders, is there any evolutionary logic to their changing substantive character? Gilpin argues that each leading state that wins a hegemonic war brings its own ideas, values, and interests to order building. One can think of a range of possibilities. At one extreme, there is no connection or evolutionary logic to the rise and fall dynamic. A state wins a hegemonic war and builds an order that is congenial with its interests and ideological impulses. A hegemonic state constructs a political formation around it, but these postwar efforts are all distinct, discrete, and unrelated to what came before or what will come later. Some versions of realist theory would lean hard in this direction. At the other extreme is the view that some trans-historical master evolution-ary logic is shaping postwar orders and the overall direction of world politics.[10]

Between these extremes, it is possible to see ways in which a contin-gent evolutionary logic might be at play. One possible source of evolution relates to the character of the states that win hegemonic wars. It might be that the regime types of states that win hegemonic wars are not randomly distributed. Some kinds of states – for example, in the modern era, it might be liberal democracies – are more likely to emerge predominant after these watershed wars than others. Or it might be that the character of the population of states is changing over time (for reasons independent of wars), and this has an indirect effect on the types of states that are likely to be involved in order building. Or it could be that the nature of hegemonic wars share characteristics that lead winning states to take similar sorts of order-building steps after the war – and to respond to and learn from prior postwar steps. After all, as Gilpin notes, hegemonic wars have been triggered by the same cause, namely aggressive states that seek to break out of and impose mastery over the wider state system. Charles V, Louis XIV, Napoleon I, post-Bismarck Germany – these were the protagonists who all sought in one way or another to establish imperial dominance over other states. What unites the experiences of postwar order-building states is that they were all responding to a similar

---

sort of geopolitical aggression. The functional tasks of order building are shared, and so – like Bill Murray in the movie *Groundhog Day* – states build on and learn from the sequence of prior efforts. Moreover, as Gilpin emphasizes, postwar order-building states – particularly Britain after 1815 and the United States in the twentieth century – have also been focused on promoting and managing an open capitalist world economy. The functional tasks associated with doing this – as the world economy itself is evolving over the centuries – also allow us to see an unfolding logic at work in order building.

Taking this argument one step further, there are two major macro-historical order-building projects that are operating in the background as specific states at specific postwar moments struggle to shape and run international order. One is associated with the Westphalian state system, where great powers over the centuries have been building on and developing rules, institutions, and practices for managing the state system and great-power relations. The other is associated with the liberal ascendency, where liberal democratic states have risen up in power and influence and engaged in repeated efforts to build international order.

The Westphalian project has involved the development of rules and institutions that enshrine the system of sovereign states. At the heart of this order is the notion of state sovereignty and great-power restraint and accommodation. The founding moment of this project was, of course, the Westphalian peace of 1648, but the rules and norms of state relations have continued to evolve. The founding location of this project was Western Europe. Great powers, empires, and universal religious authority competed for dominance on the Continent. Through wars and peace settlements, rules and norms of the Westphalian order took shape and evolved. The result has been the rise and evolution of the so-called Westphalian system of states. The great powers compete, cooperate, and balance each other within a wider framework of rules and norms. In the background, Westphalian norms of sovereignty reinforce the idea that states are formally equal and independent, possessing the ultimate authority over their own people and territory.[11]

Over the centuries, the Westphalian system has evolved as a set of principles and practices and expanded outward from its European origins to encompass the entire globe. Despite this unfolding, however, states have retained their claims of political and legal authority. The founding principles of the Westphalian system – sovereignty, territorial

---

[11] For depictions of the Westphalian state system, see F.H. Hinsley, *Power and the Pursuit of Peace* (Cambridge University Press, 1963); and Hedley Bull, *The Anarchical Society* (New York, NY: Columbia University Press, 1977).

integrity, and non-intervention – reflected an emerging consensus that states were the rightful political units for the establishment of legitimate rule. Norms and principles that subsequently evolved within the Westphalian system – such as self-determination and non-discrimination – served to further reinforce the primacy of states and state authority. These norms and principles have served as the organizing logic for Westphalian order and provided the ideational source of political authority within it. Under the banner of sovereignty and self-determination, political movements for decolonization and independence were set in motion in the non-Western developing world. Westphalian norms have been violated and ignored but they have, nonetheless, been the most salient and agreed-upon rules and principles of international order in the modern era.

The succession of postwar settlements also provided moments for the great powers to develop principles and practices that have shaped and updated the functioning of great-power relations.[12] Particularly paradigmatic is the Vienna settlement that followed the Napoleonic Wars. This settlement is widely seen as particularly successful because it was based on great-power restraint and accommodation.[13] In contrast, the Versailles settlement was famously less successful. Its punitive character violated the restraint principles that had been so critical to the earlier settlement. The settlement of World War II was more complicated than that of previous settlements. Nonetheless, the great powers – at least in the West – rebuilt their relations in innovative ways, engaging in restraint through institutional and economic binding. Germany and Japan were rebuilt as liberal democratic states, and they were integrated into the postwar American-led international order. France and West Germany tied themselves together through the Coal and Steel Community and to the other European states in wider European and Atlantic institutions. Along this historical pathway – through war and settlement, learning and adaptation – it is possible to see an evolution in how the great powers have operated within a multipolar balance of power system. The source of order remained rooted in a decentralized states system in which major states compete with and balance each other. But the practices

[12] On the evolving norms of great-power authority, see Andreas Osiander, *The States System of Europe, 1640–1990: Peacemaking and the Conditions of International Stability* (Oxford: Clarendon Press, 1994).
[13] For accounts of the Vienna settlement that emphasize its evolving practices of great-power restraint and accommodation, see Paul Schroeder, *The Transformation of European Politics, 1763–1848* (New York, NY: Palgrave Macmillan, 2002); and Charles A. Kupchan, *How Enemies Become Friends: The Sources of Stable Peace* (Princeton University Press, 2010), pp. 188–217.

and principles of competition and balance have evolved to incorporate strategic notions of restraint and accommodation.

The liberal order-building project followed from and built upon this evolving system of Westphalian relations. Fundamentally, the liberal project has entailed a commitment to international order that is open and at least loosely rule-based. Beyond this, the liberal vision is wide ranging and diverse. Open markets, international institutions, cooperative security, democratic community, progressive change, collective problem solving, shared sovereignty, the rule of law – all are aspects of the liberal vision that have made appearances in various combinations and changing ways over the decades and centuries.

In the nineteenth century, liberal internationalism was manifest in Britain's championing of free trade and freedom of the seas. But the liberal project in international relations was limited and coexisted with imperialism and colonialism. In the twentieth century, liberal order building was pushed forward by the United States and it went through several phases. After World War I, Woodrow Wilson and other liberals pushed for an international order organized around a global collective security body in which sovereign states would act together to uphold a system of territorial peace. Open trade, national self-determination, and a belief in progressive global change also undergirded the Wilsonian world view – a "one world" vision of nation-states that trade and interact in a multilateral system of laws creating an orderly international community. "What we seek," Wilson declared at Mount Vernon on July 4, 1918, "is the reign of law, based on the consent of the governed and sustained by the organized opinion of mankind." Despite its great ambition, the Wilsonian plan for liberal international order entailed very little in the way of institutional machinery or formal great-power management of the system. It was a "thin" liberal order in which states would primarily act cooperatively through the shared embrace of liberal ideas and principles.[14] In the end, this experiment in liberal order building failed and the world soon entered an inter-war period of closed economic systems and rival imperial blocs.

After World War II, the Roosevelt Administration again engaged in liberal order building, embracing a vision of an open trading system and a world organization in which the great powers would cooperate to keep the peace. Beyond this, American architects of postwar order – drawing lessons from the Wilsonian failure and incorporating ideas from the New Deal period – also advanced more ambitious ideas about economic and

---

[14] See Thomas Knock, *To End All Wars: Woodrow Wilson and the Quest for a New World Order* (New York, NY: Oxford University Press, 1992).

political cooperation embodied in the Bretton Woods institutions. But the weakness of postwar Europe and rising tensions with the Soviet Union pushed liberal order building toward a much more American-led and Western-centered system. As the Cold War unfolded, the United States took command of organizing and running the system. In both security and economic realms, the United States found itself taking on new commitments and functional roles. Its own economic and political system became, in effect, the central component of the larger liberal hegemonic order.

A more recent phase of liberal internationalism was quietly launched after World War II. This was the elaboration of universal rights of man, enshrined in the United Nations and the Universal Declaration of Human Rights. This human rights revolution is deeply embedded in the postwar liberal international project. It was liberals – wielding liberal ideas about world order – who pushed forward the campaign for international recognition of human rights. The breakthrough was the Universal Declaration adopted by the UN General Assembly in December 1948. Championed by liberals such as Eleanor Roosevelt and others, this document articulated a notion of universal individual rights that deserved recognition by the whole of mankind and not simply left to sovereign governments to define and enforce.[15] A steady stream of conventions and treaties followed that together constitute an extraordinary vision of rights, individuals, sovereignty, and global order. In the decades since the end of the Cold War, these norms of human rights have been further articulated, and notions of "responsibility to project" have given the international community legal rights and obligations to intervene in the affairs of sovereign states.

Taken together, the Westphalian and liberal internationalist projects have unfolded over the centuries and given shape to the modern international order. The result has been a layer cake of ideas, norms, rules, and institutions – most of which are complementary but some of which conflict. The Westphalian logic has given world politics organizational principles built around state sovereignty and norms of great-power restraint and accommodation. Norms of self-determination and non-discrimination have also been enshrined in the Westphalian vision. Most of these rules and norms have provided the foundation for the liberal international project. Liberal internationalism in both the nineteenth and twentieth centuries has been premised on a stable system of states. Wilsonian-era liberal internationalism coopted Westphalian notions of

---

[15] See Mary Ann Glendon, *A World Made New: Eleanor Roosevelt and the Universal Declaration* (New York, NY: Random House, 2002).

sovereignty and self-determination, even if Wilson himself did not fully acknowledge nationalist aspirations outside of the West. Roosevelt-era liberal internationalism went further and sought to empower states to pursue progressive goals of social and economic rights and protections. FDR's Four Freedoms speech and the Atlantic Charter offered visions of a modern state system in which governments actively promoted and protected their citizens. In more recent decades, the human rights agenda has become more inconsistent with Westphalian sovereignty, as it articulates rationales for intervention in the otherwise sovereign affairs of states.[16]

Seen in this light, we can make several general observations about hegemonic states and the rise and fall of international order. First, international orders, at least in the modern era, do exhibit a sort of contingent evolutionary logic. Specific historical moments are created by hegemonic wars, but the "problem of order" that is thrown up at these instances is defined and shaped by the longer-term problems generated by the Westphalian state system and the liberal ascendancy. Order-building states have found themselves building upon, extending, and modifying these deeply entrenched state-system and liberal internationalist frameworks of world politics. In building order, leading states are seeking to capitalize on their power advantages and build an order congenial with their interests, but they have tended to do so by trying to reestablish and strengthen the Westphalian state system and reestablishing and strengthening open, rule-based order.

Second, the sequence of international orders has evolved in another sense – they have become increasingly sophisticated and complex. The norms of Westphalian order evolved by becoming more elaborate. The norm of state sovereignty is the core idea but other norms – including self-determination and non-discrimination – were added. Westphalian norms started out as tools for early-modern European states to protect their autonomy in the face of bids for universal dominance but they eventually became tools for non-Western peoples in the colonial and post-imperial world seeking independence and statehood. Along the way, great powers also established themselves as a class of states with a special role in governing the system. After World War II, regional orders also found important subsidiary roles as security and economic entities. The organization of the world economy also became a more elaborate and institutionalized affair. Multilateral institutions provided mechanisms for ongoing management of trade, monetary, and financial relations. In both

---

[16] See Charles R. Beitz, *The Idea of Human Rights* (New York, NY: Oxford University Press, 2009).

the security and economic aspects of post-WWII international order, states were drawing explicit lessons from past failures and successes.

Third, the Westphalian and liberal ascendency projects exhibited deep compatibilities – along with more recent tensions. More so than some liberal theorists might admit, the liberal internationalist project has required and been built upon a realist-style state system. In both the nineteenth and twentieth centuries, liberal ideas about collective security were premised upon a functioning state system. In both 1919 and 1945, the proposed postwar peace systems defined war as a violation of the norms of state sovereignty. Liberal democratic statesmen sought ways to protect and advance the prospects of their nation-states. Systems of free trade and managed economic openness were built around states. The post-WWII vision of an "embedded liberal" order had its origins in efforts to strengthen the ability of national governments to manage modern economic interdependence. It was a state-strengthening move. Overall, the liberal internationalist project has had more to do with shaping the "environment" within which states operate than with the transformation or diminishment of the state.

The tensions between Westphalian and liberal international norms are decidedly partial and of relatively recent origin. Implicit in post-WWII human rights proclamations – most clearly expressed in the Universal Declaration – were ideas about contingent sovereignty. Yet even the Universal Declaration offered a vision of a state system in which governments acted in accord with shared universal norms. But there was also the idea that the rights of individuals were not necessarily only to be secured and protected by the nation-state. If gross violations occur, the international community has a stake in redressing and protecting these rights. These tensions between sovereignty and human rights remain unresolved.[17] It is, however, worth recalling that it is the UN Security Council – a traditional Westphalian political site – that is widely understood to be the most appropriate venue for the debate and practical resolution of disputes between sovereignty and liberal interventionism.

Power, legitimacy, and functionality

Why do some international orders endure for decades and even centuries while others do not? This is one of the classic questions of international relations. Scholars have long debated why the Roman Empire and the

---

[17] On the emerging norm of the "responsibility to protect" and its relationship to traditional principles of sovereignty, see Gareth Evans, *The Responsibility to Protect: Ending Mass Atrocity Crimes Once and For All* (Washington, DC: The Brookings Institution, 2008).

British Empire, each in its own era, lasted so long.[18] The American liberal hegemonic order has also lasted longer than many expected – outlasting the Cold War and the rise and decline of rival great powers. Certainly, the sources of persistence partly depend on the type of international order in question. A balance of power order will rise and fall with changes in the distribution of power and the degree to which states adjust to these changes. The persistence of an order built on command will depend on the degree to which the lead state continues to possess capabilities with which to enforce order. Likewise, the durability of a consent-based order will depend on whether participating states within the order continue to acquiesce to the bargains and agreements that underpin it.

But it is possible to go beyond these initial observations. When we think of international order as Gilpin does – as a state-led hegemonic political formation – we can identify at least three factors that matter most. One, of course, is the *configuration of power*. A leading state needs to be powerful in the first instance to create an international order. Gilpin suggests that winning a hegemonic war is critical because war itself vanquishes competitors, delegitimates the old order, and levels the ground for a new effort at order building. The leading state needs unmatched material capabilities to force other states to make adjustments. Power – military, economic, technological, political – provides the tools to push and pull other states into the order.

Power provides the carrots and sticks of diplomacy. But beyond this instrumental view of power, the sheer aggregation of power in the hands of one state makes it necessary for other states to adjust. It creates a reality that other states face as they make strategic decisions, undertake investments, and think about the future.

As such, the greater the power of a leading state after a hegemonic war, the more ambitious it can be in building order. FDR and Truman were sitting on top of a more powerful state – relative to the rest of the world – than Wilson was. As a result, a more thoroughgoing reorganization of the international system was possible. Britain in 1815 had to share order building with other great powers who were less powerful but not that much so.[19]

Once an international order is established, the question is: how much relative power does the lead state need to retain so as to ensure the

---

[18] See Paul Kennedy, "Why Did the British Empire Last So Long?" in *Strategy and Diplomacy, 1870–1945: Eight Studies* (London: George Allen & Unwin, 1984), pp. 197–218.

[19] I develop this point in Ikenberry, *After Victory: Institutions, Strategic Restraint, and the Rebuilding of Order after Major Wars* (Princeton University Press, 2001).

ongoing viability of that order? Presumably not as much power as it needed to build the order. Hegemonic power was used to get other states to participate in the order. All parties have made investments in the existing order. So power – as an instrumental tool – should be less needed – that is, it can decline off its peak, up to some point, without consequence. Moreover, other countries may take on some of the responsibilities for managing the order. Gilpin argues that decline of the leading state takes the form of a diffusion of wealth and power to other states, driven by laws of uneven development. This can go on for some time before a breakpoint emerges. Moreover, the breakpoint is not some sort of threshold of power – it is a hegemonic war. The road to war is paved by incremental shifts in power, but the road can be long and winding, and hegemonic war also depends on the degree to which diffusion of power is combined with the buildup of power in a singular global peer competitor. If the diffusion of power is diffused across many or several states and not a single rival state, this may not create the dyadic conflict needed to trigger a hegemonic war, and therefore the old system will continue to persist.

What if great-power war is removed as a cause of hegemonic transitions? Gilpin speculates about this at the end of *War and Change in World Politics*. If nuclear weapons have made war between the great powers profoundly irrational and unlikely, the opportunities for building new orders after hegemonic wars will disappear. Hegemonic wars will disappear. Power may continue to shift, but the critical factor that destroys the old order – massive violence – will be missing. A rising state may have the power to reshape the system but not the opportunity. This introduces yet another factor that might generate an evolutionary logic in the rise and fall of international orders – nuclear weapons and deterrence. The effect is to give an advantage to the declining status quo state and to reinforce continuity in international order.[20]

Even under these conditions, there is one remaining factor that might allow a rising state to usher in a new international order. This relates to the structural features of power. As I noted earlier, the very fact that a powerful state has risen up and overshadowed other states creates circumstances that foster order. This is the structural impact of concentrated power.[21] Smaller and weaker states are forced to make

---

[20] These ideas are explored in Daniel Deudney's chapter in this volume.

[21] See Susan Strange, "The Persistent Myth of Lost Hegemony," *International Organization*, Vol. 41, No. 4 (Autumn 1987), pp. 551–574. See also Stefano Guzzini, "Structural Power: The Limits of Neo-realist Power Analysis," *International Organization*, Vol. 47, No. 3 (Summer 1993), pp. 443–478.

thousands of little decisions about how to relate to the powerful state. In the decades after World War II, countries around the world made decisions to adjust to American predominance. Corporations made investment decisions. People in societies made decisions to learn English and seek educational opportunities in the United States. The United States became a sort of global "hub" around which other countries connected and organized their lives.[22] America's open and liberal democratic character no doubt facilitated this macro-incremental process. The point is that part of the order-building process after World War II was not directly a reflection of American strategy and plan. It followed from diffuse responses to the circumstances of American concentrated power.

It is possible that this same logic could apply to the rise of a rival state, such as China. A hegemonic war would not be needed. It is simply the long-term incremental shift in how people around the world – corporations, groups, students, etc. – decide where and how to invest and affiliate. If during the last half century "all roads" led to the United States, it is possible that in the next half century "all roads" will lead to China.[23] But this dynamic seems to be driven by more than simply the concentration of hard power. People tied themselves to the United States because it had the largest economy and military, but also because it was stable, open, and rule-based. If this is true, there will be limits on the ability of China to repeat the American experience.

The second factor influencing the durability of international order is the *legitimacy of its rules and institutions*. Legitimacy refers to the normative appeal of a political order. It is a subjective judgment that political actors make. Legitimacy does not reside in rules and institutions themselves. It resides in the sentiments and viewpoints of those who encounter the rules and institutions.[24] An international order will be more stable and enduring to the extent that states within that order – strong, weak, rising, and declining – see that order as normatively appealing. A state that has won a hegemonic war and peddles unappealing ideas and principles of order will have a hard time creating or sustaining an order.

There are several characteristics of a political order that influence judgments about its legitimacy. One aspect relates to the normative principles of the international order. An international order is more likely

---

[22] I develop this argument in Ikenberry, "The Liberal Sources of American Unipolarity," in Ikenberry, Michael Mastanduno, and William Wohlforth, eds., *International Relations Theory and Unipolarity* (New York, NY: Cambridge University Press, 2011).

[23] See Martin Jacques, *When China Rules the World: The End of the Western World and the Birth of a New Global Order* (New York, NY: Penguin, 2009).

[24] See Ian Clark, *Legitimacy in International Society* (Oxford University Press, 2005).

to be seen as legitimate if its principles accord with those of the participating states. For example, it is very unlikely that a liberal democracy will find a despotic or imperial international order legitimate – unless, of course, as in the case of the British Empire, it runs such an order. At least in the postwar era, liberal democracies have sought to create global institutions that are imbued with the same political values they embrace at home. Indeed, reflecting the dominance of liberal democracies around the world, essentially all the leading institutions of the global system do enshrine democracy and the rule of law as the proper and just form of governance.

The rules and norms of the Westphalian system have had universal appeal over the centuries because they are easily reconciled with diverse domestic political principles. Westphalian norms acknowledge the autonomous authority that states possess – up to some quite extreme point – to decide their own regime type. Sovereign independence and self-determination is celebrated. A thousand ideological flowers can bloom within a Westphalian system. However, order building during the liberal ascendency has resulted in rules and institutions that adhere more closely to the liberal democratic vision. Building on but also going beyond the Westphalian logic, the United States and the other liberal democracies have presided over an expansion of global rules and institutions. The legitimacy of this expanded system of global governance hinges in part on the ability of these states to reconcile these rules and institutions with domestic liberal democratic principles. If rising non-Western, non-liberal states want to propose new global institutions, they will need to contend with this reality.

A second source of legitimacy stems not from the principles of international order but from the political character of the order. If participating states are allowed to play a role and have a voice in what happens within the international order, they are more likely to see it as legitimate. States are more likely to give their consent if they have a say. Some orders, more than others, are organized in ways that allow states to become stake holders and pursue their own interests. It is in these various ways that liberal-oriented international order has characteristics that help foster a sense of its legitimacy.[25]

All international orders dominated by a powerful state have been based on a mix of coercion and consent. But the American-led postwar order – and liberal international orders more generally – has characteristics that

---

[25] These characteristics of liberal international order are explored in Ikenberry, *Liberal Leviathan*.

allow for participation and mutual gain. First, more so than with imperial orders of the past, the American-led order is built around rules and norms of non-discrimination and market openness – creating conditions for a wide range of states to participate within the order and advance their economic and political goals within it. Across history, international orders have varied widely in terms of whether the material benefits that are generated accrue disproportionately to the leading state or the material benefits of participation within the order are more widely shared. In the American-led system, the barriers to economic entry are low and the potential benefits are high. China has already discovered the massive economic returns that are possible through operating within this open market system.

A second feature of the American-led order is the coalition-based character of its leadership. This is an order in which a group of advanced liberal democratic states work together and assert collective leadership. It is not just an American order. Increasingly over the decades, a wider group of liberal democratic states have bound themselves together and governed the system. These leading states do not always agree but they are engaged in a continuous process of give and take over economics, politics, and security. This too is distinctive – past orders have tended to be dominated by one state. The stake holders in the current order include a coalition of status quo great powers that are arrayed around the United States. Not all states have an equal voice in the operation of the order, but a wide grouping of states do, and this helps foster consent and legitimacy.

As noted earlier, a third feature of the US-led order that facilitates participation and consent is the unusually elaborate and far-flung set of negotiated rules and institutions. International order can be rigidly hierarchical and governed by coercive domination exercised by the leading state or it can be relatively open and organized around reciprocal, consensual and rule-based relations. Within a wide variety of multilateral institutions, alliances, governance coalitions, and informal special relationships, states have access and voice.

In combination, these features of the liberal hegemonic order have made it relatively open and accessible – and therefore legitimate, and therefore durable. Its rules and institutions are rooted in and reinforced by the evolving global forces of the liberal ascendancy. It has a wide and widening array of participants and stake-holders. In all these ways, in comparison with past international orders, it is easier to join and harder to overturn. It is hard to envisage how a rival hegemonic state could offer an alternative set of ideas or organizational arrangements that could generate an equal amount of access, consent, and legitimacy.

A final factor influencing the durability of an international order is its *functionality*. Functionality refers to the ability of an international order to solve problems that states want solved.[26] This is really a question about the practical capacity of an international order to get things accomplished. International orders can be seen as more or less able to do things that bear on the ability of states to solve problems. They may be more or less able to facilitate cooperation, organize relationships, generate capacities, overcome conflicts, empower experts, and so forth. The specific challenges that states face will differ across the centuries – and not all states will agree on the problems that need solving. But all states do face practical challenges, and not all international orders will be equally endowed with the ability to tackle these practical challenges.

Those international orders that are particularly good at arraying rules and institutions in ways that facilitate problem solving will be favored and are likely to endure longer than those that are less good in this regard.

There are several ways that functionality of an international order can matter. One relates to the ways in which rules and institutions strengthen the ability of governments to act capably and accomplish goals. Does the international order enhance or diminish state capacity? Orders that enhance state capacity will be seen as more functional – and more desirable. For example, the rules and arrangements for monetary order after World War II created international capacities that allowed the United States and European governments to pursue more effective pro-growth economic policies. The Bretton Woods agreements did not so much create new realms of international authority "above" the state as create new capacities for states to act at home in the context of an open world economy. In this sense, the international order was functional from the perspective of national governments. If the rules and institutions of the international order undermine the ability of national governments to accomplish goals, the international order is less functional.

Another way that functionality can vary is within the international order's hierarchical setting. Here the question is: to what extent does the international order make life better for states that are at the lower levels of the global hierarchy? Does the international order facilitate the spread of technology and investment downward? Does the order

---

[26] International relations scholars have not offered systematic explorations of variations in the "problem-solving capacities" of international orders. For an effort to apply this idea to the European Union, see Fritz Scharpf, "Introduction: The Problem-Solving Capacity of Multi-level Governance," *Journal of European Public Policy*, Vol. 4 (1997), pp. 530–538; and Scharpf, *Governing Europe: Effective and Democratic?* (Oxford University Press, 1999).

facilitate trade upward? Do subordinate states benefit from participation in the order? One of the classic explanations for the longevity of the Roman Empire is that the Romans improved the infrastructure and social conditions of societies that were incorporated into the empire. Aqueducts, sanitation, roads, water supplies, public health – the empire was good for a lot of subordinate peoples on the periphery. A similar argument has often been made about the British Empire, at least in terms of some of its colonial holdings. In regard to American postwar hegemony, numerous scholars have noted its "empire by invitation" characteristics.[27] The United States has provided security protection and access to markets in ways that have drawn states into rather than away from the American orbit.

A third way that functionality may be manifest is in the "system effects" that are created by the order. Liberal orders seem to have a functional advantage over alternative types of orders that are not open and rule-based – i.e., orders organized around spheres, blocs, or imperial hierarchies. This is primarily a point about the organization of liberal capitalism. In particular, a system of open trade – championed by liberal polities – facilitates growth and wealth creation among the trading states. This in turn expands the scope of the world capitalist system and creates incentives and opportunities for other states – transitional and non-capitalist states – to join in. The functional logic of liberal capitalism leads states to seek economic gains from specialization and operation within the global division of labor. States outside this expanding order become increasingly weak in relative terms and marginalized – and so they face increasing incentives to seek liberal reforms and accommodate to the liberal capitalist system.[28]

Another system effect relates to the character of the rules and institutions within the order. Some international orders – more than others – create capacities for states to communicate, exchange, cooperate, overcome distrust, and mitigate security dilemmas.[29] Again, liberal orders seem to have an advantage. An open and rule-based order is one that is infused with institutional mechanisms for doing business. There is an ease and efficiency in interaction between states. Cooperation opportunities can more readily be seized. Joint gains can more quickly be realized. In a variation of this argument, Anne-Marie Slaughter

[27] Geir Lundstadt, *The American "Empire"* (Oxford University Press, 1990).
[28] See Richard Rosecrance, *The Resurgence of the West: How Transatlantic Union Can Prevent War and Restore the United States and Europe* (New Haven, CT: Yale University Press, 2013).
[29] See Robert Keohane, *After Hegemony: Cooperation and Discord in the World Political Economy* (Princeton University Press, 1984).

suggests that the United States and other liberal democracies experience "network advantages" over other sorts of states.[30] Open and rule-based international orders encourage and facilitate networks that allow states and other actors to engage in collective action and tackle common problems.

In these various ways, the functionality of an international order will have an impact on the durability of that order. If states have a choice, they will choose to operate in an international order that is most functional for their purposes. They will choose to participate in an order that strengthens their hand – that is, their ability to accomplish goals. They will choose to participate in an order that generates flows of benefits in their direction. They will choose to participate in an order that provides a congenial institutional environment for doing business. Once such an order is in place, a rising state seeking to replace the existing order faces a daunting task. China might someday find itself in this situation. It will need to offer a vision of order that is more functional than the existing one. It will need to show that the international order it wants to build will have real practical attractions for other states. If the existing order is a liberal international order, it is hard to imagine what sort of rival order would in fact be more functional. But even if such a China-led international order could be imagined, the sunk costs and system effects that are generated by the existing order create higher barriers to change. As the liberal international order gains in its global scope, it becomes more powerful and wealthy relative to the alternatives. This places rising states seeking to construct an alternative international order at an increasing disadvantage.

Conclusion

How durable is the American-led international order in the face of the rise of non-Western developing states, particularly China? In asking this question, it is important to distinguish between the fate of the liberal hegemonic order led by the United States and liberal internationalism. As we have seen, liberal international order has come in many varieties – and it has evolved over the last two centuries. Liberal internationalism is order that is open and at least loosely rule-based. After World War II, the United States stepped forward to build liberal international order around itself. It took ownership of the system. It provided "hegemonic services" to other states. It built and operated an order that gained

---

[30] Anne-Marie Slaughter, "America's Edge: Power in the Networked Century," *Foreign Affairs*, Vol. 88 (January/February 2009), pp. 94–113.

the participation and acquiescence of an expanding grouping of liberal democracies and various client states.

With the rise of non-Western great powers, the American control or management of liberal international order is slowly giving way. The distribution of rights and authority within the existing international order is shifting. But a decline in American hegemonic control will not necessarily doom liberal internationalism. The demand for American leadership will wax and wane. But the demand for liberal internationalism seems to be, if anything, growing.

This chapter has argued that international orders do not just rise and decline, they also evolve. Powerful states that win wars build order, but they do not build it simply as they please. They confront a set of postwar challenges. Order-building states are powerful but they are not all powerful. If they are unwilling or unable to maintain order simply on the basis of coercion, they will need to enter into a world of bargains, negotiations, and institutions. In the modern era, leading states also find themselves positioned – even after hegemonic wars – within a larger world historical setting defined in terms of the Westphalian system and the liberal ascendancy. Postwar orders have evolved as leading states have built upon and learned from prior efforts. The Westphalian system has provided the political framework in which great powers have operated, developing along the way an evolving array of norms and practices through which states can manage their relations. The rise to dominance of liberal democracies has provided another layer to order building over the last two hundred years. Liberal democratic states have engaged in repeated efforts to infuse the state system with rules and institutions that promote openness and stable peace.

Out of this world historical process, the notion of rise and decline of international order misses the mark. There is evolution, accumulation, expansion, and path dependency operating in the background. The liberal democracies have created a global political-economic complex that is wider and deeper than seen in past international orders. The existing international order is less tightly connected to one state, in this case the United States, than past international orders. In Gilpin's formulation, the international order is a political formation tied to the power and leadership of the state that creates it. With the advent and maturation of post-WWII liberal international order, this logic of power and order seems to have weakened. Liberal states may rise and decline but the order itself goes on. The sources of durability, as we have seen, are multiple and mutually reinforcing. With the rise of nuclear weapons and the potential end of hegemonic wars, the bias in favor of continuity over change is further reinforced.

Even if China surpasses the United States in power capabilities, it is not clear that it will be able to overturn the existing international order. This is true not only because the United States is just one of many stake holders in the existing order. China will need to offer the world a vision of international order that is legitimate and functional. As China becomes more powerful, it will certainly seek greater authority and rights within the existing order – and the existing order is configured in a way that can allow this to happen. But can it preside over an epochal transformation of liberal international order into something radically new? Not likely.

Part II

Power transition and the rise and decline
of international order

4 Hegemonic decline and hegemonic war revisited

William C. Wohlforth

Introduction

The rise and decline of hegemonic states remains a central concern of scholars and policy makers. To be sure, most international relations scholars long ago abandoned the quest for a simple causal relationship between the distribution of power and major political phenomena like war and cooperation. But as Robert Gilpin wrote three decades ago, one need not "accept a structural or systems theory approach to international relations such as Waltz's in order to agree that the distribution of power among the states in a system has a profound impact on state behavior."[1] Witness the outpouring of commentary and analysis following the 2008 financial crisis and subsequent great recession debating the extent and possible effects of American decline. For many, the world seemed to stand before a "Gilpinian moment," when the basic material underpinnings of the American-led global order were rapidly shifting toward some new as-yet undefined equilibrium.

Gilpin's *War and Change in World Politics* posited a conditional but nonetheless general relationship between the distribution of capabilities among major states and the stability of any given interstate order. States, Gilpin argued, use their material capabilities to foster a strategic environment congenial to their interests. If conditions permit, especially capable states thus may seek to create and sustain rough forms of political order over an international system. Gilpin identified a tendency for such hegemonic states to do just that, but, he stressed, no state can expect to lock in a favorable position in the distribution of capabilities. Indeed, tendencies intrinsic to being a hegemonic state will cause the distribution of capabilities to shift away to other actors. As a result, the expected net benefits to rising states of challenging the existing order will increase,

---

[1] Robert Gilpin, *War and Change in World Politics* (New York, NY: Cambridge University Press, 1981), p. 87.

causing system instability and potentially a major war reestablishing equilibrium between underlying power and the political order.

Is *War and Change* truly relevant to a world in which the United States is experiencing relative decline and China and other rapidly rising states are expressing varying levels of dissatisfaction with the US-led global order? Most scholars would answer with a qualified "yes and no." Yes, because Gilpin's focus on the ultimately self-defeating nature of hegemony applies in spades.

As Christopher Layne put it, "the United States now is facing the dilemmas that Gilpin and the other declinists warned about."[2] Scores of scholars, analysts, and pundits agree that America's hegemonic grand strategy of leadership or "global engagement" has long since become a losing proposition, imposing ever-higher costs and yielding dwindling benefits. Confronting a punishing budget crisis, an exhausted military, balky allies, and a public whose appetite for global engagement is waning, the United States appeared to be experiencing the general tendency Gilpin identified for "the economic costs of maintaining the status quo to rise faster than the economic capacity to support the status quo."[3]

But many would doubt the book's relevance simply because a hegemonic war – an all-out military slugfest among the word's most powerful states – seems exceedingly unlikely to serve as a mechanism for reorganizing the international system. Gilpin's focus on hegemonic war strikes observers as so distant from the real concerns of an age of nuclear deterrence, the declining benefits of conquest, and numerous other factors that conspire against major-power war that the posited links between order, change, and war seem relics of an unfortunate past. Indeed the word "war" is absent even from the title of this volume, and the titles of every other chapter in it.

This chapter turns the conventional wisdom about hegemonic decline and war on its head. The received theory of hegemonic decline exemplified by Gilpin's *War and Change* is far less relevant to contemporary contestation over the American-led global order than scholars assume, while the role of hegemonic war in explaining systemic change is far more relevant. Scholarship on hegemonic decline and war is voluminous, but it is striking how little is written about two fundamental relationships: between hegemonic grand strategies and hegemonic decline, and between war and systemic leadership. Concerning both of these relationships, this chapter makes a strong negative case that scholars know far less than they think they do, and a more preliminary positive case that what we do

---

[2] Christopher Layne, "This Time It's Real: The End of Unipolarity and the *Pax Americana*," *International Studies Quarterly*, Vol. 56, No. 1 (2012), pp. 203–213, 207.
[3] Gilpin, *War and Change*, p. 156.

know runs directly against most post-2008 analysis of American decline, imperial overstretch, and the need for grand strategic retrenchment.

Hegemony, hegemonic grand strategies, and decline

The central claim in scores of scholarly works is that once past some identifiable inflection point hegemonic grand strategies become losing propositions. Writing in the 1980s, Robert Gilpin, Paul Kennedy, and many other so-called "declinists" argued that the United States had reached this stage. The Soviet collapse, Japan's time of troubles, and comparatively robust levels of US growth and technological innovation in the 1990s pushed those arguments aside for a time. Many now argue that the 1990s were but a brief reprieve, and the rise of China and the post-2008 financial collapse and great recession mean that "this time it's real."[4]

In this section, I show that these claims rest on weak foundations.[5] Scholars have failed to distinguish between causes of decline that are exogenous to hegemony and the international system and those that are causally connected to being the hegemon or pursuing hegemony. Mechanisms of decline that really stem from being the hegemon or pursuing hegemony have rarely been identified, and those that have are weakly grounded in logic and poorly supported by evidence. A new wave of scholarship has emerged over the last two decades showing that, if anything, hegemons can use their position to slow decline and mitigate its effects. The implications for the debate on US grand strategy are straightforward: think long and hard before giving up hard-won positions of systemic leadership.

Realism and the debate over US grand strategy

Gilpin defines hegemony as "the leadership of one state (the hegemon) over other states in the system."[6] Hegemony emerges from a set of policies that assert and maintain leadership – a hegemonic grand strategy. Those policies require material capabilities, but hegemony is relatively independent of the distribution of capabilities, occurring across multipolar, bipolar, and unipolar systems. A state need not even be the most powerful in the system in order to pursue a hegemonic grand strategy successfully. Britain effectively pursued policies of hegemonic leadership

---

[4] Layne, "This Time It's Real."

[5] A revised and condensed version of this section appears in S. G. Brooks, G. J. Ikenberry and W. C. Wohlforth, "Don't Come Home, America: The Case Against Retrenchment," *International Security*, Vol. 37, No. 3 (2012–13), pp. 24–28.

[6] Gilpin, *War and Change*, p. 116, n. 6.

for many decades during which it did not surpass other states on key dimensions of power, including military capabilities and the size of its economy. The United States successfully pursued policies of hegemonic leadership for four decades after 1945 even though it was at times inferior to the Soviet Union in conventional military landpower. The post-1991 unipolarity was the first time in modern history that a government pursued policies of hegemony backed up by predominance in all relevant dimensions of state capabilities.[7]

Even though the United States' relative decline on many key indices of capabilities appeared to accelerate after 2008, it remained strongly committed to its hegemony. Woven through the speeches of President Obama, Secretary of State Clinton, and other top US officials was a robust restatement of the traditional US grand strategy of global leadership:

1. America's multifarious security commitments to partners and allies make core regions more secure – which makes the world safer for the US.
2. The commitments also allow Washington to shape the security environment facing potential rivals to induce them to accommodate its core interests and, should that fail, constitute a hedge against the need to contain a future peer rival.
3. The commitments are a necessary condition of US leadership. Without the commitments, US leverage for leadership declines.
4. Leadership is a necessary condition of institutionalized cooperation to address classical and new security challenges, and that cooperation promotes US security.
5. US leadership also facilitates cooperation on the global economy, and moves the cooperative equilibrium closer to US preferences.
6. The commitments and associated leverage are necessary pillars of a larger institutional and normative order whose maintenance will make the United States more secure and prosperous over the long term. Embedding US leadership in these institutions has major benefits for Washington and its partners: the classical functional benefits (focal point, reduced transaction costs, monitoring, etc.); and political and legitimacy benefits (mitigating politically awkward aspects of hegemony). Because the US is not strongly constrained by its institutional commitments, the benefits far outweigh the costs.

---

[7] Stephen G. Brooks and William C. Wohlforth, *World out of Balance: International Relations and the Challenge of American Primacy* (Princeton University Press, 2008); G. John Ikenberry, Michael M. Mastanduno, and William C. Wohlforth, eds., *International Relations Theory and the Consequences of Unipolarity* (Cambridge University Press, 2011).

Even as China's ascendance continued apace, America's war-weariness grew, and its budget woes mounted, scant evidence emerged of any weakening in official or elite commitment to these precepts.[8] In growing numbers, however, international relations scholars – predominantly self-described realists – insist that US hegemony is "self-abrading," in Barry Posen's phrase.[9] Their case is complex but at its core is the contention that America's hegemonic grand strategy exacerbates the problem of decline and leads to imperial overstretch. Washington thus confronts a trade-off between policies of hegemony and its real national interests in prosperity and security. American elites must wean themselves of their intoxication with leadership and scale back their country's manifold security commitments, whose economic and security costs far outweigh the benefits.

Realists so frequently and vociferously criticize America's "over-ambitious" foreign policies that it is easy to miss the seeming paradox in their arguments. After all, realism generally follows Thucydides in positing that "the strong do what they can while the weak suffer what they must." Normally, realist theories would lead to the expectation that powerful actors tend on average to get what they most want, and weaker ones are compelled to adjust. Yet the case against hegemonic grand strategy is built upon the proposition that the strong hegemon is often incapable of doing what it wants, and is systematically exploited by weaker players free riding on its efforts or conspiring to undermine its leadership. Similarly, most realist theories posit that states respond more or less

---

[8] Michelle Flournoy and Janine Davidson, "Obama's New Global Posture," *Foreign Affairs*, Vol. 91, No. 3 (July/August 2012), pp. 54–63.

[9] Barry Posen, "From Unipolarity to Multipolarity: Transition in Sight?" in Ikenberry, Mastanduno, and Wohlforth, *International Relations Theory and the Consequences of Unipolarity*. For a sampling of this literature, see also Barry Posen, "The Case for Restraint," *American Interest*, Vol. 3, No. 1 (November 1, 2007); Barry Posen, "A Grand Strategy of Restraint," in Michele A. Flournoy and Shawn Brimley, eds., *Finding Our Way* (Washington, DC: Center for a New American Security, 2008); John J. Mearsheimer, "Imperial by Design," *The National Interest*, Vol. 111 (Jan/Feb 2011), pp. 16–34; Stephen M. Walt, *Taming American Power* (New York, NY: Norton 2005); Stephen M. Walt "In the National Interest," *Boston Review*, Vol. 30, No. 1 (Feb/Mar 2005); Eugene Gholz, Daryl G. Press, and Harvey M. Sapolsky, "Come Home, America," *International Security*, Vol. 21, No. 4 (1997), pp. 5–48; Eugene Gholz, Daryl G. Press, and Benjamin Valentino, "Time to Offshore Our Troops," *New York Times*, December 12, 2006; Christopher Layne, *The Peace of Illusions* (Ithaca, NY: Cornell University Press, 2006); Christopher Layne, "From Preponderance of Offshore Balancing," *International Security*, Vol. 22, No. 1 (Summer 1997), pp. 86–124; Christopher Layne, "Offshore Balancing Revisited" in *Washington Quarterly*, Vol. 25 (2002), pp. 233–248; Benjamin Schwarz and Christopher Layne, "A New Grand Strategy," *Atlantic Monthly*, Vol. 289, No. 1 (January 2002), pp. 36–42; Richard Betts, *American Force: Dangers, Delusions and Dilemmas in National Security* (New York, NY: Columbia University Press, 2012).

rationally to systemic incentives. If hegemonic grand strategies are so clearly suboptimal, why has Washington followed this course for so long? US foreign policy for the twenty years since the Cold War's favorable end must therefore constitute one of the greatest anomalies for realism. And, indeed, according to these scholars, the anomaly can only be explained by inertia, pathologies of domestic politics, or the pernicious influence of liberal ideology and imperial myths, all against the backdrop of the permissive strategic environment fostered by unipolarity.[10]

This realist anti-hegemonism is grounded in two bodies of scholarship best exemplified by Kenneth Waltz and Robert Gilpin, with the emphasis shifting from the former to the latter over time. For a decade and a half after 1991, realists highlighted counterbalancing as the causal mechanism linking pursuit of hegemony with relative decline.[11] Derived from established theories of the balance of power and threat, the argument posits a direct connection between the United States' position as the most capable state in the system, its strategic choice to sustain hegemony, and the twin problems of overstretch and decline. The systemic concentration of capabilities in the United States primes other potential great powers to ramp up their power in order to restore balance, the argument goes, and a forward-leaning hegemonic grand strategy is just the trigger needed to get the process going. Being Number One is thus a dubious honor, and the temptation to establish and sustain hegemony should be resisted, for the result is likely to be a more rapid decline as other major powers' capabilities rise faster than they would if the United States cut a lower profile on the world's stage.

Needless to say, the problem with this argument is that there is no evidence of counter-hegemonic balancing against the United States.[12] Slowly but steadily, most realists are coming to understand that while balancing may be a constraint on the *rise* of hegemony, it is not a significant

---

[10] Stephen Walt: "...the United States allowed its foreign policy to be distorted by partisan sniping, hijacked by foreign lobbyists and narrow domestic special interests, blinded by lofty but unrealistic rhetoric, and held hostage by irresponsible and xenophobic members of Congress..." "In the National Interest." Christopher Layne: "More than most, America's foreign policy is the product of ... ideas. US foreign policy elites have constructed their own myths of empire to justify the United States' hegemonic role..." "Graceful Decline: The End of Pax Americana," *American Conservative*, Vol. 9, No. 5 (May 2010), p. 30. See also Michael Desch, "America's Liberal Illiberalism: The Ideological Origins of Overreaction in US Foreign Policy," *International Security*, Vol. 32, No. 3 (Winter 2007/08), pp. 7–43; and Richard K. Betts, "The Political Support System for American Primacy," *International Affairs*, Vol. 81, No. 1 (2005), pp. 1–14.

[11] See especially Christopher Layne, "The Unipolar Illusion: Why New Great Powers Will Rise," *International Security*, Vol. 17 (1993), pp. 5–51; and Kenneth N. Waltz, Structural Realism after the Cold War," *International Security*, Vol. 25 (2000), pp. 5–41.

[12] Brooks and Wohlforth, *World out of Balance*, Chapters 2–3.

contributor to hegemonic *decline*. As a result, the case against the current US grand strategy has moved away from reliance on Kenneth Waltz's *Theory of International Politics*, which elevated balancing to the status of the central equilibrating force in world politics, and toward the kind of arguments associated with Gilpin's *War and Change in World Politics*, which discounted the role of balancing as a constraint on expansion in favor of other factors, and accorded it no role whatsoever in explaining hegemonic decline. The newfound vogue of these arguments puts a new premium on understanding what they actually are and how, if at all, they are connected to the strategic choices the United States now confronts.

Hegemonic grand strategy and hegemonic decline

As noted, Gilpin joins many other theorists of hegemonic rise and decline in stressing the tendency "for the economic costs of maintaining the status quo to rise faster than the economic capacity to support the status quo."[13] He explains this by reference to a set of factors, mechanisms, or processes, dividing them into two categories: internal and external. That division made sense for his sweeping analysis encompassing pre-modern empires as well as states. But many processes and arguments that are relevant for empires do not apply to states. This is one of several issues on which it is analytically profitable to do what Gilpin himself failed to do (and what most realists who use his work also neglect to do): integrate the insights of the theory developed in *War and Change* with other rise-and-decline schools, notably power transition theory and leadership long cycle theory.[14] For, as long cycle scholars Karen Rasler and William Thompson stress, processes of decline that are relevant to continental landpowers may not apply to offshore seapowers.[15] More relevant for the contemporary discussion are three categories: those that are entirely exogenous to the international system; those that are caused or influenced by being the system's most capable actor; and those that are caused by pursuing policies of hegemonic leadership. Only the third category has any relevance to the debate over US grand strategy.

Five processes fall into the exogenous category: declining rates of economic growth; the rising costs of military power; the tendency of private and public consumption to grow; the tendency for economic

---

[13] Gilpin, *War and Change*, p. 156.
[14] See, e.g., A.F.K. Organski, *World Politics* (New York, NY: Knopf, 1958); and George Modelski, *Long Cycles in World Politics* (London: Macmillan, 1988).
[15] Karen Rasler and William Thompson, *The Great Powers and Global Struggle, 1490–1990* (Lexington, KY: University Press of Kentucky, 1994).

activity to shift to services; and the "corrupting influence of affluence."[16] These can be expected to bedevil any rich state regardless of its position in the international system. They all affect a state's ability to sustain hegemony, but none is caused by being a hegemon or pursuing policies of leadership. Indeed, they would presumably all conspire to hinder any state on the same growth path as the hegemon from mounting a challenge. For example, were the European Union to become a state and seek hegemonic leadership, it would be just as susceptible to these processes as the United States – as would China if it were to become rich. These five processes describe a pattern that may affect a hegemon's ability to continue in that role, but they are not in any sense the result of pursuing hegemony. While they may conspire to induce a hegemon to scale back its global role, there is nothing about them that implies that retrenchment will arrest or slow relative decline.

The main link between hegemonic grand strategy and decline that figures in Gilpin, as well as in the works of scholars such as David Calleo and Paul Kennedy, is diversion of resources away from productive investment toward system maintenance and protection.[17] In a nutshell, paying the costs of protecting clients and maintaining the system – military expenditures, wars, subsidies to allies, etc. – exacerbates the larger growth-sapping trend toward consumption and away from investment. This amounts to a claim that the opportunity cost of its grand strategy will cause a hegemon's rate of growth to slow more markedly than a non-hegemonic state as it proceeds along the internally driven course from poor and rapidly growing to rich and slowly growing. Conversely, other states whose security and prosperity are underwritten by the hegemon will be spared these opportunity costs and perform relatively better. Always present in realist arguments for strategic retrenchment, this argument began to figure more prominently as US defense expenditures skyrocketed after 2001.[18]

The problem with this argument is that subsequent research has found virtually no evidence for it. Research in economics has yielded no

---

[16] Gilpin, *War and Change*, Chapter 4. Gilpin's discussion of declining rates of growth is roughly consistent with neoclassical growth models in economics, and also has foreshadowings of some of the arguments developed in Mancur Olson's *The Rise and Decline of Nations* (New Haven, CT: Yale University Press, 1982). Key is that causes of declining growth in Gilpin, Solow, and Olson are all internal to a country's economy, unrelated to its positioning in the international system.

[17] Paul M. Kennedy, *The Rise and Fall of the Great Powers* (New York, NY: Random House, 1987); David P. Calleo, *The Imperious Economy* (Cambridge, MA: Harvard University Press, 1982).

[18] See, e.g., Press, Gholz, and Sapolsky, "Come Home, America"; Posen, "The Case for Restraint."

consensus theory or accepted empirical finding to support the assumption that reduced US military spending would improve its economic
growth or that the economic performance of US allies is attributable to
lower military expenditures. On the latter question, the economic trajectory of US allies is indicative. Their relative position vis-à-vis the United
States essentially stopped improving right about when Gilpin, Calleo,
and Kennedy were publishing their signature books. Over the past twenty
years, the United States' total and per capita GDP relative to key European allies and Japan have either held steady or improved despite a
growing gap in respective military efforts.

This pattern would come as no surprise to economists. As one review
summed it up, the "literature in economics has not found military
expenditure to be a significant determinant of growth."[19] This finding
is robust to all three major growth models in economics, a huge array of
identification strategies, and various country groupings (e.g., developed
vs. developing), and concerning the United States itself. Indeed, when
considered in aggregate, the most common finding is a positive relationship between military spending and growth.[20] Unlike the broader
research in economics, Rasler and Thompson conducted a study tailored
to the specific claims about the costs of hegemonic grand strategies. Their
findings "do not support the argument that consumption-driven investment tradeoffs are critical to an understanding of the relative decline of
system leaders."[21] Obviously, there are some limits to this overall claim: if
the US were a dramatic outlier among the advanced economies, spending
Soviet Union-type levels on defense (20–25%), this would surely complicate its growth trajectory and relative competitiveness. But even in 2010 –
still fully engaged in the Afghan war and with many expensive militarized
responses to 9/11 still in place – the United States was not spending an
historically high proportion of its GDP on the military (4.5%) either in
absolute terms or in relation to its primary economic competitors.

In sum, there is scant theoretical or empirical reason to link rates of
growth to either the distribution of power or the specific policies the US

---

[19] J.P. Dunne and R.P. Smith, "Models of Military Expenditure and Growth: A Critical
Review," *Defence and Peace*, Vol. 16, No. 6 (December 2005), pp. 449–461.

[20] See Aynur Alptekin and Paul Levine, "Military Expenditure and Economic Growth:
A Meta-Analysis," MPRA Paper No. 28853, posted February 21, 2011, available at:
http://mpra.ub.uni-muenchen.de/28853/; Betu Dicle and Mehmet F. Dicle, "Military
Spending and GDP Growth: Is There a General Causal Relationship?"*Journal of
Comparative Policy Analysis*, Vol. 12, No. 3 (June 2010), pp. 311–345. On the US, see
Uk Heo, "The Relationship between Defense Spending and Economic Growth in the
United States, 1947–2007," *Political Research Quarterly*, Vol. 63, No. 4 (December
2010), pp. 760–770.

[21] Rasler and Thompson, *Great Powers and Global Struggle*, p. 134.

pursues to sustain its leadership. As William Thompson notes, it is unclear "why uneven growth should be viewed as a function of unbalanced power."[22] No scholarly theory or empirical findings clearly link the financial collapse, great recession, and consequent ballooning of the US budget deficit to the international system at all (at least, as scholars of international security construe it). Nor does any established research finding show a connection between any US security commitment and the causes of the economic downturn. Nor is there reason to expect that resources freed up from global commitments would necessarily be diverted to uses more advantageous for long-term US growth. The downturn might affect the United States' willingness to sustain defense spending in the range of 4% of GDP and may even prompt Washington to reevaluate some of its security commitments, but that does not mean that defense spending or security commitments or any other policy associated with US hegemony caused the downturn in the first place.

Gilpin discusses a second, closely related factor that is a consequence of hegemonic policies, as opposed to the position of material dominance or exogenous manifestations of affluence: free riding. Gilpin stressed that as exogenous changes raise the costs of political dominance, the constant problem of free riding would become relatively more significant. That is, though hegemons always "overpay" by absorbing a disproportionate share of the costs of system maintenance, the relative significance of this cost rises as exogenous changes generate higher overall costs of protection. The strong implication is that the more insistently the hegemon pursues leadership, the greater other states' incentives to free ride.

There are two major problems with this argument. I have already established the first: the absence of evidence for a link between military expenditures and growth. Given the lack of connection between protection costs and economic growth, allied free riding will not likely affect relative US long-term economic performance and so will not conspire to make the pursuit of hegemony self-defeating. On the contrary, US security provision may reduce other states' investments in military modernization and thus serve to entrench US military dominance. So even if we accept that allies do in fact free ride, the main implication lies in the realm of norms (fairness) and welfare (shifting resources from the Pentagon to other consumption might improve Americans' welfare). Both of these potential implications may well turn out to matter in domestic politics, but they do not matter for the key issue at hand: US relative decline.

---

[22] William P. Thompson, "Systemic Leadership, Evolutionary Processes, and International Relations Theory: The Unipolarity Question," *International Studies Review*, Vol. 8, No. 1 (2006) pp. 1–22, 17.

The free-riding argument faces a second, even bigger challenge, however: it is probably wrong. Free riding is a phenomenon derived from the collective goods theory. We should expect the phenomenon to occur in some real world setting to the degree that the setting matches the theory. The theory applies to goods that have two key properties: non-rivalry and non-excludability. But as recent scholarship stresses, the most expensive and visible manifestation of America's hegemonic grand strategy – security guarantees to key allies and partners – violates these two assumptions.[23] The consumption of US security guarantees by some states (e.g., NATO) arguably can reduce the security of others (e.g., Russia). And Washington can, in principle, exclude any state it wants, which means its bargaining leverage is greater than the theory implies. Moreover, Michael Beckley demonstrates that foreign aid and peacekeeping more closely resemble true public goods, and there the United States is the free rider, contributing far less than its allies.[24]

Once it is clear that the theory that best approximates the real conditions of US hegemony is not collective goods but bargaining, the possibility emerges that allied undersupply of conventional military capabilities and oversupply of foreign aid and post-conflict peacekeeping are part of a complex hegemonic bargain. And, according to recent scholarly research, that bargain links the security and the economic realms. For, as Michael Mastanduno has shown in detail, for the global economy the United States is more of a "privilege taker" than a "system maker," routinely using its hegemonic position to solve its domestic political problems at others' economic expense.[25] This is in part the result of the asymmetric interdependence conveyed by America's large size, which Washington can use to wangle favorable deals and avoid the constraints of its allies' and rivals' economic statecraft.[26] That influence might obtain even if the United States eschewed the costs of a hegemonic grand strategy. But some portion of these economic benefits accrues as the direct or indirect result of US military commitments. As Carla Norrlof argues, security commitments help skew bargaining outcomes in Washington's favor, and constitute an important security bulwark of the US dollar's status as global reserve currency, from which it extracts

---

[23] Carla Norrlof, *America's Global Advantage* (Cambridge University Press, 2010), Chapter 6; Beckley, "Hegemony; Self-Sustaining or Self-Defeating?" paper presented at American Political Science Association Annual Meeting, September 2011.

[24] Michael Beckley, *The Unipolar Era: Why American Power Persists and China's Rise Is Limited*, PhD dissertation, Columbia University, New York, 2012.

[25] Michael Mastanduno, "System Maker and Privilege Taker," *World Politics*, Vol. 60, No. 1 (January 2009), pp. 121–154. See also Norrlof, *America's Global Advantage*.

[26] Brooks and Wohlforth, *World out of Balance*, Chapter 5.

major economic benefits.[27] Again, low levels of allied defense spending look less like free riding and more like a part of a complex hegemonic bargain that works to America's advantage.

Gilpin identifies a final process that results at least partly from the hegemon's position of primacy: the diffusion of the techniques of power. Military, organizational, technological, and economic innovations that facilitate the hegemon's leadership naturally attract attention and emulation by other states in the system. Gilpin's discussion notes the complexity of diffusion, which depends in part on the recipient polity's capacity to adopt, but focuses on the "advantages of backwardness"; that is, the capacity of late developing rising states to leapfrog stages of development by adopting the power-generating practices and techniques of the early-developing dominant state.

Subsequent research has underscored the complexity of diffusion, complicating its implications for today's debate over US grand strategy. The historical tendency for states to fail to adopt successful power-generating practices may be much stronger than Gilpin implies.[28] Relatedly, new research underscores that there are some settings in which the first-mover's innovations are unlikely to be adopted successfully.[29] *War and Change*'s focus on the advantages of backwardness slights the problems of path dependence and barriers to entry in the production of high-end military power.[30] Indeed, the post-World War II decades have if anything witnessed a shift toward the military *disadvantages* of backwardness: poor countries are very bad at generating military capabilities.[31] In many areas, moreover, the hegemon can control and regulate diffusion as suits its political interests.[32] The US successfully prevented many technologies from diffusing to the Soviet Union and it is noteworthy that the most modern and effective militaries in the world (e.g., Israel, UK) are close US allies.[33]

---

[27] Norrlof, *America's Global Advantage*, Chapter 6.
[28] Stuart Kaufman, Richard Little, and William Wohlforth, eds., *The Balance of Power in World History* (New York, NY: Palgrave Macmillan, 2007).
[29] Michael Horowitz, *The Diffusion of Military Power* (Princeton University Press, 2010).
[30] Stephen Brooks, *Producing Security* (Princeton University Press, 2005); Jonathan D. Caverley, "United States Hegemony and the New Economics of Defense," *Security Studies*, Vol. 16, No. 4 (October–December 2007), pp. 597–613.
[31] Michael Beckley, "Economic Development and Military Effectiveness," *Journal of Strategic Studies*, Vol. 34, No. 1 (February 2010), pp. 43–71. Analysts frequently miss this trend by comparing rich states' militaries to insurgents or other non-state actors rather than to poor states' militaries.
[32] Mark Zachary Taylor, "Toward an International Relations Theory of National Innovation Rates," *Security Studies*, Vol. 21, No. 1 (March 2012), pp. 113–151.
[33] Michael Mastanduno, *Economic Containment: COCOM and the Politics of East-West Trade* (Ithaca, NY: Cornell University Press, 1992). See also Joanne Gowa, *Allies, Adversaries and Free Trade* (Princeton University Press, 1994).

America's potential rivals – notably China and Russia – are denied access not only to military industries of the US but also to those of all its allies.

It is difficult to see how these anti-diffusion policies could succeed if the US did not follow its hegemonic grand strategy. The implication is that there may be settings in which a hegemon can prevent or delay diffusion by doubling down on expensive or organizationally complex power-generating technologies while selectively controlling diffusion. Britain's policy of naval dominance, pursued well into its decline phase, may be one example. More controversially, Reagan's military buildup of the 1980s – when Gilpin and other prominent scholars were focused on the problem of hegemonic decline – may be another case in point. Current high levels of US defense expenditures have been explained in this way.[34]

This scholarship raises the possibility that diffusion is *less* of a problem for hegemons than it is for smaller states because systemic power and influence offer opportunities to regulate absorption by others and deter entry. Smaller states that innovate power-generating technologies lack these advantages. After all, successful power-generating practices can diffuse away from any state, whether it is a hegemon or not. Prussian military technology and organizational innovations diffused throughout the system even though the country was far from attaining primacy. A hegemon may face strong incentives to maintain leadership precisely in order to control diffusion – this is indeed the thinking that informs US policy on counter-proliferation. A US less committed to global leadership, the standard Washington view has it, would have less leverage to control proliferation.

In light of this analysis, US grand strategy since 1991 does not appear to be an anomaly for realism that requires elaborate investigations of the peculiarities of American ideology or domestic politics. Nor is there necessarily much of a paradox of power condemning the mighty to be humbled by the weak. The story that emerges would be unsurprising were we not so accustomed to realists from Morgenthau, Waltz, and Gilpin on down to today warning Americans about the dangers of having too much power. In the end, a strong case can be made that the United States as a uniquely powerful actor tends to act rationally in its self-interest by ruthlessly pursuing hegemony as long as its benefits outweigh its costs.

---

[34] Joanne Gowa and Kristopher W. Ramsay, "Gulliver Untied: Entry Deterrence in a Unipolar World," Working Paper, Princeton University Department of Politics.

Hegemonic war

Scores of papers assess the origins of hegemonic wars and/or the connection between concentrated capabilities distributions and war, but few analyze the *function* of great-power war in ordering world politics.[35] As a result, scholars know remarkably little about the precise causal mechanisms and processes by which war might actually make it possible for states to facilitate a new, more stable order. This knowledge deficit matters even if we discount the probability of hegemonic war. A "hegemonic war is characterized by the unlimited means employed and by the general scope of the warfare," Gilpin writes. "Because all parties are drawn into the war and the stakes involved are high, few limitations, if any, are observed with respect to the means employed . . ."[36] Such a war is exceedingly unlikely to emerge among states armed with secure second-strike nuclear forces. We need to know what function these wars served in establishing hegemonic orders of the past to assess the full implications of their expected absence in the future.

Two functional arguments are most prominent in the literature. For Gilpin, the core function of hegemonic war is to resolve the contradiction between the underlying distribution of capabilities in the system and the hierarchy of prestige. His theory relies on a major lag between the diffusion of system capabilities away from the hegemon, on the one hand, and states' ability to revise the order accordingly, on the other hand. As capabilities shift to rising states, their dissatisfaction increases, as does their putative bargaining leverage, but the dominant state faces incentives to hold fast defending the existing order. The gap between the system's material "base" and its governance superstructure is resolved by a major war, which clarifies the distribution of capabilities and prestige, setting the stage for efficient bargaining over a new order. John Ikenberry stresses a second function: "Major or great-power war is a uniquely powerful agent of change in world politics because it tends to destroy and discredit old institutions and force the emergence of a new leading or hegemonic

---

[35] Empirical tests have focused on two relationships: the connection between power transition and major war (e.g., Woosang Kim and James D. Morrow, "When Do Power Shifts Lead to War?" *American Journal of Political Science*, Vol. 36, No. 4 (November, 1992), pp. 896–922) and the connection between power concentration and peace (e.g., K. Edward Spiezio, "British Hegemony and Major Power War, 1815–1939: An Empirical Test of Gilpin's Model of Hegemonic Governance," *International Studies Quarterly*, Vol. 34, No. 2 (June 1990), pp. 165–181. Neither relationship directly tests Gilpin's theory, which posits a complex set of links between systemic preconditions (a disequilibrium between underlying capabilities and the hierarchy of prestige), psychological processes (fear, sense of massive stakes), and contagion.

[36] Gilpin, *War and Change*, p. 200.

state."[37] The first part of Ikenberry's argument seems intuitive, but it is not clear exactly how war "forces the emergence" of a new hegemon.

To date, scholars have yet to produce focused empirical studies dedicated to testing these arguments. For his part, Gilpin ignored the actual processes wrought by war, focusing almost exclusively on causes. Ikenberry's narrative studies of postwar order building implicitly refer back to his arguments about war's effect but they are not structured around an investigation of these processes.

An initial review yields some evidence for both scholars' arguments, but the major implication is that the conditions for hegemonic emergence are very hard to produce. Over the last two centuries, such conditions only truly obtained once, and, while it took a cataclysmic war to create them, neither Gilpin's nor Ikenberry's argument fully captures the major mechanisms leading to American hegemony and the creation of a new institutional order. Consider four "ordering moments": 1815, 1914, 1945, and 1991.

After 1815, Russia was preeminent on land, and Britain ruled the seas and dominated global finance. Nearly a quarter century's fighting in the wars of the French Revolution and Napoleon failed to clarify the relation between these elements of power. After all, Britain had been an unexceptional military contributor to the grand coalitions against Napoleon, but the decisive naval and financial power, while Alexander I's Russia emerged as the preeminent military power on the Continent. Hence, the war's implications for the overall capabilities of these two empires was debatable – and indeed has been debated ever since, as scholars cannot agree who emerged as the "hegemon" after 1815. If power is measured in financial and naval terms and the domain of theory is global, Britain is seen as the hegemon. If power is viewed as military and the domain is focused on continental Europe, Russia comes out on top. In reality, neither empire was unambiguously the top dog.[38]

---

[37] G. John Ikenberry, *After Victory: Institutions, Strategic Restraint, and the Rebuilding of Order after Major Wars* (Princeton University Press, 2001), p. 254, n. 134.

[38] I rely most on Paul W. Schroeder, *The Transformation of European Politics* (London: Oxford University Press, 1993); Paul W. Schroeder, "The 19th Century International System: Changes in the Structure," *World Politics*, Vol. 39, No. 1 (October 1986), pp. 1–26. See also Adam Watson, *Evolution of International Society: A Comparative Historical Analysis* (London: Routledge, 1992), p. 243. See also Paul Kennedy, *The Rise and Fall of British Naval Mastery* (London: Macmillan, 1983), Chapter 6 for a discussion of the nature and limitations of British power in this period. Kennedy, *Rise and Fall*, Chapter 4; Ikenberry, *After Victory*, Chapter 4; Ian Clark, *Hegemony in International Society* (Oxford University Press, 2011), Chapter 5. Paul W. Schroeder, "Did the Vienna Settlement Rest on a Balance of Power?' *American Historical Review*, Vol. 97 (1992), pp. 683–706; Richard Elrod, "The Concert of Europe: A Fresh Look at an International System," *World Politics*, Vol. 28, No. 2 (1976), pp. 159–174.

The war, in short, did not "force the emergence of a new leading or hegemonic state," as Ikenberry puts it, but rather clarified the emergence of two co-hegemons whose comparative strength was not tested until the Crimean War a generation later: the British and Russian Empires. They were clearly firsts among putative great-power equals. On the fringes of Europe, with extensive non-European resources at their disposal, both empires had proved their relative invulnerability in the war, as well as their superiority in different categories of power. They were, in Adam Watson's phrase, the two "bookends" that propped up the Concert of Europe, and they were recognized as such by their contemporaries.[39] While detailed reconstructions of the Vienna negotiations and the Concert's functions do show how London's financial and naval power gave it bargaining leverage over some negotiations, it had to defer to St. Petersburg on core continental questions.[40]

Moreover, if the Napoleonic Wars had yielded one clear lesson, it was that it took grand coalitions of all the other powers to beat France, which was left intact and ready to vie with St. Petersburg or London for hegemonic status. Only in hindsight do the Napoleonic Wars stand as the last gasp of France's claim to top dog status. Contemporary statesmen perceived the gap between the two bookend empires and France as precariously small. Hence, the Concert bargaining was muddled by the existence of two empires in a special but unacknowledged class of "co-hegemons," each in possession of a different mix of power resources whose ultimate superiority had not been tested, and both perilously close in power to next lower ranked state.

As a result, two perennial problems dogged the Concert. First, Britain and Russia were continually courting rivalry as the two expanding empires came into contact in Central and South Asia. The asymmetries in the nature of the two empires' power resources complicated matters mightily, especially for Russia, whose main resource – its massive army – lacked the signaling flexibility of the Royal Navy. If St. Petersburg wanted to indicate its strong interest in some interstate dispute, it generally could not simply dispatch a few warships and expect any kind of local or general European deference. In many cases, only the army would do, and that risked sparking serious security fears and dangerous spirals.[41] The second recurring problem was France, whose power and status were

---

[39] Adam Watson, *Evolution of International Society*, p. 243.
[40] See, e.g., Harold Nicholson, *The Congress of Vienna: A Study in Allies Unity: 1812–1822* (New York, NY: Harcourt, Brace, 1946).
[41] For more, see William C. Wohlforth, "Status Dilemmas and Inter-State Conflict," in Deborah W. Larson, T.V. Paul and William C. Wohlforth, ed., *Status and World Order* (Cambridge University Press, forthcoming 2014).

close enough to those of the two top dogs that either could rationally view Paris as a revisionist bent on hegemony for itself.

A generation of war quite simply failed to settle the power and status hierarchy and clarify bargaining among the key actors. As to sweeping clean the institutional slate by destroying or discrediting the old order, this, too, remained ambiguous. After all, the main discredited order was that of Napoleon and the very idea of any state seeking singular as opposed to shared hegemony – not a propitious normative setting for any state seeking singular hegemony.[42] True, as Paul Schroeder has argued, eighteenth-century norms about how sovereigns ought to compete were indeed discredited for a time, but that negative conclusion could not lead to positive consensus on anything other than a highly constrained new institutional order. As Ikenberry observes, "the institutional arrangements were of dramatically less breadth and depth than those that were proposed or employed after 1919 and 1945."[43]

World War I did a more effective job of discrediting old institutions and practices – particularly the classical nineteenth-century approach to the balance of power and alliances – but is justly famous among scholars for its failure to settle European power relations. As E.H. Carr stressed, Germany and the Soviet Union were knocked down but not out – each retained fearsome power potential and was poised to grow fast and stake claims to revise the order.[44] Even worse, the United States was by far the world's greatest industrial and economic power, but its role in the actual fighting was minimal and its military and naval capabilities comparatively modest.[45] Woodrow Wilson cut a large figure at Versailles and the United States was the only major power whose overall capabilities were actually increased by the war, but a recurrent theme of accounts of the negotiations in Paris is the massive gap between the US president's expectations and the actual influence he wielded.[46]

Even had domestic politics not intervened to thwart Wilson's vision for postwar order, the underlying power asymmetry would have frustrated bargaining. American power was simply not perceived in 1919 in the way it began to be thought of in the Cold War – as relevant to the actual workings of European and Eurasian security. As Ikenberry notes, "Wilson wanted to transform European politics without getting too

[42] Clark, *Hegemony in International Society*, Chapter 5.   [43] Ikenberry, *After Victory*, p. 81.

[44] E.H. Carr, *The Twenty Years' Crisis: 1919–1939: An Introduction to the Study of International Relations* (London: Macmillan, 1951).

[45] Kennedy, *Rise and Fall*, Chapter 6.

[46] See, e.g., Alan Sharp, *The Versailles Settlement: Peacemaking in Paris, 1919* (Basingstoke and London: Macmillan, 1991); Harold Nicolson, *Peacemaking 1919* (Boston, MA: Houghton Mifflin, 1933).

involved in actually working with or protecting Europe."[47] Even an unambiguous and consistent American posture backed by a united domestic political scene would not have been effective without credible security guarantees to European partners for which the United States lacked not only the will but also the means. Thus, the world war at least partially fulfilled Ikenberry's function of discrediting past institutions and creating demands for new ones, but failed utterly to "force the emergence" of a hegemon. And the most comprehensive war the world had known also failed to perform Gilpin's function of settling power relations and establishing a new hierarchy of power and prestige. The result of strongly discredited old institutions coupled with deep power asymmetries and resultant bargaining problems was the well-known story of the fatally compromised implementation of lofty postwar visions.

World War II is widely seen as the most shattering of modern history. Less widely recognized is the fact that while it knocked several great powers down, it yielded ambiguous lessons concerning the relative importance of American sea, air, and economic capabilities versus the Soviet Union's proven conventional military superiority in Eurasia.[48] The war's failure to clarify power and bargaining relations between the two superpowers and the resultant struggle for security and prestige constitute the key backdrop of the postwar American order-building project. Postwar American hegemony was inextricably intertwined with the bipolar Cold War struggle.[49] It was the war's manifest *failure* to clarify the US–Soviet power balance that aided and abetted the creation of the Pax Americana.

At the same time, the war wrought a series of other changes that cumulatively created hothouse conditions for forcing the emergence of the United States as the hegemon of its portion of the world. Consider the features it possessed that the other major wars lacked:

- Though it failed to clarify relative US and Soviet military power, it radically increased the economic gap in the United States' favor not only by giving it history's greatest Keynesian boost but also by physically destroying or gravely wounding all of the world's other major economies.
- It created the preconditions for the Cold War, without which America's order-building project could never have been as elaborate and

[47] Ikenberry, *After Victory*, p. 139.
[48] William Wohlforth, *Elusive Balance: Power and Perceptions in the Cold War* (Ithaca, NY: Cornell University Press, 1993).
[49] Simon Bromley, *American Power and the Prospects for International Order* (Cambridge: Polity, 2008).

extensive. It left the Soviet Union's armies in the center of Europe, creating the conditions for a plausible threat of Eurasian hegemony. This in turn enabled history's most ramified and long-lasting counter-hegemonic coalition – NATO – by giving Washington the incentive to overcome domestic resistance to the costs of building hegemony while conferring unprecedented US leverage over its allies to bend them to its will.

• It left in its wake unprecedented humanitarian and economic crises that only the United States had the wherewithal to address in a timely fashion.

The Second World War, in sum, did indeed foster a Gilpin/Ikenberry order-building moment, but for reasons lying outside either thinker's theoretical set-up. Precisely because it did not clarify power relations, it did not create a truly global order in the Gilpin/Ikenberry sense. Rather, it yielded a roughly bipolar distribution that created perfect conditions for a Gilpin/Ikenberry-style order in one part of the world. The Cold War and American hegemony over its part of the world were inextricably linked.

It is impossible to assess the relationship between hegemonic war and the emergence of hegemony without examining cases that do not feature major war. Hegemony may emerge as a result of processes other than hegemonic war, such as smaller wars or even peaceful changes.[50] After all, past hegemonic order-building moments were grounded in war outcomes that were much more ambiguous than traditional scholarship allows. Perhaps other kinds of phenomena perform functions scholars such as Ikenberry and Gilpin attribute to war? 1991 is a case in point. John Mueller described the changes of 1989–1991 as "the functional equivalent of World War III."[51] As Mary Elise Sarotte shows, many policy makers and observers outside the corridors of power sensed that the circumstances were ripe for constructing a new order.[52]

I have established elsewhere that, despite their comparatively peaceful nature, the events that gave rise to the current hierarchy were unusually diagnostic for power relationships.[53] Only Germany in the Second World War suffered as unambiguous a decline as the Soviet Union after 1989.

---

[50] Bruce Bueno de Mesquita, "Pride of Place: The Origins of German Hegemony," *World Politics*, Vol. 43, No. 1 (October 1990), pp. 28–52.

[51] John Mueller, *Quiet Cataclysm: Reflections on the Recent Transformation of World Politics* (London: Longman, 1992), p. 1.

[52] Mary Elise Sarotte, *1989: The Struggle to Create Post-Cold War* Europe (Princeton University Press, 2009).

[53] William C. Wohlforth, "The Stability of a Unipolar World," *International Security*, Vol. 21, No. 1 (Summer 1999), pp. 5–41.

The gap between the power and status of the superpowers, on the one hand, and all other major powers, on the other hand, was greater in the Cold War than any analogous gap in the history of the European states system. Since the United States and the Soviet Union were so clearly in a class by themselves, the fall of one from superpower status left the other much more unambiguously "number one" than at any other time since 1800.

Thus, the comparatively peaceful events of 1989–1991 yielded an interstate power hierarchy that was unusually clear.[54] Yet no ordering moment occurred.[55] The reason that leaps from the pages of the documents and other evidence of the period is that while the Gilpin conditions (clarity of power relations) were in place, Ikenberry's were not. Far from sweeping away and discrediting the old order, the events of 1989–1991 seemed to those decision makers with the most power to be a stunning affirmation of the order's essential robustness and rightness.[56]

There is a lot scholars do not know about the relationship between war and the emergence of hegemony. Further study may yet yield subtler processes or events that yield hegemonic authority, or ways in which hegemony can emerge slowly and subtly rather than at the dramatic junctures that have attracted scholars' attention. Yet it is hard to identify better candidates for hegemonic ordering moments over the last two centuries than those discussed here. And this admittedly preliminary examination yields three conclusions directly relevant to current debates about US decline.

First, the strength and salience of the emergence of a new hegemon appears to be associated with the existence and strength of the functions stressed by both Gilpin and Ikenberry: discrediting the old order and clarifying relations of power. Second, the most comprehensive hegemonic wars in history routinely perform these functions much less effectively than existing scholarship would lead one to believe. Third, standard

---

[54] William C. Wohlforth, "Unipolarity, Status Competition and Great Power War," *World Politics*, Vol. 61, No. 1 (January 2009), pp. 28–57.

[55] Mary Elise Sarotte, "Perpetuating US Preeminence: The 1990 Deals to 'Bribe the Soviets Out' and Move NATO In," *International Security*, Vol. 35, No. 1 (2010), pp. 110–137; Daniel Deudney and G. John Ikenberry, "The Unraveling of the Cold War Settlement," *Survival*, Vol. 51, No. 6 (December 2009–January 2010), pp. 39–62.

[56] In addition to Sarotte, *1989*, see James W. Davis and W. C. Wohlforth, "German Unification," in Richard K. Herrmann and Richard Ned Lebow, ed., *Ending the Cold War: Interpretations, Causation, and the Study of International Relations* (New York: Palgrave, 2004); and William C. Wohlforth, "German Reunification: A Reassessment," in Arthur L. Rosenbaum and Chae-Jin Lee, ed., *The Cold War – Reassessments*, Monograph Series #11 (Claremont, CA: The Keck Center for International and Strategic Studies, 2000).

treatments of hegemonic emergence do not capture crucial effects that conspired to facilitate the current hegemonic order that emerged under US auspices. For uniquely in modern history World War II yielded a combination of the Gilpin/Ikenberry conditions (destroying old order, clarifying power relations between hegemon and allies) and the Waltzian condition (credible Soviet threat of hegemony producing unusually strong counterbalancing imperative).

If these conclusions withstand further scrutiny, it follows that scholarly and popular discussions radically underestimate the difficulty of hegemonic emergence and therefore overestimate the fragility of American hegemony.[57]

Conclusion

Once it was clear that a properly construed neo-realist theory predicted no balancing under unipolarity and that there was actually zero evidence for balancing, realist critics of US grand strategy began to shift from arguments grounded in Kenneth Waltz's *Theory of International Politics* to propositions associated with Gilpin's *War and Change in World Politics*. Gilpin's work, as well as that of other distinguished theorists of hegemonic cycles, remains a gold mine of middle-range hypotheses and propositions relevant to explaining the causes and consequences of change in the distribution of power. Careful study of these works, however, yields far less direct relevance to current US grand strategy than most assume. Propositions that might at first glance seem to impugn the pursuit of hegemonic grand strategies late in a leading state's career have not withstood further scholarly scrutiny. Given mounting theory and evidence for the proposition that current American hegemony might be "self-sustaining rather than self-defeating," simple citations of the "declinist" works of the 1980s are insufficient to support a recommendation for US grand strategic disengagement.[58]

One of the most important implications of Gilpin's work, moreover, might be the exact opposite of the "declinism" for which he is so well known. For if Gilpin was right that "hegemonic war historically has been the basic mechanism of systemic change in world politics," and if most scholars are right that such a war is exceedingly unlikely in the

---

[57] For an analysis of the international political economy aspects of US hegemony that reaches similar conclusions, see Richard Saull, "Rethinking Hegemony: Uneven Development, Historical Blocs, and the World Economic Crisis," *International Studies Quarterly*, Vol. 56, No. 2 (2012), pp. 323–338.
[58] Beckley, "Hegemony; Self-Sustaining or Self-Defeating?"

nuclear age, then systemic change is much harder now than in the past. And as this chapter has shown, it was exceedingly hard in the past, when even some of the most destructive wars in human history failed to establish key preconditions. It is difficult to imagine what sort of event might generate such conditions under contemporary circumstances. In this light, expectations of a coming "Chinese century" or "Pax Sinica" seem fanciful.

5 Gilpin approaches *War and Change*: a classical realist in structural drag

Jonathan Kirshner[1]

Introduction

Robert Gilpin's *War and Change in World Politics*, flirting with its twentieth printing three decades after it was first published, is much more than a classic text dutifully absorbed by graduate students preparing for their comprehensive exams – it remains a work of enduring, theoretical insights that are immediately relevant for understanding contemporary international relations. Why does *War and Change* remain vital, for both scholars and statesmen, after all these years? A tempting and fashionable answer might be that as a deductive, structuralist argument, it is free from the minutiae of the current events of its day, or any day, and is thus timeless. And it is possible to read the book this way, encouraged by the author's occasional resort to stentorian, deterministic prose ("it has always been thus and always will be," p. 210[2]). But in fact, *War and Change* endures in spite of its structuralism, not because of it. That structural machine, so carefully pieced together over the course of the volume, like many "deductive" frameworks proffered by scholars of international relations then and now, was in fact much rooted in (and shaped by) the transient concerns of its time – and it got those concerns wrong. *War and Change* was motivated by the late 1970s alarm about American decline in comparison with the "rising challenger" of the Soviet Union.[3] These themes also inform the book's incongruous epilogue, which concludes on a "cautiously optimistic note"[4] that belies the inescapable (and compelling) pessimistic logic of the preceding chapters.[5] Epilogue notwithstanding, the machine expected hegemonic war, and the machine was wrong.

[1] Thanks to Rawi Abdelal, John Ikenberry, Robert Keohane, Sarah Kreps, and Alison McQueen for comments on earlier versions of this chapter.
[2] Robert Gilpin, *War and Change in World Politics* (Cambridge University Press, 1981), p. 210.
[3] *Ibid.*, pp. 1, 241.   [4] *Ibid.*, p. 243.
[5] After arguing persuasively that neither nuclear weapons nor economic interdependence altered the basic nature of world politics, the epilogue holds out hope that these factors might forestall "real danger" of hegemonic war.

But there was always more – much more – to *War and Change* than the derivation of a deductive theory to be judged on its predictive power. The book – unlike, in my view, its author – reflects an uneasy mixture of structural and classical elements. This tension is suggested in the book's important preface, which considers the distinct but in some ways parallel dilemma of negotiating the strengths and weaknesses of economic versus sociological conceptions of how to study international politics.[6] *War and Change* seeks to split the difference, and "draw on both the sociological approach and the economic approach"; similarly if implicitly, the book is characterized by a discord between the structural apparatus of its theory and the classical instincts of its theorist. The trajectory of intellectual fashions in political science in the decades that followed the book's publication obscured the extent to which *War and Change* is a product of those instincts. But what endures from *War and Change* are the timeless lessons of classical realism, and those insights are crucial to understanding essential problems in contemporary international politics.

This chapter proceeds in four parts: First I situate Gilpin, and *War and Change*, in the context of classical realism, which is distinct from and often at odds with its wayward, widely celebrated cousin, structural realism. In particular, they part ways over politics, history, ideology, and the motivations of states and relevance of statesmen. The second section contrasts classical realism with another defining element of contemporary international relations theory – the hyper-rationalist turn – which is characterized by an extremely strict (and misguided) definition of "rationality" that it imposes on the actors whose behavior it aims to model. In particular, classical realists hold radically different (and more empirically defensible) assumptions about rationality – and from there, about the predictive capabilities both of rational actors in world politics and of the scholars that hope to model them – than does the hyper-rationalist approach. Armed with these two clarifications (the rejections of strict structuralism and hyper-rationality), I revisit two of the book's key assumptions – the suspect assumption 3 and the enigmatic assumption 4 – and address some of the lingering puzzles generated by them, in particular, some crucial theoretical anomalies that pertain to the book's core concerns about rise and decline. Privileging variables associated with classical realism, I argue, resolves some of those loose ends otherwise left dangling about the logic of expansion and the tendency for overexpansion, and why relative decline and the emergence of rising challengers present enormous political challenges and threaten the stability of the

---

[6] See esp. pp. x–xiii of Gilpin, *War and Change*.

international system. To understand and apply Gilpin's model as a general theory and for contemporary international politics it is necessary to highlight (and jettison) these deviations from classical realism that muddy the analytical waters. A concluding section briefly summarizes some of the enduring lessons of *War and Change*.

War and change as classical realism

Robert Gilpin is readily characterized (and self-identifies) as a "realist"; somewhat less appreciated is the extent to which he is a *classical* realist, although he wears this identity plainly on his sleeve. According to Gilpin, "there have been three great realist writers ... Thucydides, Machiavelli, and Carr." Of these Gilpin cites two in particular as having a great influence on his own thinking: Thucydides, of course, and Carr, his "second favorite realist."[7] Classicals all, and these influences are clearly reflected in *War and Change*; Thucydides is invoked sixteen times and Carr twelve, others show up much less frequently. Machiavelli and Morgenthau, for example, are cited four times each, and even these are limited to essentially cameo roles.

But what does that mean? Classical realism, which, certainly and necessarily, shares numerous basic attributes with structural realism (such as an emphasis on the consequences of anarchy, the possibility of war, the absence of ultimate constraints on behavior, and, as a result, a need to be attentive to security and thus to basic variables that affect security, such as the balance of power), is nevertheless fundamentally different from structural realism in its analysis of world politics. Four attributes distinguish classicals from the structuralists: for the former, (1) structure matters, but is irretrievably indeterminate; (2) attention to aspects of domestic politics, including ideational variables, is necessary to understand state behavior; (3) great powers seek more than just security, and they are instinctively opportunistic; (4) international politics – that is, the choices made by states – are uncertain, contingent, and consequential. Each of these four either violates core tenets of structural realism or attends to factors it deems superficial or ephemeral. But they are the stuffing of classical realism, and these differences merit scrutiny.

Classical realists have an acute sensitivity to the balance of power, which must be recognized and attended to, since it establishes the

---

[7] Robert Gilpin, "The Richness of the Tradition of Political Realism," in Robert O. Keohane, ed., *Neorealism and Its Critics* (New York, NY: Columbia University Press, 1986), pp. 301–321, 306, 309.

constellation of potential security threats. But unlike Waltzian neo-realism, which became the hegemonic voice of realism in the 1980s (to the extent that, even among specialists, neo-realism is often conflated with realism), classical realism aims to "put structure in its place" – that is, to understand its strengths and (considerable) limitations as a tool for understanding world politics.[8] But from a classical perspective, to insist that analysis be limited to the systemic level (a consideration as states as like units differentiated only by their relative capabilities) is to demand the sound of one hand clapping. Waltz, however, is dismissive of any appeal to variables at other levels of analysis – "it is not possible to understand world politics simply by looking inside of states," he insists, "The behavior of states and statesmen . . . is indeterminate."[9] This may be true. But, it need be emphasized, this is also true for the system.[10] Thus, although as noted, classical realists are very alert to the structure of the system, because in the context of anarchy and the possibility of war the balance of power conditions states' fears and expectations and influences the pattern of interactions between them. But classical realists also hold that it is simply impossible to understand world politics solely by looking outside of states. The implications of systemic forces are inherently and irretrievably indeterminate.

This is the case for international relations – just as it is true for the microeconomic theory (as applied) that serves explicitly as the intellectual template for neo-realism. The international system does indeed impose constraints on states in a way analogous to how market forces limit the range of choices available to firms. And the market (like the international system) on the one hand derives from the collective behavior of its participants but on the other generates pressures that are beyond the control of any particular actor. But this analogy is imperfect, and upon reflection, self-negating as it applies to international relations. Even assuming an idealized abstract market, with similar firms seeking singular goals (maximizing profits or market share), the deterministic

---

[8] Additionally, as discussed in the final section of this chapter, in another departure from structural realism as it is commonly practiced, even when operating at the systemic level, classical realists tend to place much more emphasis on dynamics (that is, changes to the balance of power), rather than statics (such as whether the system is multipolar or bipolar). Relatedly, it is worth noting that Gilpin has well-argued reservations about Waltz's conclusions that bipolar systems are more stable than multipolar ones, in favor of an indeterminacy regarding polarity that suggests that the explanatory action will be found more in dynamics than statics (*War and Change*, pp. 90–93).

[9] Kenneth Waltz, *Theory of International Politics* (New York, NY: Addison Wesley, 1979), pp. 65, 68.

[10] On this point, see Robert Jervis, *Perception and Misperception in International Politics* (Princeton University Press, 1977), pp. 19–21.

implications of systemic market pressure are dependent on very strict assumptions of perfect competition – which hold when there are very large sets of actors, each so small that they have no market power but instead are price takers. But as the idealized assumption of perfect competition is relaxed, market forces remain vital but individual choices – idiosyncratic choices – become increasingly central to explaining behavior. In particular, large firms in oligopolistic settings, while certainly not unconstrained by market forces, nevertheless enjoy considerable discretion as to how they will pursue their goals.[11]

Shifting now to international relations, that considerable discretion is especially true for great powers, which, it should be noted, attract the lion's share of analytical attention from realists of all stripes – and Waltz in particular, who holds that "a general theory of international politics is necessarily based on the great powers."[12] But most states generally, and great powers in particular, look *much* more like large oligopolists regarding the behavior of each other than tiny firms facing disembodied constraints under perfect competition. This is, of course, especially true of those states at the center of the analysis of *War and Change* – hegemons and their would-be challengers. Gilpin quotes Raymond Aron approvingly on this point: "the structure of the international system is always *oligopolistic*. In each period the principal actors have determined the system more than they have been determined by it."[13]

Oligopolistic competition implies indeterminate outcomes, and also means that agents' choices actually shape the systemic environment.[14] This is a crucial point, because it means that the choices made by states *matter* – not simply for filling in colorful or minute details, but in shaping the pressures that affect other states.[15] In international relations, that indeterminacy, and system-shaping behavior, are even greater still, because despite their common attributes, states in world politics are less similar to each other than are firms of the same industry, and despite a

---

[11] For a good discussion of some of these issues, see Joseph Nye, "Neorealism and Neoliberalism," *World Politics*, Vol. 40, No. 2 (January 1988), pp. 235–251, esp. pp. 235, 242, 245.

[12] Waltz, *Theory of International Politics*, p. 73.   [13] Gilpin, *War and Change*, p. 29.

[14] Waltz occasionally invokes the concept of oligopoly, but never acknowledges the implications of oligopolistic competition for his argument. See *Theory of International Politics*, pp. 105, 115, 134; see also Waltz, "Reflections on *Theory of International Politics*: A Response to My Critics," and Robert Keohane, "Theory of World Politics: Structural Realism and Beyond," both in Keohane, ed., *NeoRealism and Its Critics*, pp. 331, 161.

[15] To be clear, from a classical realist perspective, the choices of great powers shape, but do not determine, the nature of systemic forces that influence other states (and themselves). Here the microeconomic analogy holds; oligopolistic firms are not price takers, but neither are they free from the constraints of and incentives created by the market.

common desire for survival, as classical realists have observed in the past, states pursue a broad range of goals (certainly more diverse than goals of firms), the content of which will very likely vary from state to state.[16] And even in pursuit of that most narrow, common goal – survival – states are still less predictable than firms, because they typically have more latitude – firms are selected out of the system with much greater frequency than are states. Perhaps most subversive of all (to structural realism, that is) is that although all realists expect that great powers will tend to balance against each other, according to oligopoly theory, such actors – even duopolists – might easily collude with each other. Appeals to metaphors of market competition alone can't even tell us about the most fundamental choices made by states.

In sum, the balance of power (and changes to it), and the systemic pressures generated by an anarchic political order more generally, inform importantly the environment in which all states act. But in that context, all states, and especially great powers, enjoy considerable discretion with regard to how they will pursue their goals and what sacrifices they will make in the face of constraints. It is thus impossible to understand and anticipate the behavior of states by looking solely at structural variables and constraints. As Gilpin writes, "both the structure of the international system and domestic conditions of societies are primary determinants" of state behavior.[17] To explain world politics, it is necessary to appeal to a host of other factors, including domestic politics, history, ideology, and perceptions of legitimacy. To many modern ears this sounds incongruous, because the dominance of structural realism has left the impression that "realists can't do that." But classical realists can and have taken domestic politics seriously. And they also understand that state behavior is shaped by the lessons of history (right or wrong), ideas (accurate or not), ideology (good or bad), and that (as discussed further below) states are not best understood as hyper-rationalist automatons, but make choices influenced by fear, vulnerability, and hubris, usually in the context of considerable uncertainty.

This leaves classical realists with dirty hands, digging, necessarily, through domestic politics, which are informed by historical experience and filtered through ideological lenses. These are necessary to understand the choices made by both hegemons and their challengers as they interpret and respond to apparent trends and political maneuvers in the international arena. Thus *War and Change* leans heavily on domestic

---

[16] Arnold Wolfers, "The Goals of Foreign Policy," in Wolfers, *Discord and Collaboration* (Baltimore, MD: The Johns Hopkins University Press, 1962).

[17] Gilpin, *War and Change*, p. 87.

political variables, noting that, in addition to external pressures, choices in the international arena also "depend ultimately on the nature of the state and the society it represents," and highlights the key role of "differing domestic social arrangements." Cost/benefit analysis is at the heart of the book's explanatory mechanism, but it is domestic social relations that answer the crucial question, "Profitable (or costly) for whom?"[18] As Gilpin notes with approval, Thucydides routinely appealed to regime type (and factional conflict within regimes) in his explanation of why actors behaved a certain way in world politics.[19] Indeed, Gilpin's commitment to domestic politics goes "all the way down," to the building blocks of realist analysis. When he writes that "shifts in domestic coalitions may necessitate redefinition of the 'national interest,'"[20] Gilpin, as suggested in the preceding quotes as well, is explaining that the definition of the national interest is not unique, inviolable, and determined by external forces. Rather (although, again, the national interest and its pursuit must reflect the constraints and realities presented by an anarchic and potentially dangerous world), the expression of that interest – its content, directionality, and style of pursuit – can be articulated in a number of plausible and distinct ways. It remains the case that realists insist that the national interest is a distinct phenomenon, not reducible to some aggregation of particularistic interests.[21] But classical realists expect (within some plausible, circumscribed range) that the national interest is malleable, contested, and evolving.

Throughout *War and Change*, domestic factors are essential: their "social, political or economic organization"[22] determines how well states will adapt new military technologies (a crucial mechanism via which the balance of power changes in the model); large sections of the book are devoted to "domestic sources of change";[23] and Gilpin repeatedly emphasizes domestic social changes (as opposed to a raw accounting of military hardware and economic capacity) in explaining changes to state power. As a hegemon reaches the apogee of its power and enters relative

---

[18] *Ibid.*, p. 54.

[19] Robert Strassler, *The Landmark Thucydides: A Comprehensive Guide to The Peloponnesian War* (New York, NY: Simon and Schuster, 1996), i.e., pp. 14, 318, 328, 346, 348, 481; Robert Gilpin, "The Theory of Hegemonic War," in Robert Rothberg and Theodore Rabb, *The Origin and Prevention of Major Wars* (Cambridge University Press, 1989), pp. 15–37, p. 23.

[20] Gilpin, *War and Change*, p. 13.

[21] On the centrality of the national interest for the realist tradition see Hans Morgenthau, *In Defense of the National Interest* (New York, NY: Knopf, 1951); George F. Kennan, *American Diplomacy, 1900–1950* (University of Chicago Press, 1951); and Stephen Krasner, *Defending the National Interest* (Princeton University Press, 1978).

[22] Gilpin, *War and Change*, p. 63.   [23] E.g., *ibid.*, pp. 96ff.

decline, it is "limited by internal transformations in society," such as increased interest group competition and other forms of social conflict, reduced innovation and tolerance for risk, and – a key Gilpinesque theme – "moral decay and the corruption of the original values that enabled the society to grow in the first place."[24]

War and Change also invests its domestic politics with history and ideology, two factors explicitly rejected as impermissible by neo-realists. But for Gilpin (and classical realists more generally), they are formative. Thus, although *War and Change* is heavily invested in cost/benefit analysis, as noted above, the book takes one step back from neo-realism by noting that this analysis is filtered through domestic politics. It then takes another giant step away by observing that the assessment of costs and benefits is also "highly subjective," and depends on "perceived interests." What shapes those perceptions? According to Gilpin, "foremost among the determinants of these perceptions is the historical experience of society … what lessons has the nation learned about war, aggression, appeasement, etc.?"[25] In sum, history matters. Additionally, *War and Change* presumes that the behavior of great powers will also be informed by ideology – which also influences how states define their interests, the character of a given hegemonic order, and the prospects for war and peace.[26] In Gilpin's assessment, for example, the ideological character of the superpowers was "a greatly underappreciated factor in the preservation of world peace" during the Cold War.[27] The counter-factual argument is thus that if, even while holding all material factors constant, had the superpowers held different ideological views, a shooting war would have been more likely.

Classical realists, then, place great emphasis on domestic politics, and take seriously the role of historical experience, and of ideas, norms, and legitimacy in explaining international relations. Indeed, Gilpin, in one of the founding statements of the subfield of international political economy, distinguished realism from liberalism and Marxism by noting the distinct realist emphasis on "national sentiment" and "political values." (Here Gilpin again reveals his affinity with John Maynard Keynes, author of the epigraph that opens *War and Change*.)[28] Other classicals routinely

[24] *Ibid.*, pp. 152–154. See also his emphasis on "the decay of bourgeois middle class work ethic" in explaining state behavior; Robert Gilpin, "Economic Interdependence and National Security in Historical Perspective," in Klaus Knorr and Frank Traeger, eds., *Economic Issues and National Security* (Lawrence, KS: University Press of Kansas, 1977), pp. 19–66, p. 59.
[25] Gilpin, *War and Change*, p. 51.   [26] *Ibid.*, pp. 8, 37–38.   [27] *Ibid.*, p. 240.
[28] Robert Gilpin, "The Politics of Transnational Economic Relations," *International Organization*, Vol. 25, No. 3 (Summer 1971), pp. 398–419, 401, 403. Keynes, in the

deployed these variables. Carr took very seriously the role of public opinion ("power over opinion ... is a necessary part of all power"); Morgenthau attributed many of the pathologies of US foreign policy to ideology and domestic politics; Kennan's most famous and influential work rooted the "Sources of Soviet Conduct" to internal Russian politics, historical experience, and the nature of the Russian character.[29]

This remains, it need be stressed, robustly realist, with all the reassuring darkness and pessimism that implies. Classical realists do not assume ideas are "good" or that lessons are learned accurately; they anticipate with dispositional cynicism that very often ideas, instrumentally or even perhaps unwittingly, often serve interests (what Carr called "the relativity of thought to the interests and circumstances of the thinker"). Nor do they expect norms to prevent states from pursuing radically dangerous foreign policies. But they do expect that all of these things nevertheless affect, significantly, politics and behavior. Realists may withhold moral judgment on the merits of competing ideologies, but states' choices will nonetheless be deeply affected by the influence of one or the other. Norms will not stop states from engaging in horrifying acts of barbaric aggression, but historical experience and perceptions of legitimacy nevertheless condition the way in which states interpret the meaning of each others' actions; certainly this view was central, for example, to Carr's thinking.[30] Established hegemons are likely to imbue the international order that they have shaped with a rosy glow of "legitimacy," and view many challenges to that order as disreputably subversive; whereas others, especially those once weaker and now becoming strong, are more likely to chafe under the tyranny of a status quo imposed by an arrogant (and fading) power that happened to get there first. Such contestations over the legitimacy of the status quo are the stuffing of classical realism.

Classical realists are also distinguished by their assumptions about the motivations of states and the influence of statesmen. Neo-realism

---

memoir that summarized much of his own personal philosophy, even more pointedly critiqued "an over-valuation of the economic criterion," which he saw as the source of "the final *reductio ad absurdum* of Benthamism known as Marxism." John Maynard Keynes, "My Early Beliefs," in his *Two Memoirs* (London: Rupert Hart-Davis, 1949). Keynes remains an underappreciated thinker in contemporary political science, to its impoverishment. See Jonathan Kirshner, "Keynes, Legacies, and Inquiry," *Theory and Society*, Vol. 38, No. 4 (2009), pp. 527–541.

[29] E.H. Carr, *The Twenty Years' Crisis, 1919–1939*, 2nd edn. (New York, NY: St. Martin's Press, 1946 [1939]), pp. 108, 132, 138; 145 (quote); Morgenthau, *National Interest*, pp. 4, 13, 115–116, 208, 223, 229, 234, 237; George F. Kennan, "The Sources of Soviet Conduct," *Foreign Affairs*, Vol. 25 (July 1947), pp. 566–582; see also George F. Kennan, "Russia – Seven Years Later," (1944) reprinted in Kennan, *Memoirs 1925–1950* (Boston, MA: Little, Brown & Co., 1967), pp. 503–531.

[30] Carr, *Twenty Years' Crisis*, pp. 69 (quote), 92, 97, 98, 101, 108, 143, 152, 220–222.

assumes that states are motivated by a desire for survival and crave security in order to assure that survival. Other than survival, their desires are, in Waltz's words, "endlessly varied." This "survival plus agnosticism" is the way in which structural realists model states. Even John Mearsheimer, touting a brand of structural realism ominously branded "offensive realism," explicitly models states as seeking nothing more than to ensure their own security and survival. The "Tragedy" of "Great Power Politics" derives from the (postulated) awful consequences of rational, dispassionate attempts to satisfy these understandable and fairly benign instincts.[31]

Classical realists, on the other hand, think states want more than survival. Indeed, they think that great powers want ... more. And in the pursuit of more, they seek status, deference, and primacy – all positional goods. (In *War and Change*, Gilpin repeatedly stresses the importance of states jockeying for position in the "hierarchy of prestige," and how status-seeking behavior is part of that struggle.[32]) This suggests a more dangerous world than is implied by neo-realism, because, challenging as it may be, it is possible to imagine settings in which two or more great powers can plausibly feel secure. But secure actors – hegemons and their challengers, for example and in particular – can still clash over primacy. For classical realists, then, politics is less a struggle for survival (most great powers, most of the time, are not faced with threats to their survival), and more about the clash of interests, with outcomes determined by power. And more than just security, this perspective emphasizes that men covet what others have; and worse still, as instinctively political actors, they are motivated by more than simply the accumulation of material things – they have a desire for power as an end in itself. In this envisioning of politics, there is no end zone, no ultimate goal achievement. Carr observes that "the exercise of power always appears to beget the appetite for more power"; Machiavelli concurs, concluding that "it does not appear to men that they possess securely what a man has unless he acquires something else new." Gilpin cites

---

[31] Waltz, *Theory of International Politics*, p. 91; John Mearsheimer, *The Tragedy of Great Power Politics* (New York, NY: Norton, 2001), p. 30. For a comprehensive critique of Mearsheimer, see Jonathan Kirshner, "The Tragedy of Offensive Realism: Classical Realism and the Rise of China," *European Journal of International Relations*, Vol. 18, No. 1 (March 2012), pp. 53–75,

[32] *War and Change*, pp. 30–31, 215. Gilpin is splitting the difference a bit here; prestige "rests on power," and thus arguably is derivative of it. But prestige is "the everyday currency of international relations," has an important reputational component, and challenges to prestige make war more likely. Thus states seek (and seek to defend) prestige as an end in itself.

approvingly Thucydides' emphasis on "greed" as a motivating force in world politics and a building block of realist analysis. Not surprisingly, then, in *War and Change* it is axiomatic that "as the power of a state increases, it seeks to extend ... its political influence."[33]

This emphasis on politics – and from there, on contingency, choice, and, consequentially, diplomacy, distinguishes classical from structural realism. For the classicals, the trajectory of state choices – especially of great powers, which have the most room for maneuver – is uncertain, and influenced by domestic politics, historical legacies, and, importantly, the choices made by other great powers, whose behavior shapes the nature of the opportunities and constraints presented by the system. By contrast, in considering the international political dynamics of rising states for example, structural realists, of course, cannot distinguish between the Japan of the 1920s and the Japan of the 1930s; for them the former was necessarily pregnant with the latter. Nor can they distinguish between Weimar Germany and Nazi Germany; or mourn the blunders of the Western powers in the 1920s. Classical realists, on the other hand, looking back tend to see the catastrophes of the 1930s not as the inevitable consequences of physical laws, but rooted in the dismal political choices of the 1920s.

For classical realists, politics matters, and the future is largely unwritten. Ironically, the classical realist vision of an unwritten future, but a written (and consequential) past, is the opposite of the approach taken by neo-realism, which insists on the absence (or at least the irrelevance) of history, and a more determined future. Structural realists model their states as amnesiacs, innocent of historical legacies; they model their statesmen as caretakers, arranging the deckchairs on ships guided by inexorable currents beyond their control. Gilpin, in *War and Change*, sees it differently: "Ultimately, international politics still can be characterized as it was by Thucydides: the interplay of

---

[33] Gilpin, *War and Change*, p. 106. Gilpin here echoes Spykman: "the number of cases in which a strong dynamic state has stopped expanding or has set modest limits to its power aims has been very few indeed." Nicholas J. Spykman, *America's Strategy in World Politics: The United States and the Balance of Power* (New York, NY: Harcourt, Brace, and Co., 1942), p. 20. Carr, *Twenty Years' Crisis*, p. 112; Niccolo Machiavelli, *Discourses on Livy* (University of Chicago Press, 1996, trans. Harvey Mansfield and Nathan Tarcov), p. 4; Gilpin, "Richness of the Tradition of Political Realism," p. 305. See also Miles Kahler, "External Ambition and Economic Performance," *World Politics*, Vol. 40, No. 4 (July 1988), pp. 419–451, 451; Hans Morgenthau, *Scientific Man vs. Power Politics* (University of Chicago Press, 1946), pp. 5, 42, 168, 195; Hans Morgenthau, "The Evil of Politics and the Politics of Evil," *Ethics*, Vol. 56, No. 1 (October 1945), pp. 1–18, 1, 13, 16–17.

impersonal forces and great leaders." "Though always constrained, choices always exist."[34]

Classical realism and the hyper-rationalist turn in international relations theory

Classical realism also dissents from what can be called the "hyper-rationalist turn" in contemporary international relations theory, which draws its sustenance from the (theoretically still dominant but nevertheless intellectually in tatters) rational expectations approach to macroeconomic theory. Classical realism parts company from the hyper-rationalist approach in three fundamental ways: it is more modest with regard to aspirations about what research in international relations can hope to achieve; it holds a broader definition of rationality (which can be called "realistic expectations"); it is profoundly skeptical of the possibility of prediction, and, as such, wary of an approach to inquiry that is oriented around the project of improving predictive power. These last two points in particular speak directly to the contributions of *War and Change* and to our ability to understand international relations in general and the political dynamics of conflict and contestation between rising and declining states in particular. Gilpin models his actors mostly (but not always) with a baseline expectation of modest rationality – they can order their preferences and go about the pursuit of them with a logic (however apparently flawed to future observers) that can be understood in retrospect. But they do not share knowledge of the same, essentially correct, model of politics. This in turn informs the classical realist rejection of prediction – the ability to predict future state behavior, and, distinctly, the expectation that actors in world politics share the same set of expectations about the future. These theoretical divergences are crucial, because these distinct classical perspectives on rationality and prediction drive the logic of Gilpin's model. I consider each of these elements (analytical modesty, realistic rationality, repudiation of prediction) in turn.

Classical realism, as founded and practiced, has been committed to the "scientific" study of world politics. But this does not suggest the resort to test tubes and Bunsen burners. Rather, it reflects a commitment to the objective, dispassionate analysis of international political behavior. The fundamental realist emphasis on acknowledging the reality of power gives pride of place to seeing the world as it is, not as one might like it to be; it requires, *from an analytical perspective*, a recusal from labeling actions "good and bad" or "right and wrong." Critical theorists are skeptical of

---

[34] Gilpin, *War and Change*, p. 228.

whether analysts can really achieve such objectivity; ethicists might suggest implicit, inescapable moral choices (and culpability) attendant to the enterprise.[35] Nevertheless, as Carr plainly describes (and endorses), "Consistent realism ... involves acceptance of the whole historical process and precludes moral judgment on it."[36]

But beyond this dyed-in-the-wool commitment to the objectivity and dispassion of a scientist, classical realists recoil from what Hans Morgenthau called "the illusion of a social science imitating a model of the natural sciences." Central to this disposition is the issue of *unpredictability*, a key source of "the practical weakness of a political science which aims at emulating the natural sciences."[37] Orientation around a predictive model is at the heart of much contemporary social science, but is incompatible with classical realism. It also, it should be noted, is an approach rejected by many of the seminal figures of twentieth-century economics. Frank Knight saw a belief in prediction as the basic flaw in economic theory, stressing instead "the inherent, absolute unpredictability of things, out of the sheer brute fact that the results of human activity cannot be anticipated." One important source of this "is the variation in the power of reading human nature, of forecasting the conduct of other men, as contrasted with the scientific judgment in regard to natural phenomena." Friedrich von Hayek also emphasized the distinction between the natural and social sciences, which informed his insistence that "in the study of such complex phenomena as the market," economists could expect to offer no more than "only very general predictions about the *kind* of events which we must expect in a given situation."[38]

Similarly, in *War and Change*, from the very start Gilpin stresses how "unique and unpredictable sets of developments"[39] render prediction beyond the means of the student of world politics. Once again a microeconomic analogy (and its limits) shows the insurmountable difficulties involved. In the study of consumer choice, for example, causal factors

---

[35] Teaching realism and proffering policy prescriptions based on realist analysis runs the risk that *assuming* states behave amorally might *contribute* to amoral policies, just as teaching microeconomic theory, which models actors as if they are selfish egoists, actually "teaches" undergraduates to become more selfish. (See Robert Frank, Thomas Gilovich and Dennis Regan, "Does Studying Economics Inhibit Cooperation?" *Journal of Economic Perspectives*, Vol. 7, No. 2 (Spring 1993), pp. 159–171.)

[36] Carr, *The Twenty Years' Crisis*, p. 91.

[37] Morgenthau, *Scientific Man vs. Power Politics*, pp. 121, 139 (quotes), 150; see also Gilpin, "Richness of the Tradition of Political Realism," p. 307.

[38] Frank Knight, *Risk, Uncertainty and Profit* (University of Chicago Press, 1971/1921), pp. 241, 311; Friedrich Hayek, "The Pretence of Knowledge," (Nobel Memorial Lecture, December 11, 1974), pp. 267, 271, 272. On these themes see also Emanuel Derman, *Models Behaving Badly: Why Confusing Illusion with Reality Can Lead to Disaster, on Wall Street and in Life* (New York, NY: Free Press, 2011).

[39] Gilpin, *War and Change*, p. 3.

can often be limited to a few, relatively pristine independent variables; there is commonly an enormous universe of nicely homogeneous data available for analysis; and it can be comfortably assumed that behavioral relationships are stable.[40] Yet even in this most favorable of analytical settings, "prediction" nevertheless refers to predicting the *average* behavioral response of a random actor drawn from a large population making similar choices, and not to predictions about the behavior of any one specific individual, which can, and will, vary broadly. Yet in international relations, the ultimate goal of the enterprise is capturing that elusive *individual* behavior (the behavior of a particular state at some significant moment in time) as opposed to the behavior of a hypothetical average state. Moreover, it should be recalled, our imagined consumers in that microeconomic setting are drawn randomly from a vast sea of tiny actors operating under perfect competition – as opposed to the market-shaping oligopsonists that states in world politics are more properly modeled as.[41]

And even in economics – which arguably would offer settings more analytically hospitable to forecasting future outcomes – there is good reason to be wary of prediction. Alfred Marshall, one of the founding fathers of the marginal revolution in economics, with all of the analytical precision that implied, was nevertheless profoundly skeptical of prediction, and this informed his approach to the discipline. Marshall explained how the problem of contingency – something even more prevalent in international politics than in economics (what Morgenthau called "the interminable chains of causes and effects") – severely circumscribes the prospects for all but the most limited efforts at prediction: "Prediction in economics must be hypothetical. Show an uninterrupted game at chess to an expert and he will be bold indeed if he prophesies its future stages. If either side make one move ever so little different from what he expected, all the following moves will be altered; and after two or three moves more the whole face of the game will have become different."[42]

---

[40] Such as elasticities of income and demand and the market sensitivity to complements and substitutes.

[41] On the challenge of complexity in international relations, and in particular with reference to the challenges of predicting the behavior of individual states, see Charles P. Kindleberger, "A Monetary Economist on Power Politics," *World Politics*, Vol. 6, No. 4 (July 1954), pp. 507–514, 509–510, and Charles P. Kindleberger, "Scientific International Politics," *World Politics*, Vol. 11, No. 1 (October 1958), pp. 83–88, 86.

[42] Alfred Marshall, "Fragments," in A.C. Pigou, ed., *Memorials of Alfred Marshall* (London: Macmillan, 1925), pp. 358–368, 360 (quote); Alfred Marshall, *Principles of Economics* (8th edn.) (London: Macmillan, 1920), esp. Book I, Chapter III, "Economic Generalizations or Laws," pp. 30–33. Morgenthau, *Scientific Man vs. Power Politics*, p. 129. On the limits to prediction in economics, see also Frank H. Knight, "'What is Truth' in Economics?" *Journal of Political Economy*, Vol. 48, No. 1 (1940), pp. 1–32, 29–31, and Andrew Rutten, "But It Will Never Be Science, Either," *Journal of Economic History*, Vol. 40, No. 1 (March 1980), pp. 137–142, 139, 141–142.

Once again, these types of obstacles are even more problematic (and intractable) in the vastly more complicated analytical setting of world politics. Consider for example theories designed to explain the causes of war – three additional challenges immediately emerge. First are the larger number of explanatory variables, some of which can be quite mercurial and idiosyncratic (such as the personal attributes of leaders – would there have been a Falklands War absent Margaret Thatcher?), and of which many are intricately interdependent rather than independent variables. Second is the lack of stability of these behavioral relationships over time, meaning that exactly the same set of circumstances that led to war in one period might not cause war in another, due to any number of factors. Third is the heterogeneity of the "dependent variable," that is, war. States choose to go to what we routinely (and accurately) call "war" for very different reasons.[43] The resort to war with different social meanings and purposes (compare, for example, the causes, motivations, and purposes associated with the first and second Gulf Wars) is likely the result of distinct (and, again, contingent) causal logics.

Each one of these individual analytical challenges might, in theory, be addressed (with the likely exception of contingency, wedded as that is to uncertainty, discussed below). But can a "general equilibrium theory" of world politics be derived? For the classical realist the answer is a plain "No." "The first lesson the student of international politics must learn and never forget," Morgenthau lectured, "is that the complexities of international affairs make simple solutions and trustworthy prophecies impossible."[44] Classical realists, then, do not share a conception of inquiry that imagines a sequence of the stepping stones of "description, explanation, and prediction," with prediction as the end goal and crowning achievement. From this perspective, prediction absent explanation is not problematic, as poor explanation is irrelevant. If that poverty of explanation (or the unrealistic nature of assumptions) was consequential, then a better theory with superior explanation or more realistic assumptions would do a better job of predicting.[45] But the classical

---

[43] Consider for example the (very distinct) motivations and goals associated with the US invasion of Panama in 1989, China's attack on Vietnam in 1979, Great Britain's declaration of war on Germany in 1939, and Chile's decision to take on Bolivia and Peru in 1879.

[44] Morgenthau, *Politics Among Nations: The Struggle for Power and Peace*, 3rd edn (New York, NY: Alfred A. Knopf, 1960), pp. 20 (quote), 21; see also Morgenthau, *Scientific Man vs. Power Politics*, pp. 129 ("interminable chains of causes and effects"), 139, 146–148, 150 (contingent elements), 220, 221.

[45] Milton Friedman's paper, "The Methodology of Positive Economics," in his *Essays in Positive Economics* (University of Chicago Press, 1953), remains an excellent articulation and defense of this perspective.

realist, although committed to rationalism, causality, generalizability, and hypothesis testing, nevertheless views forecasting the future as *impossible*, and thus redirects effort away from prediction – and away from orienting scholarship aimed at the idealized goal of prediction. Rather than describe, explain, and predict, the classical realist agenda is characterized by a different sequence: *describe, explain, understand, anticipate.*

Anticipation might suggest a narrower and more easily bridgeable distance from the narrow predictive approach than suggested above, if it implied a fall-back to a probabilistic conception of forecasting. That is, we can't predict the outcome of one roll of the dice, but we can know for certain the specific odds of rolling the number three, and act accordingly. But although this is certainly true (for dice), it does not capture the basis upon which the classicals reject prediction. It is not simply that the dauntingly numerous, interdependent, behaviorally unstable variables and complex chains of contingency reduce in practice the appeal of a retreat to probabilism to the moral equivalent of grasping in the non-falsifiable darkness (which it does). It is that probabilism (and the hyper-rationalist project more generally) requires a world of risk, whereas, as Gilpin concludes in *War and Change*, "in truth it must be said that uncertainty rules the world."[46] Risk implies that the underlying probability distribution is known (as it is with dice). Uncertainty describes a world characterized by crucial unknowns and unknowables (as it is with war). As Keynes described in his crucial 1937 paper,

> The orthodox theory assumes that we have a knowledge of the future of a kind quite different from that which we actually possess. This false rationalisation follows the lines of the Benthamite calculus. This hypothesis of a calculable future leads to a wrong interpretation of the principles of behavior which the need for action compels us to adopt, and to an underestimation of the concealed factors of utter doubt, precariousness, hope and fear.[47]

In a world of uncertainty, as Keynes argues, rational actors need to reach for decision-making rules that are at odds with much of what might be called "rational" by a strict, narrow version of the way rationality is often modeled in contemporary social science. In the absence of a future characterized by risk – that is by a known, proper (or at least reasonably accurate and widely understood) underlying probability distribution – the

---

[46] Gilpin, *War and Change*, p. 205.
[47] John Maynard Keynes, "The General Theory of Employment," *Quarterly Journal of Economics*, Vol. 51, No. 2 (February 1937), pp. 209–223 (*Collected Writings*: XIV, pp. 109–123, 122 (quote); see also pp. 113–114 for a discussion of the importance of uncertainty, such as "the prospect of a European war" or "the rate of interest twenty years hence" or "the obsolescence of a new invention," matters where "there is no scientific basis on which to form any calculable probability whatsoever").

rational actor becomes the rational muddler, who needs to draw on a larger bag of tricks. Sharing this perspective with Keynes were Hayek and Knight (who vehemently disagreed with Keynes about most other things). For Knight, "Uncertainty must be taken in a sense radically different from the familiar notion of Risk." He saw this as the engine of economic activity; Hayek similarly stressed the limits of what could possibly be known and the distinct perspectives of disparate market actors.[48] Similarly, in the context of uncertainty, classical realists tend to model states in the abstract as rational muddlers: essentially rational, purposeful, and motivated – but not as hyper-rationalist automatons. They will often guess, fall back on personal experiences, received conventional wisdom, and various rules of thumb to help steer them through the confusion. Thus, as Gilpin writes in *War and Change*, even though his model is built around the rational calculation of costs and benefits, "decisions are made under conditions of uncertainty," the "rush of events" and buffeted by "unintended consequences." Calculations, although "profoundly influenced by objective factors," are "ultimately subjective in nature."[49] Gilpin actually extends this further, including psychological factors as important for understanding the causes of war, including "gnawing fear" and "anxiety." Revisiting his emphasis on the rational calculation of costs and benefits, he concludes that "up to a point, rationality does appear to apply . . . but it is equally true that events, especially those associated with the passions of war, can easily escape from human control."[50]

In sum, fundamental uncertainty, radical contingency, and inherent unpredictability lead classical realists to embrace a different definition of the rational actor than is associated with much contemporary international relations theory. In particular, with regard to explaining war, classical realism is at odds with its baseline, predominant, theoretical formulation: the rationalist explanations for war (REW) approach. The central premise of this approach is that "given identical information, truly rational agents should reason to the same conclusions about the probability of one uncertain outcome or another. Conflicting estimates should occur only if the agents have different (and so necessarily) private information."[51] Classical realism rejects this proposition – and here it is

---

[48] Knight, *Risk, Uncertainty and Profit*, p. 19, see also p. 233; Friedrich Hayek, "The Use of Knowledge in Society," *American Economic Review*, Vol. 35, No. 4 (September 1945), pp. 519–530; John Maynard Keynes, *The General Theory of Employment, Interest and Money* (London: Macmillan, 1936), pp. 156–158.
[49] Gilpin, *War and Change*, p. 51.   [50] *Ibid.*, p. 201–202.
[51] James Fearon, "Rationalist Explanations for War," *International Organization*, Vol. 49, No. 3 (Summer 1995), pp. 379–414, 392.

not simply a matter of intellectual disposition. Although the core REW proposition has a coherent internal logic, it crumbles under the weight of competing deductive claims, and, not surprisingly, is easily falsified when put to an empirical test. Thoughtful, dispassionate experts looking at an identical, extremely rich information set, *routinely* come to markedly different expectations about the probability of various possible outcomes.[52] This is a crucial engine of conflict in world politics, and especially between hegemons and their challengers.

The fundamental flaw of the REW approach (and of the hyperrationalist turn in international relations theory more generally) can be found in its uncritical and intimate (if often implicit) embrace of the rational expectations revolution in macroeconomic theory. A central tenet of rational expectations theory is that actors process information quickly, efficiently, and correctly – and, crucially, that they share knowledge of the correct underlying model of the economy.[53] This approach took the economics profession by storm, seemed to overthrow a preceding, Keynesian logic, and presented a raft of empirically testable implications. But rational expectations did not test well; even leading anti-Keynesians concluded that "the strong rational expectations hypothesis cannot be accepted as a serious empirical hypothesis." Other mainstream economists concluded that "the weight of the empirical evidence is sufficiently strong to compel us to suspend belief in the hypothesis of rational expectations"; most attributed the empirical failure of rational expectations to the flawed underlying assumptions of the approach. These dissents have only increased as mistakes in the treatment of expectations and rationality came home to roost, as the limits to its deductive logic and empirical applications were exposed by the global financial crisis of 2007–2008. Critics, armed with ever more evidence, have increasingly observed that rational expectations models have "turned out to be grossly inconsistent with actual behavior in real world markets."[54]

---

[52] Jonathan Kirshner, "Rationalist Explanations for War?" *Security Studies*, Vol. 10, No. 1 (Autumn 2000), pp. 143–150.

[53] A good introduction to this literature is Preston Miller, ed., *The Rational Expectations Revolution* (Cambridge, MA: MIT Press, 1994).

[54] Karl Brunner and Allan H. Meltzer, *Money in the Economy: Issues in Monetary Analysis* (Cambridge University Press, 1993), p. 42; Michael C. Lovell, "Tests of the Rational Expectations Hypothesis," *American Economic Review*, Vol. 76, No. 1 (1986), pp. 110–124, 122; Benjamin Friedman, "Optimal Expectations and the Extreme Information Assumptions of 'Rational Expectations' Macromodels," *Journal of Monetary Economics*, Vol. 5 (January 1979), pp. 23–41, 26–27; Roman Frydman and Michael D. Goldberg, *Imperfect Knowledge Economics: Exchange Rates and Risk* (Princeton University Press, 2007), p. 54; see also pp. 126, 132, 138, 140, 151, 203, and Roman Frydman and

A classical realist perspective would typically model actors with what could be called "realistic expectations": that actors aim to advance relatively stable, ordered preferences by drawing thoughtfully and logically on implicit models of how the world works. But REW's hyper-rationalist approach, grafted from rational expectations theory, holds the view that rational actors must know and share the same (more or less) correct model of international politics (and so if they have the same information, they must reach the same conclusions[55]). In a world of rational expectations, in the words of founding father John Muth, "expectations, since they are informed predictions of future events, are essentially the same as the predictions of the relevant economic theory." Or as Thomas Sargent explains, "you simply cannot talk about" differences among people's models in the context of rational expectations. "All agents inside the model, the econometrician, and God share the same model."[56]

Rational expectations – and the rationalist explanations for war approach – assumes that "the representative individual, hence everyone in the economy, behaves as if he had *a complete understanding of the economic mechanisms governing the world*." But they don't. "No economist can point to a particular model, and honestly say 'this is how the world works,'" explains Mervyn King, Governor of the Bank of England from 2003 to 2013. "Our understanding of the economy is incomplete and constantly evolving."[57] And that's in economics, where many theoretical relationships, like that between the money supply and the inflation rate (which has its own problems in practice), are at least solid enough to allow rational agents to make informed predictions about future price levels.[58] In the fantastically more complex setting of international relations, however, leaders, statesmen, and experts walk around with different, and competing (and typically implicit) theoretical models of world politics in their heads. And when confronted with the same information, they will thus make different guesses, based on those

---

Michael Goldberg, *Beyond Mechanical Markets: Asset Price Swings, Risk, and the Role of the State* (Princeton University Press, 2011), "gross empirical failures," p. 52; see also pp. 102, 139, 196.

[55] With variations representing random errors distributed around the correct underlying model.

[56] John Muth, "Rational Expectations and the Theory of Price Movements," *Econometrica*, Vol. 29, No. 3 (July 1961), pp. 315–335, 316; George Evans and Seppo Honkapohja, "An Interview with Thomas J. Sargent," *Macroeconomic Dynamics*, Vol. 9 (2005), pp. 561–583, 566.

[57] David Colander, et al., "The Financial Crisis and the Systemic Failure of the Economics Profession," *Critical Review*, Vol. 21, No. 2–3 (2009), pp. 249–267, 256; Mervyn King, "Monetary Policy – Practice Ahead of Theory," speech given on May 17, 2005, p. 4.

[58] Again, as noted in FN 55, differences across experts could still occur, but they would be randomly distributed around the mean implied by a shared underlying model.

disparate implicit models and theories. "Bad" or "inferior" theories will not be selected out, because of the enormous complexity of the assessments involved, the small number of cases to draw on, the heterogeneity of the relevant "sample" (and even possible disagreements about what is a relevant data point and what conclusions to draw about it[59]) – and here even assuming behavioral stability among the variables over time (which is extremely unlikely).[60]

War, in particular (as well as the steps taken towards its approach), is a plunge into radical uncertainty, and rational experts can and will disagree, profoundly, with regard to their expectations about its cost, course, and consequence, even in the most complete and symmetrical information environments conceivably imaginable. Indeed, elite decision makers *within* states, sharing the same information, disagree about the implications of war – how much it will cost, how it will unfold, how it might widen, what will be its ultimate outcome – as a perfunctory scanning of the minutes of cabinet meetings or military planning sessions on the eve of any conflict makes clear.[61] Even a virtually omniscient vantage point fails to ensure a convergence of expectations. Consider, for example, the fall of France in 1940. Expert historians, with unlimited access not only to reams of comprehensive evidence but the actual outcome of the battle itself, *still* disagree about whether Germany's victory was virtually inevitable or an unlikely stroke of luck.[62] These disagreements are not the result of private information, but due to the multiplicity of causal models deployed by the experts, which are sustained by the absence, and practical impossibility, of a singular predictive model of war.[63]

---

[59] Given a probabilistic world, the meaning of outcomes can be contested. An outcome that a theory suggests has a 70% chance of occurring won't happen 30% of the time. So when a "failure" is observed, was it the result of a flawed model or just a case of bad luck? Either is possible, and it is very hard to tell with very small, heterogeneous "samples." As a result, competing theories are not easily selected out.

[60] For example, the US went to war in Korea in 1950, Vietnam in 1965, and Iraq in 1990 – each setting, obviously, involving different troops, weapons, leaders, terrains, adversaries, and politics. Was this data adequate to produce a singularly accurate theory designed to "predict" the capaciousness of US troops or the choices made by US leadership in wartime in the 2000s?

[61] Recall, for example, the radically differing assessments and expectations of members of the elite Executive Committee during the Cuban missile crisis.

[62] Ernest May, *Strange Victory: Hitler's Conquest of France* (New York, NY: Hill and Wang, 2000), looks at the evidence and reaches conclusions that are the opposite of Marc Bloch, *Strange Defeat* (New York, NY: Norton 1999 [1940]). Tony Judt, *Reappraisals: Reflections on the Forgotten Twentieth Century* (New York, NY: Penguin, 2008), looks at the evidence and reaches conclusions that are the opposite of May's.

[63] On the eve of any war, for example, both sides will be making guesses (again, drawing on different implicit models) about crucial variables that are unknown, and unknowable, to *both* sides, and will only become apparent when the war is underway.

This is, at the very least, the classical realist position. Morgenthau emphasized the inherent unpredictability of military campaigns, with outcomes turning on factors which cannot "be foreseen with any degree of certainty." Gilpin's favorite realist Thucydides held a similar view, citing "the vast influence of accident in war," one reason why "the course of war cannot be foreseen."[64] These sentiments are readily seen in *War and Change*, which observes that "actors can seldom predict the train of events they set in motion."[65] Gilpin drives home the point that statesmen rarely "anticipate the consequences of hegemonic war," repeating the claim three times in the space of two pages. "They do not get the war they want or expect."[66]

Revisiting the assumptions of war and change

An emphasis on these distinctions between classical realism and both strict structuralism and hyper-rationalism informs a revisitation and reassessment of the five core assumptions of *War and Change*.[67] Three of these assumptions are entirely consistent with classical realism (and a number of other perspectives as well). Two others, however, are problematic, and are the source of unresolved puzzles in the book. And they speak to the heart of the matter, from both a theoretical and a practical perspective, as they are the source of the *deus ex machina* leap from expansion to overstretch, and of the vexing elusiveness of peaceful adjustment to change. These paradoxes and contradictions are rooted in the book's vestigial structuralism and hyper-rationalism, and are resolved by the shift to a classical perspective.

As noted, assumptions 1, 2, and 5 are uncomplicated:

(1) A system is stable ... if no state believes it is profitable to attempt to change [it].
(2) A state will attempt to change the international system if the expected benefits exceed the expected net costs ...
(5) If the disequilibrium in the international system is not resolved, then the system will be changed ...

These assumptions are rooted in the expectations that states are ambitious, essentially rational, and uninhibited in the pursuit of their goals. If states perceive opportunities in the international system, which typically

---

[64] Morgenthau, *Scientific Man vs. Power Politics*, pp. 138–140; Strassler, *The Landmark Thucydides*, pp. 44, 97.
[65] Gilpin, *War and Change*, p. 74.   [66] *Ibid.*, pp. 202–203.   [67] *Ibid.*, pp. 10–11.

arise from economic change, they will pursue them with all of the means at their disposal, including the resort to force.

Assumptions 3 and 4, however, are problematic:

(3) A state will seek to change the international system through territorial, political and economic expansion until the marginal costs of further change are equal to or greater than the marginal benefits.
(4) Once an equilibrium between the costs and benefits of further change and expansion is reached, the tendency is for the economic costs of maintaining the status quo to rise faster than the economic capacity to support the status quo.

From the perspective of classical realism, assumption 3 is inconsistent with its expectations of how states behave; and assumption 4 (and the dangerous disequilibria it generates in world politics) can only be understood by the resort to explanations inconsistent with structuralism and hyper-rationality. I consider these in turn.

A classical recasting of assumption 3 would be that states tend to systematically overreach. That is, they don't stop expanding until they are *clearly beyond* the point where costs equal benefits, because it is only when they are well past the point that they belatedly realize that costs have considerably exceeded benefits. Why? Because the data and evidence used to assess costs and benefits is noisy and lagged (and, as a technical point, almost always discontinuous). These claims are not at all controversial – the classical departure is to expect that in this context states, and especially great powers, will typically overreach. Because all that data will not simply be noisy, but contested in its interpretation, a rising power, especially one near the height of its power (and thus long accustomed to winning and having things go its way), will be primed to interpret setbacks as temporary, and aberrant.[68] Stated plainly, great, rising powers near their apogee are almost certain to suffer from a hubris cultivated by a long string of successes.[69] They will be naturally overconfident, and slow to process experiences that suggest anything to the contrary. Or as boss Jim Gettys said to a similarly disposed Charles Foster Kane, who simply did not understand that he had been beaten: "If it was anybody else, I'd say what's going to happen to you would be a lesson to you. Only you're going to need more than one lesson. And

---

[68] For a modestly formalized model of why great powers will tend to err (and disagree with others) on the trajectory of their relative power, see Charles Doran, "War and Power Dynamics: Economic Underpinnings," *International Studies Quarterly*, Vol. 27, No. 4 (1983), pp. 419–441.
[69] Or, at least, to be systematically biased towards such a predisposition.

you're going to get more than one lesson."[70] So it is true for hegemons at the apogee of their power, overconfident and utterly unprepared to process the fact that they stand at the precipice of relative decline. Again, crucially, this alternate, classical assumption 3 is inconsistent with security seeking, affectless structuralism, which would assume dispassion and expect much more prudence from a great power; it is also fundamentally at odds with a hyper-rationalist approach which cannot abide systematic biases. At the heart of rational expectations theory, it should be recalled, is the idea that any errors made are unbiased; that is, randomly distributed around the correct (or at least best) model. Thus hegemons should be just as likely to stop too short as expand too far, and certainly sentiments like hubris are expressly presumed *not* to influence decision making.

But classical realists *expect* hubris. Warning against such folly can be seen as one of Thucydides' main agendas in his *History of the Peloponnesian War*. Gilpin's favorite realist is often hard to decipher, as he moves back and forth from his own voice to the speeches of others, players whom he chooses to present in one light or another, at times even presenting what he assumed they likely said. Nevertheless, in writing of the long war that Athens lost, a number of themes plainly emerge from a work explicitly designed to offer timeless lessons to history – and prominent among them is a warning against hubris. Thucydides calls attention to two key blunders, which, more than anything, contributed to Athens' ultimate defeat – and each an example of foolish overreach. The first occurred in year seven of the war, when Sparta offered Athens peace on generous terms. "The Athenians, however, kept grasping for more," Thucydides reports. Three years later, however, Athens "began to repent having rejected the treaty." The second occurred in year seventeen, with the disastrous campaign to conquer Sicily. The reluctant mission commander labeled the enterprise "folly" in the public debates on the topic, arguing that "the Sicilians, even if conquered, are too far off and too numerous to be ruled without difficulty." But his warnings were not heeded, because, as Thucydides in his own voice explained, of Athenian overconfidence, rooted in "their general extraordinary success, which made them confuse their strength with their hopes." And so, "being ambitious," the Athenians were "bent on invading" Sicily, despite the fact of "most of them being ignorant of its size and of the number of its inhabitants." As a majority rallied to the cause, "the few that did not like it feared to appear unpatriotic by holding up their hand against it, and so

---

[70] Citizen Kane (RKO, Orson Welles, 1941), written by Herman Mankiewicz and Orson Welles.

kept quiet." But this overreach was the decisive blunder of the war, and ultimately resulted in "the despondency of the Athenians ... [and] greater still their regret for having come on the expedition."[71]

It is not necessary to look into the distant past to find behavior that contradicts assumption three as written – the most recent US hegemonic cycles provide ample evidence as well. Into the 1960s, the US was still near the height of its post-World War II hegemony (the economic strengthening of its allies in Western Europe and Japan reduced US share of world GDP, but that was surely not a blow to its relative power in the context of the Cold War). What occurred in that decade was not an example of increasing costs of defending the status quo (a key driver of *War and Change*'s structural machine), but the foolish blunder of a hegemon unwilling to recognize the limits of its own power – and one so secure that it could throw bad money after good long past the point that a state with real security concerns possibly could. Vietnam mattered to the US not due to the inherent significance of that obscure, geopolitical backwater; it mattered solely in its Cold War context. But as the US poured blood and treasure into that war – 23,000 US ground troops introduced in January 1965 became 180,000 by December, and then 380,000 one year later, and finally over 500,000 troops at the end of 1967 – it was no closer to winning the war, and it had hollowed out its military, damaged its economy, weakened its defenses in Western Europe, and undermined its political standing around the world. In other words, a war fought solely to advance US interests in the Cold War had undermined those interests considerably and across the board. Even if the Vietnam War had somehow, against all odds, been "won" – it still would have thus been lost. Proof of this is that, stranded among the ruins of 1968, it is hard to imagine that President Johnson (or any American leader, for that matter) would not have wished that he had made different decisions in 1964 and 1965.[72] American hegemony was not undone by

[71] Strassler, *The Landmark Thucydides*, pp. 22, 233, 234, 238, 246, 255, 258, 309, 361, 368, 375. Warnings against overconfidence can be found throughout the book. ("Not that confidence is out of place in an army of invasion, but in an enemy's country it should also be accompanied by the precautions of apprehension," p. 97).

[72] The Vietnam War literature is obviously enormous; on the trip from 1964 to 1968 and subsequent regrets, see Fredrik Logevall, *Choosing War: The Lost Chance for Peace and the Escalation of War in Vietnam* (Berkeley, CA: University of California Press, 1999), pp. 73–74, 78, 145, 298, 314, 388, 393; George McT. Kahin, *Intervention: How America Became Involved in Vietnam* (New York, NY: Anchor Books, 1987), pp. 260, 262, 286, 306, 366, 393, 399, 423, 426, 432; Herbert Y. Schandler, *Lyndon Johnson and Vietnam: The Unmaking of a President* (Princeton University Press, 1977), pp. 98, 109, 119–120, 129, 140–141, 197–198, 258, 263–264; George C. Herring, *America's Longest War: The United States and Vietnam, 1950–1975* (New York, NY: Knopf, 2nd edn., 1986), pp. 144–145, 146, 151, 161.

costs rising faster than benefits; it was undone by the US obtusely grasping for too much, and trying to extend its power long past the point that the costs of doing so exceeded the benefits.

Similarly, another cycle of American hegemony met with a similar fate. With the unanticipated collapse of the Soviet Union, the end of the Japanese miracle, and the renaissance of the US economy in the 1990s, the American decline widely forecast since the late 1970s did not come to pass. Instead, the US entered the twenty-first century more powerful than ever before – the hegemon, the hyper-power, the colossus of a unipolar world.[73] Ten years later the US was bloodied, overextended, debt-ridden, and exhausted. But this change in fortunes did not come about because the US expanded until benefits touched up against costs, after which costs rose – it occurred, once again, due to hubris. Embarking upon its disastrous Iraq War, the US radically overestimated its ability to use force to remake the world as it would have liked it to be. The US only "stopped" expanding long past the point where costs had clearly exceeded benefits, evidence, again, that the structuralist/hyper-rationalist version of assumption 3 in *War and Change* is empirically suspect, at least compared to a more classical conception.

Assumption 4 also presents problems – indeed it presents the paradox that has always gnawed at the psyche of *War and Change*: if at equilibrium costs will begin, cumulatively, to outweigh benefits, why does the hegemon – modeled up to this point as a savvy, efficient, rational calculator – fail to anticipate this, or, at least, aptly adjust to it?[74] Gilpin is aware of this puzzle, and, leaning heavily on his classical side (in addition to reviewing a number of external factors that work to the hegemon's disadvantage), introduces a host of debilitating domestic political and social changes that are common to mature hegemons.[75] But two big puzzles remain, despite the external and internal problems Gilpin elucidates: the failure of a hegemon, in ascendance (when it is rationally and efficiently calculating costs and benefits), to anticipate problems on the horizon; and the failure of the hegemon in decline to properly adjust.

Far-sightedness presents a paradox that Gilpin wrestles with on several occasions. He argues that (liberal, capitalist) hegemons will bear the costs of establishing and maintaining an open international order, for the good realist reason that, given their economic advantages and position, they

---

[73] See for example G. John Ikenberry, ed., *America Unrivaled: The Future of the Balance of Power* (Ithaca, NY: Cornell University Press, 2002).

[74] For a thoughtful attempt to address this paradox, see Charles Kupchan, *The Vulnerability of Empire* (Ithaca, NY: Cornell University Press, 1994).

[75] Gilpin, *War and Change*, pp. 152–154, 162–163, 165, 167.

expect "to benefit *relatively* more than other states."[76] This is the basic motivation of the hegemon, as Gilpin and others have emphasized.[77] Yet he also notes that "trade and investment between advanced economies and less developed economies tend to favor and develop the latter."[78] Subsequently Gilpin acknowledges this apparent contradiction, noting although he had argued that "a world market economy tends to favor and to concentrate wealth in the more advanced and more efficient economy," this is only the case for the "short run."[79] In the long run, "a world market economy fosters the spread of economic growth," and "new centers of economic growth … frequently overtake and surpass the original center."[80] This may be true, and Gilpin gives good reasons why. But it leaves open the question of why the hegemon did not act more forcefully to preserve its advantages, or perhaps behave in a more predatory fashion during that period when it was reaping most of the advantages. More generally, structural and hyper-rationalist approaches might appeal to "time inconsistency" or a "discounting of the future." But this is somewhat unsatisfying in that it remains a systematic error (an error biased in one direction, repeatedly), that contrasts with the hegemon's previously modeled unbiased forecasting of costs and benefits; additionally, from a realist perspective, the state is supposed to have a long time horizon – that is one of the public goods it provides to society. A classical realist approach is less troubled by this paradox, as it anticipates systematic errors based on overconfidence. Even more important, a classical realist approach is untroubled by the apparent puzzle of why an equilibrium point suddenly becomes a disequilibrium point. As discussed, it offers a different engine for the hegemon's troubles at this stage: having expected the hegemon to overextend, by the time it stops expanding, it has already fomented the disequilibrium. Costs have already run far ahead of benefits, presenting formidable burdens for the hegemon and opportunities for potential challengers.

The second lingering puzzle in *War and Change* that flows from assumption 4 is why hegemons entering relative decline typically fail to restore equilibrium through retrenchment, which would bring costs back into line. Gilpin notes that disequilibrium is most commonly resolved by hegemonic war, which is obviously horrifying and extremely costly. Moreover, he does not see hegemonic war as a rational war, but something that is brought about by "gnawing fear," "anxiety," and "passions"

---

[76] *Ibid.*, p. 138 (emphasis added).
[77] Stephen Krasner, "State Power and the Structure of International Trade," *World Politics*, Vol. 28, No. 3 (1976), pp. 317–347, esp. p. 320.
[78] Gilpin, *War and Change*, p. 142.   [79] *Ibid.*, p. 177.   [80] *Ibid.*, p. 178.

that "can easily escape from human control." Gilpin holds out hope that mankind will find a mechanism for bringing about peaceful change, and he cites his second favorite realist, Carr, approvingly on this point. Carr argued that "defense of the status quo is not a policy which can be lastingly successful," and, as Gilpin summarizes his argument, the dominant state, not the challenger, has "a moral obligation to make the greater concessions."[81] But despite this, and Gilpin's praise for British retrenchment before World War I, he argues that it is "a course seldom pursued by a declining power."[82] Why is this? Gilpin finds the answers in politics, hubris, and fear. Retrenchment is *"politically* difficult"[83] even if it is the wisest course of action. One source of the political difficulties derives from the classical assumption that declining powers and their challengers – as well as various political actors *within* those states – will look at exactly the same information and reach different conclusions about its implications. There will thus be basic disagreements, both within and between states, about whether, and how much, retrenchment and adjustment is needed. And beyond that is the hubris/fear paradox: "Until a state is pressed by others, it has little incentive to make concessions for the sake of peace." But once faced with a real challenge, it fears that such concessions "will only whet the appetite for still greater concessions."[84] Hegemons are too arrogant to make concessions when they should and too frightened to make them when they must. Despite its structural machine, *War and Change* thus roots its central problem – the difficulty of adjustment – in a classical grounding.

The enduring lessons of war and change

Isms matter. They reflect underlying philosophical points of departure, and are rooted in specific, explicit assumptions about how the world works. The very different expectations and conclusions of different theories often stem from the fact that those theories derived from distinct, and contrasting, paradigmatic roots. To be self-conscious about those foundations is to understand the likely strengths, weaknesses, limitations, controversies, and specific attributes of various theories. In contemporary international relations scholarship, there is a common claim that we are "past paradigms"; many younger scholars are expected to recite this.

---

[81] Carr, *Twenty Years' Crisis*, p. 169, 222 (quote); Gilpin, *War and Change*, p. 206 (quote).
[82] Gilpin, *War and Change*, p. 194.   [83] *Ibid.*, p. 192 (emphasis added).
[84] *Ibid.*, p. 207. On the wisdom hegemonic restraint, see G. John Ikenberry, *After Victory: Institutions, Strategic Restraint, and the Rebuilding of Order after Major Wars* (Princeton University Press, 2001).

But that is a political act, not an intellectual one. It reflects the hegemony of one particular paradigmatic perspective – what I have elsewhere dubbed HIM: hyper-rationalism, individualism, and materialism – which *is* a paradigm. Power, not science, has led to the disciplinary hegemony of HIM (especially in international political economy), to the intellectual impoverishment of international relations theory.[85]

Classical realism matters. As a point of departure for the study of world politics, it is distinct from schools of thought such as liberalism and Marxism, especially with regard to the reductionist materialism of those perspectives. It is also distinct from its realist cousins – such as structural realism or neo-classical realism.[86] All of these realisms share common orienting principles regarding the significance of the role of anarchy, fear, the balance of power, the national interest, and the central role of politics in explaining the behavior of actors in world politics. Unlike its brethren, however, classical realism is distinguished by the expectation that great powers are motivated by more than security seeking, and that the national interest is contested and evolving. In addition, although classical realism, true to its roots, does not expect that norms, ideology, and legitimacy will limit the potential barbarism of states or transcend the amoral, empty darkness of anarchy – it nevertheless does expect that such things will affect behavior, the content of ambition, and the way that actions are interpreted by others. Finally, and, perhaps, most important, classical realism holds that history matters and that the future is very much unwritten. This means that politics matters: domestic politics within states, and, especially, the foreign policy *choices* made by great powers, which, despite the real constraints of anarchy, enjoy considerable discretion with regard to the choices that they will make. Those choices not only reflect the constraints suggested by the system but (like the market power of large oligopolists) also influence the nature of the systemic environment in which they dwell.

War and Change in World Politics matters, because, especially as interpreted here, it offers a baseline, contemporary articulation of a classical realist approach to world politics. Gilpin, most would agree, is ill suited

---

[85] Jonathan Kirshner, "The Second Crisis in IPE Theory," in Nicola Phillips and Catherine Weaver, ed., *International Political Economy: Debating the Past, Present and Future* (London: Routledge, 2011), pp. 203–209; see also Kathleen McNamara, "Of Intellectual Monocultures and the Study of IPE," also in Phillips and Weaver.

[86] Neo-classical realism is essentially modified neo-realism, and more accurately called neo-neo-realism. For an overview see Steven E. Lobell, Norrin M. Ripsman, and Jeffrey W. Taliaferro, *Neoclassical Realism, The State, and Foreign Policy* (Cambridge University Press, 2009), and Gideon Rose, "Neoclassical Realism and Theories of Foreign Policy," *World Politics*, Vol. 51, No. 1 (October 1998), pp. 144–172.

to be a cross-dresser. Better to shed the trendy, designer distractions of strict structuralism and hyper-rationalism that Gilpin rashly draped around his classical argument. Modifying assumption 3, reinterpreting aspects of assumption 4 and its implications, and abandoning the forecasts and qualifications towards the end, reveals even more clearly why the book is an enduring masterpiece, littered with gems for the classical realist scholar to study and polish. "Realism," Gilpin explains, "must be seen as a philosophical disposition and set of assumptions about the world rather than as in any strict sense a 'scientific' theory." It assumes that international affairs are "essentially conflictual," that the "building blocks" of analysis are groups, not individuals, and "power and security" are basic motivations. "World politics is still characterized by the struggle of political entities for power, prestige, and wealth in a condition of global anarchy."[87] From this point of departure, beyond its enduring insights into the perennial problems caused by the rise and decline of great powers in world politics, *War and Change* offers additional timeless lessons and emphasizes numerous classical themes, including the expectation of continuity over change, the importance of dynamics over statics, and the irreducibility of the inherently intertwined political and economic spheres.

Continuity over change. Gilpin, like Thucydides, did not intend to write a work "of the moment, but as a possession for all time."[88] Rather, he holds "the basic assumption of this study" is that "the fundamental nature of international relations has not changed over the millennia,"[89] a recurring theme that becomes the main point of the book's final chapter. Changes that appear transformative – like nuclear weapons or economic interdependence – do little more than change calculations about the costs and benefits of cooperation and conflict. Autonomous states (or conflict groups) still pursue their interests in the context of anarchy, and remain willing to fight over their differences.[90] Thucydides would have "little trouble in understanding the power struggle of our age."[91]

Dynamics over statics. Gilpin also calls upon his favorite realist to chastise neo-realism for missing the driving engine of international relations, even on their own terms; that is, at the most abstract, systemic level of analysis. Waltz and his followers focused on the distribution of power

---

[87] Gilpin, "Richness of the Tradition of Political Realism," pp. 304, 305; Gilpin, *War and Change*, p. 230.
[88] Strassler, *The Landmark Thucydides*, p. 16.
[89] Gilpin, *War and Change*, p. 7, also p. 211.
[90] *Ibid.*, pp. 16, 18, 24; Gilpin, "Theory of Hegemonic War," pp. 17–18, 35–36.
[91] Gilpin, *War and Change*, pp. 211, 227.

between states. Gilpin is skeptical of Waltz's conclusions about the likely implications of bipolarity and multipolarity which he suggests are indeterminate.[92] And, more forcefully, he insists that "the most important factor for the process of international political change is not the static distribution of power in the system (bipolar or multipolar) but the dynamics of power relations over time." In either setting, it is the "changes in relative power among the principal actors in the system" that are key.[93] Thucydides famously wrote that the "real" cause of the Peloponnesian War was that "the growth of power in Athens, and the alarm which this inspired in Sparta, made war inevitable." This phrase has been repeated so often it has become a cliché; nevertheless, for Gilpin, Thucydides' most important contribution is to have identified "that the uneven growth of power among states is the driving force of international relations."[94]

Political economy. With the uneven growth of power as the central causal mechanism of change in world politics, Gilpin, and *War and Change*, insist that politics and economics are inseparable, intimately co-joined twins. This, again, is distinct from the approach most commonly seen in contemporary international relations theory – where many PhD programs in IR separate out "international political economy" from "security studies," and in some cases even let students master one and not the other – which is simply incoherent from a classical perspective. For Gilpin, "the distribution of power itself ultimately rests on an economic base," and "the struggle for power and the desire for economic gain are ultimately and inextricably joined."[95] Moreover, it is folly to fail to understand, and attend to, the political context of *all* economic relations. Gilpin quotes E.H. Carr on this point approvingly: "the science of economics presupposes a given political order and cannot be profitably studied in isolation from politics."[96] And, finally, a main theme of *War and Change*, that hegemons envision and forge an international economic order to advance their interests, is in accord with the classical position that international politics fundamentally shapes the pattern of economic relations, which in turn consequentially affect political relations between states.[97]

---

[92] *Ibid.*, pp. 88–90, 93.   [93] *Ibid.*, p. 93, see also pp. 4, 6, 13–14, 96.
[94] Strassler, *The Landmark Thucydides*, pp. 16, 44, 49; Gilpin, "Theory of Hegemonic War," pp. 15, 19, 25–26.
[95] Gilpin, *War and Change*, p. 67.   [96] *Ibid.*, p. 133.
[97] The Carr quote is from *Twenty Years' Crisis*; on this point see also Morgenthau, *Scientific Man vs. Power Politics*, p. 84. On politics shaping economics, see Albert Hirschman, *National Power and the Structure of Foreign Trade* (Berkeley, CA: University of California Press, 1980 [1945]), and Rawi Abdelal and Jonathan Kirshner, "Strategy, Economic Relations, and the Definition of National Interests," *Security Studies*, Vol. 9, No. 1–2 (Autumn 1999–Winter 2000), pp. 119–156.

In sum, *War and Change in World Politics* is a landmark work of classical realism, and endures because of that fact. Classical realism matters because it is informed by a distinct point of departure: the past is relevant, the future is unwritten, and, above all, *politics matters*: expressed as the choices made by great powers acting with discretion, and as a motivation for human behavior.

6   Order and change in world politics: the financial crisis and the breakdown of the US–China grand bargain

Michael Mastanduno

Introduction

War and Change reflects in intellectual terms both the remarkable ambition and pessimistic inclination of Robert Gilpin. Although much of his academic reputation has rested on work in international political economy, Gilpin focuses in *War and Change* on what he considers the core problem in international politics, hegemonic war. He views power transitions as inherently dangerous and searches for the elusive formula for peaceful change. He appreciates the value of stable international orders, while his analysis consistently demonstrates that over time the "law of uneven growth" and an array of other factors ensure that orders do not remain stable. International order is the key theme running through Gilpin's work – how it is created and sustained, how and why it inevitably breaks down, how to survive the breakdown without the catastrophe of hegemonic war, and how to reconstruct order after major war.[1]

Gilpin is a methodological pluralist but at its core his approach is that of a classical realist. *War and Change* focuses on the great powers. It is about the always precarious predicament of dominant states in a competitive environment, and about the calculations and strategies of rising challengers. It is about the integration of economics and security; written when the professional study of international relations developed a division of labor across these two subfields, Gilpin insisted that their synthesis and interplay was vital to comprehend world politics.[2] *War and Change* emphasizes both the material and non-material aspects of national power. It highlights relative material capabilities but continually returns to the importance of prestige, reputation, and legitimacy as driving forces

---

[1] Gilpin's insights on order building inspired the vast literature on hegemonic stability and have been foundational for recent work on the reconstruction of order, e.g., G. John Ikenberry, *After Victory: Institutions, Strategic Restraint and the Rebuilding of Order after Major Wars* (Princeton University Press, 2001).

[2] Michael Mastanduno, "Economics and Security in Statecraft and Scholarship," *International Organization*, Vol. 52, No. 4 (1998), pp. 825–854.

in great-power competition. Rather than adhering slavishly to the international level of analysis, Gilpin finds room for the meaningful impact of domestic structures and politics on the calculations and strategies of competing states.[3] William Wohlforth argued recently that had *War and Change* received equal billing alongside Waltz's seminal work, "scholars would not have been bewildered by change, bewitched by the balance of power, [or] blind to numerous potentially powerful realist theories."[4]

Although written in the language of social science theory-building (internal chapters, for example, open with rational choice style "assumptions"), *War and Change* is more a sweeping intellectual treatise than a tightly developed and tested theory. Gilpin observes in the preface that the basic dilemma of social science is "whether to explain trivial matters with exactitude or to treat significant matters with imprecision."[5] The book and Gilpin's contributions more generally fall decisively on the latter side of that dilemma.

This chapter draws on Gilpin's understanding of order and change to examine the most important bilateral relationship in contemporary world politics, that between China and the United States. Throughout the postwar era, the United States has pursued the hegemonic project of building an international order that reflects its values and interests on an increasingly global scale. The management of this US-centered order has been based on a series of special relationships with key supporters. During the Cold War, those supporters were found among America's NATO allies in Europe and, in East Asia, Japan. After the Cold War, China emerged as the key US supporter, and the United States and China struck a tacit deal, or "grand bargain," that served symbiotically both the economic and security interests of each side.

The great financial crisis that began in 2008 served as a catalyst for the unraveling of the US–China grand bargain. The financial crisis, in turn, reflects and reinforces gradual shifts in relative power and, equally important, in the harder to measure yet critical Gilpinian factor of international prestige. The overall result is that the US–China relationship is moving from the seemingly stable bargain of the initial post-Cold War years to a transitional era of uncertainty, risk, and potential danger.

---

[3] *War and Change* manages to praise and draw upon Kenneth Waltz's *Theory of International Politics*, which was published just two years prior to *War and Change*, while simultaneously offering a classical realist alternative to it.

[4] William Wohlforth, "Gilpinian Realism and International Relations," *International Relations*, Vol. 25, No. 4 (2011), pp. 499–511.

[5] Robert Gilpin, *War and Change in World Politics* (Cambridge University Press, 1981), p. xiii.

In discussing the concept of prestige, Gilpin argues that lesser states are inclined to follow an international leader as long as they "accept the legitimacy and utility of the existing order" and "prefer the certainty of the status quo to the uncertainties of change."[6] Today's China, to be sure, would prefer a stable status quo and is not seeking fundamental change in the international order. But the status quo no longer appears stable, and over time the benefits of supporting the US-centered order are likely to decrease as China becomes more powerful and if US prestige continues to decline and the world economy remains unstable.

The argument proceeds as follows. In the next section I explore the idea of "grand bargains" and apply it to the US-centered international order and the arrangement involving economics, security, and even identity that evolved between the United States and China over the decades since the end of the Cold War. The third section explains how the financial crisis has undermined this bargain, forcing both China and the United States to confront an uncertain process of adjustment. The likely result will be greater economic friction and a gradual move away from the extraordinarily mutual dependence that has characterized their grand bargain.

The fourth section takes up US–China security relations, arguing that the financial crisis has altered US prestige, and also both Chinese and American perceptions of China's rise. The likely result will be a more "normal" great-power relationship characterized more by competition and friction than by cooperation. That growing competition will take place in the context of China's continued rise and the winding down of America's preoccupation with the war on terrorism which, for at least a decade, deflected US attention away from traditional great-power politics and toward the periphery of the international system. The concluding section briefly explores, in the spirit of Gilpin's analysis, competing images of future US–China relations.

The political management of hegemony: grand bargains and the US–China relationship

War and Change tells us a great deal about how dominant powers rise and fall. Gilpin devotes considerable attention to the incentives for rising states to change the international order, focusing in particular on the cost-benefit calculations that make a hegemonic challenge more profitable than continued support for the status quo. Domestic factors – the historical experience of the rising state and its coalitional politics – and

---

[6] *Ibid.*, p. 30.

environmental factors such as changes in military technology or in the nature of international economic exchange loom large.[7] In later chapters Gilpin shifts attention to the beleaguered dominant state and explains why economic constraints make it increasingly difficult to maintain its preferred international order.

War and Change focuses more on the forces impinging respectively on the leading and potentially challenging states than on interactions among them. Put differently, Gilpin tells us why orders come and go, but says very little about the political management of hegemony. What techniques or strategies do hegemonic states employ in relations with both supporters and challengers in an effort to maintain their dominant position?

Over time other scholars have picked up what Gilpin left unattended on the inner workings or mechanics of hegemony. The hegemonic stability literature has long debated the relative efficacy of benign hegemonic techniques centered on the production of public goods versus coercive techniques that rely on the purposeful exercise of preponderant power.[8] John Ikenberry's recent work focuses on hegemonic management through institutional lock-in, self-restraint on the part of the dominant state, and the creation of durable constitutional orders.[9] David Lake asks why states comply with biased international orders and emphasizes the key role of authority and legitimacy in hierarchical relationships.[10] A prominent line of argument in the recent literature on US grand strategy after the Cold War highlights the technique of selective engagement as a way to prolong hegemony while sidestepping and minimizing the mounting costs and burdens that accompany the effort.[11]

My emphasis is on a different technique for hegemonic management, what I term the "grand bargain." Leaders need followers; hegemonic states need supporters. Generally the more supporters the better, but dominant states will tend to rely most heavily on a small number of critical supporters.[12] Supporters are states with the potential to

---

[7] *Ibid.*, Chapters 2 and 3.

[8] For example, see Timothy McKeown, "Hegemonic Stability Theory and 19th Century Tariff Levels in Europe," *International Organization*, Vol 31, No. 1 (1989), pp. 73–91.

[9] G. John Ikenberry, *After Victory*, and *Liberal Leviathan: The Origins, Crisis, and Transformation of the American World Order* (Princeton University Press, 2011).

[10] David Lake, *Hierarchy in International Relations* (Ithaca, NY: Cornell University Press, 2009), and "Dominance and Subordination in World Politics," this volume.

[11] For example see Robert Art, *A Grand Strategy for America* (Ithaca, NY: Cornell University Press, 2003).

[12] This line of argument is related to, but different from, arguments that suggest hegemonic leadership can be provided by collective or co-leaders, i.e., by more than one state. See David Lake, "Leadership, Hegemony, and the International Economy," *International Studies Quarterly*, Vol. 37 (1993), pp. 459–489, and Duncan Snidal, "The Limits of Hegemonic Stability Theory," *International Organization*, Vol. 39 (1985), pp. 579–614.

challenge an existing order, yet which choose instead, because the order serves their own interests, to accept and reinforce its basic principles. Hegemonic states strike tacit deals, or bargains, with these supporters, deals that serve both the economic and security interests of each side.[13] Grand bargains enable the dominant state both to run its preferred order and to manage the domestic political and economic costs associated with it. Unfortunately for the dominant state, and in the spirit of Gilpin's analysis, grand bargains do not last forever. They ultimately break down either because they no longer adequately serve the economic and security interests of either side, or because they produce side effects (e.g., economic crises) that jeopardize the very order on which they are based.

An historical example of a grand bargain to manage hegemony was prompted by the Cobden-Chevalier Treaty of 1860 between Great Britain and France.[14] Britain needed France's help to establish its preferred liberal economic order and maintain the balance of power on the European continent. France desired preferential access to Britain's large home market. The economic deal encouraged and reinforced bilateral security cooperation between the two powers. Their bargain was sustained until the 1880s when the rise of a unified Germany led to protectionism on the Continent and a British-German security competition that led ultimately to war and the end of British hegemony.

Postwar grand bargains

Power in world politics is multidimensional and relational.[15] America's postwar dominance was never simply a matter of capabilities, e.g., maintaining the largest economy or deploying better ships and planes than other states. And, although US officials were certainly willing and able to do so, US hegemony was never simply a matter of coercing other states to do what America wanted, politically, economically, or strategically. More fundamentally, hegemony involved establishing and maintaining the rules of the global political and economic game, getting other states to abide by and embrace those rules (even as the United

---

[13] Michael Mastanduno, "System Maker and Privilege Taker: US Power and the International Political Economy," *World Politics*, Vol. 61, No. 1 (2009), pp. 121–154.

[14] See Arthur Stein, "The Hegemon's Dilemma: Great Britain, the United States, and the International Economic Order," *International Organization*, Vol. 38, No. 2 (1984), pp. 355–386, and Daniel Verdier, *Democracy and International Trade: Britain, France, and the United States, 1860–1990* (Princeton University Press, 1994).

[15] Michael Barnett and Raymond Duvall, "Power in International Politics," *International Organization*, Vol. 59 (Winter 2005), pp. 39–75.

States reserved for itself the right to alter or break those rules), and even shaping the identities of the players themselves.

The US-centered or "Western" order of the Cold War era was limited geographically yet nonetheless hegemonic, centered around American-led alliances in Western Europe and East Asia with the dual purpose of rebuilding the liberal world economy and preserving the balance of power against the global influence and aspiration of the Soviet Union. That order came to include numerous states, but was based on a set of tacit bargains between the United States and a small number of supporting countries. These bargains served the economic and security interests of each side.[16] In the initial Bretton Woods arrangement of the 1950s and 1960s, the United States opened its markets, asymmetrically, to its war-ravaged and export-dependent partners in Europe and Asia. It also provided security, in the form of nuclear guarantees and commitments institutionalized in NATO and the US–Japan Security Treaty, to defend those states against the conventionally superior armies of the Communist bloc. NATO members and Japan received market access and security protection; in exchange, the United States gained the support of a core coalition for its global struggle with the Soviet Union. Specific benefits included loyal allies, forward bases from which to project power, and the ideological advantage of having partners that resembled the United States institutionally with shared commitments to democracy and some form of liberal capitalism. Economically, the United States enjoyed the special privileges that accompanied the dollar's role as international exchange and reserve currency. It could pursue both "guns and butter" without making hard and time-sensitive trade-offs across domestic priorities and international obligations. The US commitment to defend a dollar link to gold, in turn, enabled and even obliged America's partners to maintain undervalued currencies and the associated advantages for their export sectors.

The dollar and the navy were the lynchpins of US hegemony. After the war, America enjoyed undisputed naval superiority. It controlled and protected global trade routes – the very routes on which its allies depended for their exports to the United States. Control of the seas, coupled with the US nuclear umbrella as the ultimate guarantor of alliance security in the face of the Soviet land threat, essentially ensured that no US ally would be tempted to adopt an independent foreign

---

[16] Mastanduno, "System Maker and Privilege Taker." Although *War and Change* does not develop the theme of hegemonic management, Gilpin does describe the logic of America's hegemonic order in earlier work. See *US Power and the Multinational Corporation* (New York, NY: Basic Books, 1975), especially Chapter 4.

policy.[17] The special role of the dollar was a key source of US prestige and reinforced the indispensability of the United States in the Western economic system. It is not surprising that President Johnson feared devaluation of the dollar as much as losing the Vietnam War. US allies were in effect obliged to hold dollars; as the key European supporter, West Germany, recognized, any reluctance to do so would lead the United States to undertake agonizing reappraisals of its security commitments.[18]

The economic side of the deal broke down in the late 1960s and collapsed in August 1971 because the United States took its privileges too far, threatening the stability of the global economy, and because its partners in Europe and Japan became too strong, making it difficult to justify the currency-induced export advantages to which they had become accustomed. America's prestige as a global and alliance leader was also shaken by the debacle in Vietnam. But by the 1980s the bargain was reconstructed, institutionally with the G-7 and politically with the United States partnering most closely with West Germany and Japan, the two allies with the strongest economies and most important regional security roles. The overall terms remained essentially the same. America's partners enjoyed security protection in the final intense phase of the Cold War, when the Soviet Union appeared to become an even more formidable global threat. They maintained access with undervalued currencies to the large American consumer market. The United States, in turn, managed to enjoy during the Reagan years deep tax cuts, a massive defense buildup, trade deficits, and budget deficits – all without having to endure painful adjustments in its domestic economy. The dollar remained the world economy's key currency in a new floating exchange rate regime and America's partners continued to accumulate dollars in reserve.

For the United States, hegemony has meant never having to say you are sorry. As tacit compensation for shouldering the burden of system management, US officials reserved the right to modify the specific terms of the bargain on short notice. The United States was strong enough to force any necessary adjustments on its loyal partners, as it did during the Nixon Shock of 1971, when it unilaterally closed the gold window, imposed trade restrictions, and ended Bretton Woods, and in the Plaza Agreement of 1985, when it forced Japan into a painful currency revaluation as a way to address the US trade deficit.

---

[17] Barry Posen, "Control of the Commons: The Military Foundation of US Hegemony, *International Security*, Vol. 28 (Summer 2003), pp. 5–46.

[18] Francis Gavin, "Ideas, Power and the Politics of US Monetary Policy during the 1960s," in Jonathan Kirshner, ed., *Monetary Orders: Ambiguous Economics, Ubiquitous Politics* (New York, NY: Cornell University Press, 2003).

Hegemony and the US–China bargain after the Cold War

In the epilogue to *War and Change*, Gilpin writes that in 1980 the Pax Americana was in "a state of disarray."[19] The United States faced a military challenge from the Soviet Union and the rise of new centers of economic power. It was struggling to scale back its security commitments and regain its economic footing. Gilpin, like Paul Kennedy after him, perceived the US experience as fitting the larger historical pattern of hegemonic decline. His pessimism at that time was unfounded; the US economy survived the 1980s and rebounded well in the 1990s, while that of its most plausible economic challenger, Japan, entered a twenty-year period of stagnation. The European Union turned inward, absorbed by its ambitious integration project. Most importantly, the Soviet Union offered international politics a double historical surprise – it abruptly terminated its military challenge to the United States, and it also collapsed peacefully without bringing on hegemonic war as an instrument of change.

After the Cold War, the United States emerged as a unipolar power with an ambitious grand strategy to match. In the international economy it sought through the so-called Washington Consensus to expand the American-centered liberal order to include as much of the developing world and the former Soviet area as possible. It sought to deepen the liberal economic consensus by convincing states to liberalize not just trade but also finance and investment. In the security arena it positioned itself as a regional stabilizer in Europe, the Middle East, and East Asia. It punished (e.g., Iraq) or tried to buy off (e.g., North Korea) smaller states it perceived as having the potential to undermine regional stability. In great-power relations, US policy makers sought to reassure Japan and major NATO powers, most importantly a reunified Germany, that the American system of security protection still prevailed and therefore that they had no pressing need to transform themselves into independent military powers. The United States also tried to coax other potential challengers, especially Russia and China, into becoming supporters of the US hegemonic order. When the dust began to clear a decade or so after the Soviet collapse, it was apparent that the United States had succeeded in holding together Cold War alliances but had failed to coax Russia into joining the liberal club. China, however, was on a more promising path.

The integration of China is critical to the longer-term viability of the US hegemonic project. In the great-power politics of the current era, China is both a potential supporter and the most plausible rising challenger in terms of its size of population, geographical footprint, historical

---

[19] Gilpin, *War and Change*, p. 231.

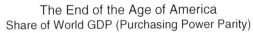

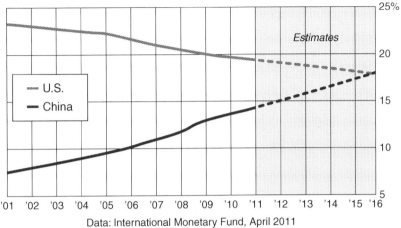

Data: International Monetary Fund, April 2011

Figure 6.1: The end of the age of America: Share of world GDP
(purchasing power parity).
Source: www.marketwatch.com/story/imf-bombshell-age-of-america-
about-to-end-2011-04-25

ambition, and economic growth trajectory. In April 2011, the IMF
predicted provocatively that in terms of purchasing power parity, China's
economy would catch up to that of the United States by 2016 (see
Figure 6.1). Unlike the Soviet Union, China is a potential challenger
that is simultaneously critical to the success of the world economy.
Whatever its impact on world politics, the Soviet Union was never a
serious player in the world economy, save perhaps as a supplier of energy
to Western Europe. China's large and dynamic economic is a much-
anticipated engine of growth for a world economy no longer sustained by
the collective efforts of the United States, Germany, and Japan.

In light of America's ongoing hegemonic ambition, and China's critical position, it is not surprising that by the late 1990s China emerged as
the newest and most important US partner. It is remarkable that even in
the absence of the Cold War, and even though China is not a US ally, the
basic US–China bargain looks very similar to the Cold War partnerships
described above. The similarities are striking enough for some analysts to
label the core economic relationships of the 1990s and 2000s as "Bretton
Woods II."[20] As was the case for American partnerships during the Cold

---

[20] Michael Dooley, et al., "The Revised Bretton Woods System," *International Journal of
Finance and Economics*, Vol. 9 (October 2004), pp. 307–313.

War, the US-China partnership, or grand bargain, has served both the economic and security interests of each side.

On the economic side, China has enjoyed an accommodating international environment for the externally oriented growth strategy that has fueled its economic miracle. Since 1978, when China essentially abandoned its national version of the Soviet-style command economy, its Communist leaders have followed the example of other Asian tigers and Japan in pursuit of export-led growth. This strategy has been remarkably successful, resulting in sustained and rapid growth rates for the better part of three decades. The value of China's exports was a mere $10 billion in 1978; by 1992 it was almost $70 billion, by 1995 about $150 billion, by 2003 almost $500 billion, and by 2007 approached $1 trillion. China's exports as a percentage of GDP reached 38% in 2005. By comparison, the relevant figure for Japan was 13%, and for the United States, 10%.[21] Armed with an undervalued currency, China has gained access to global markets and most importantly to the large, relatively open, and seemingly insatiable US consumer market, while offering selective access and maintaining control over its domestic markets for goods and services. Like Japan during the 1980s, China during the first decade of the 2000s accumulated sizable surpluses in trade with the United States. Japan's bilateral surpluses with the United States reached the neighborhood of $50 billion annually; China's bilateral surplus exceeded $200 billion by 2005 and reached a record $315 billion at the end of 2012.[22]

For its part, the United States has managed to retain the special benefits – what French leaders in an earlier era termed the "exorbitant privilege" – in the world economy due to the special status of the dollar. Chinese holdings of American Treasury securities have expanded dramatically from about $100 billion in 2000 to over $1.2 trillion by 2012.[23] With others, led by China, willing to build up their reserves of the US currency, the United States has continued to enjoy extraordinary autonomy in its domestic and foreign policies. The Bush Administration pursued tax cuts, significantly increased defense spending to fight the global war on terrorism, and produced a consumer boom fueled by cheap credit, massive fiscal and current account deficits, and sufficient investment to sustain economic growth – all at the same time. Ordinary economies must make trade-offs and adjust their domestic economies in a timely

---

[21] *The Economist: Pocket World in Figures*, 2007 edn. (London: Profile Books, 2007).

[22] "China," Office of the US Trade Representative (www.ustr.gov), and US Census, Foreign Trade, "Trade in Goods with China," available at: www.census.gov/foreigntrade/balance.

[23] US Treasury, "Major Foreign Holders of U.S. Treasury Securities," available at: www.treasury.gov.

manner to the realities of their external accounts. The United States, with the help of willing supporters and at least until the financial crisis, did not. The grand bargain enabled the United States to remain addicted to borrowing and spending, while its supporting partner China could remain addicted to lending and exporting.[24]

The more underappreciated part of the US–China grand bargain is on the security side. In Bretton Woods I, the United States struck a deal with economic partners who were simultaneously security allies. China is a deep economic partner yet a possible security challenger. Nevertheless, the grand bargain still served the security interest of each side.

The principal security benefit for China has been the maintenance of a benign global environment. China's long-term strategy of economic development and "peaceful rise" has required cooperation, rather than confrontation, with the dominant power in the international system, and that is precisely what the grand bargain has delivered. China has needed the United States to restrain itself rather than place China in the cross-hairs and employ its preponderant capabilities and influence to thwart China's gradual rise. A hostile security environment would be detrimental to an economic development strategy that relies on sustained international openness and access. China is a patient challenger and economic development is the key to China's future geopolitical success.

Peaceful rise requires stability in China's East Asian neighborhood as well as globally. China has needed to assure its neighbors that its rise will be neither disruptive nor threatening; its partnership with the United States helped serve that objective. For China, the grand bargain has meant that the United States may be allied with Japan but also restrains Japan, serving as the "cork in the bottle" that contains possible Japanese militarism and dampens the historical Japan-China rivalry for regional dominance. The grand bargain has also implied that although the United States fashions itself as the regional stabilizer in East Asia, it can also make room for China to play a constructive diplomatic role – for example, in the Six-Party Talks on North Korea – that reinforces China's preferred image as a rapidly growing but non-threatening neighbor. Although China and the United States differ fundamentally over Taiwan, their tacit bargain to "kick the can down the road" and put off any definitive resolution has enabled China to continue to draw Taiwan in economically and Chinese leaders hope eventually politically as well.

[24] Stephen D. Cohen, "The Superpower as Super-Debtor: Implications of Economic Disequilibria in U.S.-Asian Relations," in Ashley Tellis and Michael Wills, eds., *Strategic Asia 2006–07: Trade, Interdependence and Security* (Seattle, WA: National Bureau of Asian Research, 2006), pp. 29–63.

The grand bargain has offered security benefits to the United States as well. Deep economic interdependence and an accommodating foreign policy hold out the possibility that a rising China, unlike a more discontented Russia, will be integrated into the US-led security order. In the post-Cold War era the United States has sought to discourage peer competitors and convince would-be challengers that they are better off operating within an American-centered order, in effect as junior partners, than standing outside of that order and seeking to undermine it.[25] This is the essential message conveyed to China when US officials urge it to become, in the now famous phrase of the State Department's Robert Zoellick, a "responsible stakeholder." In exchange for economic and security benefits, US policy makers are asking that China act "responsibly," that is, in a manner consistent with the interests, priorities, and values of the United States.

For the United States, the grand bargain has offered a possible solution to the classic dilemma of economic interdependence with a possible future rival. On the one hand, promoting China's integration into the global capitalist economy strengthens China's *capabilities*, by accelerating its economic growth and affording it access to advanced technology. The more the United States engages economically with China, the more quickly China will become a formidable potential rival. On the other hand, American officials have been placing the liberal bet that the more China becomes integrated economically, the more likely it will become transformed domestically and change its foreign policy *intentions* – in a direction preferred by the United States.[26] As China engages the world economy, progressive and ultimately democratic forces will gain in strength, transforming not only China's domestic politics but also, since democracies tend to be peaceful in relations with each other, its foreign policy. From an American perspective, the grand bargain opens the possibility of having one's cake and eating it – that is, enjoying both the economic benefits of interdependence with the world's now second-largest economy, and the security benefits of a supportive partner whose foreign policy reflects broadly America's own global priorities.

War and Change reminds us to appreciate the non-material as well as material dimensions of political relationships. For Gilpin, prestige stands alongside power as critical elements of hegemony; each is vital in

---

[25] Michael Mastanduno, "Preserving the Unipolar Moment: Realist Theories and U.S. Grand Strategy After the Cold War," *International Security*, Vol. 21, No. 4 (1997), pp. 49–88.

[26] The basic logic is spelled out in Albert Hirschman's classic, *National Power and the Structure of Foreign Trade* (Berkeley, CA: University of California Press [1945], 1981).

ensuring that supporting states embrace the hegemonic order.[27] In social terms, the political bargains struck by the United States have been as asymmetrical as the power relationships on which they rest. The United States has positioned itself and has acted as the dominant and more autonomous partner, setting agendas and establishing expectations and rules for others to follow, though not necessarily feeling the need to follow those rules itself. It has expected its partners to be supportive, and it prefers that they share US values and resemble the United States institutionally by being or becoming market economies and liberal democracies. In this sense Japan proved to be the ideal postwar partner, gradually transforming its international identity from that of a competing great power explicitly challenging the existing international order to that of a loyal client state embracing a "civilian" or partial great-power identity and playing a supporting role in America's hegemonic project. As postwar Japan became more powerful it struggled, without much success, to become more assertive in its bilateral partnership with the United States in the hope of being treated as a more equal partner. The struggle was well captured by the controversy created in Japan during the early 1990s by the publication of a book authored by a prominent politician with the title *The Japan That Can Say No*.[28] Some sixty years after the end of the war, Japan remains a loyal supporter that still seems incapable of saying no to the United States.

In this respect China has always promised to be a more challenging partner. Postwar China has proven more resistant than Japan to great-power efforts to shape its identity. In the early Cold War era Mao defied Stalin and refused to allow China to play a subordinate role as the *second* most important Communist power. During the 1970s, China's leaders resisted the Nixon Administration's attempts to play the "China card" in the larger US–Soviet struggle. China's leaders believed they represented a player rather than a card.[29] Nevertheless, for the United States a key attraction of the grand bargain is that it has held out the promise of gradually transforming China into a like-minded supporting partner rather than a rising and eventual peer competitor. The US designation of China as a responsible stakeholder is a call, in effect, for China to

---

[27] Gilpin, *War and Change*, p. 30. Gilpin overstates the point: "Both power and prestige function to ensure that the lesser states in the system will obey the commands of the dominant state or states."

[28] Shintaro Ishihara, *The Japan That Can Say No: Why Japan Will be First Among Equals* (New York, NY: Simon & Schuster, 1991).

[29] Kissinger emphasizes this more assertive Chinese streak in his comparative experiences with Chinese and Soviet leaders during the Cold War. See Henry A. Kissinger, *White House Years* (Boston, MA: Little, Brown, 1979), p. 1141.

self-identify as a supporter and follow the US lead on an array of issues such as the correction of global economic imbalances, the maintenance of regional stability in East Asia, the proper response to climate change, and the sanctioning of states (e.g., Iran and Sudan) that the United States has designated as rogue actors. It is not clear that a rising China would ever be comfortable in a secondary, supporting role.[30] Until the financial crisis, however, US officials at least held out the hope that by offering an array of economic and security benefits they might gradually transform China's identity and coax it into playing the part. After the crisis the prospects are considerably more uncertain.

Catalyst for change: the financial crisis and US–China economic relations

For Gilpin, international change is more likely the product of gradual shifts in the relative distribution of power than it is the result of a dramatic single event.[31] However, particular shocks or crises may serve as catalysts for change and at the same time illuminate and reinforce patterns that are already underway. The financial crisis that began in 2008 has magnified and accelerated ongoing shifts in the US–China balance of power and prestige.

By the middle of the 2000s, many economists warned that the great macroeconomic imbalances as a consequence of extraordinary amounts of Chinese and other country lending and US borrowing were creating financial instability and could spark a global crisis. The great financial crisis that did arrive in 2008 was ignited by the availability of cheap credit within the United States, which led to a housing bubble, which encouraged consumers and financial institutions to borrow and lend aggressively as each took on considerable risks in the belief that housing prices would never fall and in the hope of reaping great benefits. Housing prices of course did fall, and the resulting steep losses brought down key players in the US financial sector and led banks to curtail lending. The crisis spread around the world due to America's central place in international finance and the fact that equity markets and financial institutions are deeply interconnected globally. The resulting recession became the deepest, most sustained, and most widespread since the Great Depression of the 1930s.

---

[30] A book by Chinese authors, similar in spirit to Ishihara's book (fn. 28) appeared in 1996: Zhang Zangzang, et al., *China Can Say No: Political and Emotional Choices in the Post-Cold War Era* (Beijing: Zhonghua gongshang lianhe chubanshe).
[31] Gilpin, *War and Change*, p. 93.

The breakdown of the US–China grand bargain is among the most profound consequences of the financial crisis and recession. The breakdown is not immediately apparent, decisive, or dramatic. Understandably, neither the United States nor China will be quick to concede that it is over. Neither country is prepared to abandon the considerable benefits that each has reaped from the grand bargain, and we should expect each to try to hold on as long as possible to what became a mutually reinforcing arrangement. But the bargain will end nevertheless because the crisis and recession have undermined its structural foundations. The United States and China will remain economically interdependent. But the crisis and its aftermath will force the United States to break its addiction to excessive borrowing and consumption, just as China will be forced to rely less for economic growth on exports to Western consumer markets and thereby will have less incentive to continue accumulating US dollars. Their special economic relationship, on which their uneasy security partnership has rested, will no longer be as special.

China's predicament

For China, the global crisis and recession have ushered in a new international environment, one that, in the developed world, is no longer as accommodating to its export-driven growth strategy. As Japan learned three decades ago, export-led growth works only as long as others are both willing and able to accommodate it. Japan until the end of the 1970s, like China until the crisis, was tolerated as an extremely successful mercantilist state operating in a liberal world economy. The tolerance of the United States and others ran out once the world economy slowed down, the United States faced unemployment and sizable external deficits, and Japan became the world's second-largest economy. US attention then focused not so much on its own home-grown problems, but on Japan's privileged position and the unfairness of its rise. US politicians responded by pressuring Japan to limit its exports, open its own markets, revalue its currency, and consume more at home.[32]

By 2010 China had replaced Japan as the world's most successful exporter and second-largest economy, and its political predicament has become similar to that of Japan's at the peak of its economic success.

---

[32] Gilpin devoted considerable attention in his writings after *War and Change* to the Japanese challenge to US economic hegemony. He viewed the challenge in both material and ideational (liberal vs. developmental capitalism) terms. See for example Robert Gilpin, "Sources of American-Japanese Economic Conflict," in G. John Ikenberry and Michael Mastanduno, ed., *International Relations Theory and the Asia-Pacific* (New York, NY: Columbia University Press, 2003), pp. 299–322.

At the beginning of the post-financial crisis era China has the dubious distinction of wearing the same "unfair trader" target on its back that Japan wore during the 1980s and 1990s. Deep recession has meant slower growth and high levels of unemployment in the United States and European Union, and, particularly in the United States, there is often a strong political temptation to "blame the foreigner" for economic pain at home. China's insistence on maintaining an undervalued currency, its unwillingness to provide intellectual property protection, and its pursuit of neo-mercantilist policies of "indigenous innovation" all serve to reinforce that political temptation.

In the typical US pattern, the pressure on "unfair traders" comes most directly from members of Congress, who, in an era of slower growth, face political pressure themselves to do something to alleviate the economic pain of their constituents. The standard political narrative is not that the United States overextended itself and now needs to pay the price, but that other countries have taken advantage of America's economic beneficence and willingness to provide global public goods.[33] For example, at congressional hearings in September 2010 on China's currency policy, US Senator Charles Schumer (D-NY) stated that "China's currency manipulation is like a boot on the throat of our recovery, and this administration refuses to try to get China to remove that boot."[34]

In response to this type of political pressure, sitting executive branch officials typically talk tough but try to deflect protectionism and mitigate conflicts with US trading partners. Whether the Obama Administration and its successor will continue to do so, or, as the Nixon Administration did in an earlier era, exploit the political pressure and take up the unfair trader narrative as its own, remains to be seen. It is clear that over the past twenty years, the US executive has found itself in a weaker position domestically to champion freer trade. As the failure of the Doha Round suggests, US presidents no longer have the political will, domestic support, or international clout to bring complicated multilateral trade agreements to conclusion. Both the Bush and Obama Administrations struggled to complete even far more modest bilateral trade agreements with Panama, Colombia, and South Korea. The key Obama Administration trade initiatives were at the regional level, and it is revealing

---

[33] This narrative was powerful during the early 1970s collapse of Bretton Woods. See John Odell, *US International Monetary Policy: Markets, Power, and Ideas as Sources of Change* (Princeton University Press, 1982).

[34] "Geithner Stuck in the Middle on China," *Wall Street Journal*, September 17, 2010, p. A12.

that its Asian initiative, the Trans-Pacific Partnership, was crafted either to exclude China or to make it politically difficult for China to participate.[35]

As a result of the crisis and recession, China faces a more uncertain and less accommodating US political environment for its preferred economic strategy. Of even greater concern for China, as discussed below, is the structural reality that the US economy and consumer are no longer in a position to serve as the global market of last resort. Thus, even if US political pressure on China dissipates or the executive branch manages it effectively, over time the US economy is being forced by the depth of the financial crisis to make fundamental adjustments that will slow the pace of consumption and by implication the demand for China's exports. Put differently, even if the United States still proves willing politically to accommodate China's export-led growth strategy, it will likely no longer be able economically to do so.

In this new global environment China cannot simply turn to its other most important market, the European Union, to sustain export-led growth. The crisis forced EU governments also to grapple with political pressures generated by high unemployment and slower growth, with the structural need to unwind debt, and with the risk of plummeting collectively into a deeper financial and even political crisis. EU members became more wary of China's exports and more willing to criticize China's mercantilist restrictions on its home market. The EU's 2020 trade strategy, unveiled in 2010, focuses among other things on China's exclusionary and WTO-inconsistent public procurement practices which are designed to support indigenous innovation and give home-grown Chinese enterprises an advantage in the vast domestic market. In a transparent reference to China, the 2020 strategy calls for "improved symmetry in access to public procurement markets in developed and large emerging economies."[36] Rather than being able to substitute greater penetration of European final markets for less penetration of US markets, China's leaders face political and structural pressure that limits access to both. And, as Japan found during the 1980s, China might need to brace itself for coordinated US and European pressure to

---

[35] Guoyou Song and Wen Jin Yuan, "China's Free Trade Agreement Strategies," *Washington Quarterly*, Vol. 35, No. 4 (2012), pp. 107–119.

[36] *Trade, Growth, and World Affairs: Trade Policy as a Core Component of the EU's 2020 Strategy* (Brussels: European Commission, 2010), available at: http://trade.ec.europa.eu/doclib/docs/2010/november/tradoc_146955.pdf, p. 6. The economic stakes in public procurement programs were considerably higher in the context of the financial crisis as governments put together large economic stimulus programs – China's was valued at about $600 billion.

open its home markets and to abandon the types of industrial policies that confer what are perceived as unfair advantages in its home market and in others around the world.

China will continue to be a global export powerhouse. Its share of world exports jumped from 2% in 1990 to over 10% in 2010. Sluggish demand in the United States and Europe has led it to rely increasingly on trade with developing countries; between 2000 and 2010, the developing country share of China's trade jumped from 20% to 30%. By 2012, China was already the number one trading partner of South Korea, India, and South Africa, and the number two partner of Indonesia, Mexico, and Brazil. But even in the developing world concerns mounted that China's exports, fueled by an undervalued currency, was depressing wages, displacing workers, and distorting local economies.

As the crisis unfolded Chinese leaders exhibited awareness that, with the overall international economic environment less accommodating, China would be forced to rely more on domestic consumption to maintain high growth rates. In the initial phase of the crisis private consumption as a proportion of GDP in China rose significantly, from 41% in 2007 to 52% in 2009, as government stimulus funds replaced export receipts. Discussion in the G-20 and elsewhere points to China's large and growing domestic market as a key future engine of growth not only for China but for the entire world economy.

Greater reliance on domestic consumption eventually may prove viable as a core growth strategy, though it is likely to pose challenges to China along the way. For example, to what extent will Chinese consumers be prepared to spend more and save less in the absence of a more developed social safety net? Will state leaders manage to find alternative pools of saving, perhaps by accepting the risks of liberalizing Chinese capital markets faster than they otherwise would have? Will Chinese firms be able to provide not only the goods but also the kinds of services demanded by consumers in a modern, knowledge-intensive economy – and can a knowledge-intensive economy flourish in a political context in which state leaders prefer to maintain control over the flow of information? The shift from an export-oriented to a domestic consumption–oriented growth strategy will not be as simple as flipping a switch. China, nevertheless, will be forced to move in that less time-tested and more uncertain direction.

In the context of the grand bargain, the important point is that the transition to more diversified export markets and a more consumption-based growth strategy means that China will necessarily become less dependent on the US market – and thus less inclined to hold US dollars in reserve. China would be prudent to diversify its reserve holdings away from the dollar in any event; less reliance on the US market will only hasten its move in that direction. By 2012, initial evidence of Chinese diversification came to light; China's dollar holdings as a share of its foreign exchange reserves in 2011 fell to a decade low of 54%, down from 65% one year earlier.[37] The grand bargain was built on the expectation of a special G-2 relationship marked by deep, mutually binding, and ever-growing bilateral economic interdependence – interdependence so deep and restraining that it created the economic equivalent of "mutual assured destruction," a situation in which neither side could afford to jeopardize economic cooperation without harming itself significantly. The longer-term impact of the financial crisis and its aftermath is not that China and the United States will become economically isolated from each other. But they will become relatively less dependent on each other and therefore less mutually constrained than they have been during the era of the grand bargain.

America's predicament

In the wake of the crisis the United States, like China, has found that it can no longer sustain its economic side of the grand bargain. America's post-crisis problem is deeper than simply managing the political pressures emanating from the ups and downs of the business cycle – or managing the business cycle itself. The recession spawned by the financial crisis was not a normal recession, and it is not surprising that the US recovery from it was more sluggish than recoveries from other postwar recessions.

What might be called a balance-sheet recession, prompted by the collapse of a sustained, bubble-induced spending binge, requires a longer period of adjustment as private and eventually public actors are forced to reduce debt and restore solvency. That process was underway in the household sector by 2010. US household debt as a percentage of disposable income dropped from a peak of 130% in 2007 to 116% in 2010 – still a considerable distance from the 90% level of 2000. The US personal savings rate hit a low of 1.4% in 2005; it increased to 5.8% in 2010, a level last seen during the early 1990s.[38] In response to the crisis and ensuing recession, public sector borrowing and spending continued to increase to what many economists view as dangerously unsustainable

---

[37] Tom Orlik and Bob Davis, "Beijing Diversifies away from US Dollar," *Wall Street Journal*, March 2, 2012, p. A1.
[38] Justin Lahart and Mark Whitehouse, "Families Slice Debt to Lowest in Six Years," *Wall Street Journal*, March 11, 2011.

levels. This simply puts off the day of reckoning, with the important question being whether the political process will find a way to engineer a softer landing or financial markets will force a harder landing in the adjustment process.

The era of the United States as the primary engine of growth for the world economy is nearing its end. Notwithstanding its best intentions, the United States will not be positioned in the short or perhaps even medium term to play its traditional postwar role as global consumer of last resort. That role was welcomed by American citizens as well as America's economic partners, but was propped up, with the complicity of America's dollar-holding partners, by an extraordinarily accommodating monetary policy and by other government policies that encouraged citizens and public entities to borrow, spend, and live well beyond their means. The financial crisis disrupted this pattern, and the ensuing recession has placed the United States at the very beginning of what is likely to be an extended rebalancing adjustment in the direction of less consumption and borrowing and more savings and debt reduction.[39]

The international environment will likely become less accommodating to the United States as well. America's external borrowing binge led the leading state in the world economic system to take on record-setting external deficits. That position is sustainable only as long as other major players in the world economy are confident in the US economy, the US dollar, and in the capacity of the United States for global leadership. Here, too, we see echoes of the early 1970s. In the wake of the recent financial crisis the United States and the US dollar no longer inspire that type of confidence. The US economic model, which appeared so triumphant during the 1990s, is now one that other countries approach with some skepticism and a high degree of caution. The dollar is a source of widespread concern around the world, and among monetary experts there is no consensus that it will maintain its dominant global role.[40] To be sure, there is as yet no viable alternative to the dollar's global exchange and reserve role. The dollar even has strengthened during the crisis as governments and private actors predictably sought it out as a relative safe haven. But that strengthening in the short term should not be mistaken for enduring confidence or stability. The combination of over-reliance on the dollar and uncertainty about the US economy means that other

---

[39] For example, Roger Altman and Richard Haass, "American Profligacy and American Power: The Consequences of Fiscal Irresponsibility," *Foreign Affairs*, Vol. 89 (November–December 2010), and Michael Mandelbaum, *The Frugal Superpower: America's Global Leadership in a Cash-Strapped Era* (New York, NY: Public Affairs, 2010).

[40] Eric Helleiner and Jonathan Kirshner, ed., *The Future of the Dollar* (Ithaca, NY: Cornell University Press, 2009).

actors would prefer alternatives to the dollar, even if at present there are few viable ones – except perhaps for gold, which continued to hit record price highs during and after the crisis.

In the short term, international dollar holders, China included, are unlikely to make a mass exit for fear of precipitating the very crisis they are hoping to avoid. But the US–China grand bargain requires others not simply to hold dollars, but to continue to accumulate them as Americans keep consuming foreign goods and services. It is this continued rapid accumulation that is no longer viable. The situation is reminiscent of the late 1960s, when the structural foundations of the original Bretton Woods deal had washed away and confidence in the dollar and in the ability of the United States to lead the world economy waned. With the exception of France, which made a political point of selling dollars for gold, the major trans-Atlantic partners sought to make incremental adjustments in the hope, ultimately unrealized, that they could patch together and prolong the life of the bargain that had served each of them so well.

We should expect, in similar fashion, China and the United States to try to preserve the aspects of the grand bargain that have worked best for them. China will look to sustain its export levels by searching for new markets or finding new products for old markets.[41] The US government, as the early Obama years demonstrated, will look to double down, moving deeper into debt, in an effort to shock the consumer sector back to life. The United States will look to its partners to continue amassing US debt. These temporary patches may hold, but not for long, for the reasons explained above. The financial crisis signals the demise of the economic foundations of the grand bargain. By implication, the United States and China will become relatively less dependent on each other even as their economic relations become more contentious because China is not yet prepared to relinquish its identity as a developing country and the privileges which follow from that status, while the United States, unwilling to give up its own privileges, grows increasingly less tolerant of China's.

Power and prestige: the financial crisis and US–China security relations

The transformations in the US–China economic relationship both motivates and plays out in the context of changes in the bilateral security relationship. During the era of the grand bargain, US–China security

---

[41] Stephen Roach, "Manchurian Paradox," *The National Interest*, Vol. 101 (May/June 2009), pp. 59–65.

relations were generally cooperative. In the aftermath of the financial crisis, two developments render the security relationship more competitive and potentially more conflict-prone. The first is the continued rise of China and changing US and Chinese perceptions of it – perceptions affected directly by the financial crisis. The second is the winding down of America's more than decade-long obsession with the war on terrorism.

Changing perceptions of China's rise

China is the rising power in the international system and possesses the classic attributes of a great-power challenger. It has a continental land mass, a very large population, a rapidly growing economy, and a modernizing military. China's leaders are geopolitically ambitious and sensitive to China's long history as the dominant Asian power yet one disrespected by Western great powers. They believe China has earned its rightful place among the contemporary global great powers. The circumstances of China today inspire comparisons to the rising powers of earlier eras, including imperial Germany, which challenged Britain's European and global dominance in the late nineteenth century both economically and militarily. But China's rise might also be compared plausibly to late-nineteenth-century America – a massive country that viewed itself primarily as a regional power, whose economy grew rapidly to the point of overtaking, peacefully, the previously dominant economies of the prior era, and whose security relationship with the prior dominant power was a cooperative one.

Will China's continued rise ultimately resemble Germany's more alarming path, or America's more reassuring one, or perhaps neither? No one can know for sure. *War and Change* is preoccupied with precisely this question of whether rising powers can be accommodated peacefully. Yet, Gilpin does not provide clear guidance on this question, even after struggling with key developments such as the advent of nuclear weapons that might alter history's cyclical pattern. He is on firmer ground in identifying the emergence of hegemonic struggles in the changing balance of power and prestige, and his argument suggests that after the financial crisis, US-China relations have begun to take on the material and relational attributes characteristic of prior hegemonic struggles.[42]

Between 1990 and 2008, US policy makers kept a wary eye on China's rise, but found reasons not to be alarmed by it. One reason is that in military terms the gap between US and Chinese capabilities remained,

---

[42] In this spirit see Aaron Friedberg, *A Contest for Supremacy: China, America, and the Struggle for Mastery in Asia* (New York, NY: Norton, 2012).

from the US perspective, comfortably large.[43] China's military is impressive in relative numerical terms, but relative military capability is not simply a matter of numerical comparisons. China has lagged significantly in the training, sophistication, and experience of its fighting forces and has been far behind in the ability to equip its forces with modern equipment. Chinese ground forces last saw significant action against Vietnam three decades ago; by comparison, US forces have been deployed in numerous missions around the world since 1979, and have fought significant wars twice in Iraq and in Afghanistan.

Since the middle of the 1990s, China has committed to a comprehensive improvement in its military capabilities. Military spending doubled between 2000 and 2005, and then doubled again to about $60 billion annually by 2008. China has developed its own fighter aircraft and has improved the accuracy and reliability of its ground-based missile systems. It has made considerable investments in space systems and in other defense-related sectors such as information technology and shipbuilding.[44] Chinese officials have been aggressive in acquiring military equipment and technology from abroad. And, although Taiwan has remained the Chinese military's most pressing concern, Chinese officials recently have begun to think of military power in more global terms. They are developing a blue-water naval capacity, and the associated air forces, to project Chinese military power beyond coastal waters. China's military efforts over the past decade have attracted the attention and concern of the US defense establishment, which now publishes annual reports on developments in Chinese military power, similar to the ones it produced on Soviet military power during the latter stage of the Cold War.[45]

But even with the recent commitments and improvements, US officials have recognized that China has a long way to go before it can credibly challenge the military forces of other major powers, much less the United States. Even the US Defense Department conceded in 2009 that China's limited ability to deploy forces beyond its borders had not improved meaningfully since 2000. Defense also estimated that even after recent developments and acquisitions, only 20% of the

[43] See, for example, "US-China Relations: An Affirmative Agenda, A Responsible Course," *Independent Task Force Report #59* (New York, NY: Council on Foreign Relations, 2007), pp. 47–54.
[44] Evan Medeiros, Roger Cliff, Keith Crane, and James Mulvenon, *A New Direction for China's Defense Industry* (Santa Monica, CA: The RAND Corporation, 2005).
[45] See US Department of Defense, Office of the Secretary of Defense, *Military Power of the People's Republic of China 2009*, Annual Report to Congress (Washington, DC: Government Printing Office, 2009).

weapons systems used by the Chinese air force could reasonably be characterized as "modern," along with only 30% of the navy's surface ships and 40% of its submarines.[46] Given continued improvements in US military capability, during the era of the grand bargain US defense officials monitored China's military progress but had good reason to be confident it would take China a long time to catch up.

A second reason that US officials proved less distressed by China's rise concerned not China's capabilities but its intentions. By the middle of the 1990s, and particularly after the Taiwan Straits crisis of 1995–1996, it became clear to Chinese leaders that China's rise promised to create anxiety regionally and globally. Their response was to adopt a grand strategy of reassurance, centered on non-threatening rhetoric (e.g., "peaceful rise"), support for international initiatives, participation in multilateral institutions, and avoidance of provocative foreign policy behavior.[47] China's message to its neighbors, and to the United States, was intended to signal clearly that its rise was intended to be patient and peaceful, its foreign policy would be system supportive, and that it did not threaten anyone. This strategy of reassurance complemented nicely America's aspiration that a rising China would develop over time into a country "more like us" economically and politically and be transformed into a cooperative supporter of the US-centered international order.

Perceptions matter in international politics. The financial crisis disrupted both China's reassuring image and America's belief in it. It is not surprising that the financial crisis tempted China to feel more assertive about its global role. After all, the self-appointed leader of global capitalism badly mismanaged its own economy and brought the entire system to the brink of collapse. China did not cause the problem, and in fact much of the world looked to China to help rescue the system from the ensuing damage. China's response at home to the crisis – a massive government-led stimulus program – seemed to work far better than the initial response of Europe or America, reinforcing the view that China's distinctive mix of capitalism and authoritarianism offered a superior model than the discredited versions of Western capitalism. All of this took place in the afterglow of the Beijing Olympics – China's carefully choreographed, global coming out party – and in the context of America's apparent inability to manage its economy or to shape global

---

[46] A. Browne and G. Fairclough, "China: Friend or Foe?" *Wall Street Journal*, April 18–19, 2009, pp. W1–W2.

[47] Avery Goldstein, *Rising to the Challenge: China's Grand Strategy and International Security* (Palo Alto, CA: Stanford University Press, 2005).

politics. Bogged down in Iraq and Afghanistan, America could not prevent or even respond credibly to Russia's invasion of Georgia in 2008. For China, peaceful rise began to look like inevitable rise, and perhaps sooner than anyone anticipated. A Brookings Institution report in 2012, co-authored by the influential Chinese thinker Wang Jisi, pointed to key structural changes in the post-financial crisis international system:

the feeling in China that since 2008 the PRC has ascended to be a first-class global power; the assessment that the United States, despite ongoing great strength, is heading for decline; the observation that emerging powers like India, Brazil, Russia and South Africa are increasingly challenging Western dominance and are working more closely with each other and with China in doing so; and the notion that China's development model of a strong political leadership that effectively manages social and economic affairs provides an alternative to Western democracy and market economies to learn from.[48]

So it may not be surprising that against the backdrop of the financial crisis, China succumbed to the temptation and began to act more assertively, on the presumption that global momentum was shifting decisively in its favor. It played what was viewed as an obstructionist role in global climate change negotiations, fought with Google over internet freedom, worked to soften sanctions against Iran, and alarmed its neighbors, including the most powerful one, Japan, by expanding its claims in the South China Sea and elsewhere.[49] A foreign policy of reassurance gave way to one characterized more by assertiveness and swagger.[50]

China's new assertiveness prompted regional anxiety, and in light of that reaction we might expect Chinese leaders eventually to dial back the more provocative tone, just as they did following the 1995–1996 Taiwan crisis. But the damage may already be done in that China's behavior and rhetoric in the aftermath of the financial crisis have re-shaped US perceptions of future China's intentions. Moderates in US foreign policy debates find it harder to sell China as a responsible stake holder, while hardliners feel that their view of China as an eventual revisionist

---

[48] Kenneth Lieberthal and Wang Jisi, *Addressing US-China Strategic Distrust* (Washington, DC: The Brookings Institution, March 2012), pp. vii–viii.

[49] See Thomas Wright, "How China Gambit Backfired," *The Diplomat*, July 28, 2010, and Robert Sutter, "China's Rise, the United States, and Asia's Angst," *PacNet #41*, September 13, 2010.

[50] Foreign policy experts debate whether China was actually more assertive or just perceived as such, and how the United States should respond. See Alastair Iain Johnston, "How New and Assertive is China's New Assertiveness?" *International Security*, Vol. 37, No. 4 (2013), pp. 7–48, and Robert Ross, "The Problem with the Pivot," *Foreign Affairs*, Vol. 91, No. 6 (2012), pp. 70–82.

challenger, one steadily translating its economic into military power and extending its global reach, is being affirmed.[51] Among US defense specialists, the reassuring argument that China has a long way to go to catch up gave way by 2012 to more anxious discussions of China's determination to develop the capacity to deter or frustrate US global interests and actions, for example, by using lasers to blind US satellites or cyberattacks to disrupt military communications. Part of the Pentagon's response, a strategy called Air-Sea Battle designed to prevent adversaries from using anti-access and area-denial (A2/AD) tactics against US forces, alarmed some observers with its potential to spark a destabilizing action-reaction cycle in the event of an East Asian crisis.[52]

It would not surprise Gilpin to find that the United States pushed back in East Asia. It has longstanding economic and security interests in the region – China's immediate neighborhood – and is not prepared to cede regional dominance. It considers itself a resident power in East Asia and the self-appointed stabilizer of crises that erupt periodically in the region. It has allies in the neighborhood who are worried about both China's growing capabilities and changing intentions, and who react by trying to pull the United States more deeply into the region as a defender and balancer. All this is not to say the United States is moving decisively towards "containment," or that China and the United States are entering the equivalent of the Cold War. It is to say that the relative stability in US-China security relations during the era of the grand bargain has given way to greater uncertainty, a higher level of mistrust, and in all likelihood episodes of regional competition and perhaps even brinksmanship as each side probes the other's conception of its vital interests and willingness to defend them.

Gilpin observes in *War and Change* that international order and relations among great powers are most stable when the balance of power in the system matches the balance of prestige.[53] Problems emerge when the balance of prestige no longer accurately reflects the distribution of power. The balance of economic power between the United States and China clearly has shifted over the past 10–15 years. The balance of military power has shifted more slowly. America still enjoys a comfortable lead but after the financial crisis found itself glancing uneasily over its shoulder, wondering if China might figure out how to frustrate America's

---

[51] For example, John Ikenberry, "Rise of China and Future of the West," *Foreign Affairs*, Vol. 87 (Jan–Feb 2008), pp. 23–37, and John Mearsheimer, "China's Unpeaceful Rise," *Current History*, Vol. 105 (April 2006), pp. 160–162.

[52] David Gompert and Terence Kelly, "How the Pentagon's New Strategy Could Trigger War with China," *Foreign Policy*, August 2, 2013, available at: www.foreignpolicy.com.

[53] Gilpin, *War and Change*, p. 33.

projection of power even if China is not quite ready to project regional or global power itself. China's rapid economic growth continued to generate resources that might be devoted to improved military capacity or geopolitical influence, while the United States, still the undisputed global leader in military spending, faced post-crisis pressure to cut all types of government spending, including defense.

China's recent assertiveness may simply be an early sign that it no longer believes that the balance of prestige is commensurate with a gradually shifting balance of power. It is not unreasonable to expect more challenges ahead, as Chinese leaders probe to discern whether and to what extent to push back. Although it is difficult to predict how conflict-prone the US–China relationship may become, it is safe to consider the US hope of locking China down as a compliant stakeholder in a US-centered order a casualty of the crisis and its aftermath.

Winding down the war on terrorism

An additional factor driving US–China security relations in a more competitive direction is the winding down of the more than decade-long US priority commitment to the war on terrorism. That effort both deflected US attention from China's rise, and gave US officials additional incentives to cooperate with China. As the war on terrorism winds down, the attention of US policy makers has shifted emphasis from threats posed by smaller states and non-state actors to the more traditional challenge of managing great-power relations.

The war on terrorism was beneficial to US–China relations in two ways. First, this seemingly new threat from the periphery of the international system prompted US policy makers to seek cooperation and support from other major powers, including China. President Bush, in his first National Security Strategy, went as far as to assert that terrorism was a global challenge that had placed all the major powers "on the same side" in a key battle of good against evil.[54] Conflict among great powers was a thing of the past, having been replaced by a struggle with a new and more elusive adversary that threatened all of them. This line of argument also complemented the Bush Administration view that as a unipolar power the United States no longer faced the challenges from peer competitors that defined earlier eras of international politics.

Second, the war on terror deflected priority US attention from East Asia and Europe to the Persian Gulf and Southwest Asia. America's allies

---

[54] *The National Security Strategy* (Washington, DC: The White House, September 2002), p. 1.

in East Asia openly worried during the 2000s that the United States was a distracted power paying insufficient attention to developments in a rapidly changing region. US officials sought to counter that perception by emphasizing enduring US commitments to the region and the US role, in the words of Defense Secretary Robert Gates, as a "resident power."[55] The fact of the matter of course is that priority attention is necessarily limited and the United States was paying more attention elsewhere. This worked to the benefit of China for the simple reason that someone else (not China!) was the focus of US foreign policy mobilization. The distraction of US attention also meant that the United States was prepared to cede some initiative on regional diplomacy (e.g., the Six-Party Talks), which gave China more opportunities to pursue its own regional strategy of multilateralism and reassurance.

After ten years, the intensity of the US commitment to combating terrorism has waned. In 2011 US combat operations ended in Iraq. The Obama Administration expanded the US commitment to Afghanistan, yet at the same time made clear that for both political and economic reasons it preferred an exit strategy. The United States "led from behind" on Libya, and agonized, even after evidence of chemical weapons use, over whether to become involved militarily in Syria. A second, major terrorist attack on the United States of course could change this trajectory and provide new fuel for the war on terrorism. In the absence of that tragic scenario, however, terrorism is likely to remain an ongoing concern at a lower level of intensity.

The waning of the war on terrorism has coincided with the return of great-power politics. Russia has made clear for some time that it is not a junior partner of the United States, particularly in its own neighborhood and increasingly outside of it. China, more carefully, has signaled the same. As US officials, however reluctantly, recognized this reality, they "pivoted" in the direction of China, not necessarily as an enemy but as the most eligible potential peer competitor.

Conclusion

The era of good feelings between the United States and China is drawing to a close. But does this mean a Gilpin-like hegemonic struggle will ensue, with its attendant risks and dangers? If the analysis of this article is correct, the drama that plays out between these two leading actors on

---

[55] Robert Gates, "Challenges to Stability in the Asia-Pacific," Address at the 7th IISS Asia Security Summit Shangri-La Dialogue, May 31, 2008.

the current international stage is likely to reflect neither the US liberal dream nor the realist nightmare. Liberals envision a cooperative bilateral partnership – a G-2 or its functional equivalent – that jointly provides collective goods to the world economy while solving global problems and maintaining stability among major powers in world politics. This vision presumes that China will grow, but also anticipates that its growth within the existing order will gradually transform China into a supporter rather than a challenger. This vision, however attractive, may be time-bound. It was most plausible when the US and China, for their own good reasons, enjoyed an extraordinary type of mutual dependence economically and pursued complementary and mutually reinforcing, cooperative strategies in the security realm. Moving forward, those conditions are less likely to hold. The hope that China cannot pose a serious challenge to a US-led order because it currently lacks a clear alternative vision fails to appreciate, as the logic of *War and Change* makes clear, that as China's capabilities increase so too will its interests and its conception of how to satisfy them.

The realist nightmare is that of a nasty power transition and new Cold War. But that may be unnecessarily alarmist. Even if economic interdependence between the United States and China is scaled back from the extraordinary grand bargain, it will remain in absolute terms far greater than that which characterized economic relations between the United States and Soviet Union, or between West and East, during the Cold War. A new Cold War would require other states to choose sides and line up behind one or the other dominant powers. But even America's closest security allies in East Asia wish to hedge – they prefer the regional security presence of the United States to balance China, but they also wish to reap the economic benefits of deeper integration with a growing China. Even more important is that the United States and China themselves prefer to hedge. Each prefers bilateral cooperation and especially the economic benefits that accompany it, while preparing quietly but steadily for the possibility of future conflict.

If neither the dream nor nightmare scenario proves plausible, the expectation looking ahead is for a more "normal" great-power relationship characterized by a mix of wary cooperation, competition, and at times significant conflict. The key area of potential conflict is of course East Asia. Like any emerging great power, China wishes to call the shots in its immediate neighborhood, even if it does not go as far as to declare explicitly the Chinese equivalent of a Monroe Doctrine. The United States, however, a longstanding global power with a global grand strategy, is not prepared to accept a secondary role in a region long deemed vital to its own economic and security interests.

Among the most important lessons to derive from *War and Change* is the inevitability of international change. It is understandable that, after the stress and cost of the Cold War, US policy makers would be interested, if not in ending history, at least in freezing it by expanding an order in which all major powers lined up behind it and on the same side. As Gilpin wisely shows, the real challenge of international order is not stifling change, but in finding ways to accommodate it peacefully.

Part III

Systems change and global order

7   Hegemony, nuclear weapons, and liberal hegemony

Daniel Deudney

Introduction

Hegemony, nuclear weapons, and the American liberal order

The topic of hegemony has been of central concern to theorists of world politics at least since Thucydides, many of the leading figures of international theory have written about it, contemporary international theorists are still keenly thinking about it, and, with the relative decline in American power, it seems more relevant than ever. One of the leading works on the topic of hegemony, Robert Gilpin's magisterial *War and Change in World Politics* was published at the end of the tumultuous decade of the 1970s in which it appeared that American power and the American liberal hegemonic order was waning fairly rapidly.

Often overlooked, however, is Gilpin's larger project to understand large-scale and important change in human political life. Gilpin's work on the logic of hegemonic systems, for which he is perhaps best known among IR scholars, was but one part of his larger body of work in which he addressed the range of theories about nuclear weapons, the implications of scientific-technological change for state power, and the ways in which state power and markets were changing in the era of American liberal hegemony and rapid economic "globalization." What unites these works is Gilpin's general quest to understand the interplay between changing material circumstances, particularly ones propelled by technological change, and various forms of political orders, internally and externally, particularly hierarchies and their interplay with more horizontal arrangements, particularly markets. And as an American writing in the American century, Gilpin has been keenly interested in exploring the prospects for the American liberal hegemony and the ways in which this order is like and unlike previous orders which have arisen and declined across history.

Questions and arguments

In this chapter I investigate how the advent of nuclear weapons and nuclear deterrence, and then the prospect of their diffusion, interacts with hegemony in general and the liberal order of the United States in particular. Like American hegemony and its liberal order, nuclear weapons is on the very short list of the major features of world politics. And theorizing about the implications of nuclear weapons for world politics has been at the very center of international theory, particularly for realists. But the extensive literatures on hegemony and on nuclear weapons, both of which realists have done so much to contribute to, if not dominate, have surprisingly little overlap, almost at times as if they were exploring phenomena from different eras rather than one. This chapter seeks to contribute to closing this gap by exploring the ways in which US hegemony might be different in important ways from all previous hegemonies because it has occurred alongside the arrival of nuclear explosives into the human scene.

The question of just what nuclear weapons mean for world politics has been hotly debated since their arrival, but it is nearly universally held that nuclear weapons are "revolutionary" in their implications, and that they raise greatly, perhaps prohibitively, the costs of major great-power war. The fact that nuclear weapons are so widely thought to have importantly shaped world politics over the nearly seven decades of their existence poses the possibility that many of the effects widely attributed to hegemony or to the liberal aspects of American hegemony may in fact be the result of nuclear weapons or nuclear weapons deterrence rather than hegemony. There are several ways in which this might occur. The fact that nuclear weapons as forms of power seem so unlike in important ways previous forms of power also raises the possibility that the concentration of power upon which hegemonies ultimately rest may be importantly different for a hegemon in the nuclear era. And if nuclear weapons do greatly lower the willingness of states to embark upon major wars, what does this entail for the hegemonic succession arguments at the heart of realist theories of hegemony, and the prospects for hegemonic challenges and hegemonic wars? And, looking ahead across the "second nuclear era" marked by the growing possibilities for the risk of their wide diffusion to other actors, even outside the state club, it seems all plausible the implications of nuclear weapons for hegemony will be considerably different from what they were in the "first nuclear age" when they were confined to the possession of only a handful of the leading states.

This chapter advances four main arguments about the relationship between hegemony and nuclear weapons. First, I argue that nuclear weapons profoundly alter power and what it can accomplish, and this has far-reaching and cross-cutting implications for hegemonic political orders that rest on concentrations of power and upon the potential influences of different kinds of power. Following the standard division of power into at least four types (central military balance, conventional forces, economic capacity, and soft power), I argue that if nuclear weapons define the central balance of power, then the current international system cannot be marked by much of a concentration of power. Even further, nuclear deterrence also diminishes the relevance of power distribution, as there is strong logic and evidence to suggest that and nuclear weapons largely paralyze the first two types of power, robbing concentrations of these types of power of much of the influence that states in pre-nuclear times derived from them. At the same time, there are reasons to think that nuclear weapons as war deterrents may unexpectedly enhance the potential influences of economic power and soft power in ways that are particularly favorable to a hegemonic state, such as the United States, that is also liberal and capitalist.

Second, I argue that nuclear weapons as war deterrents greatly decrease the likelihood of several well-known syndromes of hegemonic power concentration (encroachment and counterbalancing, overextension, and hegemonic transitions). If nuclear weapons deter major war, then they significantly mitigate many of the power political patterns inimical or subversive of hegemony based on concentrated power. While hegemonic states in the nuclear age may be less able to influence or coerce than in pre-nuclear times, they are also spared many of the costs and risks and problems traditionally associated with hegemony. In short, a hegemonic state in the nuclear era cannot do some things they used to do, but they do not have many of the things that were ultimately most difficult for them to do. This also suggests that the durability of American hegemony is likely to be much higher than many hegemonic theorists believe, not because of any liberal feature of this order, but rather due to the simple historical accident that the United States achieved its hegemonic position just as nuclear weapons came on the scene, effectively making the path to hegemonic challenge much more difficult. Furthermore, if nuclear weapons are broadly effective in preventing great-power war, then the prospects of the broad liberalization of states are improved, suggesting that the expansion of democratic states across the nuclear era may in part be the result of the nuclear peace, and less the result of the many other factors that theorists use to explain the spread of democracy.

Third and fourth, I argue that there are several important ways in which nuclear proliferation and nuclear terrorism alter the relationship between nuclear weapons and hegemony, and particularly the American liberal hegemony. The key feature of the emerging "second nuclear era" is that deterrence failure is much more likely than during the Cold War. The implications of these trends and possibilities for a hegemonic state that is also liberal and capitalist are mixed, but largely negative. Proliferation is likely to further reduce the leverage and raise the costs of American military influence. Potential leakage of nuclear capability to non-state actors is likely to be even more damaging to the position of a hegemonic state, particularly a liberal hegemonic unipolar state such as the United States. But containment of this threat may be possible, and could be facilitated by the liberal character of the American hegemonic state and its liberal order.

This chapter proceeds in four main steps. The first part of the chapter surveys and summarizes theories of nuclear weapons and of hegemony. The second part looks in detail at what the apparently distinctive features of nuclear weapons as forms of power mean for the concentrations of power that hegemonies are understood to rest upon. The third part explores the ways in which nuclear weapons as deterrents of great-power war may effect the various syndromes of power transitions and hegemonic successions, and the prospects for hegemonic war. And the fourth and fifth parts extend the investigation of the relations between hegemony and nuclear weapons into the emerging "second nuclear age."

Theories of nuclear weapons and theories of hegemony

Gilpin does not extensively consider nuclear weapons in *War and Change*, but he does offer reflections on them and their implications in the closing pages of the book. Gilpin's closing thoughts are different in style and tone from the rest of his book. Here Gilpin nervously worries about whether the overall patterns he identifies in the historical interstate system will tragically precipitate a cataclysmic nuclear war that could destroy civilization and perhaps humanity.[1] He perceives the age-old pattern of hegemonic rise and fall, and challenge and thus a real threat of war in the Cold War rivalry between the United States and the Soviet Union. But he is very anxious that the vast destructiveness of nuclear weapons, combined with the hegemonic dynamics he is sure will continue to operate, will produce a civilizational catastrophe. He is anxious that deterrence could fail, but he makes no reference to arms control, and never mentions it as holding promise or importance. Gilpin's anxieties are those of a traditional realist pessimist, a general posture that pervades all of his writings.

---

[1] Robert Gilpin, *War and Change in World Politics* (Cambridge University Press, 1982).

Gilpin's "realist pessimism" about nuclear weapons differs in basic ways from the two views of the nuclear revolution that are most extensively developed and held by IR theorists and security analysts. Nuclear weapons are a relatively recent part of international politics, theorizing about them has gone on for well under a century, and many of the most important questions remain very contested. And an extremely diverse array of claims about nuclear weapons and world politics have been advanced, and there are fundamental epistemological problems in actually proving the superiority of one position over another.[2] Despite these problems a great majority of nuclear theory and thought is in two clusters. The first view, centered around deterrence, holds that the prospects for nuclear war are very low, simply because nuclear use would be so catastrophic. The proposition that nuclear weapons deter conflicts by vastly raising the cost of war is both theoretically robust and widely held. According to this view, nuclear deterrence has made international politics much more peaceful than in pre-nuclear times. In this view nuclear weapons profoundly alter the incentives of states to use military force, and particularly their paramount military force, to achieve political effects.[3] Nuclear weapons are so destructive that they readily deter attacks. Thus the revolutionary destructiveness of nuclear weapons also revolutionizes the relations among states with regard to war-making, and this is the "nuclear revolution." This view thus provides a very optimistic reading of the relationship between the state system and nuclear weapons, and one which makes the pursuit of significant international institutional change unnecessary.

The second view also holds that deterrence has greatly reduced the likelihood of war, but also holds that the prospects for the failure of deterrence are sufficiently high to require significant arms control measures between states. These measures, if fully implemented, would entail both great alterations in the practices and structures of states, as well as of

---

[2] This assumption that nuclear deterrence has brought about a system change comes, however, with an important caveat, because it is also widely recognized that the arguments about both deterrence and arms control rest on thin empirical ground. Great-power war has not occurred in the nuclear era, but it is impossible to say with high confidence that this non-event results from the presence of nuclear weapons or from some other source, or combination of sources. Indeed, arguably the two most important questions about nuclear weapons (How likely is deterrence failure? What will happen after nuclear use?) are unanswerable with any assurance. The detonation of nuclear weapons would shatter the deterrence consensus, and possibly catalyze far-reaching changes in international order. Given these uncertainties, theorizing about the political effects of nuclear weapons has an inescapably provisional character.

[3] Influential statements and versions of this position have been made by Bernard Brodie, Robert Jervis, and Kenneth Waltz. Kenneth Waltz, "Nuclear Myths and Political Realities," *American Political Science Review*, Vol. 84, No. 3 (September 1990), pp. 731–744.

international anarchy. This view, which is not treated as seriously as it should be by the proponents of the first view, holds that the combination of hierarchical states, interstate anarchy, and nuclear weapons is a security system prone to potentially catastrophic failure. Advocates of this view look at the empirical history of the nuclear confrontation during the US-Soviet Cold War and see several near misses, most notably the Cuban missile crisis of 1962. They also point to the many leaders of nuclear states who, contrary to the confidence and optimism which deterrence alone should inspire, have made very strong statements to the effect that a nuclear-armed anarchy poses an unacceptably high level of risks. Advocates of this view also point out the important, but still significantly incomplete, ways in which minor and major arms control treaties, stretching from the 1950s to the present, have contributed to security. And they also look to the ways in which the end of the Cold War and the erection of a settlement giving unprecedented centrality to arms control took place in significant measure because of the influences of the global nuclear arms control movement, and the extremely strong anti-nuclear views held by Gorbachev and Reagan, views which were far outside the conventional deterrence-centered view of the security requirements of the nuclear age. This view is thus pessimistic about the relationship between nuclear weapons and the state system, and in effect holds that the nuclear revolution has only partially occurred.

Thus, exploring in the pages ahead the relationships between nuclear weapons and hegemony and liberal hegemony must involve both of the competing readings of the implications of nuclear weapons for world politics. In the first two parts, in thinking about the implications of nuclear weapons for power concentrations and hegemonic dynamics, I will mainly employ the deterrence view. But in the third and fourth arguments, I will give the arms control reading of the nuclear problem greater attention.

Gilpin's theory about hegemonic change is what he refers to as a "systemic" change in contrast to "system" and "process" grades of change. Gilpin's definition of "system" change is a change in the basic character of the units, and he identifies city-state, nation-state, and empire as the three main types of units.[4] In contrast, most IR theorists understand system change to entail either changes in the density and character of interactions and interdependence, or change in the "structure" of the system, understood typically as a move beyond anarchy. Both those who view the nuclear revolution as having already occurred

---

[4] Gilpin, *War and Change in World Politics.*

(due to deterrence), and those who believe it has occurred only incompletely (due to the partial completion of the nuclear arms control project) are advancing what should be seen as claims about "system" change.

Theories of hegemony

Theorizing hegemony and power concentrations has been occurring for centuries, but consensus on this topic has been elusive, despite the apparent abundance of the empirical historical record. Speaking broadly, theorists of hegemony split into three main camps. First are those realists who believe hegemony and power concentrations in international systems are rare and "unnatural," likely to produce encroachment and counterbalancing, and thus not last very long.[5] Second are those realists who see concentrations of power as both historically widespread and intrinsically prone to stability and durability.[6] Thus there are two main branches of realist theory, one seeing balances and counterbalancing as typical of stable and durable international orders, with the other seeing stable and durable order (both internally and externally) arising from concentrations of power.[7] A third position, more recently developed, claims contemporary hegemony is stable in large part because of the liberal and capitalist character of the American hegemon, and the various restraints and incentives for restraint produced by the liberal aspects of the international system.[8] In this view, significant counterbalancing against the unipolar state is less likely due to the self-restraint of the liberal unipolar state, as well as the restraining features of its liberal hegemonic system.

Power assessment, hegemony, and nuclear weapons

At first glance assessing the relationship between nuclear weapons and hegemony seems quite straightforward. Hegemony requires a distribution of power in which power is relatively concentrated. This is to say that

---

[5] Kenneth N. Waltz, "The Emerging Structure of International Politics," *International Security*, Vol. 18, No.2 (Fall 1993), pp. 44–79; and Stephen M. Walt, *Taming American Power: The Global Response to US Primacy* (New York, NY: Norton, 2005).

[6] William C. Wohlforth, "The Stability of a Unipolar World," *International Security*, Vol. 24, No. 1 (Summer 1999), pp. 5–41; and Stephen G. Brooks and William C. Wohlforth, *World Out of Balance: International Relations and the Challenge of American Primacy* (Princeton University Press, 2008).

[7] For historical cases of the failure of balancing and presence of preponderance, see Stuart J. Kaufman, Richard Little, and William C. Wohlforth, eds., *The Balance of Power in World History* (London: Palgrave, 2007).

[8] G. John Ikenberry, *After Victory: Institutions, Strategic Restraint, and the Rebuilding of Order after Major Wars* (Princeton University Press, 2001); and G. John Ikenberry, *Liberal Order and Imperial Ambition* (Cambridge: Polity, 2006).

a state is hegemonic when there is something approximating a unipolar distribution of power. Thus the United States is said to have been hegemonic in the Western subsystem during the Cold War, and in the global system after the Cold War because in both these situations, the United States had a distinct preponderance of power. Nuclear weapons are power assets, and so their distribution should be readily measured and assessed as part of the general distribution of power. However, this type of calculation essentially obscures or ignores the main effect of nuclear weapons, as understood by the deterrence revolution view of nuclear weapons: their tendency to paralyze their possessors from recourse both to nuclear arms as well as use of non-nuclear arms which might lead to the use of nuclear arms.

Power analysis and nuclear weapons

If nuclear weapons do provide such a ready and robust ability to deter at least major war among great-power states equipped with nuclear weapons, can the system be usefully characterized as having significant polarity? If the deterrence argument is correct, then it is doubtful that the system is actually and meaningfully characterized as polar. Polarity is about power and nuclear weapons change the implications of power for politics. In some ways, nuclear weapons are power, indeed a paramount form of power. But in other ways they greatly inhibit the expression of power. Assuming they mainly deter war, nuclear weapons greatly diminish the ability of power to do what power has traditionally done, namely achieve outcomes, and particularly military outcomes, favorable to more powerful states.

The distribution of power has traditionally been viewed as very relevant in explaining what states would tend to do, because power distribution is thought to be an indicator of what states could do. States mobilize and deploy power assets in order to achieve their objectives in conflicts with other states. States with relatively more power can be expected to achieve relatively more of their objectives than states with relatively less power. Power thus matters because it shapes outcomes and the overall distribution of power among states roughly determines which outcomes occur. To say "power" is to imply use of power, and nuclear weapons as war deterrents render nuclear power unusable. Thus, if nuclear weapons significantly deter war, then their implications for the meaning of hegemony and unipolarity are potentially very far-reaching. Nuclear deterrence robs a unipolar state of what in the pre-nuclear era would have been the reasonably expected fruits of its relative power over other states.

Relative power and concentrations of power traditionally mattered because they indicated a particular balance or configuration of capacity to do something of importance. However, the presence of nuclear weapons makes the balance of power very much unlike the pre-nuclear pattern. Nuclear weapons make the *balance* of power between nuclear-armed states so robust that *balancing* ceases to matter much (except perhaps in a very dangerous way). Nuclear weapons, by making states secure against direct military encroachment and aggression, solve the problem that balancing was previously relied upon to address. In pre-nuclear times, balancing to achieve security from aggression was necessary, often difficult, and sometimes impossible. In the nuclear era, the balance is so robust that strenuous balancing is largely unnecessary.

In order to gain a fuller appreciation of the extent and limits of the paralytic effects of nuclear deterrence on the potential political influence of a hegemonic state, it is useful to employ a rough list of the major components of power. Broadly speaking, there are at least four contemporary categories of power assets: (1) central nuclear military forces; (2) non-nuclear conventional forces (land, naval, air) and their various supports; (3) economic assets, necessary for generating and sustaining military force structures, as well as directly potentially influential; and (4) a significant but conceptually ill-defined category of soft power assets such as culture, ideological appeal, and prestige.[9]

Given these distinctions, there are four main questions, each about a type of power asset, and each addressed in a subsequent section. First, what are the implications for unipolarity of the deterrence revolution view that Type 1 power assets are paralyzed by nuclear deterrence? Second, to what degree does the shadow of the paralysis and war avoidance produced by nuclear weapons in Type 1 shadow or spill over into the realm of Type 2 (conventional forces) power assets? Third, what is the relationship between nuclear capabilities and Type 3 (economic capacity) power assets? And fourth, what are the effects of nuclear weapons on the exercise of Type 4 (soft power) assets?

The nuclear military balance, polarity, and hegemony

The central military balance has historically been accorded top status in power calculations because of the role such assets play in shaping war

[9] Ashley Tellis, Janice Bially, Christopher Layne, and Melissa McPherson, *Measuring National Power in the Postindustrial Age* (Santa Monica, CA: RAND Arroyo Center, 2000); and Richard J. Stoll and Michael Ward, eds., *Power in World Politics* (Boulder, CO: Lynne Rienner, 1989).

outcomes, which in turn frequently decisively shaped the survival and security of states. This fact justifies ranking these power assets at the top of the list. The central military balance is composed of actually existing military capacities, roughly measured as an aggregate of paramount weaponry and aggregate military expenditures. The other assets of state power also matter in part because of their potential contribution to the central military balance, and thus the survival and security of states. Historically, the entire calculus of power analysis is centered on military capacity, and the factors that shape the ability to generate military capacity. Thus factors such as the size of a state's economy, the size of its population, and its organizational capacity matter because they are indicators of the overall military capacity which a state could generate to make war.

Scholars making military power assessments acknowledge that their enterprise has ambiguities and uncertainties, and inevitably involves "comparing apples and oranges," the aggregation of at least partially qualitatively incommensurate assets and capabilities. How many triremes equal how many hoplites? How many battleships equal how many tanks? Acknowledging these difficulties, analysts of the military balance of power routinely place more weight on larger military violence capabilities than smaller ones. For example, an analysis of the balance between Germany, France, and Britain in 1914 would acknowledge the difficulty of weighing battleships against army divisions, but would center on the distribution of battleships more than destroyers, and on heavy artillery more than machine guns. Better armed and trained divisions of ground forces are weighed more heavily than less armed and trained ones. The basic counting rule is "more bang, more weight." This rough basic counting rule had the added feature that the more capable ("more bang") cost roughly proportionately more than the less capable. Battleships not only did more than destroyers, they also cost roughly proportionately more.

Nuclear weapons are, and are nearly universally recognized to be, the paramount destructive capability deployed by states since the end of the Second World War. It is the vastness of their destructive power that seems to make them "absolute" and this is the source of their being widely seen as having "revolutionary" implications for interstate relations.[10] The one bomb dropped on Hiroshima by one bomber was as

---

[10] Bernard Brodie, "War in the Atomic Age," and "Implications for Military Strategy," in Brodie, ed., *The Absolute Weapon: Atomic Power and World Order* (New York, NY: Harcourt, Brace & Co., 1946); Robert Jervis, *The Meaning of the Nuclear Revolution: Statecraft and the Prospect of Armageddon* (Ithaca, NY: Cornell University Press, 1989); and Patrick M. Morgan, *Deterrence Now* (Cambridge University Press, 2003).

destructive as the many thousands of conventional high explosive bombs previously dropped on Tokyo by hundreds of bombers. For the first half century of the nuclear era, the strategic balance between the United States and the Soviet Union, a topic of intense and continuous concern for both states, was centered on nuclear weapons and the various systems to deliver them.

Given this very traditionally realist view of the paramount role of deployed military force, what happens to assessment of the system's polarity if nuclear weapons and the balance of nuclear forces are put into the center of calculus? The answer, of course, is that the current supposedly American hegemonic system is not plausibly classified as having anything approaching a unipolar distribution of power.[11] If nuclear weapons matter as much as the nuclear revolution hypothesis asserts, then putting the nuclear assets of the central military balance at the center of calculations of system polarity would seem warranted. But with such a move, the system does not look unipolar. The United States does have the most extensive and capable nuclear arsenal, but Russia is not far behind. Russia (inheriting most of the nuclear arsenal of the Soviet Union), possesses nuclear forces capable of rapidly obliterating the United States.

Russia's nuclear forces are less extensive than the Soviet Union's. The broad scope of Russian decline has severely hobbled Russia's ability to sustain a full spectrum military competition with the United States, but it has not appreciably reduced the ability of Russia to obliterate the United States. The large decreases in Russian conventional forces, economic output, population size, organizational capability, and territorial size have not been the main cause of the decline in Russia's nuclear forces since the end of the Cold War.[12] The decline in Russian strategic forces since the collapse of the Soviet Union has resulted from mutually agreed upon arms control and disarmament agreements that were central parts of the settlement of the Cold War.

The fact that the most decisive violence capacity in the international system is distributed in this bipolar pattern poses severe limits on viewing the system as unipolar. Furthermore, this characterization of the system

---

[11] Some maintain that the United States has usable nuclear superiority as well, but only within the very circumscribed scenario of a "bolt from the blue" attack. Kier A. Lieber and Daryl G. Press, "The End of MAD? The Nuclear Dimension of U.S. Primacy," *International Security*, Vol. 30, No. 4 (Spring 2006), pp. 7–44. For the difficulties associated with the brief period of American nuclear monopoly, see George Quester, *Nuclear Monopoly* (New Brunswick, NJ: Transaction, 2000).
[12] William E. Odom, *The Collapse of the Soviet Military* (New Haven, CT: Yale University Press, 1998).

as bipolar may overstate the degree of concentration. Secondary great powers with nuclear weapons (China, Britain, and France) have enough deployed nuclear capability to wreck catastrophic damage on other major states, suggesting that the system is, at least in this important regard, multipolar.[13]

Conventional military forces, nuclear deterrence, and hegemonic power

Nuclear weapons dominate and paralyze the central military balance, but they certainly are not the only military power asset that matters. The prominent and well-developed argument of Brooks and Wohlforth that the system is unipolar in ways that matter, essentially concedes that nuclear weapons have a paralytic effect on great-power war, but still thinks that asymmetries in other military capacities, and the concentration of non-nuclear conventional forces, provide their possessor (the United States) significant sources of influence on international political outcomes. This argument assumes, however, that there is not a significant paralytic "shadow" or "spillover" from the nuclear to the non-nuclear realm. To what degree do nuclear weapons as war inhibiters also inhibit the use of conventional forces?

The question of the relationship between nuclear and conventional forces was a topic of extreme interest during the Cold War. The United States and Soviet Union at least partially behaved as if they thought that both nuclear *and* conventional forces had major roles to play, as evidenced by the vast conventional forces they deployed, at an economic cost that considerably exceeded the cost of their strategic nuclear forces. Yet at the same time, both the United States and the Soviet Union also behaved as if they believed that nuclear weapons provided a major paralyzing effect on the willingness to use conventional forces. Both did use their vast conventional forces in a number of wars, invasions, and interventions (Korea, Hungary, Vietnam, and Afghanistan). During this period many other states, including the other nuclear weapon states, also used conventional forces on several occasions. Overall, however, the superpowers seemed to exercise extreme caution in employing their conventional forces against each other, or close allies. While both the United States and the Soviet Union seemed to partially view conventional forces as substitutes or supplements for nuclear forces, they also

---

[13] For the deterrence capabilities of secondary nuclear powers, see Avery Goldstein, *Deterrence and Security in the 21st Century: China, Britain, and Enduring Legacy of the Nuclear Revolution* (Palo Alto, CA: Stanford University Press, 2000).

seemed to view a clash of conventional forces against each other (or core allies) as a very dangerous precursor to a nuclear exchange that could readily escalate into a catastrophic general war of unprecedented destructiveness. Given these stakes, both the United States and the Soviet Union took extreme caution to avoid clashes of conventional arms.[14] Thus, generalizing from the Cold War experience of the United States and the Soviet Union seems strongly to support the claim that there is (or at least was) a significant shadow or spillover of paralysis from the nuclear to the conventional realm. This conclusion must be partly provisional because of the small number of actors in play, and the possibility that these inhibiting effects of nuclear weapons might have been lesser or greater with different actors.

But what is the relationship between nuclear weapons and conventional forces after the Cold War? The basic logic of the argument for a nuclear shadow of paralysis on conventional forces should also largely apply after the Cold War. States with nuclear weapons, whatever their other asymmetries of capability, can be expected to be extremely cautious in employing conventional forces in ways that significantly risk clashes with the conventional forces of other nuclear weapons states. If this continuity is present then the use of conventional forces is unlikely in a great many of the possible combinations of potentially clashing states. This means that for a wide range of contemporary interstate relations the nuclear shadow makes improbable the exercise of conventional military force to achieve political outcomes.

What potential for influence does this leave for conventional forces that is not substantially inhibited by the nuclear shadow? The record of US foreign and military policy since the end of the Cold War is in its main features a continuation of many of the patterns of the Cold War and before, but with far less inhibition. The United States has pronounced advantages in conventional forces, particularly in the logistical capacities to sustain military activities with global reach.[15] The United States has repeatedly used its conventional forces against a variety of non-nuclear weapons states (Persian Gulf War, Bosnia, Haiti, Somalia, Kosovo, Iraq War, Afghanistan). Fear of escalation to nuclear use has largely been absent in these cases. These uses of conventional forces have been a significant feature of overall US foreign policy since the end of the Cold

---

[14] Part of the reason for this caution was the intermingling of conventional and nuclear forces, analyzed in Barry R. Posen, *Inadvertent Escalation: Conventional War and Nuclear Risks* (Ithaca, NY: Cornell University Press, 1991).

[15] Barry Buzan, *The United States and the Great Powers: World Politics in the Twenty-First Century* (Cambridge: Polity, 2004).

War. Several of these interventions and wars employed substantial portions of total US conventional forces, absorbed significant leadership attention and diplomatic energy, and sometimes imposed major economic costs.[16] Given all of this, it is clear that the inhibiting effect of nuclear weapons on conventional forces is far from complete. The United States behaves as if it believes it can employ conventional forces to gain its preferred outcomes with minimal risk to its core security interests. However, it is notable that the United States has not used its conventional forces against any state with nuclear weapons or against the close ally of any state with nuclear weapons. This suggests that either conventional forces remain substantially inhibited by the possibility of nuclear use and escalation, or perhaps that conflicts with other nuclear weapon states have simply not arisen.

However, within the fuller historical spectrum of the use of military capability for political gains, these conventional military activities of the United States in the post-Cold War era do not look very impressive or significant. None of them really touched upon core American national interests, or even the core national interests of significant American allies (with the possible exceptions of Kuwait for Saudi Arabia, and Iraq for Israel). Although vastly destructive by the standards of historical policing activities by great powers, these American uses of its conventional forces are best viewed as policing activities because of their limited aims and in their marginal role in shaping international politics. Also, there are serious doubts as to whether these US efforts accomplished very much compared to their direct and indirect costs.

Economic hegemony, nuclear weapons, and liberal-capitalist hegemony

Economic capabilities are next on the list of the power assets weighed in calculating the international balance of power and polarity. Historically, economic capacity has been a powerful indicator of potential military capacity. Particularly during the long modern era in which the military and naval employment of gunpowder weaponry (across successive technological iterations) has been militarily paramount, economic capabilities to produce and sustain capital- and technology-intensive warfare have tightly linked military power potential to overall economic capability.[17]

---

[16] Derek Chollet and James Goldgeier, *America Between the Wars* (New York, NY: Public Affairs, 2008).

[17] William McNeill, *The Pursuit of Power: Technology, Armed Force, and Society, AD 1000–1945* (University of Chicago Press, 1982).

In the nuclear era, however, the relationship between economic power and the ability of state access to violence capacity has changed in significant ways. The key fact is that nuclear weapons are, relative to the violence capacity they provide, very cheap. Although nuclear weapons are relatively inexpensive, they are still beyond the reach of many poor states in the international system. But they are still readily available to a very large number of states, most of whom have chosen not to actually acquire them. Because the nuclear world is so power access abundant, variations in economic capacity have a diminished role as a restraint on the acquisition of the paramount violence capacity in the system.

The case for the contemporary existence of a concentration of power that still shapes important international political outcomes rests significantly upon claims about the impacts of relative economic power. The case for the United States being the current unipolar state rests heavily on the claim that the United States possesses a substantial concentration of economic power. While the United States is seen as having a balanced portfolio of power assets compared to major potential competitors, its economic assets are central to its abilities to influence significant political outcomes. The overall US economic position is one of slow relative decline, but nevertheless it is still quite far ahead economically, and appears to be even more so when per capita averages are factored in. The second-largest economy, Japan (closely followed or roughly equaled by China), is less than half the aggregate size of the American economy. Whatever is going on with regard to the strategic military balance of major deployed capital weapons, the United States can reasonably be said to have something approaching economic unipolarity in the current system. On the other hand, the high levels of public and private debt diminish the ability of the United States (and many of its main allies) to derive influence from its relatively preponderant economic capabilities.

Does American economic superiority matter as much in the nuclear world as in the pre-nuclear modern state system? Certainly economic assets still matter in a variety of important ways, both directly and indirectly. Economic assets can be used to induce other states to produce political or other outcomes to the interests of the wealthier state. Conventional military forces, whatever the degree of inhibition produced by nuclear weapons, remain expensive, particularly at the upper end of capabilities (naval and air and heavy ground forces).

Overall, however, the relative cheapness of nuclear weapons limits the advantages of economic superiority. The key fact is that the costs of achieving robust nuclear deterrence capability are low in comparison to the overall wealth of a very large number of states in the international system. States have, of course, demonstrated widely variable abilities to extract and mobilize economic resources and convert them into actual military capability. Sometimes states are woefully constrained in this effort, typically for some domestic reason, and sometimes have suffered severely as a result. But a great many modern states have demonstrated the ability to mobilize and deploy a substantial fraction of their aggregate economic output on military expenditures, and much more for shorter periods of time.

In short, aggregate economic output calculations are importantly misleading with regard to military power potential because they fail adequately to take into account how relatively little nuclear weapons and their various support systems cost as a share of overall military expenditure and national wealth. Starting at the top, the United States and Russia (as the core of the Soviet Union), the two most nuclear capable states, have over the course of the six decades of the nuclear era spent enormous aggregate amounts on nuclear weapons.[18] This expenditure has produced quantities of nuclear weapons, nuclear materials, and support capabilities with astoundingly large destructive capabilities. But this staggeringly destructive power has been purchased by a relatively small share of their military expenditures and national wealth. Over the course of the Cold War, these two states have spent about 10% of their military expenditure on nuclear weapons and their support systems. For these two states, there has been a significant de-coupling of the indicators of general asset power analysis and the achievement of very robust nuclear forces.

Further evidence for this de-coupling of economic and nuclear military potential is found in the less powerful states with nuclear weapons. There are now thought to be nine states with nuclear weapons (United States, Russia, United Kingdom, France, China, Israel, India, Pakistan, and North Korea). At the top of the list are many (but not all) of the leading states in economic output. However, Germany, Japan, and Brazil have large economies but no nuclear weapons. But the states at the bottom of the list are quite different. Several of them are extremely small, poor, and weak by the indicators of general asset power analysis. Looking at the lower end of the spectrum, Israel has a tiny population (well under ten million), and a modest aggregate GDP, but has acquired several hundred nuclear weapons, a force capable of essentially obliterating the other

---

[18] For the American effort, see Stephen I. Schwartz, ed., *Atomic Audit: The Costs and Consequences of US Nuclear Weapons since 1940* (Washington, DC: Brookings Institution, 1998).

states in its regional state system.[19] Similarly, Pakistan is very poor, cannot even exercise control over large parts of its territory, but has fielded a potent nuclear arsenal.

Ideological hegemony, liberal hegemony, and nuclear weapons

Finally, what is the relationship between nuclear weapons and Type 4, soft power, or ideological power, and its operation in a hegemonic system in which the paralytic effects of nuclear weapons loom so large? At first glance the connections between the nuclear world and the exercise of soft power would seem to be negligible, and little attention has been paid to this relationship.[20]

Prestige provides one possible link between nuclear weapons and soft power. Traditional realist analysis of power relations (recently extended by realists influenced by conventional approaches) holds that states seek various advantages from reputation and prestige, and so do things to enhance their prestige and reputation.[21] Nuclear weapons, being paramount destructive capabilities, might thus be seen as providing their possessors with advantages of prestige that are independent of their actual use. France would appear to be a prominent example of a state which gains, or at least thinks it gains, status advantages from the possession of nuclear weapons. With its great-power position institutionalized as one of the five permanent and veto-bearing members of the United Nations Security Council, France can plausibly view possession of nuclear military forces as vital for sustaining its great-power role and status. Yet at the same time, other major states that forego nuclear acquisition may also be seen as gaining status and prestige advantages of a different kind. Japan and Germany may be the leading examples of such states. Prestige exists in the minds of observers, and what is viewed as prestigious may be highly variable, and subject to change. Overall, this possible link between nuclear weapons and status and soft power is difficult to assess, but does not seem to be particularly significant.

---

[19] For a description of Israel's nuclear capabilities and their origins, see Seymour M. Hersh, *The Samson Option: Israel's Nuclear Arsenal and American Foreign Policy* (New York, NY: Random House, 1991).

[20] For this concept, see Joseph Nye, *Soft Power: The Means to Success in World Politics* (New York, NY: Public Affairs, 2004).

[21] For a strong statement of the relevance of prestige, see William C. Wohlforth, "Unipolarity, Power Competition, and Great Power War," in G. John Ikenberry, Michael Mastanduno, and William C. Wohlforth, eds., *International Relations Theory and the Consequences of Unipolarity* (Cambridge University Press, 2011).

However, there may be another link, overlooked and unexpected, between nuclear weapons and both economic power and forms of soft power. If nuclear weapons do paralyze and restrain the use of military power among states, and Great Powers in particular, then there may be reasons why economic power and soft power assets might be *more effective* than in previous international systems. If nuclear weapons extensively paralyze the use of military capabilities measured against historical patterns, then most states in the international system are secure in their pursuit of the historically core national interests of physical survival and political independence. A world with nuclear weapons raises the costs of conquest to inhibiting degrees and so states of lesser overall capabilities are more secure than they were in pre-nuclear times. States which in the past would have been subject to significant military attack and conquest enjoy an unprecedented degree of easy security.

A world of states secure in this traditionally very central way might be one in which states are much more willing to open themselves to the various types of outside influence and suasion that in the past they would have reasonably associated with positions of vulnerability that could be exploited to the detriment of their core security interests. In this secured world, states are not driven by core security interests to strenuously avoid political, economic, or cultural influences from more powerful states. Outside influences no longer jeopardize their core security influences, and so they can decide to open themselves to such influences. Allowing outsiders to wield influence is no longer a sign of weakness jeopardizing security. Outside influence does not have to be viewed as a bridgehead for a potential "fifth column" that could be employed by a more powerful state to weaken and divide. Secure states can also accept extensive levels of economic interdependence without fear that asymmetries of interdependence might be exploited in ways inimical to survival and independence.

In short, a world secured by the effects of nuclear paralysis of war making is likely to favor a more liberal international order marked by various forms of openness to outside political, economic, and cultural influences. Of course, this sort of multi-sided openness, interdependence, and penetration is widely viewed as a hallmark of the contemporary American liberal project and system. Theorists and advocates of the contemporary liberal international order emphasize the American interest and role in exporting and promoting a package of political, economic, and cultural forms. They also emphasize the great absolute gains (particularly in wealth) that states in such arrangements can reap in the contemporary world. If nuclear weapons do make states secure, and if this security lowers fears of security losses from openness, interdependence, and penetration, then the overall liberal project may be much easier to realize in a world with nuclear weapons. This suggests that the character of world politics may be appreciably more liberal due to these indirect effects of nuclear weapons. Furthermore, because the contemporary unipolar state is also particularly liberal, the paralytic effects of nuclear weapons may make the exercise of American soft power hegemony much easier than it would have been (or was) in the pre-nuclear era of insecure states.

In sum, nuclear weapons may be simultaneously weakening and enhancing the ability of a hegemonic state to shape international outcomes, making for a world in which the main traditional vectors of power (in central strategic balance, conventional balance, and economic foundations of the central strategic balance) in their ability to shape outcomes is diminished at the same time that soft power can be more effective than ever before.

Liberal hegemony and the arms control project

Another dimension of the relationship between liberal hegemony and nuclear weapons is the relationship between the arms control project and liberal hegemony. As we saw earlier, the view of the nuclear revolution centered around deterrence accords little importance to arms control. Conversely, its main rival view of the nuclear revolution holds that nuclear arms control is vital for achieving security in the nuclear era, and that the extensive, but incomplete, nuclear arms control that has occurred has made an important contribution to security. If this second view is correct, then the role of the liberal character of the United States and its relationship to nuclear arms control may be of very great importance. The United States has never pursued a grand strategy which was solely focused on advancing nuclear arms control, and many measures pursued by the United States were quite contrary to the arms control agenda. But it also seems clear that the United States has been more significantly supportive of the arms control project than any other major state in the nuclear era, and that the arms control project has deep links to the general liberal character of the American hegemony. If nuclear arms control has, as its advocates maintain, lowered significantly the likelihood of deterrence failure and general war, and if the United States has made such significant contributions to international arms control because of its significantly liberal character, then the fact that the hegemon during this period was a liberal state has made a significant, perhaps crucial, contribution to the avoidance of nuclear war and civilizational collapse.

Hegemonic systemic change and nuclear weapons

Theorists of international politics have also advanced a cluster of arguments about how they expect hegemonic states with power preponderance to interact with the other states in the system. These expectations about hegemonic states and their orders are several, and in disagreement. Four clusters of argument are most important. First, some theorists, building on a long line of balance of power theory, argue that a preponderant hegemonic state will tend to encroach (or be seen as threatening to encroach) upon the interests of other states. These balance of power theories suggest that encroachment, both actual and prospective, will stimulate various counterbalancing actions against the paramount state. Second, building on a long line of theory about hegemonic orders, other realist theorists, among them Gilpin, argue that a hegemonic state will tend to become overextended. Eventually overextension is expected to undermine the foundations of its hegemonic position. Third, a related body of theory about power transitions argues that inevitable changes (from many sources) in the relative power of states will trigger systemic power transitions in which a rising power comes to displace, or attempts to displace, the previously dominant state. The expectations of all three of these power-centered clusters of argument are all largely pessimistic about the prospects for peaceful international orders and the persistence of hegemonic orders. A fourth body of argument, very different in its expectations, argues that the contemporary American hegemony, due to several of its liberal features, is less likely to encroach and trigger counterbalancing, less likely to suffer from debilitating overextension, and less likely to be subject to hegemonic challengers.

Nuclear weapons as war deterrents have significant, but very different, implications for all four of these claims about unipolar concentrations of power. Nuclear weapons greatly diminish all the problems or syndromes traditionally associated with concentrations of power in international politics. Nuclear weapons reduce the likelihood that hegemonic states will trigger counterbalancing. Nuclear weapons reduce the likelihood that a hegemonic state will become overextended. Nuclear weapons also reduce the likelihood that hegemonic states will be subject to violent challenges and transitions stemming from relative power shifts. But if nuclear weapons provide such benefits to the hegemonic state, it may also be the case that deterrence provides at least some of the international stability that theorists attribute to the liberal theorist features of the American hegemon and its international order.

Encroachment, counterbalancing, and nuclear weapons

For theories of international equilibrium, the existence of a hegemonic and unipolar concentration is an unnatural, and likely to be a temporary, occurrence. This variant of balance of power theory, most developed over the course of the modern European and modern global state system, anticipates that a state which has a relative concentration of power over other potential rival states will come to be seen, simply because of its power, as potentially threatening to their core interests and ultimate independence.[22] In this view, a disproportionate concentration of power in the hands of one state is likely to alarm other states by posing the possibility that international anarchy will be replaced by empire, or what used to be called "universal monarchy." In the face of this prospect, balance of power theorists expect other states to counterbalance against the paramount state, with some combination of external alliance and internal power mobilization. During the period of bipolar Soviet-American competition, American hegemony within the anti-Soviet coalition was seen by balance of power theorists as helping to sustain the global balance. With the near collapse of the Soviet pole of the Cold War bipolar order, and the resulting American "unipolar moment," neo-realist balance of power theorists have, consistent with their overall theory, predicted the occurrence of various types of balancing against American power.

The expectation that hegemonic power concentrations will stimulate counterbalancing is further strengthened by a corollary argument about the relationship between power and foreign policy goals. In this view, states with a disproportion of relative power will tend to expand the scope of their foreign policy interests in ways that encroach upon other states. With a relative concentration of power, a hegemonic state has surplus power beyond what is necessary to secure its core interests, and will tend to broaden its foreign policy goals, and seek to export its preferred domestic political system and ideology in ways that other states will find threatening and intrusive.

There are, however, strong reasons to think that the presence of nuclear weapons makes both encroachment and counterbalancing less likely. Deterred from making war against other great powers, a hegemonic state in a nuclear world is much less threatening to the other states of the system. Secondary states with nuclear weapons will have little fear

---

[22] Edward V. Gulick, *Europe's Classical Balance of Power* (New York, NY: Norton, 1967); and Kenneth N. Waltz, *Theory of International Politics* (New York, NY: Random House, 1979).

of aggressions from the hegemonic state and thus will have little or no need to counterbalance against the paramount state. In effect, the existence of nuclear weapons in the hands of secondary states provides a very robust check on the ability of the paramount state to use its relative preponderance of power in ways that encroach on other states. This argument does not imply, however, that balance of power theory is inaccurate. Rather, this nuclear revolution argument holds that further balancing of the sort predicted by balance of power theorists is not necessary because nuclear weapons are already such powerful counterweights. In short, the *balance* with nuclear weapons is so robust that further *balancing* is redundant and unnecessary, and perhaps dangerous. This argument may also apply to states that could readily possess nuclear weapons but do not actually possess them.

This argument also has implications for the debate over the durability of unipolarity and American hegemony. In a world with nuclear weapons, contemporary American hegemony may have a durability that is significantly de-coupled from its level of power concentration. Similarly, the absence of balancing against the United States, which was expected by countervailance balance theory (particularly contemporary neo-realism), may result from the existence of widely diffused and robust nuclear deterrence among the great powers. In short, nuclear weapons provide American hegemony with enhanced durability that is quite distinct from American unipolarity.

Overextension and nuclear weapons

A third set of arguments, also realist and based on substantial historical experience, points to hegemonic self-subversion through overextension. Where balance of power theorists see such hegemonic ordering efforts as either doomed to fail or very difficult to achieve due to counterbalancing, theorists of hegemony view hegemonic ordering as generally beneficial to other states, who are seen as receiving the benefits of the hegemonic state's efforts.[23] The expectation is that most states with a disproportionate share of relative power will attempt to order their international system in ways compatible with their security interests, as well as with domestic interests and ideology. Hegemonic theorists point to the ways in which both Britain in the nineteenth and early twentieth centuries, and the United States in the second half of the twentieth century, behaved in

---

[23] Gilpin, *War and Change in World Politics*; and Paul Kennedy, *The Rise and Fall of the Great Powers: Economic Change and Military Conflict, 1500 to 2000* (New York, NY: Random House, 1987).

ways consistent with these theoretical expectations by providing various "public goods" that benefited secondary states, but sapped the power of their hegemonic provider.

Theorists hypothesize that there is an important source of instability in hegemonic systems that is rooted in the tendency for a hegemonic state to overextend and overcommit. In this view, hegemony is more beneficial to the recipients of hegemonic ordering than to the hegemon. The expectation of hegemonic theorists is that hegemonic states will tend to take on more responsibilities and roles than their power capabilities can ultimately support. Hegemony burdens the hegemon and saps the foundations of hegemony. Overextension and the related free riding of secondary states eventually create a crisis of solvency for the hegemonic state as resources become insufficient to meet the responsibilities and sustain the roles that the hegemon has assumed.

As with encroachment and counterbalancing, the existence of nuclear weapons reduces the likelihood of hegemonic overextension and insolvency. Nuclear weapons are relatively cheap and so diminish the likelihood that resources will be outstripped by responsibilities. Nuclear weapons as deterrents of major military conflicts with other major states also reduce the costs which the hegemonic state must bear to sustain its position.

Power transitions and nuclear weapons

A third set of arguments about power distribution, concerning power transitions, also generates expectations about hegemony and power concentrations. The basic assumption of power transition theory is that power diffuses and that the relative power of states inevitably changes as technology, population, and political systems change.[24] Whether or not hegemony undermines hegemony, changes in relative power caused by other factors will undermine hegemony. As the relative power of states is altered, the expectation is that states rising in relative power will come to challenge the position of states, particularly hegemonic states, with declining power. The general line of thinking in power transition theory is that such changes trigger wars in which the challenger attempts to convert its rising strength into greater international security or influence (and thus further augment its strength) while the declining defender of the status quo finds its capacities to maintain its position diminished.

---

[24] Ronald L. Tammen, Jacek Kugler, Douglas Lemke, Carole Alsharabati, Brian Efird, and A.F.K. Organski, *Power Transitions: Strategies for the 21st Century* (New York, NY: Chatham House, 2000)

Nuclear weapons make wars stemming from power transitions much less likely. Given the relative cheapness and vast destructiveness of nuclear weapons, status quo states in decline will be able to sustain their position against rising challengers much more easily. Conversely, states with rising capabilities will find it much more difficult to convert their rising relative power into military gains. Assuming nuclear weapons significantly deter major war, the status quo is likely to persist long after the distribution of power that led to its formation has changed. In effect the major mechanism for translating additional capacity into additional gain is blocked when nuclear weapons greatly raise the costs and thresholds of conflict.

In sum, this assessment of the implications of nuclear weapons for the three major syndromes traditionally associated with hegemony and power concentration suggests that these dynamics are likely to be greatly diminished. Nuclear weapons may largely rob states with power concentrations of the advantages and benefits they provided in pre-nuclear times. But this diminishment of hegemony power is accompanied by important advantages to hegemonic states as well. Encroachment, counterbalancing, hegemonic overextension, and power transitions are likely to be much less salient features of international politics in a nuclear world, making the overall international system less tumultuous and conflictual than in pre-nuclear times. With these problems reduced, hegemonic states and orders in the nuclear era may persist much longer than in pre-nuclear times.

Proliferation and hegemony

Thus far this examination of nuclear weapons and hegemony has focused almost entirely on the effects of nuclear weapons as deterrents of war among the leading and most powerful states. Throughout the long nuclear Cold War, the diffusion or proliferation of nuclear weapons to less powerful states seemed far less important than the topic of general war among major nuclear armed states. And for the many decades of the Cold War, the politics of nuclear weapons could largely ignore the security problems posed by non-state actors because only states and major states had access to nuclear weapons capability.

Since the end of the Cold War, however, the nuclear issue in world politics has changed, ushering in what many refer to as a second nuclear age.[25] In this new phase of the nuclear era, both states and international

---

[25] This is dated by some beginning with the proliferation after China's nuclear test in 1964, but now more widely dated from the end of the Cold War. For example, see Colin S. Gray, *The Second Nuclear Age* (Boulder, CO: Lynne Reiner, 1999)

relations scholars attach much greater importance to interstate proliferation and the prospect for "nuclear terrorism" (or more precisely the use
of nuclear weapons by non-state actors). In part this is because the
prospects for a nuclear war ending civilization and perhaps all human
life appear to have become a much more remote possibility than during
the Cold War. But in part this shift in concern is because of the
widespread perception that the prospects for both proliferation and
nuclear terrorism are increasing. Many aspects of proliferation and
terrorism have been extensively examined by IR theorists, and there
are many important differences in thinking on these topics. This and
the following parts of this chapter explore the relationships between
nuclear proliferation and terrorism on hegemony, and particularly
American hegemony. Both the effects of hegemony on proliferation
and terrorism, and the effects of proliferation and terrorism on hegemony are examined.

Ascertaining these effects is a complex undertaking. One difficulty
arises from the fact that two very different sets of logics are involved,
relative power and deterrence failure. It seems likely that proliferation
and the prospect for terrorism will significantly diminish the ability of the
hegemonic state to employ its non-nuclear military assets for political
gains, while increasing the potential costs and risks associated with its
hegemonic alliance system. But beyond implications of relative power
and the costs of sustaining hegemony, there is also the question of
deterrence failure. Since the beginning of the nuclear era, skeptics of
deterrence, both the "hawkish" nuclear war fighters and the "dovish"
advocates of international arms control, have advanced a range of ways in
which deterrence among the major states might fail. But the ways in
which deterrence failure might occur in the second nuclear age are
significantly different than in the first. In particular, non-state actors
are widely seen to be significantly less deterred than territorial states
(although they have compensating weaknesses and vulnerabilities due
to their statelessness). If nuclear capability leaks into the hands of non-
state, less readily deterred actors, then the prospect for nuclear use rises.

Because of the increased likelihood of deterrence failure, hegemony in
the second nuclear era can be expected to have costs and benefits that are
quite different than in the first nuclear era. As we have seen, the implications of nuclear weapons during the first nuclear age were largely favorable to a hegemonic state, particularly a liberal hegemon. Assuming the
hegemonic state is not revisionist in its ambitions, the effects of nuclear
weapons on it are largely positive, avoiding problems, solving problems,
and lowering costs. However, these conclusions depend crucially upon
the premise that deterrence failure is extremely unlikely.

Overall, there are good reasons to think that proliferation and nuclear terrorism which raise the likelihood of deterrence failure may be *disproportionately disadvantageous* to the hegemonic state. And a liberal hegemonic state, such as the United States, is likely to be disproportionately vulnerable. A liberal hegemonic state thus has higher incentives to combat or eliminate this problem, and it may also have greater capabilities to address the problem. But whether these incentives and capabilities are sufficient remains very much in doubt.

The effects of hegemony on proliferation

Technology, and thus power based on technology, tends to diffuse.[26] The diffusion of nuclear weapons capability, privileged with the special term "proliferation," has been subject to extensive study – and anxiety – since the beginning of the nuclear era.

But perhaps the single most important fact is that the diffusion of nuclear weapons has been much less than anticipated, and is greatly less than is possible. The gap between the number of actual nuclear states (nine) and the potential number of nuclear states (certainly several dozen, if not more) is commonly referred to as the "nuclear overhang." The nuclear overhang is large and inexorably growing. Most states that could have nuclear weapons do not now appear to want them.[27] Given that so many states can readily acquire nuclear weapons, motive becomes paramount. What effects do hegemony and American liberal hegemony have on the incentives of states to acquire nuclear weapons? And what are the effects of proliferation on American liberal hegemony? The diffusion of nuclear weapons in the international system is significantly entangled with the role of the hegemonic state in several very different, even opposing ways.

First, hegemony can stimulate proliferation. From the beginning of the nuclear age, proliferation has been motivated by the desire of other states to check American power and influence. Soviet and Chinese acquisition of nuclear weapons was certainly motivated by this goal. And in the second nuclear age, states and regimes which perceive themselves to be threatened or potentially threatened by American power and influence continue to find nuclear weapons an appealing means to check American

---

[26] Geoffrey L. Herrera, *Technology and International Transformation: The Railroad, the Atom Bomb and the Politics of Technological Change* (Albany, NY: SUNY Press, 2006).

[27] Michael Reiss, *Bridled Ambition: Why Countries Constrain Their Nuclear Capabilities* (Washington DC: Wilson Center Press, 1995).

influence and intimidation.[28] The nuclear acquisition efforts of North Korea, Libya, Iraq, and Iran all appear to be motivated, at least in significant part, by the desire to establish restraints on American power. In some of these cases, the desire to deter American military power is rooted in agendas of regional revisionism. In others it appears based on fears that the United States would intervene to overthrow the regime.

Several distinctly liberal-democratic and capitalist features of the American hegemon and its order may also contribute to proliferation. To the extent the American liberal hegemonic state pursues the expansion of its preferred domestic regime type by coercively imposing the domestic regime type of democracy upon non-democratic states, such states have a heightened incentive to acquire nuclear weapons.[29] Other features of the liberal hegemonic order, particularly its expansive trade, travel, and educational opportunities, may also facilitate ease of access to nuclear weapons.[30] And as more states become wealthier and technologically sophisticated due to the growth of world trade facilitated by the liberal economic order, their ability to acquire nuclear weapons grows as well.

The existence of a liberal hegemonic state has also arguably been a major constraint on the rate and extent of proliferation. Hegemons tend to have many alliances, liberal hegemons appear to be particularly adept at forming alliances, and the United States has the largest system of alliances in the modern state system. The extended military alliance system of the United States is widely seen as a major reason why many potentially nuclear states have foregone acquisition. Starting with Germany and Japan, and extending to a long list of European and East Asian states, the American alliances are widely understood to provide a "nuclear umbrella." Overall, without such a state playing this role, it seems likely that proliferation would be much more extensive.

---

[28] Derek D. Smith, *Deterring America: Rogue States and the Proliferation of Weapons of Mass Destruction* (Cambridge University Press, 2006); and Peter R. Lavoy, Scott D. Sagan, and James J. Wirtz, eds., *Planning the Unthinkable: How New Powers Will Use Nuclear, Biological, and Chemical Weapons* (Ithaca, NY: Cornell University Press, 2000).

[29] Despite realist claims to the contrary, almost all contemporary liberal internationalists are opponents of the use of American military power to overthrow non-democratic governments, but other forms of broadly liberal thinking, most notably neo-conservatives and what Henry Nau refers to as "conservative internationalists" continue to support such measures. Henry Nau, *Conservative Internationalism: Armed Diplomacy under Jefferson, Polk, Truman and Reagan* (Princeton University Press, 2013).

[30] for accounts of the interface between the international market and the spread of nuclear weapons technology, see Gordon Corera, *Shopping for Bombs: Nuclear Proliferation, Global Insecurity, and the Rise and Fall of the A.Q. Khan Network* (Oxford University Press, 2006); and William Langewiesche, *The Atomic Bazaar: The Rise of the Nuclear Poor* (New York, NY: Farrar, Strauss & Giroux, 2007).

Other liberal features of the American hegemonic state may also help restrain the rate and extent of proliferation. To the extent the United States is non-aggressive, even accommodating, toward the interests of other states, the incentives for other states to acquire nuclear weapons is reduced. Also American leadership contributed to the establishment of the non-proliferation regime, and the general liberal internationalist vision of law-governed cooperative international politics infuses it. While the non-proliferation treaty and its regime have limited abilities to prevent the acquisition of nuclear weapons by states that seek them, it does raise the cost of nuclear acquisition. Similarly, the robust and inclusive liberal world trading system that has been a distinctive and salient feature of the American liberal hegemonic system offers integrating states paths to secure themselves that make nuclear acquisition less attractive.[31]

The effects of proliferation on hegemony

However shaped by these and other inhibitions and incentives, proliferation has slowly but surely occurred, thus posing the question of the consequences of proliferation for American hegemony. Overall, like the cross-cutting effects of hegemony on nuclear proliferation, the effects of proliferation on American hegemony appear to be very mixed. On the one hand, the spread of nuclear weapons may make hegemony more costly and risky to maintain.

The proliferation of nuclear weapons into the hands of additional states has been a feature of world politics since the acquisition of nuclear weapons by the Soviet Union in 1949.[32] Without proliferation, only one state (the United States) would have nuclear weapons. Indeed, the premise of the dominant nuclear age view that nuclear weapons deter major war is that enough proliferation has occurred to enough major states to deter great-power war. But because nuclear weapons are so powerful, their proliferation, more than any other historical case of the diffusion of other military technologies, has the ability to alter decisively the balance of military power between states. This fact, coupled with the fact that nuclear weapons are so relatively cheap, and thus not prohibitively difficult to obtain, means that the proliferation of nuclear weapons is likely to further diminish the ability of concentrations of conventional military force to shape outcomes favorable to a hegemonic state.

[31] Etel Solingen, *Nuclear Logics: Contrasting Paths in East Asia and the Middle East* (Princeton University Press, 2007).
[32] Thomas C. Reed and Danny B. Stillman, *The Nuclear Express: A Political History of the Bomb and Its Proliferation* (Minneapolis, MN: Zenith Press, 2009).

There are several reasons why proliferation is likely to be disadvantageous to the American hegemonic state and its international order. While there would be more proliferation without a hegemonic state, the proliferation which is most likely to occur next diminishes the power and influence and role of the hegemonic state.

The acquisition of nuclear weapons by revisionist states in the regions in which the extended American alliance system operates (Europe, Northeast Asia, and the Middle East) is likely to raise the costs and create uncertainties for the American position. To the extent such proliferation occurs, it reduces the conventional military superiority which the United States has acquired at such great cost. Nuclear proliferation will thus further narrow the usable influence which a hegemonic state can derive from its preponderance of non-nuclear power.[33] Furthermore, proliferation may seriously raise the cost of the extended American alliance system. The presence of extensive American conventional forces in these unsettled regions means that US forces become targets at greater risk of devastating attacks. A nuclear attack on a major American base (Guam, Diego Garcia, etc.) or a capital naval asset (particularly large aircraft carriers) would produce many thousand American casualties.

Proliferation may also diminish hegemony by making it more likely that a hegemonic state will launch a preventive war to prevent proliferation. Coercive non-proliferation, via sanctions as well as military strikes, has been a prominent part of the response of the United States to the revisionist state proliferation, as well as nuclear terrorism threats. Coercive counter-proliferation was considered, but not pursued, by the United States in the years the Soviet Union was acquiring nuclear weapons. The Soviet Union and the United States briefly jointly considered pre-emptive counter-proliferation when China was acquiring nuclear weapons, but did not exercise this extreme option. The largest effort of coercive counter-proliferation, the invasion of Iraq by the United States in 2002, was in part a "war of choice" enabled by American hegemony. But it was powerfully motivated by the vulnerability created by nuclear weapons in the hands of a state viewed as regionally revisionist and potentially a sponsor of non-state terrorist groups. In the view of the Bush Administration, the United States was both vulnerable and powerful, and the preventive war against Iraq was seen as a means to employ its power to reduce its vulnerability. And before the invasion, the United States government believed Iraq did (or soon would) have nuclear weapons, and judged this a serious threat to its regional hegemonic

---

[33] Barry Posen, "US Security Policy in a Nuclear-Armed World, or What If Iraq Had Had Nuclear Weapons," *Security Studies*, Vol. 6 (Spring 1997), pp. 1–31.

order, and perhaps eventually to the United States itself. American preponderance of conventional force enabled the Iraq War, but the vulnerability associated with nuclear weapons (and other weapons of mass destruction, particularly bioweapons) seems to have been a signifi-cant motivation (both to the leadership and the public) for the war. A combination of hegemonic strength (conventional forces, global basing network, economic resources, allies) and nuclear vulnerability shaped American policy.

In retrospect, Iraq did not, in fact, have nuclear weapons (or even make much of an effort to acquire them). And the United States, while power-ful enough to quickly depose the regime of Saddam Hussein, did not have the power to create a viable successor regime in Iraq. Unfortunately for this effort, the Iraq War both diminished American preponderance (cost, alienation of allies, etc.) and the public credibility of nuclear vulnerability as a paramount problem for US grand strategy to address. Quite aside from the potentially large direct costs of coercive counter-proliferation is the strong possibility that such strategies are also counter-productive because they stimulate other states to seek nuclear capabilities to deter American attack.

But there may also be benefits for the United States as hegemon from further proliferation. A world with more nuclear states might also make the extended US military alliance system much less necessary. American influence would decline, but so too might American costs and vulner-abilities. If major American allies acquired nuclear weapons, the value of their alliance with the United States would be significantly reduced. Protection of the American homeland does not depend on the United States playing the role of hegemonic protector of the system in a world with many nuclear armed states. Prevention of consolidation of Eurasia by one state, a major reason for the extensive American involvement and willingness to forge extension and costly alliance security commitments, presumes that such a consolidation would occur in the absence of American balancing. Extensive nuclear proliferation in the rimlands of Eurasia might evoke an American retrenchment to an "off-shore balancing" posture advocated by isolationists, some realists, and anti-big-government libertarians.[34] But such an American withdrawal would probably stimulate further proliferation. This is likely to increase the

[34] Eric A. Nordlinger, *Isolationism Reconfigured: American Foreign Policy for a New Century* (Princeton University Press, 1995); Christopher Layne, "From Preponderance to Offshore Balancing: America's Future Grand Strategy," *International Security*, Vol. 17, No. 4 (Spring 1993), pp. 5–51; and Christopher Preble, *The Power Problem* (Ithaca, NY: Cornell University Press, 2009).

probability of deterrence failure, but reduce the likelihood that use would occur against the United States or American military forces.

Nuclear terrorism and hegemony

The second defining feature of the emerging second nuclear age is the prospect of nuclear terrorism, which may ultimately be more far-reaching in its impact on American hegemony than proliferation. Unlike proliferation, nuclear terrorism has not yet occurred. Nuclear terrorist acts were recognized as a possibility during the first nuclear age, but were widely discounted as very improbable. Since the early 1990s, however, the plausibility of such acts has risen considerably. Nuclear terrorism, like nuclear war more generally, is essentially a speculative and hypothetical construct. Unfortunately, due to its relatively recent arrival as a serious concern, and due to the non-state character of the prospective nuclear actors, theories are relatively underdeveloped, especially in comparison with the topics of deterrence, power assessment, balance of power, hegemony, and power transitions. Unfortunately, no treatment of nuclear weapons and their implications for world politics can now be complete without a consideration of the problem of non-state weapons of mass destruction (WMD) and particularly nuclear terrorism. Over the long Cold War period, the study of both hegemony and nuclear weapons largely operated from the assumption that states (and particularly great-power states) were the sole or primary object of analysis. Long viewed as very implausible, the prospect of nuclear terrorism by small non-state actors is increasingly seen as a major possibility, with dire implications. In the wake of the attacks by the Japanese Aum Shinrikyo cult in Japan, the 9/11 attacks in New York and Washington, and the anthrax letters shortly afterward, the threat of nuclear terrorism has come to be widely perceived to be a major national security threat, particularly in the United States.[35] It is now widely feared and anticipated that non-state actors, groups the size of criminal gangs, could obtain or construct a nuclear weapon and employ it in a devastating attack to achieve various political goals. Lacking a state territorial base, such actors may not be readily deterred by the threat of retaliation.

---

[35] Among the vast literature, see Graham Allison, *Nuclear Terrorism: The Ultimate Preventable Catastrophe* (New York, NY: Henry Holt, 2004); Richard A. Falkenrath, Robert D. Newman and Bradley Thayer, *America's Achilles Heel: Nuclear, Biological and Chemical Terrororism and Covert Attack* (Cambridge, MA: MIT Press, 1998); and particularly Charles D. Ferguson and William C. Potter, *The Four Faces of Nuclear Terrorism* (New York, NY: Routledge, 2006).

The nuclear terrorism problem is a continuation of the proliferation problem, namely diffusion to more actors.[36] To capture this new situation, it has become conventional to speak of nuclear capability leaking into the hands of an altogether different type of (non-state) actor, posing the altogether novel situation of "omniviolence." Given that there is enough reprocessed plutonium (the preferred key ingredient in nuclear explosive devices) to make some 400,000 Hiroshima-sized bombs, this prospect has considerable credibility. However, leakage differs from proliferation because it alters not just the relations among states, but the monopoly (or near monopoly) of capital weapons by states that has been a stable feature of world politics for many centuries.

Anticipation and response to the threat of nuclear terrorism has emerged as a factor of significance in American foreign policy. The Bush Administration's policy that led to the Iraq War had many dimensions, but the threat of nuclear terrorism was widely voiced as a motive for the invasion of Iraq and the overthrow of the regime.[37] The American invasion of Iraq was in part a war of counter-proliferation, of coercive disarmament in order to reverse the perceived, or at least anticipated, Iraqi nuclear acquisition. It also appears to have been significantly motivated by the prospect of nuclear terrorism, because many key decision makers in the Iraq War policy making in and around the Bush Administration thought that there was a significant risk that Iraq would transfer nuclear weapons capability to non-state proxies for use in terrorist attacks against the United States and its allies.

Nuclear terrorism and American hegemony

What does this new security environment of leakage and omniviolence mean for the American state and its hegemonic order? The empirical basis to substantiate claims on this topic is thin and ambiguous, and it could be that these threats are greatly exaggerated.[38] Two arguments are advanced. First, a hegemonic is likely to have particularly high vulnerabilities to this threat. These vulnerabilities are further amplified by the internally liberal democratic constitutional features of the United States. As a result of this greater vulnerability, a hegemonic state, and particularly a liberal hegemonic state like the United States, should have very

---

[36] Terrorist groups may also be supported by states. Daniel Byman, *Deadly Connections: States that Sponsor Terrorism* (Cambridge University Press, 2005).

[37] For critical analysis of the Iraq War justifications, see Robert Jervis, *American Foreign Policy in a New Era* (New York, NY: Routledge, 2005).

[38] John Mueller, *Overblown: How Politicians and the Terrorism Industry Inflate National Security Threats and Why We Believe Them* (New York, NY: Free Press, 2006).

high incentives to prevent nuclear terrorism. Second, the capabilities of a liberal hegemonic state, while substantial, may be insufficient to adequately contain this threat. The liberal features of the American unipolar state both decrease and increase capabilities to respond to this threat.

First, the diffusion of nuclear weapons capability to non-state actors with revisionist or revolutionary political objectives is likely to disproportionately diminish the security of a hegemonic state, particularly one playing the role of liberal hegemon. The United States' extended system of alliances (many with domestically repressive regimes) makes it a target of numerous grievances, as does its general military, economic, and cultural preponderance. The American role as guarantor of various regional systems with numerous client states increases the prospect that the United States will be targeted by revisionist and revolutionary non-state actors. For example, al-Qaeda and its affiliates target the United States because of the role of the United States in defending the Saudi Arabian regime, which the group aims to overthrow. Also, the corrosive effects of terrorism and anti-terrorism on limited government and civil liberties add further incentive for a liberal-democratic state to contain the nuclear terrorist threat.[39] Overall, it seems likely that the prospect of nuclear terrorism by non-state actors raises the cost of maintaining the American system.[40]

Liberal hegemony against nuclear terrorism

Given this vulnerability, the United States has a very strong incentive to combat this threat. At the same time, American hegemony and its liberal features provide important capabilities to combat nuclear terrorism. Three possible responses to the threat of nuclear terrorism[41] are considered: (1) defense via border control and internal policing; (2) inter-state cooperative policing and intelligence; and (3) nuclear arms and fissile material control regimes. Over the first decade in which the nuclear terrorism threat has been of primary concern to US national security, each of these options has been pursued to some extent, but none has

---

[39] Fred Charles Ikle, *Annihilation from Within: The Ultimate Threat to Nations* (New York, NY: Columbia University Press, 2006).
[40] Richard Betts, "The Soft Underbelly of American Primacy: Tactical Advantages of Terror," *Political Science Quarterly*, Vol. 117, No. 1 (2002), pp. 19–36.
[41] For the fuller range of possible responses, see Audrey Kurth Cronin and James M. Ludes, ed., *Attacking Terrorism: Elements of a Grand Strategy* (Washington, DC: Georgetown University Press, 2004).

been fully or consistently pursued. Each has major limitations and each faces major impediments.

First, the nuclear terrorism threat can potentially be countered by increased border controls and internal policing. Terrorism long pre-dates nuclear terrorism, and border controls and internal policing have been widely employed to combat it. As the nuclear terrorism threat has emerged, the United States has greatly increased the resources and authorities of its internal policing and border surveillance. But these measures may fall significantly short of what is necessary to contain the threat. Furthermore, such measures are resisted by a wide array of powerful domestic interest groups, who are particularly influential in the formation of policy in the American polity due to its liberal, demo-cratic, and constitutional features. It also may be the case that liberal democratic constitutional states committed to international openness in trade and travel are at a serious disadvantage to authoritarian states that close themselves to extensive international intercourse.

Second, the nuclear terrorism threat can potentially be countered by increased cooperative policing and intelligence. In response to the emerging threat of non-state nuclear terrorism, almost all states in the international system arguably have a strong security interest in prevent-ing leakage and implementing measures, both unilateral and multilateral, to secure themselves and sustain the primacy of states. There have been significant steps in this direction, but they may fall far short of what is needed. This suggests either that the threat is overblown, or states are slow learners about qualitatively new threat vectors, or perhaps that minor relative gains considerations still outweigh high absolute gains from cooperation. Cooperation among states to combat various criminal activities has a long history, being a salient part of the Concert of Europe, and playing a major role in the development of international cooperation to combat a wide array of criminal activities.[42] The emergence of dyna-mite bomb terrorism in the late nineteenth century provided a substantial impetus to interstate police cooperation.[43] Over the last several decades air hijacking and terrorism have stimulated a major increase in cooper-ation between the policing agencies of states, with the United States playing a major leadership role. The liberal character of the United States and its system of international regimes has greatly facilitated these

[42] Peter Andreas and Ethan Nadelmann, *Policing the Globe: Criminalization and Crime Control in International Relations* (Oxford University Press, 2006).
[43] For historical overviews of terrorism and counterterrorism, see Matthew Carr, *The Infernal Machine: A History of Terrorism from the Assassination of Tsar Alexander II to Al-Qaeda* (New York, NY: New Press, 2006); and Walter Laqueur, *The New Terrorism: Fanaticism and the Arms of Mass Destruction* (Oxford University Press, 1999).

international cooperative efforts,[44] while domestic liberal and constitutional features have impeded them.[45]

Third, the nuclear terrorism threat can be potentially countered by strengthened regimes for nuclear arms control and fissile material. The fact that the current unipolar state is also a liberal hegemonic state increases the prospects for the expansion and deepening of the global nuclear control regime.[46] Over the decades of the nuclear era, arms control has been a much more significant feature of the international system and of great-power grand strategy than ever before. But, with the very significant exception of the end of the Cold War period during the late 1980s and early 1990s, nuclear arms control has played a secondary role in American grand strategy.[47] Rejecting the emphasis on coercive counter-proliferation of the Bush Administration, the Obama Administration has put greater emphasis on international arms control as a means of reducing the nuclear terrorist threat. Building on efforts stretching back to the beginning of the nuclear era, the Obama Administration has launched a variety of initiatives (renewed calls for abolition, Europe missile defense pull-back, START follow-on negotiations, terrorism-centered Nuclear Posture Review) that are advanced in large measure as responses to the threat of nuclear terrorism.

But a reinvigorated global nuclear arms control project cannot succeed solely with American efforts. Nearly universal compliance will be needed and the ability of other states to resist, whether actively or passively, is large. Over the last several decades, and even more so after 9/11, virtually all states have condemned and outlawed (via domestic criminal sanctions) nuclear and other WMD terrorism and expressed this consensus in a variety of UN Security Council resolutions and other instruments.[48] Yet, it also seems clear that other states place a much

---

[44] Barak Mendelsohn, *Combating Jihadism: American Hegemony and Interstate Cooperation in the War on Terrorism* (University of Chicago Press, 2010).

[45] Matthew Kroenig and Jay Stowsky, "War Makes States, But Not As It Pleases: Homeland Security and American Anti-Statism," *Security Studies*, Vol. 15, No. 2 (2006), pp. 225–270.

[46] For robust international arms control as a support for the survival of limited government constitutionalism, see Daniel Deudney, "Omniviolence, Arms Control, and Limited Government," in Stephen Macedo and Jeffrey Tulis, ed., *The Limits of Constitutionalism* (Princeton University Press, 2010).

[47] For the extent of the arms control and disarmament at the end of the Cold War, see Joseph Cirincione, *Bomb Scare: The History and Future of Nuclear Weapons* (New York, NY: Columbia University Press, 2007).

[48] Jane Boulden and Thomas G. Weiss, ed., *Terrorism and the UN: Before and After September 11* (Bloomington, IN: University of Indiana Press, 2004); and David Cortwright and George A. Lopez, eds., *United Against Terror: Cooperative Nonmilitary Responses to the Global Terrorist Threat* (Cambridge, MA: MIT Press, 2007).

lower priority on this problem than does the United States. With a focused effort, the United States could plausibly make headway in this direction, but subordinating competing foreign policy goals and interests (notoriously difficult in large fractious liberal democracies) may make this grand strategy unrealizable. Also, other states, particularly rising potential rivals (China) or resentful former rivals (Russia) may see the problem of mass terrorist attacks as a preponderantly American problem and passively obstruct US initiatives. The difficulties faced by the Bush and Obama Administrations in orchestrating sanctions against Iran for its nuclear activities supports the argument that states do not uniformly view this threat as very great. The diffusion of nuclear capabilities into the hands of more states is also amplifying the collective action barriers to global nuclear arms control. Finally, the still largely hypothetical character of the nuclear terrorist threat makes it difficult to sustain attention and support for the often costly measures of containing it.

Given the significant limits to these four strategies, the question of what a nuclear terrorist attack on the United States or allied soil would mean for the American position as a liberal hegemonic state warrants consideration. A nuclear terrorist attack would produce far less destruction than a general nuclear war between nuclear-armed states. But such an attack is likely to have severe consequences for the political order of the United States and for the American relationship with the world. Internally, it is widely expected that such an attack would lead to the great expansion of policing and intelligence activities, and tightening of borders to the flow of people and material. A nuclear terrorist attack is also likely to reduce greatly the liberal, democratic, and constitutional features of the American political order. Externally, if the historical record of American reaction to military attacks is any guide, the American response is likely to be both rapid and violent.

At the same time, a nuclear terrorist attack might also be a catalytic event internationally, creating a widespread realization (or perception) of the salience of this threat by many states. Thus, a serious nuclear terrorist attack might harden hierarchy internally at the expense of traditional broadly liberal, constitutional regime features in the liberal hegemon, while at the same time stimulating major international institutional change to alter, if not authoritatively abridge, interstate anarchy. Effective international collective action in this domain may not require much more than the active consensus of five major states (or actors) (the United States, Russia, Europe, China, and India) in a concert-like arrangement, based on minimal common security interests. If these states employed their collective economic weight, and diplomatic problem solving to induce universal compliance with a robust fissile containment regime, the threat of nuclear terrorism might be substantially reduced.

Conclusions

Five overall conclusions emerge from this analysis. First, the contemporary international system may be hegemonic, but it certainly is not unipolar. The paramount military capability of nuclear weapons is not distributed in a unipolar pattern. The system is at least bipolar and perhaps multipolar. The United States does have a significant lead over other states in secondary and tertiary power capacities of conventional military force, economic output, and soft power, but these concentrations make for a very truncated unipolarity. This means that the contemporary American hegemony rests on very different power foundations than previous hegemonies.

Second, nuclear weapons call into question the foundations of hegemony theory by calling into question the more general relevance of power distribution and polarity as a category for analyzing international systems. If the dominant view of the nuclear revolution centered around deterrence is correct, then the relationship between military power and international political outcomes has profoundly changed. If states are in fact primarily deterred by nuclear weapons, then their capacity to coercively achieve favorable outcomes is greatly reduced. In short, power as a factor in international politics has been significantly altered, producing a decreased relevance of polarity, and thus hegemony. The paralysis of power produced by nuclear deterrence robs power concentrations of their potency.

Third, contemporary hegemony is also different because the truncated power base upon which it rests is altered by the shadow of nuclear deterrence. Most importantly, conventional forces, while not completely paralyzed, are substantially circumscribed, and come to play something closer to a policing role than an arbiter of great-power interstate disputes. At the same time, the widespread security of states produced by the nuclear revolution may unexpectedly amplify the impacts of concentrations of economic and soft power. If nuclear weapons greatly diminish the threat of conquest, weaker states can more confidently open themselves to economic interdependence and cultural penetration by stronger states. This means that a nuclear world is, paradoxically, particularly favorable for the operation of a liberal international order of the sort promoted by the American liberal hegemon. But this also means that this liberal international order may be in significant measure liberal because of nuclear weapons rather than because of the influence or example of the liberal hegemon.

Fourth, hegemony is made much easier and more durable by nuclear weapons. Major syndromes and dynamics historically associated with concentrated power become much less pronounced in a nuclear world. Encroachment and counterbalancing, overcommitment and over-extension, and violent power transitions all diminish in a world with nuclear weapons. This conclusion also casts new light on the triangular debate about unipolarity among variants of realism and liberalism. If nuclear weapons mean the balance is robust, then the absence of balancing is at least partially explained. If nuclear weapons make unipolarity more durable, then it may be persisting for reasons unrelated to power asymmetries. If nuclear weapons provide security and facilitate openness to interdependence and penetration, then the liberal order may have an under-recognized source of strength and support. But this also means that the liberal character of the international order may not depend as much on its liberal hegemon as many liberal theorists believe.

Fifth and finally, the emerging patterns of nuclear proliferation and the prospect of nuclear terrorism pose major problems for both policy and theory. Most importantly, further proliferation and possible nuclear terrorism challenge the non-use of nuclear weapons produced by deterrence. Unipolarity and hegemony both inhibit and stimulate proliferation. Further proliferation is likely to further disadvantage the American hegemonic state by further truncating the already limited range of uses of its advantage in conventional forces. Nuclear terrorism, made more likely by further proliferation, poses a far-reaching threat not only to the American hegemonic position, but also to the liberal character of the hegemon's polity. Hegemony probably increases the ability of the United States and other states to address this problem, but the measures likely to be implemented may be insufficient. The trajectory of the second nuclear age opens the possibility that major shock and system change may lie ahead, a change that is likely to be profoundly subversive of both nuclear deterrence and American liberal hegemony.

Brilliant but now wrong: a sociological and
         historical sociological assessment of Gilpin's
         War and Change in World Politics

Barry Buzan

Introduction

How should one now relate to Gilpin's *War and Change in World Politics*
(*WCWP*) from a sociological and historical sociological perspective on
structural change? In its time, *WCWP* was a pretty radical project. It took
the difficult path by attempting a dynamic theory of change rather than a
static one of continuity. It attempted a grand synthesis by combining
Waltz's then fresh neo-realism with world history and a large dose of
international political economy (IPE). It was not afraid to combine holis-
tic, sociological, structural approaches with reductionist, economistic,
rational choice ones. It was a landmark in the development of the neo-
neo synthesis between neo-realism and neo-liberalism. And it anticipated
by nearly a decade both Tilly's[1] argument about "war makes the state
and the state makes war," and Kennedy's[2] argument about overstretch
and the rise and fall of great powers.

All of that said, looked at in retrospect, *WCWP* is very much a late Cold
War book in terms of both its policy concerns and prescriptions. It centers
around the US as an inevitably declining hegemon, and what if anything
might be done to avert the dangers inherent in that position. For those
inclined to think in this way, the question of US decline and hegemonic
transition is still very much on the agenda, albeit in a rather different
context from that of the early 1980s. Yet despite its impressive intellectual
breadth, and sensitivity to IPE, the book accepts Waltz's definition of
structure in terms of the distribution of power,[3] and remains captured by
the quintessentially realist assumption that "the nature of international
relations has not changed fundamentally over the millennia."[4] Although

---

[1] Charles Tilly, *Coercion, Capital and European States AD 990–1990* (Oxford: Basil
Blackwell, 1990).
[2] Paul Kennedy, *The Rise and Fall of the Great Powers* (London: Fontana, 1989).
[3] Robert Gilpin, *War and Change in World Politics* (Cambridge University Press, 1981),
pp. 85–86.
[4] *Ibid.*, p. 211.

Gilpin's[5] definition of deep systems change is different from Waltz's (the nature of the principal actors versus the organizing principle of the system), like Waltz's it is defined in such a way as to exclude this type of change from the analysis. Just as this closure forced Waltz to focus on polarity, so Gilpin consequently focuses his analysis of change on the rise and decline of hegemonic powers, and the changes to international orders that occur in the context of an apparently endless cycle of hegemonic wars.[6] Gilpin[7] is fully aware of the sociological distinction among "social formations" represented by hunter-gatherer, agrarian, and industrial modes of production, and throughout the book he discusses the impact of industrialism and capitalism on weapons, wealth generation, transportation and communication, society, and the process of rising and declining great powers. But while he sees industrial capitalism as significantly affecting the dynamics of war and change, he definitely does not see it as changing the game.

Thus although a sociological perspective is included in Gilpin's analysis, it is accorded a marginal role. Ironically, given the book's title, it is only about change *within* the essentially realist story of endless continuity shaped by the material rise and decline of great powers in a context of a competitive anarchic structure mediated by the legitimate use of war. International society is only there as an epiphenomenon, something that changes when the dominant power declines and is replaced.[8] As a consequence, and despite the fact that he was far better set up to do so than most realists, Gilpin seriously underplays the important distinction made later by Clark[9] between *primacy* (as material dominance) and *hegemony* (the consensual legitimation of the leader by its followers). Because he sees hegemony as closely derived from primacy, Gilpin excludes the opportunity to differentiate the two when thinking about US decline. The utility of this distinction became very apparent with the Bush Administration and its war on terror, which had little effect on the material power of the US, but a lot on the legitimacy of its leadership. An overemphasis on material as opposed to social structure in the current American debates about US decline (or not) is perhaps a legacy of both Gilpin's work and neo-realism more broadly.

---

[5] *Ibid.*, pp. 40–41.
[6] Gilpin (*ibid.*, pp. 39ff) is much more tentative than Waltz is about his three-tier scheme for change ("systems change," "systemic change," "and interaction change") and does not explore or develop it much. In what follows my focus is not on the internal problems of his scheme, but on its overall inadequacy as an approach to systems change.
[7] *Ibid.*, pp. 107–110.   [8] *Ibid.*, pp. 25–42.
[9] Ian Clark, *Hegemony in International Society* (Oxford University Press, 2011), pp. 23–28.

Gilpin's[10] central driving dynamic of change is differential rates of mainly economic change in the component parts of the system. World history might be differentiated by changes in the dominant mode of production, particularly that from agrarian to industrial, but this makes no fundamental difference to how the game of international relations is played. Gilpin does not use the sociological language of differentiation theory,[11] but his analysis is firmly cast around two types of differentiation: *segmentary* (into like units and anarchic structure) and *stratificatory* (into a hierarchy of powers). Segmentary differentiation is broadly taken as given, as the permanently operating condition of international relations. Stratificatory differentiation is taken as cyclical, and the main thrust of the book is to expose the dynamics underlying this. The third element of differentiation theory, *functional* differentiation, hardly features at all. There are passing mentions of the importance of the rise of modern economics[12] and, overall, economic dynamism plays a large role in Gilpin's understanding of change and the differential rise and decline of powers. But the deeper idea that functional differentiation might itself be a way of understanding change gets no play.

Gilpin[13] simply sweeps this possibility away along with the straw man target of the failure of liberal idealism to generate a harmonious world.

Interestingly, Gilpin ends on a rather confused note about how to understand the present (early 1980s) condition of world politics. His analytical scheme commits him to the realist proposition that "The fundamental problem of international relations in the contemporary world is the problem of peaceful adjustment to the consequences of the uneven growth of power among states, just as it was in the past."[14] He sees the US as a classical waning power, and the Soviet Union still as "the rising challenger."[15] He foresees the probable rise of more superpowers challenging the bipolar structure. But he also sees the impact of the global market economy and nuclear weapons as constraining the classical logic of power politics, and he cannot see a hegemonic war clearly in the making.[16] He is cautiously optimistic that hegemonic war can be avoided by wise US policy, but hangs on to the idea that such a war remains a real possibility. This final confusion about the direction of the system opens up room to question Gilpin's unwavering commitment to the permanent logic of "the struggle of political entities for power, prestige and wealth in

[10] Gilpin, *War and Change in World Politics*, pp. 44–49.
[11] Barry Buzan and Mathias Albert, "Differentiation: A Sociological Approach to International Relations Theory," *European Journal of International Relations*, Vol. 16, No. 3 (2010), pp. 315–337.
[12] Gilpin, *War and Change in World Politics*, pp. 24–25, 67–72.   [13] *Ibid.*, pp. 219–223.
[14] *Ibid.*, p. 230.   [15] *Ibid.*, p. 241.   [16] *Ibid.*, pp. 228–244.

a condition of global anarchy."[17] Is it just that the present (whenever it is) will always be substantially opaque to highly generalized analytical schemes like Gilpin's? Or is it that Gilpin's conceptualization of change is itself too narrow, locking him into a perspective that blinds him to deeper kinds of change that have in fact been underway?

In the thirty years since Gilpin wrote, there have of course been some changes. China has converted to a form of capitalist economy. The Soviet Union has died, and communism as a challenger ideology to capitalism has abandoned the field. Even though many large differences remain within the political economy of capitalism, fundamental ideological differences have thus narrowed, and in Gilpin's scheme this should reduce the pressure towards hegemonic war. Ironically, the US is once again a classical waning power. It appeared to revive for a decade or so from the mid-1990s, and still remains militarily preeminent. But the vast mistakes of the global war on terror, the collapse of the Washington Consensus, the paralyzing polarization of US domestic politics, and the weakening of the US economy have undermined both its legitimacy and its resources.[18] The rise of China, India, and "the rest"[19] mean that the diffusion of power is continuing, and the possibility of multipolarity identified by Gilpin is more clearly emergent. Except for those ideologically committed to the realist view in which assumptions of enmity and/or rivalry point inevitably to clashing great powers and hegemonic wars, the likelihood of hegemonic war seems rather remote. In Wendt's[20] terms, a world in which all the major powers are some species of capitalist feels more like one of rivals and friends rather than one of enemies and rivals. It is certainly not yet a world of democratic peace, but neither is it the world of zero-sum ideological rivalry that dominated the international relations of the twentieth century. Since Doyle[21] reopened interest in democratic peace theory, one has at least to entertain the possibility that a Kantian world could exist, and up to a point already does among the Western world and its close associates.

So the question is whether Gilpin's lack of clarity over the prospect of hegemonic war is still basically correct, albeit with the Soviet Union

---

[17] *Ibid.*, p. 230.
[18] Barry Buzan and Richard Little, *International Systems in World History* (Oxford University Press, 2000).
[19] Fareed Zakaria, *The Post-American World and the Rise of the Rest* (London: Penguin, 2009).
[20] Alexander Wendt, *Social Theory of International Politics* (Cambridge University Press, 1999).
[21] Michael Doyle, "Liberalism and World Politics," *American Political Science Review*, Vol. 80, No. 4 (1986), pp. 1151–1169.

and communist ideology removed from the mix. Or whether, already in the early 1980s, his confusion pointed to basic flaws in the realist way he conceptualized structural change. In the latter case, what can a more sociological, and historical sociological, understanding of change offer as an alternative framework? Put in another way, do structural changes observable through a more sociological approach override Gilpin's realist analysis, changing the game in a fundamental way, or do they, as his work assumes, merely change aspects of the process without fundamentally changing the realist game of great-power rivalry mediated by periodic war?

In the next section I will review the general perspective on change given by differentiation theory, bringing in not just segmentary and stratificatory differentiation, but also functional differentiation. In the third section, I will use a historical sociological perspective to fill in the detail around the bare bones of differentiation theory. This puts flesh onto the idea that the transformation from an agrarian to an industrial mode of production constituted a shift so fundamental as to void realist (and Gilpin's) assumptions that the nature of international politics has remained basically unchanged for millennia. It also allows a more detailed look at the impact of modernity on war. In the concluding section, I will return to the question of how these two perspectives on change and war stand in relation to Gilpin's framework. Do they show its conceptualization of war and change to be superficial? Or do they reinforce it by elaborating on the dynamics of inequality that reproduce endless cycles of great-power rivalry and war as rising powers struggle to replace those defining the status quo, and those in power struggle to avoid overstretch, decline, and war?

Change and war in the perspective of differentiation theory[22]

Buzan and Albert[23] argue that Waltz's particular way of transposing differentiation theory to IR largely removed functional differentiation in its full meaning from the theory. Thus followers of Waltz, including Gilpin, end up using the theory to talk only about the difference between segmentary/anarchic and stratificatory/hierarchic systems. Consequently Gilpin's notion of structural change is largely focused on the rise and fall and clash of great powers as driven by unequal development.

---

[22] The argument and some of the text in this section is largely drawn from Buzan and Albert, "Differentiation."

[23] Buzan and Albert, "Differentiation," pp. 322–326.

Differentiation theory has functional differentiation not just as a third fundamental type, but also as the dominant feature of modernity. In principle, this should open up a different way of understanding structural change and war. Let us look more closely at the three basic types of differentiation in sociological and IR perspective:

- *Segmentary* differentiation is where every social subsystem is the equal of, and functionally similar to every other social subsystem. In anthropology and sociology this points to families, bands, clans, and tribes. In IR it points to anarchic systems of sovereign states as "like units." Durkheim[24] argues that such "mechanical" societies are held together, indeed defined by, a collective conscience, which is "the totality of beliefs and sentiments common to average citizens of the same society." This totality, which today we would discuss as "identity," transcends the individuals that compose it and so operates as an independent social structure across space and time. A segmentary form of differentiation is the one most prone to be organized in terms of territorial delimitations, although this is not necessarily so.
- *Stratificatory* differentiation is where some persons or groups raise themselves above others, creating a hierarchical social order. Stratificatory differentiation covers a wide range of possibilities and can be further subdivided into rank and class forms distinguished by whether or not there is significant inequality not just in status (rank), but in access to basic resources (class). In anthropology and sociology this points to feudal or caste or aristocratic or military social orders, though it can also be about the conquest and absorption of some units by others.[25] As this suggests, stratification can occur in many dimensions: coercive capability, access to resources, authority, status. In IR it points to the many forms of hierarchy: conquest and empire, hegemony, a privileged position for great powers, and a division of the world into core and periphery, first and third worlds or, before 1945, "civilized," "barbarian," and "savage." Collective conscience applies here too, but with the additional element that stratification must be accepted as legitimate. The lower the degree of legitimacy, the higher the necessity to maintain a stratified order by force.
- *Functional* differentiation is where the subsystems are defined by the coherence of particular types of activity and their differentiation from other types of activity, and these differences do not stem simply

---

[24] Émile Durkheim, *The Division of Labor in Society* (New York, NY: The Free Press, 1986 [1893]), pp. 79–80, 84–85, 105–107. Translated by George Simpson (5th print).
[25] Allen W. Johnson and Timothy Earle, *The Evolution of Human Societies* (Palo Alto, CA: Stanford University Press, 2000), p. 35.

from rank. The idea was initially drawn from biological metaphors about the different subsystems that compose living organisms.[26] Functional differentiation is mainly studied in sociology where it is generally thought of as the essential characteristic of modernity. It is closely related to the idea of a division of labour in the sense understood by economists, but when applied to society as a whole it points to its increasing division into legal, political, military, economic, scientific, religious, and suchlike distinct and specialized subsystems or *sectors* of activity, often with distinctive institutions, actors, and discursive rules. Durkheim[27] argues that through a logic of interdependence and non-competition the functional differentiation of a division of labour itself generates a new form or social solidarity which he labels "organic." In IR functional differentiation points, *inter alia*, to international political economy, international law, world (or global civil) society, transnational actors, and the debates about deterritorialization, a set of elements that have so far lacked a unifying concept in IR theory debates (other than the extremely loose one of *globalization*).

The conceptualization of structural change in differentiation theory involves an idea of evolution in which more complex forms grow out of the simpler ones that precede them: segmentary hunter-gatherer bands preceded the stratified city states and empires of ancient and classical times, which preceded the functionally differentiated societies characteristic of modernity.[28] In this view, segmentary, stratificatory, and functional differentiation form a sequence in that the higher tiers depend for their existence on having developed out of, and overcome, the one that came before. The sequence is thus both empirical (roughly corresponding to the general pattern of human history) and qualitative (from simpler forms of differentiation to more complex ones). Although such evolution is common, it is certainly not inevitable. Specific societies can end up in stasis, or can revert back to simpler types. Evolution does not mean that higher forms of differentiation totally eliminate those below them. The logic is structural: social orders are characterized by the co-presence of different forms of differentiation. Some try to look for which form is

---

[26] Durkheim, *The Division of Labor in Society*, pp. 41, 125, 127, 271.
[27] *Ibid.*, pp. 56, 64–65, 267, 274.
[28] Niklas Luhmann, "The Paradox of System Differentiation and the Evolution of Society," in Jeffrey C. Alexander and Paul Colomy, ed., *Differentiation Theory and Social Change: Comparative and Historical Perspectives* (New York, NY: Columbia University Press, 1990), pp. 409–440, 423ff; Durkheim, *The Division of Labor in Society*, pp. 256, 277, 283.

dominant in shaping the social structure as a whole.[29] Others emphasise the complexity of co-presence, with every type of functional differentiation having within it segmentary and stratificatory differentiation, and ditto for segmentary and stratificatory differentiation each containing the other two.[30] This co-presence framing is immediately apparent in contemporary society, where it is easy to identify all three types of differentiation in simultaneous operation.[31] It puts into context the debates in IR about the nature and direction of the contemporary international system which seems to contain elements of all three forms, with the dominant segmentary one (territorial states, sovereign equality, anarchy) being questioned by both stratificatory elements (the return of empire, the privileged position of great powers, hegemony, core-periphery) and functional ones (globalization, deterritorialization, a world society of transnational actors, an increasingly autonomous global economy).

This sociological scheme of differentiation has the advantage of putting functional differentiation into the scheme in a coherent fashion, whereas in IR the elements that go to make up functional differentiation are generally discussed as separate parts (the international economy, international law, international society, and suchlike) rather than as a coherent structural whole. Functional differentiation, when properly understood, is both an additional form of structure and a radical departure from IR's obsession with the anarchy-hierarchy dyad. It opens up a concept of structure that embraces rather than denies wider understandings of international systems/societies incorporating the whole range of sectors. It also suggests that since the nineteenth century functional differentiation has become the dominant social form first within the leading states, and increasingly in the international system as a whole.

However, the sociological framing has the disadvantage that it is designed mainly for looking at the unit level. This raises the big question of what happens when it is transposed to the two-level universe of IR: how can one transpose the three basic types of differentiation onto the

---

[29] Durkheim, *The Division of Labor in Society*, pp. 260–261; Niklas Luhmann, *The Differentiation of Society* (New York, NY: Columbia University Press, 1982), pp. 242–245.

[30] Jack Donnelly, "Rethinking Political Structures: From 'Ordering Principles' to "Vertical Differentiation" – and Beyond," *International Theory*, Vol. 1, No. 1 (2009), pp. 49–86; Jack Donnelly, "The Differentiation of International Societies: An Approach to Structural International Theory," *European Journal of International Relations* (2011), DOI: 10.1177/1354066111411208.

[31] Mathias Albert, Barry Buzan and Michael Zürn, eds., *Social Differentiation as IR Theory: Segmentation, Stratification, and Functional Differentiation in World Politics* (Cambridge University Press, 2013).

unit and system levels? If there are two levels in play in IR, one needs to apply the structural questions of differentiation to both, asking not just how the individual units are differentiated internally, but also how the international system/society as a whole is differentiated. Contemporary answers to these questions might be that internally the leading units display quite advanced degrees of functional differentiation, while the international system remains mainly a mixture of segmentary (sovereign equality) and stratificatory (hegemony). Does this difference in the dominant mode of differentiation across the levels matter? Does the disjuncture create tension and constitute a driving force for change? Should we expect the leading units increasingly to project their domestic form of differentiation into the system as a whole? The suggestive evidence for such a link is strong. Colonialism, great-power management, and hegemony surely link to stratificatory differentiation; sovereign equality and nationalism to segmentary differentiation; and the market, international law, and international and world society to functional differentiation. There can be no denying that international law and the global market economy and world society have become much stronger features of the international system/society since the advent of modernity, and that this relates to the rise of functional differentiation within and beyond the leading powers since the nineteenth century.

But while it is one thing to think about the leading units being dominated by functional differentiation, it is quite another to think of the whole system in this way. Moving to the idea that there is any serious functional differentiation at the system level would have major implications for what kind of units are in play. It would almost certainly require a move away from state-centric models of the international system/society towards ones where non-state actors, whether firms or civil society associations, and even individuals, have standing as units. This points to work from IPE such as Cerny,[32] and Stopford and Strange,[33] all of whom take non-state actors more seriously than Gilpin does. It also points to "world society" thinking in the English school and elsewhere which brings both state and non-state actors into the picture;[34] and from the globalization

[32] Philip G. Cerny, "Plurilateralism: Structural Differentiation and Functional Conflict in the Post-Cold War World Order," *Millennium*, Vol. 22, No. 1 (1993), pp. 27–51; Philip G. Cerny, "The New Security Dilemma: Divisibility, Defection and Disorder in the Global Arena," *Review of International Studies*, Vol. 26, No. 4 (2000), pp. 623–646.
[33] John Stopford and Susan Strange, *Rival States, Rival Firms* (Cambridge University Press, 1991).
[34] Barry Buzan, *From International to World Society?* (Cambridge University Press, 2004), pp. 27–89; Ian Clark, *International Legitimacy and World Society* (Oxford University Press, 2007).

literature that points to deterritorialization as the principal trend in global politics,[35] and a global civil society of non-state, often transnational, actors.[36]

What the sociological perspective of differentiation theory offers to the consideration of change is thus a quite different set of benchmarks from Gilpin's. Gilpin[37] certainly acknowledges the impact of industrialization in the nineteenth century, and the way in which it not only opened the prospect of open-ended economic growth, and transformed the basic underpinnings of power, but also made the economy a much bigger feature of international relations. But he does not see these changes in themselves as being transformative of the system structure. For him they are interesting mainly as changes in the process that drive the timeless game of great-power competition, and, to the extent that it bothers to think about modernity and the nineteenth century at all, this view is common to much of the rest of IR. Mainstream IR remains largely stuck in thinking about structure in terms of segmentary and stratificatory differentiation.

From a sociological perspective, by contrast, the shift from an agrarian mode of production to an industrial one, and from tradition to modernity, is the biggest structural transformation in human affairs to have happened since the change from hunting-gathering to an agrarian mode of production gave rise to cities and civilizations 5,000–6,000 years ago. In this perspective, industrialization and the rise of the global economy are just two facets of the much broader and deeper transformation to modernity. That transformation can be captured as the steady displacement of stratificatory by functional differentiation as the dominant social form of the leading units in the system. The traditional pre-modern world was dominated by stratificatory differentiation both within the units (kings, emperors, vassals, slaves) and at the system level (empires, suzerainties), across several millennia and several distinct international systems. Despite all the fuss made about sovereign equality, the Westphalian system was also largely in this agrarian mode of stratificatory at the unit level, and a mix of segmentary (among the European great powers) and stratificatory at the system level (between those great powers and everyone else; and between European powers and their colonies). As modernity took hold, at first in Western Europe and increasingly more widely, the dominant units shifted towards functional differentiation internally. As they transformed

[35] Jan Aart Scholte, *Globalization: A Critical Introduction* (Basingstoke: Macmillan, 2000).
[36] Helmut Anheier, Marlies Glasius, and Mary Kaldor, eds., *Global Civil Society* (Oxford University Press, 2001).
[37] Gilpin, *War and Change in World Politics*, pp. 123–127.

internally, these leading units increasingly projected their new internal structures out into the international system, building up a global market economy and the transportation and communication infrastructure necessary to support it, international law, a host of intergovernmental functional organizations, and global civil society. They also transformed the meaning and practice of war. From this point of view, the international system/society is still within the massive structural transformation begun in the late eighteenth century by the American, French, and Industrial Revolutions. Modernity as functional differentiation has spread far and, by historical standards, fast, but it is still not dominant everywhere. Many states remain predominantly stratificatory, and the international system/ society is a complex and unfolding mix of all three types of differentiation. I will look more closely at this transformation in the next section using the perspective of historical sociology.

Change and war in the perspective of historical sociology[38]

Any discussion of change has to identify criteria that benchmark *significant* change. The everyday run of events all counts as change, but most of it is of little wider consequence.[39] What one sees as significant change, and therefore how one constructs a periodization of history, depends on the type of criteria chosen. Gilpin chooses hegemonic war, and the closest he gets to a set of benchmarks is a list of wars whose characteristics fit his definition[40]:

- The Peloponnesian War (431–404 BC).
- The Second Punic War (218–201 BC).
- The Thirty Years War (1618–1648).
- The Wars of Louis XIV (1667–1713).
- The Wars of the French Revolution and Napoleon (1792–1814).
- The First World War (1914–1918).
- The Second World War (1939–1945).

Should the Cold War have turned hot, that would also have counted as a hegemonic war in Gilpin's terms, but its peaceful ending in 1989 was beyond the time frame of his book.

---

[38] This section draws heavily on work done for Barry Buzan and George Lawson, *The Global Transformation: History, Modernity and the Making of International Relations* (Cambridge University Press, 2015).

[39] R.J. Barry Jones, "Concepts and Models of Change in International Relations," in Barry Buzan and R.J. Barry Jones, ed., *Change and the Study of International Relations* (London: Pinter, 1981), pp. 11–29.

[40] Gilpin, *War and Change in World Politics*, p. 200.

In their survey of world historical periodizations relevant to IR, Buzan and Little[41] note both considerable variation amongst schemes, and some consensus around a few key benchmarks, most notably:

- The transition from hunting-gathering to agrarian mode of production between 10000 and 6000 BC.
- The first creation of a planetary scale international system circa 1500.
- The transition from traditional agrarian society to modern, industrial capitalism beginning circa 1750.

There is no fit at all between these dates and Gilpin's, which suggests at the very least that he is using a rather narrow criterion for benchmarking change.

IR itself is mainly organized around a set of benchmarks distinctive to it. Although pervasive, and very influential in how the subject is taught, this set is more implicit than explicit in the self-conceptualization of the discipline.[42] The key dates in this scheme are:

- The opening of the sea lanes from Europe to the Americas and the Indian Ocean circa 1500.
- The institutionalization of sovereignty at the Treaty of Westphalia (1648).
- The First World War (1914–1918).
- The Second World War (1939–1945).
- The Cold War (with its ending in 1989 as the benchmark).
- The terrorist attacks on the US in 2001 also have some standing as an IR benchmark.

Note how these lists represent different criteria: major conflicts, major transformations in the mode of production, major changes in the scale of the international system, and major political agreements. Gilpin's list has substantial overlap of dates with the general IR one because of agreement on the significance of major wars (the Treaty of Westphalia represents the settlement of the Thirty Years War). But while Gilpin's list has the merit of consistency, it has the weakness that its narrow criteria exclude not just significant change as benchmarked by other criteria, but also types of change that register in profound ways on his key variable of war.

---

[41] Barry Buzan and Richard Little, *International Systems in World History* (Oxford University Press, 2000), pp. 393–406.
[42] For a critical discussion of this set, an investigation into the theoretical bases for defining benchmarks for IR, and an alternative set, see Barry Buzan and George Lawson, "Rethinking Benchmark Dates in International Relations," *European Journal of International Relations* (2012) (preprint), DOI: 10.1177/1354066112454553.

In the rest of this section I want to sketch out the case (space permits no more than a sketch) that the long nineteenth century (1776–1914) represents a transformative epoch in human history. This epoch is fundamentally defined by a change in the dominant mode of production from agrarian to industrial, and is therefore comparable to the previous such change from hunting-gathering to agriculture. The argument is that a change in the dominant mode of production changes almost everything of consequence in human society, both material and ideational, and that such a transformation took place during the long nineteenth century.[43] This argument would come as no surprise to sociologists, historical sociologists, international lawyers, economic historians, or modern world historians because the profound transformation to modernity during the nineteenth century provides the main foundational story for their disciplines. With his IPE-informed perspective, Gilpin is more aware of these changes than most in IR, but even he does not give them anything like the weight they deserve in thinking about the key changes that generated the world we are now in. So while this is a critique of Gilpin's scheme, it is even more a critique of IR and how it understands its subject matter. The nineteenth century began a profound process of transformation in whose backwash we are still living, and whose material, ideational, and political developments still dominate the agenda of IR. In the terms with which I opened this section, the nineteenth century represents an intense cluster of benchmarks of significant systemic change that needs to be seen as a package because it set the terms for almost all of the subsequent main lines of international relations that followed it. All of these benchmarks are of equal or greater weight to those in either Gilpin's periodization or that which defines mainstream IR.[44]

Between 1776 and 1914 the key benchmarks are:

- 1776: Publication of Adam Smith's *Wealth of Nations* as transforming ways of thinking about political economy.
- 1776: The American revolution begins the revolt of settler colonies against European empires and the first round of decolonization, leading to the expansion of European into Western international society.

---

[43] I do not mean to imply here that changes in the mode of production are somehow the primary causal driver. Exactly what caused what in the hugely complicated emergence of modernity is a source of ongoing controversy beyond the scope of this chapter. Whether technological changes caused social ones or the other way around is extremely difficult to disentangle. The core point is that a transformational package of material and social changes became the dominant feature of the global system during the nineteenth century.

[44] For a discussion of the theoretical criteria underpinning these benchmarks, see Buzan and Lawson, "Rethinking Benchmark Dates in International Relations."

- 1789: The French Revolution unleashes the new legitimizing ideas of nationalism and popular sovereignty against dynasticism and aristocratic rule.
- 1833: The victory of the anti-slavery campaign as symbolizing the rise of global civil society as a player in shaping the norms and institutions of international society.
- 1840: This date roughly signifies when the British reversed the cloth trade between themselves and India, so marking the turnaround of trade relations between Europe and Asia, and the establishment of an unequal relationship between an industrial core and a commodity-supplying periphery.
- 1841: The First Opium War in which the British easily defeat the greatest of the classical Asian powers and establish the huge inequality of military power between core and periphery.
- 1848: The springtime of peoples signifying the shift from elite to mass society with ever wider participation in the economy and politics within the leading modernist states.
- 1857: The Indian Mutiny (aka War of Independence) signifies the first major revolt of non-Western peoples against European imperialism.
- 1859: Publication of Darwin's *Origin of Species* unleashing the idea of "survival of the fittest" into thinking about race, nation, economy, and much else.
- 1859: The launching of the French ironclad warship *La Gloire* opens the era of industrial arms racing in which continuous and rapid technological improvement becomes a new central factor in great-power military relations.
- 1862: The British Companies Act marked a general shift to limited liability firms and opened the way to the formation of transnational corporations as a significant new type of actor in the international system/society.
- 1861–1865: The American Civil War as the first industrial war won by mass production and making extensive use of railways and telegraph.
- 1865: The International Telecommunications Union as the first standing intergovernmental organization symbolizing the beginnings of permanent institutions of global governance.
- 1866: The opening of the first transatlantic telegraph cable begins the wiring together of the planet with instantaneous communication.
- 1869: The opening of the Suez Canal marks the beginning of geoengineering on a planetary scale to improve interaction capacity.
- 1870: The unification of Germany as a symbol of the new standing of nationalism as an institution of international society, as well as the key change in the distribution of power creating "the German

problem" that was to dominate much of the international relations of the twentieth century.

- 1873: The onset of the Long Depression of 1873–1896 signifying the shift from agrarian to trade/industry cycles in the world economy.
- 1905: Japan defeats Russia and in becoming the first non-Western (and non-white) imperial great power makes the first big move in the "rise of the rest."

Seeing the nineteenth century as a set of benchmarks in this way tells us two things. First, very many important things happened in the nineteenth century that are on the face of it of equal weight to the other benchmarks that define IR. Second, that seeing these things as benchmarks for IR suggests strongly that the field needs to rethink in a big way how it locates its subject matter into a historical context. The structural discontinuity of the nineteenth century saw social relations recast in decisive ways. It brought to an end the long period in which human history was mainly local and contact among polities, societies, and economies fairly light, and replaced it with one in which human history became mainly global, and contact among peoples intense. All of this happened in such a way as to vault a few Western states into a period of unprecedented, if temporary, dominance over all other parts of the world.[45]

One way of grasping this kind of transformation is to see it as a *change in the dominant mode of production*,[46] and I will use that term as a useful shorthand to represent a complex package of material and social changes. A change in the dominant mode of production transforms not only the material conditions of human existence, but also the structure of human social, political, and economic relations, and the framework of basic ideas that legitimate those structures. Short of a change in the biological qualities of the dominant species, a change in the dominant mode of production is the most profound imaginable in a social order. From this perspective, the period between the last quarter of the eighteenth century and the present day is a single historical period defined by the revolutionary transformation of the human condition.[47] The transformation of the Atlantic region changed not just the *distribution* of power (by making the West more powerful than other regions in the world), but also the dominant *mode* of power itself – the technological, social, economic, and political structures which lay behind "the European miracle." IR, including Gilpin, has a great deal to say about the changing distribution

---

[45] Eric Hobsbawm, *The Age of Revolution 1789–1848* (London: Abacus, 1962), pp. 15, 44.

[46] Ernest Gellner, *Plough, Sword and Book: The Structure of Human History* (London: Paladin, 1988).

[47] Eric Hobsbawm, *The Age of Empire, 1875–1914* (London: Abacus, 1987), p. 335.

of power, but it seldom features considerations about changes in the mode of power. The hidden assumption seems to be that changes in the mode of power occur evenly (chariots, gunpowder, nuclear weapons, etc.) and therefore do not much affect the basic logic of great-power rivalry. While this may be true in the long run, a massive change like that of agrarian to industrial power has taken more than two centuries to begin approaching anything like an even global diffusion. During that time, differences in the mode of power have defined much of world politics. Looking at the nineteenth century brings this mode of power theme into sharp perspective and shows that its consequences are just as important as those arising from the (re)distribution of power. Indeed, one cannot properly understand contemporary changes in either war or the distribution of power without understanding the parallel changes in its dominant mode.

On the basis of a new mode of power, the Atlantic region came to dominate the world. It projected new forms of organization and new ideas which destabilized traditional societies and brought the classical era of human history to an end. During the nineteenth century, the West broke open and overwhelmed the remaining power bastions of the classical world (the Ottoman Empire, China, and Japan), and overcame the environmental barriers both of disease (that had restricted Europeans to coastal enclaves in Africa) and of distance. The nineteenth century was, therefore, the beginning of what we might call "the Western-global era," an era which not only empowered the West vis-à-vis "the rest," but also set loose revolutions in terms of both material capacities and ways of thinking. These revolutions are still spreading and intensifying, and Giddens[48] is quite right to argue that what we now talk about as "globalization" is in fact the ongoing outward spread of modernity. As modernity takes root ever more widely, Western dominance is being placed under increasing challenge. In the early twenty-first century, we are probably living in the beginning of the end of this Western-global era transition period. With the rise of the rest we begin to approach the other side of the transition, where modernity is the dominant social form in most places, rather than just giving a temporary, but huge, power advantage to those that first mastered it.

The earliest example of a change in the dominant mode of production is the shift from hunting-gathering to agriculture that took place in several areas more than 12,000 years ago. Within the agrarian mode of production a second epochal transformation occurred starting around

---

[48] Anthony Giddens, *The Consequences of Modernity* (Cambridge: Polity, 1990), pp. 45–54.

6,000 years ago: the emergence of cities, city-states, and eventually empires. Increasing productivity sustained a rising human population grouped into larger settlements. This first global shift in the dominant mode of production suggests that such transformations display six key characteristics:

- They trigger profound changes in both the scale and organization of human societies.
- Except for the fundamental family unit, and up to a point the wider kinship communities of clan and tribe, everything changes. Society becomes bigger, more complicated, and more differentiated in terms of stratification and function.
- They happen unevenly. They will have some point or points of origin, and spread from there to the rest of the system. The pace of this spread will vary according to the mediating effects of the social and physical environments. Unevenness of development may thus continue for a very long time after the initial breakthrough.
- As well as being uneven, the spread of the new system will produce diverse outcomes.
- Each society that encounters the change has to find its own way of adapting it to both its local environmental conditions and its social structure. Some will fail in this and collapse. Those that succeed will not be carbon copies of the original adopters but will develop their own distinctive characteristics.
- Rising productivity plus rising population plus rising complexity and sophistication in both social structure and physical technologies will generate an ever denser and more interactive international system. Whatever the socio-political units might be, they will almost certainly have more intense relationships with both their neighbors and peoples further away. Interdependence tends to rise, meaning that every society is less self-contained and more exposed to developments elsewhere. Development is thus not only uneven, but also combined.[49]

The nineteenth-century transformation certainly shows all six of these characteristics. There is a leading edge where the transformation occurs first, creating deep and profound changes in the social and political and economic structures, with large increases in productivity driving

---

[49] Justin Rosenberg, "Problems in the Theory of Uneven and Combined Development Part II: Unevenness and Multiplicity," *Cambridge Review of International Affairs*, Vol. 23, No. 1 (2010), pp. 165–189; Justin Rosenberg, "Kenneth Waltz and Leon Trotsky: Anarchy in the Mirror of Uneven and Combined Development," *International Politics*, Vol. 50, No. 2 (2013), pp. 183–230.

expansions in population, interaction, complexity, differentiation, and sophistication. From this newly empowered core the transformation is transmitted to, and often imposed upon, the rest of humankind. This outward spread results in an uneven core-periphery development, uneven both because some adopt the new mode of production earlier than others and because the early adopters have the power to impose themselves and their rules on the periphery and to control some of their options to develop. Initially Britain leads, with northwest Europe and the US following on a few decades behind and catching up by the end of the nineteenth century. Russia and Japan follow not long after. Within the nineteenth century some of the second-tier developers (Germany and the US) overtake the original core (Britain), and during the twentieth century later developers do also (Japan, Russia/USSR). In less than two centuries the core has expanded substantially further, with an increasingly differentiated periphery in stages of "late development" varying from next to nothing (many parts of Africa, Afghanistan) to knocking on the door of the developed club (China, India, Brazil). As well as being uneven, the consequences and forms of this spread are diverse. One telling indicator of the various ways in which states and societies have tried to adapt themselves to modernity is the variety of ideologies that have emerged within both the core and the periphery to define different packages of modern economy, politics, and culture: liberalism, republicanism, social democracy, economic nationalism, authoritarianism, communism, fascism.

There is increased productivity leading to both massive increases in the human population, and the development of hugely larger and more complex social structures and systems bound together in ever more dense and interdependent ways. In these denser systems, development, despite its unevenness and diversity, becomes ever more combined. The agrarian mode of production built impressive regional empires and trading systems, and even, in its final few centuries, a thin global trading system. The industrial mode of production quickly built a much more intense global economy based on hugely improved technologies of transportation and communication. These same technologies made war and politics global, producing an integrated international system and society on a global scale for the first time. The big difference between the industrial and agrarian global transformations was the speed with which their impact diffused through the body of humankind. For better or worse, industrialism massively intensified the "combined" quality of development, quickly drawing everyone into a single strong system. While the relative depth of social, economic, and political transformation generated by the shift to agriculture was probably comparable to that generated by industrialism, the agrarian transformation happened slowly, spreading its impact over centuries and millennia. By contrast, the impact of the Industrial Revolution was (and still is) concentrated into a relatively tiny historical span, with huge changes happening on a scale of mere decades. This transformation was enabled by the advent of industrial capitalism, and accompanied by the emergence of the rational, bureaucratic national state, new technologies of warfare, and novel cultural tropes ranging from individualism through nationalism to "scientific" racism and progress.

Among other things, the nature and the consequences of this transformation redefined both the material and the ideational bases of the whole war/peace problematique that is IR's, and Gilpin's, founding concern. During the nineteenth century a massive and unprecedented power gap opened up between those states and peoples who were modernizing and those who were not. As argued above, this gap was not just about a new *distribution* of power, but also about a new *mode* of power, industrial modernity. In other words, both the material and the ideational foundations of power changed, with industrial technology replacing agrarian, and nationalism, popular sovereignty, and the market replacing religion, absolutism, and mercantilism. When the mode of power stays the same or changes very slowly, as was mostly the case for agrarian civilizations, power gaps are easy to understand, and in principle simple to rectify in terms of numbers of soldiers and the amount of gold in imperial treasuries. But where the mode of power itself changes two things happen. First, the gap becomes much larger because industrialism opens a cornucopia of capabilities not available to agrarian societies. Hilaire Belloc perfectly captured the arrogance of this mode of power gap:

Whatever happens
we have got
the Maxim gun,
and they have not.

And second, the gap becomes much more difficult both to understand and to close because it is based on a different kind of social and political order. We are almost in the realm of science fiction here: as Arthur C. Clarke[50] famously remarked: "any sufficiently advanced technology is indistinguishable from magic." So it must have seemed to the many hunter-gatherers and agrarians who confronted industrial products from trains and steamships to medicines and machine guns for the first time.

---

[50] Arthur C. Clarke, *Profiles of the Future* (London: Macmillan, 1973).

To close a gap of that kind requires radical and often revolutionary changes in existing social orders. Hobsbawm[51] puts it starkly: industrialization quickly became the necessary condition for power because "Modern technology put any government which did not possess it at the mercy of any government which did."

This redefinition of the material conditions of power had profound and rapid impacts on international relations. It created a deep rift between those who succeeded fairly quickly in acquiring industrial modernity and those that, for whatever reason, were slow to acquire it (or whose societies sometimes disintegrated in the face of it). During the nineteenth century, industrialism and modernity divided the world into a core of strong, rich, developed states and a periphery of weak, poor, underdeveloped (and often colonized) peoples. The process of industrialization and modernization also caused upheaval in the ranks of the great powers. Specifically, it promoted those who were quickest to adapt (Britain, Germany, US, Japan), and demoted those that were slow (China, Ottoman Empire, Russia, France). Generally, by making power conditional on rapidly changing criteria of industrialization and technology, it induced high volatility into the relativities of the balance of power. That volatility has remained a feature of international relations down to the present day, serially reproduced in fears (or hopes) about the rise of (Germany, Russia/Soviet Union, Japan, China, India) and/or the decline of (Britain, France, US, Russia, Japan). Rises and declines are not new in world history, but industrialism both speeded up the process hugely and changed the bases on which it occurred. The impact of industrialism on the differentiation of power has thus been the central material fact dominating international relations from the nineteenth century to now, though with the spread of both, the magnitude of this impact may at last be beginning to level out.

In one sense this suggests that there are two stories about nineteenth-century international relations to be told under the heading of inequality and power. The first one is about the enormous power gap that opened up between what became the Western core of a global international society, and what became the periphery, or third world. The second one is about the destabilization of the balance of power among the great powers. A key point about these two stories is that although they tend to be told separately (one as "development," the other as "balance of power" or "polarity") both are consequences of the same cause: the onset and impact of industrialism and modernity as it spread to planetary scale.

---

[51] Eric Hobsbawm, *The Age of Capital 1848–1875* (London: Abacus, 1975), p. 100.

Industrialism and modernity changed not just the distribution, but also the mode of power by providing a host of new resources to those who mastered them. That these resources were extremely unevenly distributed explains the opening of the gap between core and periphery. That the nature of these resources was volatile and subject to continuous rapid change explains why they destabilized great-power relations. In a later book, Gilpin[52] is one of the few in IR to recognize this link, thinking that uneven development was a central feature of capitalism, involving both a core periphery structure, and instability at the core with rising and declining hegemons. In this view, inequality and instability was and is a continuous threat to the legitimacy and stability of capitalism, a problem that has worried liberals and encouraged socialists since the nineteenth century.

This point about the nineteenth century's material transformation of the war/peace problematique of IR can be equally strongly made in ideational terms. During the nineteenth century the basic framework of ideas governing, and constituting, international relations, and therefore setting the conditions for war and peace, underwent a profound change. The basic idea of the sovereign territorial state stayed in place, but its content and meaning, and thus the whole framing of the war/peace problematique, were transformed. Age-old ideas such as dynastic absolutist rule, mercantilist economics, and stratified social structures based on fixed agrarian class and caste hierarchies, all began to crumble, and the already weakened idea of religious authority in politics crumbled further in the face of rising secular ideologies. In their place, at first only in the leading edge countries of the global transformation, a new set of governing and constituting ideas began to transform both the domestic structures within states and the nature of relations between them. Nationalism redefined sovereignty, territoriality, and citizenship, providing a powerful source of political legitimacy both domestically and internationally. Its ugly twin "scientific" racism framed a powerfully unequal view of interhuman relations generally and underpinned the rise and demise of fascism in the twentieth century. Liberalism attacked the traditional structures of stratificatory differentiation and promoted those of functional differentiation. It gave the individual more status in society, legitimized the rise of the bourgeoisie as the leading class, and underpinned radically non-zero-sum ways of thinking about economic and political relations between states and societies. Socialism legitimized the consciousness and organization of the new and expanding industrial

---

[52] Robert Gilpin, *The Political Economy of International Relations* (Princeton University Press, 1987), pp. 92–111.

proletariat and offered a challenge to both liberalism and the state. And what might broadly be thought of as the idea of progress, combining science, technology, and industrialism, displaced the cyclical ideas and static expectations of agrarian society with the expectation of continuous improvement in the material capabilities, social conditions, and knowledge of humankind.

These new ideas transformed not only the ideational landscape of domestic politics in the leading-edge states, but also the principles by which states and peoples both constructed their identities and related to each other internationally. Why peoples and rulers considered each other friends, rivals, or enemies was increasingly defined in terms of these ideologies. Dynastic succession as a key cause of war gave way to nationalist and ideological causes. Not surprisingly, much of twentieth-century history was about working out the conflicts and collaborations framed by these ideologies. This task is perhaps still not quite completed, though in the long run 1989 might well take on added benchmark status as the date by which the form of political economy in which modernity was to be taken forward was resolved. Much of the twentieth century was spent in a competition amongst monarchism, liberalism, socialism, communism, and fascism for this role. By 1989 capitalism had emerged as the most effective generator of wealth and power, though diversity still remained about whether the political side should be democratic or authoritarian. These new ideas, particularly liberalism and socialism, made peace seem attainable in a permanent way that had been unthinkable before. But they also gave new grounds for war and imperialism, and they played powerfully into the material inequalities and the vast new capabilities to transform the character and utility of war. To appreciate the scale of impact of these nineteenth-century ideas, one has only to ask what the history of the twentieth century would have looked like in the absence of nationalism, racism, liberalism, socialism, and progress as the principal legitimizing ideas behind international relations. It is profoundly striking how much the ideas generated in the nineteenth century dominate the politics and international relations of the twentieth and twenty-first. Indeed, it is hard to think of any comparably weighty ideas that have their origins later than the nineteenth century.

So the material and ideational transformation of the nineteenth century set the material conditions under which a truly global international system and society came into being. It generated most of the secular ideologies over which hundreds of millions of people fought, and tens of millions died. And it generated the many inequalities within that system and society – economic, military, political, cultural, racial – that continue to define contemporary international relations. It is no exaggeration to say that the war/peace problematique of the twentieth century, and still of the twenty-first, is the one set up during the nineteenth.

Starting in the nineteenth century human history therefore moved into a different era. Modernity transformed the conditions of international relations as much as it transformed all other aspects of the human condition. In this sense there is a decisive similarity between the nineteenth century, the twentieth century, and that part of the twenty-first century that we have lived so far. The general framing of modernity makes all three of these centuries fundamentally similar, and sets them sharply apart from all of the centuries and millennia of the agrarian era. It is not that there are *no* continuities with earlier times. The European part of the late agrarian world had from the late fifteenth century generated the sovereign territorial state, mastered global navigation, and constructed a thin global economy. Religions and kinship relations are major carry-overs from much earlier times. But even these continuities, especially the state and the thin global economy, have been massively redefined by modernity. The striking similarity between the nineteenth century and the contemporary world is that both are shaped by the problem of uneven development and cultural diversity on the one hand, and the rise of an interdependent (combined) global economy and states system on the other. Cultural diversity has existed since the beginning of civilization and so have differences in development, but never on this scale, or with this intensity, or in this context of close, inescapable global interdependence. From the late eighteenth and early nineteenth centuries, the development gap between states and societies opened more widely than ever before and, at the same time (and for the same reasons), the planet was bound together far more tightly than in earlier eras. In this sense, Rosenberg[53] is correct in stressing the importance of "uneven and combined development" as a key framing for modern IR. The twentieth- and twenty-first-century world is inseparable from the nineteenth-century one, and its international relations cannot be understood without knowing how the global transformation in their predecessor set the frame for what followed. As Hobsbawm[54] notes, up to the late eighteenth century, the European powers had to deal with "the great non-European powers and civilizations on apparently equal terms," but by the middle of

---

[53] Justin Rosenberg, "Why is There No International Historical Sociology," *European Journal of International Relations*, Vol. 12, No. 3 (2006), pp. 307–340; Justin Rosenberg, "Problems in the Theory of Uneven and Combined Development Part II"; Justin Rosenberg, "Kenneth Waltz and Leon Trotsky."

[54] Eric Hobsbawm, *The Age of Revolution 1789–1848*, pp. 39, 365.

the nineteenth century there had been "an apparently wholesale and virtually unqualified revolution" in international politics in which the European powers and the US were completely dominant: "Nothing, it seemed, could henceforth stand in the way of a few western gunboats or regiments bringing with them trade and bibles." It was this disjuncture that created the modern international system. In the future, historians may well look back on the nineteenth, twentieth, and twenty-first centuries as a single period, examining the ways in which modernity spread from its Atlantic core to transform human conditions on a planetary scale. IR needs also to embed this story and its consequences into its understanding of its own subject matter.

Conclusions

Surveying these nineteenth-century global transformations tells us not just what happened then, but also shows how the events of that time define the era we are still living in. The following seven points both sum up the key developments of the nineteenth century, and set out the main international issues and agendas of the twentieth and twenty-first:

- *A massive and ongoing transformation in the interaction capacity of the system creating increased density, interdependence, and uneven and combined development.* The rise of mass air transportation that so transfixed the people of the twentieth century, and the rise of the internet that so transfixes the people of the twenty-first, are but extensions of the railways, steamships, telegraphs, and radios that transfixed the people of the nineteenth.
- *A transformation in the main ideas, actors, and institutional structures that constitute international relations.* The big social ideas of the nineteenth century (liberalism, nationalism, racism, socialism, progress) are all still powerfully in play, and no new ideas of comparable weight have arisen to join them. The twentieth century was dominated by a sustained competition about which nineteenth-century ideology should shape the future of industrial society. That now seems to have been won by liberalism, though as yet much more on the economic front than on the social and political ones: capitalism has won more or less everywhere, but democracy remains hotly contested in many places. Much other contestation remains, a good deal of it interestingly from pre-modern religious ideology. So too with new actors. The stage is still dominated by nineteenth-century creations – nation-states, limited companies, IGOs, and NGOs and INGOs – albeit in much greater profusion than in the nineteenth century.

- *A volatile set of great-power relations driven by the effects of industrialization and the competition to exploit the power gap in relation to the periphery.* The rise and fall of great powers continues in line with relative success/ failure at achieving modernity and industrialization, and military relations among them continue to be driven by concerns about technological capability. This raises the question of whether the nineteenth century has fundamentally changed Gilpin's hegemonic cycles or just added various bells and whistles to it. More on this below.

- *A huge and deep development gap between core and periphery, with great variation in the ability of different societies to deal with both the dominance of the industrial core and the requirements of modernization.* The whole agenda of development still persists as a major global component of inequality, albeit increasingly more countries are finding their way into the core and the semi-periphery. Development continues to be intensely uneven and highly combined, and the debates about it continue to reflect the mix of local cultural factors and systemic impositions by the core on the periphery.

- *A class of superpowers capable of operating extensively on a global scale and not just as major powers within their own region.* Superpowers and the polarity structures they create continue to dominate the international system, though there is now room for beginning to think that, as modernity spreads throughout the system, it will make it increasingly difficult for any state to acquire, or in the case of the US maintain, the relative superiority required for superpower status. We are not there yet, but the argument in this chapter points to a world without superpowers[55] that fits well with Kupchan's (this volume) case for looking towards a more regionalized world order.

- *An international society undergoing a profound transformation because of its expansion from Western to global scale; because of the rise of permanent IGOs, and because of the reconstitution of its institutional structure both by nationalism and by the liberal ideas of the market and human rights.* Despite decolonization, international society still has a Western-global core and a periphery varying in its degree of attachment to or alienation from the values and institutions of that core. Nationalism remains hugely influential in legitimizing political claims everywhere, and remains in tension with sovereignty and non-intervention. The struggle to incorporate the market and human rights as institutions is still a major ongoing theme.[56]

---

[55] Barry Buzan, "A World Order Without Superpowers: Decentered Globalism," *International Relations*, Vol. 25, No. 1 (2011), pp. 1–23.

[56] James Mayall, *Nationalism and International Society* (Cambridge University Press, 1990).

- A *"clash of civilizations"* between the West and the rest based on the tension
  between the expectations of political and cultural homogenization built
  into modernity, and the demands to maintain/reassert political and cultural
  difference. This clash had precursors in the Americas, and even earlier
  in the Crusades, but the main events were in Asia (Islam, India,
  China, Japan) and Africa during the nineteenth century, where the
  encounter did not wipe out the native population. This clash amplified the pre-modern issue of religion globally despite the fact that
  modernity generally weakened the position of religion in the West
  (the US excepted). Christianity, backed by Western power, challenged non-Western religions (Islam, Hinduism, animist religions).
  There was a decisive reversal of power between Christianity and Islam
  when the British took over India, and the Ottoman and Persian
  Empires weakened. Yet Hobsbawm[57] notes the effectiveness of Islam
  as an early form of resistance to the West. Similarly, Darwin[58] notes
  the emerging forms of resistance in the periphery to Western dominance in the later nineteenth century: to create European-style national
  projects, to engage in religious revivalism, and to reject the West and
  return to indigenous values. All three of these forms of resistance have
  carried forward into the twentieth and twenty-first centuries.

This continuity and depth of influence of the nineteenth-century transformations on the twentieth and twenty-first centuries suggests that there
is a very powerful case for thinking about change in terms that are wider
and deeper than Gilpin's. The nature and depth of these changes also
carry many profound implications for war and change.

The case against Gilpin's conceptualization of change is that it is too
narrow and too superficial to capture something as structurally deep as a
transformation in the dominant mode of production. Indeed, it not only
fails to see it, but actually blocks the kind of questions one has to ask in
order to see it. Given the devotion of neo-realists to capturing IR with a
few really big and important things, this is more than passingly ironic.
Gilpin's analysis is mainly materialist, thus missing or downplaying the
role of ideas or seeing them as merely epiphenomenal to changes in the
distribution of power. Yet even within a materialist framing Gilpin also
fails to make anything of the distinction between the *distribution* and the
mode of power. This is also ironic, because far more than most in IR,
Gilpin[59] does see, and up to a point take into account, the elements that

[57] Eric Hobsbawm, *The Age of Revolution 1789–1848*, pp. 273–274.
[58] John Darwin, *After Tamerlane: The Rise and Fall of Global Empires 1400–2000* (London: Penguin, 2007), pp. 339–349.
[59] Gilpin, *War and Change in World Politics*, pp. 23–27, 127–144.

compose the change in the mode of power and the impact of the rise of a global market economy on changing the behavior of powers. But he sees the impact mainly in terms of how big the dominant units can get (limits of expansion) rather than in terms of the transformation of the system itself.[60] So the charge against Gilpin is that he does not, and given his definitions of system change cannot, see changes in IR that are far wider, deeper, and more varied than those in his scheme.

The view from sociology through differentiation theory, and the complementary view from historical sociology through the idea of changes in the mode of production, provides a more profound and useful conceptualization of change for IR. They see not just dominant units (whether by power or by type), but the interplay of modes of differentiation across levels and sectors. These perspectives give a deep and durable view of change that really is about the transformation of the whole nature of international relations. It is hard to imagine that the revolution of modernity is reversible. The shift from stratificatory to functional differentiation produces too many advantages in power, wealth, status, and knowledge to make arcadian reversions attractive to more than a minority. Although the question is beyond the scope of this chapter, the underlying drivers of ever more functional differentiation are profound: the increasing size of human society, the way in which expanding knowledge forces specialization, and the powerful diversifying logic of capitalism, to name but three. And the consequences of modernity in terms of expanded populations, knowledge, infrastructure, and interdependence are now so deeply embedded that they provide an enormous inertia to the ongoing unfolding of modernity. Short of some (not unimaginable) ecological catastrophe that radically disrupts the conditions of human existence on the planet, and hugely reduces the size of the human population, modernity looks set to continue its widening and deepening. This perspective suggests a radically different periodization from either Gilpin or mainstream IR. War plays a part in this transformation, but no longer the main part. In the end, Gilpin's framework is much more about continuity than about change, and in that it shares the weakness of Waltz's neo-realism. As Tang[61] argues, realist thinking along these lines is appropriate only to an era of world history that is now many decades in the past.

The case against Gilpin's conceptualization of war is that it fails to register the full significance of large changes in the reasons for war, the constraints against war, the means by which war is fought, and its

---

[60] *Ibid.*, pp. 144–155.
[61] Shiping Tang, *The Social Evolution of International Politics* (Oxford University Press, 2013).

consequences. Changing ideas, organization, and capabilities change the meaning of and reasons for war. In the modern era war is not just about who rules (dynastic stratification), but about what ideology, what vision of progress, they represent. It is true that modernity initially increased the military capability of states, which fits comfortably into Gilpin's argument. In effect modernity accelerated and intensified the hegemonic cycle, and changed its justifications, but it did not fundamentally change its process. This was broadly true during the nineteenth century and part of the twentieth. But modernity also transformed the nature of states and the kind of international society they projected, as well as the costs and destructive consequences of war.

The transformation of war by modernity is ongoing. Partly this transformation is material. Initially, modernity supported a huge intensification of war by providing larger populations, mass production, and an endless supply of ever more destructive and expensive weapons. This was the transformation to total war manifested in the First, Second, and Third (Cold) World Wars. But from the First World War onwards, the unfolding of ever more destructive (or potentially destructive) total wars increasingly pointed towards either an end to all-out world wars, or an end to civilization, or possibly humankind. The military consequences of the Industrial Revolution increased the cost and destructiveness of total war massively beyond the point of instrumental rationality. This logic was recognized after the carnage and ruin caused in Europe by the First World War. It became manifest with the arrival of the atomic bomb in 1945, at which point the general argument in this chapter about the mode of power intersects with the specific one of Deudney (this volume) about nuclear weapons. Although total war among nuclear great powers was still possible, it was not a rational way of pursuing hegemonic transitions. A nuclear peace saw out the Cold War, and makes it rational now to suppose that we will never again see total wars amongst great powers of the kind that dominated the first half of the twentieth century.

Partly this transformation is ideational. Modernity certainly provided a wealth of new ideologies to fight about, not least nationalism and racism, but also the different interpretations of progress embodied in liberalism and socialism (and fascism). But it also provided new ideas to undermine some key reasons for fighting. Both liberalism and socialism carried the idea that the right kind of ideological homogeneity could and should generate peaceful international relations. This was a distinct departure from the agrarian world, in which dynastic homogeneity (except for universal empire under one ruler) was never associated with general peace. In contemporary IR this line of thinking is mainly carried by (liberal) democratic peace theory (DPT).

Both the material and the ideational developments of modernity thus provide increasing leverage against a perpetual cycle of hegemonic wars that was not present before the nineteenth century. Considerations of both cost and ideology weigh against hegemonic war, moreso now that the twentieth century's conflicts over ideology have boiled down largely to arguments about different versions of capitalist political economy (liberal capitalism in the US, social capitalism in Europe, authoritarian capitalism in China and Russia, and who knows what combinations emerging in India, Brazil, and elsewhere). If modernity eventually transforms war, largely wiping out the hegemonic wars of Gilpin's theory, then its understanding of transformation trumps his. Gilpin is aware of the constraints of nuclear weapons and economic interdependence, which partly underpin his moderately optimistic conclusions. But he seems blind to the material and ideational transformation of war by modernity pointing towards the end of all-out great-power war. What Gilpin sees as useful constraints, are actually elements of a much larger transformation. In a move reminiscent of E.H. Carr, he just throws this baby out along with the bathwater of the supposed failure of liberal idealism to deliver harmony.

Gilpin's book is in many ways impressive, though its weaknesses are exposed by his inability to use his framework to form a coherent view of the present as it was in 1981. That incoherence is even clearer in the perspective of developments thirty years on. I submit that a perspective on change and war rooted in differentiation theory and historical sociology offers a fuller and deeper understanding of both. It focuses on the deeper material and ideational changes that have now almost certainly brought to an end the longstanding role of great-power war as the driving force of systemic change. At the same time it reorients our attention to the profound systemic changes, economic, social, political, and military that take place apart from war. Here this chapter intersects with and supports Mastanduno (this volume) who discusses the 2008 economic crisis as a non-war transformative event in the decline of US hegemony.

If Deudney and I are right about the impact of increasingly destructive military technology; and if Kupchan and I are right about the demise of superpowers and the move to a more regionalized world politics; and if the unfolding revolution of modernity has indeed, in 1989, reached the end of its opening cycle of wars about which ideology would define the political economy of modernity, then Gilpin's model of war and change is dead. Certainly there will still be jostling amongst major powers, and certainly difficult and tense cycles of relative rise and decline will happen as they are now between the US and China. But this will happen in a world where the resort to great-power war is massively constrained by military (nuclear weapons), economic (interdependence), and ideological (DPT) considerations, and in which the spread of modernity is making both states and people more powerful. A lowering concentration of power, a degree of ideological convergence around forms of capitalism and basic institutions of international society, and a more regionalized structure of world politics all point away from Gilpin's hegemonic wars. As the revolutions of modernity unleashed during the nineteenth century continue to unfold, increasingly no power will be either able or eager to dominate world politics. This puts Lake's (this volume) argument about the US perhaps being able to draw China into a US order into a wider context. There may well be order, but it will be increasingly egalitarian, not led by anyone. If this is true then Wohlforth's (this volume) concern about the corrupting influence of dominance may pass with the fading of Western primacy, or at least be confined to dominant powers within regional systems. Some of the useful qualities of empire pointed out by Hall (this volume) may well re-emerge in this order, though empire itself most certainly will not. And Ikenberry (this volume) is correct in saying that China will not replace the US as a global hegemon, and that the future of international order will rest more on the legitimacy of its rules than on the leadership of some particular superpower.

The prospect ahead is therefore of a structure of world politics unlike anything seen before. Not like the empires, dynasticisms, recurrent cycles, and endless wars of the pre-modern world before the Atlantic revolutions. And not like the huge inequalities and ideological divisions of the transition period from agrarian to industrial society that started in the late eighteenth century and is arguably beginning to come to completion now. On this basis, I conclude that Gilpin's confusion about how to read the 1970s and 1980s in terms of his theory was not just about the intrinsic difficulty of applying broad brush theory to the present. Rather his confusion pointed to basic flaws in the realist way he conceptualized structural change in the international system.

9   Nations, states, and empires

John A. Hall

Introduction

Realism in all its forms suggests that war is always possible given the absence of any supreme Leviathan. The search for security can of course take many forms. One route is to seek total power, a search likely to be defeated and so ultimately against the logic of realism.[1] Another route is to seek the protection of the strong, and a further one to seek alliances, often bearing in mind the classic maxim that "the enemy of my enemy is my friend." For an outsider, this interrelated theoretical ensemble is a thing of beauty, on a par with classical economics, offering an elegant and parsimonious explanation of the ways in which states interact. But what is not offered by this approach is a theory of inter*national* relations. At least that is the claim of a new school of thought in the social sciences. A new data set created by Wimmer codes all wars between 1816 and 2001, and finds a strong correlation between the incidence of war and change in the institutional form of polity.[2] Of course, the general point, and the means of establishing it, is not entirely new. Holsti's *Peace and War* (1981) also counted the causes of war, over a longer time period although only in the core of world politics, and found that nationalism was ever more responsible for causing war in the late nineteenth and early twentieth centuries.[3] The

---

[1] Raymond Aron, *La tragédie algérienne* (Paris: Plon, 1957).
[2] Andreas Wimmer, *Waves of War: Nationalism, State Formation, and Ethnic Exclusion in the Modern World* (Cambridge University Press, 2013), Chapter 4.
[3] I intend on another occasion to evaluate these two approaches. There is much to recommend in Holsti's looser methodology, not least as it allows – at the expense of the statistical exercises that can then be performed on the data – for wars to have several causes. The 1864 conflict between Germany and Denmark is characterized solely as an interstate war; that is to ignore the nationalist drive of the National Liberals of Copenhagen, so unwilling to accept at any time federal arrangements that might have appeased the German ethnics of Schleswig and Holstein. And there is something to be said for caution when classifying the territorial changes involved in the unification of Italy: at least some of these were deals between states rather than the expression of nationalist pressures.

general analytic point is clear, and it deserves emphasis: wars are seen as resulting from social change rather than from the anarchic character of a multipolar world.

This dispute brings us immediately to the core of Gilpin's brilliant work. We can see why by considering the key example he gives of system change, from empire and/or city-states to a world in which nation-states compete. The analytic matrix is clear. The power of a state rests on intensity married to appropriate size. Differently put, empires were too large to be socially intensive, whilst city-states lacked the size to make the intensity of their patriotic feelings matter in power politics. Gilpin further excoriates another pre-industrial form, that of feudalism, held to be decentralized and chaotic, an obstacle to the fiscal extraction on which the sinews of states depend. In contrast nation-states are neither too small nor too large, and the presence of popular willingness to sacrifice for the nation makes them true power containers. We can see what this means for Gilpin in relation to the dispute that concerns us by noting the different logics of empires, states, and nations in abstract, ideal typical forms. Pre-industrial empires sought to be whole social worlds within which peace and order could reign. Their lack of infrastructural reach meant that they would punish harshly when they could, but their greatest desire was to leave their peoples alone, to let sleeping dogs lie in peace. This is of course utterly different from the logic imposed by Darwinian competition within a multipolar world. Change is mandated by the need to keep up, with extinction being the price of flatulence and laziness. This is the classical realist world that Gilpin exemplifies, and it is what he has in mind when talking about nation-states. The level of competition has increased because the people believe the state to be their own, but the logic at work remains realist. It is important to stress that Gilpin is right to stress all of this, for national sentiment did a great deal to strengthen many states. But there can be a different logic to the nation that causes war. When treated badly, when not allowed to "get in" to the mainstream of society, a minority can demand secession. A further cause of war can occur when such a minority has a neighboring ethnic homeland: irredentist claims from that homeland, or even the fear that such claims may come, can also start war. Bluntly put, Gilpin misses state-breaking nationalism. Nationalism of this sort has affected the historical record, and it cannot be ignored.

The central tenets of the argument can be laid out. To do so is vital, for the critics of realism have much to learn from Gilpin; differently put, the great theorist of international relations is quite often right, and in ways that have real import for nationalism studies. Much of the argument derives from the opening pages of John Hobson's *Imperialism:*

The novelty of the recent Imperialism regarded as a policy consists chiefly in its adoption by several nations. The notion of a number of competing empires is essentially modern. The root idea of empire in the ancient and medieval world was that of a federation of States, under a hegemony, covering in general terms the entire or recognized world, such as was held by Rome... Thus empire was identified with internationalism, though not always based on a conception of equality of nations... the triumph of nationalism seems to have crushed the rising hope of internationalism. Yet it would appear that there is no essential antagonism between them. A true strong internationalism in form or spirit would rather imply the existence of powerful self-respecting nationalities which seek union on the basis of common national needs and interests... Nationalism is a plain highway to internationalism, and if it manifests divergence we may well suspect a perversion of its nature and its purpose. Such a perversion is Imperialism, in which nations trespassing beyond the limits of facile assimilation transform the wholesome stimulative rivalry of varied national types into the cut-throat struggle of competing empires[4]

Obviously, states in Europe at the end of the nineteenth century felt, pace Gilpin, that scale was necessary to ensure their survival. We shall see that this did indeed lead to a very particular historical perversion. But these late-nineteenth-century empires did not create separate and distinct "worlds," as had their forebears. To the contrary, they were in continual collision and competition. That this is so means that much of their behavior can be understood in realist terms. However, the crucial consideration that matters here is the way in which scale brought with it the dilemma of how empires should treat the varied nationalities under their control. Pre-modern empires were "multicultural" and "multinational" to a fault, bound to diversity by weakness, lacking means to indoctrinate and to homogenize into a single mold. It is exactly this separation between nationalism and imperialism that was broken in modern circumstances. Modern empires often sought to become nation-states. In so doing they bred state-breaking nationalist movements. To say this is to make two claims. First, there can be no doubt but that the national question affected international relations at the end of the nineteenth century. Second, students of nationalism can gain from Gilpin an awareness of the certain fact that the movements that concern them were deeply influenced by geopolitical rivalries.

There is complexity here, a clear sense that neither side in the dispute noted at the start is a clear winner. I cannot apologize for this: the world is complex, and so must be the argument. And no apology is necessary for concentrating so much on the late nineteenth and first half of the twentieth centuries. The events of these years changed the world: the

[4] John A. Hobson, *Imperialism: A Study* (London: James Nisbet, 1902), pp. 6–7, 8.

First World War released the twin revolutions of the twentieth century, with the rise of China that so much concerns us being unimaginable without its Russian predecessor. We understand much about these tectonic shifts thanks to Gilpin's work on hegemonic rivalries; we will deepen our comprehension by placing nationalism as much at the center of our attention.

Terms of engagement

Some of the most striking pages of *War and Change in World Politics* are devoted to one particular change of "system," although hints are offered as to further changes that might be examined. Empires are seen as too large, city-states too small, and feudal politics too chaotic to allow for really effective social mobilization and penetrative rule. The European system sees the emergence of a world of continual interaction between state and society because of the pressures resulting from levels of military engagement higher than in other world civilizations. European states thus became great-power containers, intense breeders of loyalty with very considerable capacities. Further, Gilpin has made us aware that in such a world economics and politics blend together, with states needing to foster growth as their fundamental source of strength. Varied tensions accordingly arise when states of this sort live and have their being within a larger international capitalist economy. All of this seems to me profound and convincing, not surprisingly since I wrote a less developed view of this sort myself, bereft at that time of knowledge of Gilpin's particular argument.[5] European states existed, so it seemed, in a Darwinian world in which they had to swim within the larger seas of economic and military competition, with relations between these two forces being complex and in continual motion. It is only fair to mention this because the charges to be made against Gilpin apply equally to my own work. At last I can sound like a French intellectual, albeit their *autocritiques* are often facile, and certainly come all too often!

An initial difficulty with Gilpin's view is that feudalism in Europe was not replaced by nation-states – if, that is, one insists that the concept of "nation" must have some reference to the entry of the people onto the political stage. One might say that some feudal states were replaced by "national states," the preserve of a monarch but with the notion of a people referring to the inclusion of a powerful upper class. England and France fit this mold, although partial linguistic unification did come

---

[5] John A. Hall, *Powers and Liberties: The Causes and Consequences of the Rise of the West* (Oxford: Blackwell, 1985).

slowly in this world in which state came before nation. Such national states were capable of generating a good deal of power.[6] They slowly gained in authority and centrality.[7] Further, they managed over time to extract, as many empirical studies have shown, ever-higher rates of taxation.[8] This most certainly allowed them to play a part in the defeat of the imperial ambitions of Charles V and Philip II. Struggles over citizenship, caused both by the recruiting officer and the tax collector, did then lead to the creation of nation-states – as indeed did the sheer sense of belonging created, as Max Weber argued, by shared struggle against an enemy. Gilpin is thus, as noted, right to suggest that national sentiment could strengthen states – effectively when state strength came before national awakening, allowing movement of different groups towards a single national ideal. Nonetheless, the fully developed nation-state was a modern phenomenon. If there are signs of French and English nationalism in the late eighteenth century,[9] due to the imperial struggle between France and England, Eugen Weber's celebrated study of late-nineteenth-century France showed that it took the homogenizing effect of conscription to turn peasants into Frenchmen.[10]

But not all European states resembled this model, and neither, as we shall see, did Great Britain in any complete way. Before 1914 something like twenty-five million people were ruled by elites other than their own.

[6] I will not consider here what may be termed the "Clausewitz question," that is, whether nationalism increased the fighting capacity of troops, as the German theorist, who had personal experience of defeat at the hands of Napoleon's forces at Jena, claimed (Carl von Clausewitz, *On War*, edited and translated by Michael Howard and Peter Paret (Princeton University Press, 1976), pp. 591–592). There are examples (above all the *Wehrmacht* in the Second World War) where this seems veridical; in general, the claim should be doubted given a mass of evidence showing fighting effectiveness, such as it is, to be most closely related to the mini-loyalties created by intense comradeship. But if modern states did not necessarily produce better fighters, their impressive fiscal extraction rates meant that they could often win wars by putting more troops in the field, over longer periods of time.

[7] It may be useful to make a distinction here. Powerful regional nobilities could resist the state, so as to protect their liberties. But these rarely turned into popular movements until the nineteenth century. (But this did happen in Holland, where the religious enthusiasm of the sea beggars forced the nobility to become part of a societal movement.) Thus Czech nationalism began as *Landespatriotismus*, a movement led by the German-speaking nobility!

[8] The superlative reconstruction of the Roman economy provided by Peter Fibiger Bang (*The Roman Bazaar: A Comparative Study of Trade and Markets in a Tributary Empire* (Cambridge University Press, 2008)) suggests that the central state had difficulty in raising more than 6% of total product. The English state controlled a much larger share of total product by the end of the eighteenth century (John Brewer, *The Sinews of Power: War, Money and the English State, 1688–1783* (New York, NY: Alfred A. Knopf, 1989)).

[9] Michael Mann, "The Emergence of Modern European Nationalism," in J.A. Hall and I.C. Jarvie, ed., *Transition to Modernity* (Cambridge University Press, 1992), pp. 137–166.

[10] Eugen Weber, *Peasants into Frenchmen* (London: Chatto and Windus, 1979).

The great empires – Ottoman, Tsarist, and Hapsburg – had arisen out of varied mixtures of conquest and marriage. These social formations were "composite" with key provinces having or gaining "liberties" which the metropole had to respect. The crucial point to be made is simple: these were states in which national awakening came before state formation was complete – that is, in which national self-consciousness, sometimes backed by possession of a schooling system, ruled out the creation of a nation-state, that is, when understood as a situation in which each nation would have its own state, and each state its nation. The great land empires of Europe, in other words, had problems with their nationalities. The contrast with the contemporary advanced world is of course very great, for now multiculturalism in the strong sense – that is the presence of autonomous and different nations within the same polity, as compared to the presence of immigrant minorities – is all but over. Many homogeneous nation-states with which we are now familiar were created speedily and forcibly by various means. If assimilation is the American way, so too was civil war. Just as important in other cases were forcible assimilation, population movements and transfers, ethnic cleansing, secession, and mass murder. This chapter is concerned with these practices, so common between 1890 and 1945 but present too during the hideous break-up of Yugoslavia, on the grounds that Gilpin's characterization of the system change to the world of nation-states is too smooth – it concentrates on states such as France and England, and so says too little about the dilemmas that faced the Romanovs and the Hapsburgs.

Analytic progress in this field requires attention to definitions. It is possible, to begin with, to offer a simple and unitary definition of nationalism – namely that the national community should look after its own affairs so that it can survive and prosper. However, that general principle can find expression in different forms, two of which deserve special attention. Gellner's *Nations and Nationalism* represents in its essence the most striking and severe version of the first form.[11] This great modern *philosophe* was wont to claim that one should assimilate or get one's own state given that the only remaining alternative was to be killed. It is not hard to see that such a view derives from a thinker with a Jewish background (or, to be precise, with a Jewish background imposed upon him), who had experience of the full horrors of the twentieth century's dark continent.[12] Hence his definition of nationalism differed from that given in the second sentence of this paragraph, stressing the need for each state to have a single culture, and each culture to have its

---

[11] Ernest Gellner, *Nations and Nationalism* (Oxford: Blackwell, 1983).
[12] John A. Hall, *Ernest Gellner: An Intellectual Biography* (London: Verso, 2010).

own state – a view that brings to mind the hideous homogenizing practices noted in the previous paragraph. This view is represented in modern "international" relations scholarship in the work of Miller who stresses that war is likely whenever there is an imbalance in "the state to nation" ratio, that is, whenever the correspondence described by Gellner is lacking.[13] One should note an interesting and pertinent difference between the two authors. Miller suggests that war is likely at all times when an imbalance exists between state and nation; Gellner's theory pointed in that direction, but the depth of his knowledge of nationalism led him to note, indeed to accentuate, the fact that nationalism was often weak, unable to change politics, let alone to foment war.

The alternative view stresses the very varied arrangements that have allowed different ethnicities and nations to live together in peace. The key principle here is very clear, and it is best expressed in terms of Hirschman's *Exit, Voice and Loyalty*.[14] When a nation is denied voice, that is, when it is faced by a state denying it cultural rights and political representation, secessionist exit becomes attractive, even necessary. Allowing voice, in contrast, can produce loyalty, thereby undermining secessionist drives. One point that deserves emphasis here concerns the drivers of nationalism. Gellner had secession in mind in his famous parable of Ruritanians seeking to escape from Megalomania. But it was the behaviour of Megalomania when trying to build a nation-state out of disparate elements – that is, of the elite, often radical in character – that then led to demands for secession. We have here one of the key discoveries of sociology, namely that the character of social movements often results from the nature of the state with which they interact. A second point is technical in character, of great importance for those who wish to calculate the consequences of ethnic fractionalization. Bluntly put, a strong distinction needs to be drawn between nominal and politically charged ethnicity – the latter resulting most often from the discrimination and exclusion just noted. We now possess a marvelous index describing ethnicity and political life for the whole world in the postwar period.[15] What matters analytically here is that this data set records various types of political inclusion and partnership, as well as the

---

[13] Benjamin Miller, *States, Nations, and the Great Powers: The Sources of Regional War and Peace* (Cambridge University Press, 2007); Stephen van Evera, "Hypotheses on Nationalism and War," *International Security*, Vol. 18 (1994), pp. 5–39.

[14] Albert O. Hirschman, *Exit, Voice and Loyalty: Response to Decline in Firms, Organizations and States* (Cambridge, MA: Harvard University Press, 1970).

[15] Andreas Wimmer, Lars-Erik Cederman, and Brian Min, "Ethnic Politics and Armed Conflict: A Configurational Analysis of a New Global Data Set," *American Sociological Review*, Vol. 74 (2009), pp. 316–337.

discrimination that politicizes. The end result is clear: the nationalist principle can be honored, as suggested, by the provision of cultural rights and political representation within a larger polity, for all that exclusion and discrimination lead to conflict.[16] Switzerland exists, though whether it should be called a multi-ethnic nation-state[17] or a state-nation[18] is unclear. More important still, India exists. So the world in which we live has not, thank goodness, seen the complete triumph of the nation-state understood in Gellnerian terms, making it at least possible to imagine a multipolar world of competing states, important amongst them state-nations rather than nation-states.

If we move away from this point, certainly prescriptive for all that it is based in a descriptive reality, we are confronted with the undoubted fact that Gellner accurately described his own experience, that of Central Europe in the twentieth century: he wrote his autobiography, David Laitin once remarked, and called it sociology. For none of the multi-national empires and composite monarchies present in nineteenth-century Europe was able to turn itself into some form of more liberal multinational polity; all collapsed, all were replaced by a slew of new nation-states. Further, Europe since 1945 has been a zone of peace in part because the national question has been solved for the vast majority of states, though this finally only occurred, as noted, through full scale use of ethnic cleansing and mass murder. We can at least hope that this moment of nationalism was historically bounded, rather than being a permanent necessity in human affairs. But it would be as well to realize that the desire

---

[16] It is worth noting an interesting range of opinion amongst theorists who think in the alternative terms just noted. At one end of the range stand thinkers seeking an open political system so that complete assimilation can take place; at the other end are those privileging, at times for normative reasons as much as on grounds of political necessity, the deep diversity of a self-maintaining nation within some larger political frame. If the important work of David D. Laitin (*Nations, States and Violence* (New York, NY: Oxford University Press, 2007)) stands at the assimilationist of this spectrum, middling positions are provided by David Horowitz (*Ethnic Groups in Conflict* (Berkeley, CA: University of California Press, 1985)) and by Andreas Wimmer (*Waves of War*), both seeking reasonable accommodations, whilst the works of O'Leary ('Debating Consociational Politics: Normative and Explanatory Arguments,' in Sid Noel, ed., *From Power Sharing to Democracy: Post-conflict Institutions in Ethnically Divided Society* (Montreal and Kingston: McGill-Queen's University Press, 2005)), John McGarry and Brendan O'Leary ('Federation as a Method of Ethnic Conflict Regulation,' in Noel, ed., *From Power Sharing to Democracy*), and of Alfred Linz, Juan Stepan, and Yogendra Yadav (*Crafting State-Nations: India and Other Multinational Democracies* (Baltimore, MD: Johns Hopkins University Press, 2011)) recommend the greatest degree of pluralism. These are interesting and important differences, and they most certainly matter in terms of practical policy proposals.

[17] Andreas Wimmer, "A Swiss Anomaly? A Relational Account of Boundary Making," *Nations and Nationalism*, Vol. 17 (2011), pp. 718–737.

[18] Stepan, Linz, and Yadav, *Crafting State-Nations*.

to nationally homogenize a particular territory is likely to remain a possibility, a permanent temptation for some nationalizing leaders.

These comments on the nature of nationalism give the agenda for this chapter precision. Why was it that empires bred the more extreme forms of nationalism at the end of the nineteenth century? To answer that question one final preliminary definitional point must be made, in this case concerning the changing character of imperial rule.

Empires have varied over time quite as much as nations. There is an enormous difference in the pre-modern world between nomadic formations and those based on settled agriculture. The contrast between the latter type of tributary empire and modern overseas empires is greater still. The globalization of trade pioneered by Rome, for example, saw the movement only of luxury goods, and very few of them at that. In contrast, the European overseas empires totally disrupted the political economies of the areas in which they were present, building railway lines and ports so that massive amounts could be transported for general consumption.[19] The most important thing to note here, however, is that empires were considered to be the going thing, the most modern form of polity, until very recently. They were large and powerful, replete with resources. Furthermore, they could draw upon considerable reserves of loyalty. 'Imperial ethnicities' existed in all empires at the end of the nineteenth century, and often far beyond. The white residents of Canada, New Zealand, Australia, and South Africa were, above all, British, members of a larger Britannic nationalism – within whose realms social and geographical mobility was remarkably high.[20] Jews, socialists, and the officer corps were "emperor loyal" in the Hapsburg lands, just as were Baltic Germans within the Tsarist empire. For another, the rule of an empire could gain, at least for some time, through traditional practices of divide and rule. It is as well to remember the British tactic in India of setting one nationality against each other, traditional princes against Congress, and Hindus against Muslims. By the late 1920s Gandhi feared that the momentum for independence had been lost, perhaps permanently.

If we return to the text of John Hobson a final point needs to be made. The contrast of empire and nation-state can be overdone.[21] On the one hand, the nation-states of nineteenth-century Europe had once been empires. The British case is a prime example. The conquest of Wales is

[19] Peter Bang, *The Roman Bazaar*.

[20] John Darwin, "Empire and Ethnicity," *Nations and Nationalism*, Vol. 16, No. 3 (2010), pp. 383–401.

[21] Krishan Kumar, "Nation-States as Empires, Empires as Nation-States: Two Principles, One Practice?" *Theory and Society*, Vol. 39 (2010), pp. 119–143.

still evident in the castles remaining in the principality. In contrast, the attempt to conquer Scotland was less successful. But dynastic succession, the Act of Union of 1707, the repression of the rising of 1745, economic opportunity, and the warm embrace of British royalty thereafter led to notably successful incorporation. The contrast is with Ireland. Conquest certainly took place and so too did union in 1801; but incorporation was another matter. This was in part because Catholicism sustained difference, in part because the English did not want to convert so many and were certainly not prepared to dilute their identity in such a way as to allow Catholics full citizenship. On the other hand stands the central insight that follows from Hobson's text. Empires could seek to become nation-states. Seeking to do so was bound to cause tremendous difficulties. State interference with society always breeds reaction: nationalizing homogenizing policies would be bound to produce nationalist reactions.

Scale and nation

There were two types of empire extant at the end of the nineteenth century, traditional agrarian polities and overseas trading states – that is, empires within Europe itself as well as the newer ones overseas.[22] Russia and Austria clearly belong to the former type, having benefited from expansion as the result of conquest, colonization, and marriage. If Britain was the prime example of the latter, it contained the Irish, and so, as noted, had at least one element of the former type. It is of the essence of the matter that it was impossible to wholly separate these two forms of empire, although some clear-headed attempts were made to do so. The power of overseas empire could make continental imperial powers feel insignificant.

A second distinction can move the argument forward. In contemporary circumstances there is certainly something to the view that national homogeneity, especially when married to small scale, can lead to economic success. In such a world, everyone can, so to speak, sit around the same table in the face of economic and geopolitical crises, able to respond quickly and effectively, capable of bearing large burdens because they understand, not least as they speak the same language that action is required if nation-state is to survive. This is the world of modern Denmark, and of a notable number of the most competitive countries

---

[22] Dominic Lieven, "Dilemmas of Empire 1850–1918. Power, Territory, Identity," *Journal of Contemporary History*, Vol. 34, No. 2 (1999), pp. 163–200; Dominic Lieven, *Empire: The Russian Empire and Its Rivals* (London: John Murray, 2000).

of the contemporary world.[23] It is noticeable that the Danes once possessed one of the more notable European empires, with rule over Norway, southern Sweden, Schleswig and Holstein, part of the Baltic coast, and with colonies in both the West Indies and on the eastern coast of India (where the Danes founded a university, as they had already done in Lund). As the result of an extraordinary and continuing ability to lose wars, the Danes downsized; they became homogenous, freed from a nationalities problem, but blessed with state traditions from the past. This "big small state" now enjoys, by some calculations, the highest standard of living in the world.

It is very important to realize that the world did not have this character, at least for the great powers, at the end of the nineteenth century.[24] Size was then held to be the means to power, and hence to security. The awful example that proved the point to the leading powers was the slow decline of the Ottomans. Millions of Muslims had been driven from the Balkans by 1914, the first massive piece of ethnic cleansing in modern times, whilst the state was totally humiliated in a thousand ways – with its fiscal capacity farmed out to foreigners and its Greek trading elite only too willing to call in support from co-religionists abroad. The "sick man of Europe" sought to re-invent herself but there was no clear indication as to how this could be done. "Ottomanism" never had mass appeal, and the best bet – the creation of a Muslim identity that would draw in the Arab provinces – had little appeal to the Turkish military elite. The prospect of dismemberment loomed large.

The key dilemma that faced the empires of continental Europe was simple: if size was to be maintained in the circumstances of the time, as it had to be if power was to be preserved, it was necessary to deal with the national question. Homogeneity would lend cohesion and power, not least as it was believed that citizen armies had greater fighting spirit – as seems to have been demonstrated by the Japanese when fighting Russia in 1905. And homogeneity seemed necessary because a national minority might have an external national homeland, creating the possibility that it might, in war time, become a fifth column. Accordingly, state elites began to interfere with their peoples. There is ambiguity at this point. On occasion, it seems as if the actions of states actually created national

---

[23] John Campbell and John A. Hall, "Defending the Gellnerian Premise: Denmark in Historical and Comparative Context," *Nations and Nationalism*, Vol. 16, No. 1 (2010), pp. 89–107.

[24] Equally the Danish example might mislead us about the world now, at least if it is taken out of context. Small states prosper only in a world in which there is geopolitical order, and in which their preference, wholly necessary given limits to their resources and markets, for free trade is institutionally secured.

movements where none existed before. But I have no desire to deny that some national movements had already been formed, and that "official nationalisms" attempted to control something that they felt might get out of hand.[25] But in either case, the desire to homogenize gave nationalist movements a particular character, turning them from cultural affairs of professors towards popular movements all-too-capable of political agency. A classic instance of the way in which actions by the state changed the character of a pre-existing national movement is that of the Finns. Until the end of the nineteenth century, the Finns had been content within the Tsarist empire; they were largely left to their own devices, blessed with the liberties that came with the status of an imperial duchy. Rationalization policies, especially as they affected language, led a newly politicized nationalist movement to demand secession by the start of the twentieth century.

From our perspective it might seem as if Great Britain represented the furthest opposite point to the Ottomans on a range measuring state strength. She ruled over large parts of the world, balanced her accounts and paid her military thanks to the contributions made by India, had at least some hegemonic powers, especially over the sea lanes, and was soon, during both world wars, able to call on reserves of manpower that did a good deal to bring victory. Nonetheless, the fact of the matter is that the British elite felt under threat in structural terms. The country was after all but a small island, its possession of so much territory something of a freak. The defeat of the French in the great imperial contest of the late eighteenth and early nineteenth centuries had allowed Britain to expand, and the maintenance of its empire resulted thereafter from, in turn, exhaustion and then balance amongst its European rivals.[26] Most of its rule was but skin deep. Fragility also resulted from what is now seen as one of its great achievements, free trade. Food had to be imported, making naval supremacy absolutely vital. It was this that made the German challenge – directed less at the acquisition of colonies than at the capacity to strike at the British fleet – so very scary, terrifying far beyond Germany's move towards the Second Industrial Revolution. But even this understates the case. Britain was at one with Germany, and with France, in seeing the future as likely to favor Russia and the United States, powers with their own continents.

---

[25] Benedict Anderson, *Imagined Communities: Reflections on the Origin and Spread of Nationalism* (London: Verso, 1983), Chapter 6.

[26] John Darwin, *After Tamerlane: The Rise and Fall of Global Empires, 1400–2000* (London: Penguin, 2007); John Darwin, *The Empire Project: The Rise and Fall of the British World System 1830–1970* (Cambridge University Press, 2009).

One classic response was that of Sir John Seeley. It might well be the case, as Hobson (though from a different political perspective) had suggested, that not everyone could be included in a larger British entity. This certainly applied to Africans, but quite as much to Indians even though key early Indian nationalists wanted to "get in," wanted to be part of a larger Britannic entity. The empire had racial discrimination at its core, at least in its later stages, and Seeley's dream was accordingly for a Greater Britain based on the white settlers of Australia, Canada, South Africa, and New Zealand. There was certainly, as noted, a measure of shared identity in the White Dominions. But these plans nonetheless came to naught. For one thing, the settler nations were proud and independent, not at all keen to respond to calls for imperial defense given their own needs and ever more irritated by foreign policy being decided in London. Schemes for a federal empire came to naught because in the end there was insufficient interest on either side. And in this context one should remember Ireland. The varied plans for Home Rule stalemated British politics at the end of the nineteenth century and beyond, without success. Indeed, in 1914 Britain faced the possibility of mutiny in its own army, reluctant to allow a minority of Protestants to be included in Home Rule for the whole, largely Catholic island of Ireland and viscerally opposed to anything that would undermine the unity of the empire.[27] For another, the idea of imperial unity often had at its core tariff reform, that is, the creation of a closed imperial trading bloc. There was powerful resistance to this, for it seemed to guarantee more expensive food. Empire might be popular in a vague way, but not when it came to affect the living standards of the people.[28]

Tsarist Russia felt equally threatened at the end of the nineteenth century, for all that others felt scared by its sheer size, and especially by its resources of manpower. If German military prowess and industrial power were scaring, so was the alliance with Vienna, since this suggested an alliance between a single people. In these circumstances radical state nationalists sought to enhance Russian power. Industrialization mattered, but so too did the national question. Pure Russian ethnics were after all not a majority in the empire. But if Ukrainians could become Russian, that is, if they could be prevented from further creating an identity of their own, then Russia might have the chance to create at

---

[27] Lieven nicely notes that democratic pressures made it hard to create federal solutions. Franz Joseph had given great autonomy to the Hungarians in 1867 without consulting anyone; this route was barred in Britain ("Dilemmas of Empire 1850–1918," pp. 197–199).

[28] Frank Trentmann, *Free Trade Nation: Consumption, Civil Society and Commerce in Modern Britain* (Oxford University Press, 2008).

least the core of a nation-state. Harshness accordingly characterized Russian policy. And we have seen that the prospect of diminished voice raised the attractiveness of exit for the Finns.

The world of Austro-Hungary at once resembled and differed from the Russian situation. Defeat by Germany had led to the granting of autonomy for the Magyars. They were not a majority in their own territory, and so imposed very harsh assimilation conditions – close to success by 1914 – on the Slovaks. The Austrian half of the empire, Cisleithania, was very different. To begin with German had simply seemed a world language, to which other communities would accede. When this did not happen, when the Czechs started to gain political consciousness, the German community also gained consciousness as an ethnic group. But German ethnics were not a majority within Cisleithania, and certainly nothing like that in the empire as a whole.[29] In these circumstances, the empire moved very slowly to a system of accommodation. This was a world of "bearable dissatisfaction" in the words of Count Taaffe – or, to use Gellner's later formulation, less a prison-house than a kindergarten of the nations. It is important to remember that no leader of the Czech national movement, to take but one example, sought actual independence during the nineteenth century – with key leaders such as Palacky arguing strongly against such a move, fearful of becoming a petty state all too exposed to German and Russian depradations. The Moravian Compromise looked set to secure loyalty through the granting of cultural rights, and something like this was being planned for the Czechs. But herein lay a major difficulty. The empire really needed a period of peace to consolidate such reforms, all of which were anyway undermining the powers of the central government. But the Hapsburgs wished to continue to play the great game of power politics. Their world was dominated by honor, as Lebow[30] has correctly noted, making the thought of downsizing not just dangerous but wholly humiliating. The Hapsburgs were accordingly suffering from what can only be termed political schizophrenia, forced to accommodate but attracted in their heart of hearts by homogenizing policies that would enhance their geopolitical strength.

[29] German was the language of social mobility, and census returns – always political acts – sought to enhance the number of "Germans" by considering ethnicity in terms of language of daily use. But even this method – bitterly contested by the Czechs who wanted to enhance their numbers by measuring "mother tongue" – only produced 38% of "Germans" in Cisleithania, itself of course a much smaller percentage for the empire as a whole.

[30] Richard Ned Lebow, *A Cultural Theory of International Relations* (Cambridge University Press, 2008).

Perhaps the best way to characterize what is going on in general terms is by turning to Max Weber, less as a sociologist than as a political actor in his own era. Three points need to be made about the German thinker, two immediately and a third in the next section. The first is to recall that Weber's ultimate value was nationalist. The most obvious way in which this can be seen is in his obsession in his earliest work with the Polish workers in the East Elbian estates of the aristocratic Junker class. National strength would come from homogeneity and cohesion, something that Bismarck too had felt, albeit opportunistically, when opening the cultural wars against the Catholics. Weber recognized that a measure of unity had been achieved through war, but he wished to further German strength in his own time, to achieve something equivalent to the previous generation's creation of the Reich. Any doubt about Weber's nationalist leanings can be eliminated by remembering his attitude during the First World War, above all in his concern to extend German power to the east, at the expense of Poland.

The second element of Weber's own politics of concern here is his membership of the Navy League. Weber was representative of many of the statist middle class who believed that Germany deserved and needed its own place in the sun. Interestingly, his views were criticized by the Austrian marginalists in 1907 when he gave a speech in Vienna, on the immediately accurate grounds that the German economy was developing rapidly – able to overtake Great Britain in 1913, according to recent economic historians, without the benefit of imperial possessions. What matters about economics in the end is, of course, not reality, but rather what people believe to be the case. Further, in this matter there was a measure of rationality to Weber's view. The British turn to free trade and interdependence was, in fact, no such thing: food supplies might come from abroad, but the power of the Royal Navy in effect made Britain autonomous. If a continental power took the same course, it would be much more dangerous. Exactly this happened to Germany in the last years of the First World War, when the British blockade bit seriously. As it happens, we now know that this had been planned in London at exactly the time that Weber was being criticized in Vienna.[31]

It is as well to highlight what is involved. By the end of the nineteenth century, European territory was, so to speak, full up, allowing no further expansion on the Continent. In these circumstances war would necessarily be a disaster. But the intensity of geopolitical competition, the enormous insecurities of the great powers, meant that the desire for

---

[31] Avner Offner, *The First World War: An Agrarian Interpretation* (Oxford University Press, 1989).

complete autonomy was rampant. A brilliant scholarly account hinting at what was involved is that of Sen.[32] One cause of international tensions at the end of the nineteenth century lay in international trade rivalries consequent on dumping practices – themselves the result of every state determining to be autonomous in the production of steel, the base for military independence. The picture as a whole is best characterized as the marriage of nationalism and imperialism. Each state sought secure sources of supply, and secure outlets for good produced. At any particular moment in time this might seem silly, given that the British empire traded openly before 1914. But that might change, as was obvious to those on the Continent looking at British politicians from both parties talking about the need for imperial union.

The novelty of a perversion

It is time to turn to analysis of the manner in which the dilemmas noted played out in practice. Two points will be made, the first a negative, the second drawing a distinction between the character of the two world wars.

The negative point is very simple. It is not the case that the struggle for possessions overseas led in any immediate way to the First World War. Lenin was wrong. Timing disproves his theory: the division of Africa took place in the 1880s. For what always mattered most to these great powers was their security within the European heartland – and, more particularly, their determination not to let matters so get out of hand again that anything like the strains and stresses of the revolutionary and Napoleonic period would be repeated.[33] It was this background condition that made it relatively easy to settle imperial disputes, especially over the partition of Africa. After all, imperial possessions paid little – with the exception of India, which, as noted, mattered enormously for Britain. The balance within Europe is the factor that allowed Britain to gain a huge empire in the first place; equally geopolitical factors do most to explain its longevity – French resentments were never likely to lead to war given the increasing power of Germany, whilst Germany itself for long did not wish to increase French and Russian power at the expense of Britain since that would weaken its own position.[34] Besides, the British empire

---

[32] Gautam Sen, *The Military Origins of Industrialization and International Trade Rivalry* (London: Pinter, 1984).

[33] Darwin, *After Tamerlane*.

[34] Paul Kennedy, "Why Did the British Empire Last So Long?" in his *Strategy and Diplomacy 1870–1945* (London: George Allen and Unwin, 1983).

was, until the interwar period, open to trade from its rivals. In summary, imperial disputes before 1914 were always kept within bounds; they certainly did not actually cause the onset of disaster. Nonetheless, Germany clearly felt left out, as noted, and received the merest trifles despite an activist foreign policy under Kaiser Wilhelm II.

Whilst full agreement as to the origins of the First World War will never be achieved, some comments can be made that relate to the argument made to this point. Nationalism most certainly played some part in the origin of the war. Most immediately, the occasion for war was the shots fired by the Serbian nationalist Gavrilo Princip, an irredentist nationalist keen to establish a Greater Serbia. More generally there were traces of the marriage of nationalism and imperialism, not just in an intellectual like Max Weber, but also in the mind of Bethmann-Hollweg. Still more important were the feelings in Vienna. The stiff note sent to Serbia, and backed by Germany, was in part caused by the fear that the empire would not be able to compete in a world in which size and national homogeneity mattered so much if it could not control its own territory – that is, if secession by the southern Slavs meant that its power would be undermined, as had been true of that of the Ottomans. Still, the war also had the character of a normal interstate conflict within a multipolar system. "The July Crisis revealed," Darwin notes, "that the Achilles heel of Europe's global primacy was the underdevelopment of the European states system."[35] This draws our attention to the two basic factors that tend to explain escalation to the extremes in a system of states.[36] The first is that of heterogeneity in the system as a whole, the presence of different values making mutual understanding difficult. This was certainly present by 1914 in a way that it had not been when Bismarck and Lord Salisbury were conducting the foreign policies of their respective countries. The second is that of the character of the states involved, that is, establishing whether they had the capacity – so often presumed by realism to exist – to calculate rationally. There were clear deficiencies at the time. Whilst the British state had brilliantly retrenched so as to face Germany, domestic politics made it impossible to give Germany the warning, by means of an open alliance with France, that might have prevented conflict. The Hapsburg case was made endlessly difficult by Hungarian autonomy. But the key variable involved was the inability of the German state to calculate rationally. For one thing, middle class nationalists such as Weber were pressing their state for a more activist policy. But a crucial factor was that the state was really a

[35] Darwin, *After Tamerlane*, p. 373.
[36] John A. Hall, *International Orders* (Cambridge: Polity, 1996).

court, with policy determined by whoever had last gained the ear of the Kaiser, and with no priority set between a world policy directed against England and the traditional Eastern policy directed against Russia.[37] The famous "Memorandum on the Present State of British Relations with France and Germany" penned by Eyre Crowe on January 1, 1907, argued that this explained German behavior as well as any purportedly conscious, aggressive planning:

It might be suggested that the great German design is in reality no more than the expression of a vague, confused, and unpractical statesmanship, not fully realizing its own drift. A charitable critic might add, by way of explanation, that the well-known qualities of mind and temperament distinguishing for good or for evil the present Ruler of Germany may not improbably be largely responsible for the erratic, domineering, and often frankly aggressive spirit which is recognizable at present in every branch of German public life...and that this spirit has called forth those manifestations of discontent and alarm both at home and abroad with which the world is becoming familiar; that, in fact, Germany does not really know what she is driving at, and that all her excursions and alarms, all her underhand intrigues do not contribute to the steady working out of a well-conceived and relentlessly followed system of policy, because they do not really form part of any such system.[38]

And this is where the third point about Weber can be made: he realized precisely this during the war as the result of the idiotic decision to let loose submarines on American shipping. Without this Germany might have been able to establish hegemony on the Continent.

Industry applied to war together with the need of a conscription war to have grand aims ("a war to end all wars," "a war for democracy," the promise of "a land fit for heroes") meant that conflict escalated so as to make it savagely destructive and, with the benefit of hindsight, no longer a rational policy for the states concerned. As institutions were destroyed, everything changed. One important consequence crucial to this chapter was the creation of a whole slew of new nation-states in Central Europe, most of them feeble and in conflict with each other, and many of them with nationalities problems of their own. It is worth highlighting what is involved here. This chapter began by noting a challenge to traditional theory, namely the insistence that nationalism was a major cause of war

---

[37] Isabel Hull, *The Entourage of Kaiser Wilhelm II, 1888–1918* (Cambridge University Press, 1982); Michael Mann, *The Sources of Social Power. Volume Two: The Rise of Classes and Nation-States, 1760–1914* (Cambridge University Press, 1993), Chapter 21; Hall, *International Orders*.

[38] Eyre Crowe, "Memorandum on the Present State of British Relations with France and Germany," in G.P. Gooch and Harold Temperley, ed., *British Documents on the Origins of the War, 1898–1914. Volume Three: The Testing of the Entente, 1904–06* (London: Her Majesty's Stationery Office, 1928), p. 415.

in modern times.[39] That is not quite right, as the key theorist involved has also made clear.[40] The cause of the war was, as argued, in large part traditional. And it took defeat in war to allow nation-states to emerge. The caging of nations becomes impossible, at this and other times, only when states are thrown into disarray, characteristically by defeat in war. Further, the nationalist movements that then took over had gained political consciousness because of the way in which states had treated them – with Masaryk becoming certain of the need for full independence only very late, and in part in response to the new emperor's plan to "Germanify" the empire after all. In a nutshell, nationalism mattered, of course, but was largely created by the actions of states, driven to unify their territories in the belief that this was the only way to protect their power. Differently put, but for the intensity of geopolitical competition it is at least possible that the nationalities problem in some places, above all in Cisleithania, might have been solved in such a way as to allow for several nations to live under a single but necessarily more liberal political roof.

Central Europe then became a power vacuum into which larger states were always likely to be drawn. Crucially, the states involved suffered from social revolutions. The empire to the East had been recreated under new management, a significant part of it Jewish in background, as figures of this sort found that national liberation meant their eventual exclusion, so turning them into left-wing empire savers – another example of the impact of nationalism, caused in turn by prior state actions.[41] The Nazi revolution came later, but its foreign policy proved to be still more radical. All this made it impossible to create a sustainable geopolitical settlement in the interwar period. These conditions further played their part in the onset of the Great Depression, and the consequent increasing salience of the politics of economic autarchy. But if protectionism increased international disorder, as Cordell Hull believed, it is as well to remember that it was itself caused by a failure to create order in the world polity.

It was in these circumstances that the marriage of nationalism and imperialism became ever more important. One element that went into the mix in Germany was the experience by 1918 of food shortages consequent on the British blockade. This certainly made the possession of territory attractive. This is to say that Hitler's policy was entirely comprehensible. But it was aggressive and imperial, and it made the Second World War utterly different in character from the First – an

---

[39] Wimmer, *Waves of War*, Chapter 4.   [40] *Ibid.*, Chapter 3.
[41] Liliana Riga, *The Bolsheviks and the Russian Empire* (Cambridge University Press, 2012).

inter-imperial war rather than a traditional conflict in which, at the start, every state claimed war was necessary for defense and protection rather than for expansion. But one cannot leave the matter at this point, for to do so would be to miss the novelty involved. The uniqueness of the German situation was the desire for *Lebensraum*, for an expansion within Europe that would not create, as had traditionally been the case, a multinational polity but rather kill and cleanse so that new territories would be inhabited only by Aryans. The ultimate perversion of nationalism was the polity envisaged by Hitler in which extermination of difference would allow extension of a single race.[42]

Conclusion

I have argued that there is much to be said for Gilpin's view, its realist view that the activities of states determine much of social life. The challenge mounted by nationalism was not as extreme as the authors noted at the start of this chapter suggested. Peoples for long remained obedient to their states, and were most often driven to secessionist views in any case by the behavior of those states – resulting of course from high levels of geopolitical competition. Further, only the results of geopolitics allowed for massive nation-state creation. Still, Gilpin missed the phenomenology of politics at the end of the nineteenth century, failing to characterize in detail the dilemma caused by scale and nation. Hitler's empire found a way of dealing with the dilemma that was, as they say, "something else" – a perversion in Hobson's sense, standing outside the purview of Gilpin's theory, and indeed of most other theories. This adds something to Gilpin's general position. The catastrophe of modern European politics was not just due to disputed hegemony, to the Anglo-German rivalry. The national question mattered as much as political economy, albeit the latter, again, had done much to lend character to the former. This said, I have complete admiration for Gilpin's view of our current condition. We do indeed live in a capitalist world populated by nation-states over whose life a hegemon – or, as I prefer it, an empire – has considerable, if faltering, sway.

Some final reflections about the contemporary world polity may help highlight the case that has been made. Two background conditions need to be borne in mind. The first is completely clear. The nuclear revolution is a true global change whose logic – the impossibility in rational terms of using this means of destruction – has so far been generally observed. The

---

[42] Mark Mazower, *Hitler's Empire: How the Nazis Ruled Europe* (New York: Penguin, 2008).

second change is as important. The Second World War ended European empires. Nationalist (or, better, anti-imperial) militancy made empire too expensive to maintain, especially as European states slowly discovered that they could prosper without overseas territorial control. Raymond Aron made the crucial argument with characteristic lucidity.[43] If metropolitan France wished to live up to its promise to make real citizens – blessed by high standards of education, health and welfare – in all its imperial possessions, it would have to face a severe decline in its own living standards. It was not surprising to see that Paris let Algeria go so as to enjoy the standard of living to which it had become accustomed. The logic here is simple, namely that power no longer comes from the possession of territory. There is a fair measure of recognition of this logic, but it is still ignored in Moscow. Of course, it may yet be the case that ecological catastrophe again makes size, even empire, of paramount importance.

Europe has become a zone of peace, thankfully, but one should resist European self-satisfaction. The creation of peace in this part of the world was only made possible by the presence of the United States – less in the form of the Marshall Plan than through the way it solved and still solves Europe's security dilemma.[44] Then European liberalism is less impressive when one remembers that many states are liberal thanks to the efforts of Hitler and Stalin, who removed their nationalities problems. The dilemma of scale and nation is of course faced by the European Union, and there is everything to be said for the messy way in which it has become an Austro-Hungary that has worked. One hopes that it can remain, as Count Taaffe had it for the Hapsburgs, in a state of "bearable dissatisfaction." But one notes two challenges. The first is to the Euro, the result of creating a monetary system without political union. The second may prove to be still more important in the long run, and it in any case stands behind the difficulties of dealing with the first. Nationalism is a labile force, and it looks to be changing its character once again. The Danish vote on the Euro pitted two views of national identity against each other: every element of the elite was in favor of joining, with eventual rejection being entirely nativist. To be a European citizen requires facility in several languages, allowing for career and geographical mobility.[45] There is ever more evidence that those lacking these skills resent Europe, and wish integration to go no further.

[43] Aron, *La tragedie algerienne*.
[44] John A. Hall, "Europe: Banalities of Success," in T.V. Paul, ed, *International Relations Theory and Regional Transformation* (Cambridge University Press, 2013).
[45] David D. Laitin, "The Cultural Identities of a European State," *Politics and Society*, Vol. 25, No. 3 (1997), pp. 277–302.

Far more impressive than Europe is the wonderful fact that crucial parts of the world have found a route to the modern world that does not involve copying the disasters of the European past. What is most striking about India is its ability to create a state-nation rather than a nation-state. Indian leaders in the years before independence were aware of the problems of diversity, and sought to accommodate them. It would have been immensely difficult to homogenize all of India, not least as Indian civil servants had cultural capital through their knowledge of English. Accordingly, it was agreed that there would be two state languages, English and Hindi.[46] If one's state was Hindi-speaking then one only needed two languages. But three were required if one's state was not Hindi-speaking, and a fourth if one came from a minority in such a state. This linguistic regime seems to work in India, allowing for different peoples to live together under the same political roof. It is important to note that linguistic regimes of this type are not confined to India, with English serving as "neutral-speak" in several African countries. But there are of course other factors at work in the Indian case. For one thing, there is a structural skeleton to the Indian state – its army, its bureaucratic tradition, and the fact that an element of shared national identity arose from a common struggle against the British. For another, the Indian polity has shown itself to be flexible and liberal in diverse ways going beyond language. One striking example is the way in which pressures for secession in Tamil Nadu were diffused by the granting of varied political and cultural rights – in stark contrast to the situation in Sri Lanka, where homogenizing politics by the Sinhalese elite led to vicious civil war. The fact that there are areas of dissidence within India, above all Kashmir, proves the point in question: those are the areas where India is, so to speak, not true to itself – illiberal in ways that we know all too well.[47]

In contrast, there is much to be said for worrying about the situation in China where the alternative route is being taken – of homogenization through forcible assimilation and the diluting of minority populations by the traditional method of moving in large numbers of the majority population. One worry is that this route may breed violent response, the desire for secession that was present in key parts of Europe in modern times, above all in Tibet, Hong Kong, and Taiwan. One can note in this regard that the situation in China is in fact rather different from some of the cases noted above. Han Chinese are a massive majority, and it may well be that over time they can have their way; homogenization may yet

---

[46] David D. Laitin, *Language Repertoires and State Construction in Africa* (Cambridge University Press, 1992).
[47] Stepan, Linz, and Yadav, *Crafting State-Nations*.

work. A second worry is greater. There is a sense in which contemporary China resembles Wilhelmine Germany. The regime lacks legitimacy, and it may yet seek it by playing the nationalist card. Certainly new middle-class elements exist, above all the massive student population, which wishes for a more aggressive policy on the part of their state, believing in its right to a central place in world affairs. Eyre Crowe's famous memorandum suggested that Germany, for whatever reasons, wished to break up the British empire so as to supplant it. Thomas Sanderson opposed this view in an interesting memorandum of February 21, 1907, in which he saw Germany as "a helpful tough somewhat exacting friend," adding that "it is altogether contrary to reason that Germany should wish to quarrel with us."[48] Germany was prospering in 1914 within the rules of the world order of the times, and looked set to prosper much more. The same is true of China today. One hopes that the result of developments in the two countries will differ, with Chinese behavior to this point justifying worry rather than fear.

A final point concerns the fact that so many have been killed in the putatively peaceful postwar world in civil wars, very often fueled by ethnic strife – the end result in large part of European colonialism. But there are reasons to hope here, reasons to think that links between nationalism and war may weaken – and this beyond the current diminution in the numbers of such conflicts. One can at least hope that the strict version of the nation-state – each state with its own culture, each culture with its own state – may be avoided. Design may help. Much more important is a background factor, a diminution in the intensity of great-power rivalry, and of their involvement in much of the rest of the world. Relative geopolitical calm may allow states to manage their nations in a less unitary and homogenous manner.

[48] Thomas Sanderson, "Memorandum," in G.P. Gooch and Harold Temperley, eds., *British Documents on the Origins of the War, 1898–1914. Volume Three: The Testing of the Entente, 1904–06* (London: Her Majesty's Stationery Office, 1928), pp. 403–401.

Index

Printed in the United States
By Bookmasters